D0594526

The Gold in the Rings

SPORT AND SOCIETY

Series Editors
Aram Goudsouzian
Jaime Schultz

Founding Editors
Benjamin G. Rader
Randy Roberts

A list of books in the series appears at the end of this book.

The Gold in the Rings

The People and Events That Transformed the Olympic Games

STEPHEN R. WENN AND
ROBERT K. BARNEY

UNIVERSITY OF
ILLINOIS PRESS
Urbana, Chicago, and Springfield

© 2020 by the Board of Trustees
of the University of Illinois
All rights reserved
Manufactured in the United States of America
1 2 3 4 5 C P 5 4 3 2 1
∞ This book is printed on acid-free paper.

Library of Congress Cataloging-in-Publication Data

Names: Wenn, Stephen R., 1964- author. | Barney, Robert Knight,
    1932- author.

Title: The gold in the rings : the people and events that transformed
    the Olympic Games / Stephen R. Wenn and Robert K. Barney.

Description: Urbana : [University of Illinois Press], [2020] | Series:
    Sport and society | Includes bibliographical references and index. |

Identifiers: LCCN 2019018152 (print) | LCCN 2019980293 (ebook)
    | ISBN 9780252042683 (hardcover) | ISBN 9780252084522
    (paperback) | ISBN 9780252051531 (ebook)

Subjects: LCSH: International Olympic Committee. | Olympics—
    History. | Olympics—Economic aspects.

Classification: LCC GV721.5 .W44 2020 (print) | LCC GV721.5 (ebook) |
    DDC 796.48—dc23

LC record available at https://lccn.loc.gov/2019018152

LC ebook record available at https://lccn.loc.gov/2019980293

To Maynard Brichford,

*storied University of Illinois archivist,
an individual who has launched hundreds
of scholarly Olympic research missions,
including our own, each prompted by
his landmark accomplishment of creating
order, facility, and, indeed, inspiration, in the
use of one of the world's largest and most
widely employed Olympic history sources,
The Avery Brundage Collection.*

&

*In memory of
Leanne Holland Brown (1976–2019)*

*Dean of Students, Wilfrid Laurier University
Wife to Ken, Mother to Holden and Andrew
Colleague * Friend * Neighbor*

Contents

Preface

Why write this book? Why now?

At the time of Jacques Rogge's election as president of the International Olympic Committee (IOC) in 2001, we entered the home stretch of our preparation of a book manuscript titled *Selling the Five Rings: The International Olympic Committee and the Rise of Olympic Commercialism*.[1] Published by the University of Utah Press in 2002, *Selling the Five Rings* detailed the IOC's transition from an organization with a widely known and reported aversion to commercialism, best represented by the views of Avery Brundage, to the economic juggernaut staffed by people skilled in the generation of commercial revenue through the sale of television rights and the enlistment of major multinational corporate sponsors, led by Juan Antonio Samaranch. Our historical analysis of this transformation relied heavily on materials from the IOC's Lausanne archives, primarily Executive Board and Session minutes, television negotiation files, and binders of documents dealing with the emergence of the IOC's global corporate sponsorship program, The Olympic Programme (TOP).

In the 1990s, largely through the efforts of the late Dr. Karel Wendl, the genteel and thoughtful director of the IOC's Research and Archives Division, we were permitted access to certain "embargoed" primary-source files. The completion of *Selling the Five Rings* owed much to Wendl's onsite assistance and steadfast support for our project when Samaranch balked at sustaining our access in the immediate aftermath of the publication of Vyv Simson and Andrew Jennings's 1992 exposé, *The Lords of the Rings: Power, Money and Drugs in the Modern Olympics*, a highly critical assessment of Samaranch's character and leadership, which contained allegations of corruption and bad behavior within the IOC.[2]

Following our considered reflection of *Selling the Five Rings* over the years, we believe that we provided a thorough treatment of the IOC's activities pertaining to television rights negotiations and corporate sponsorship during the Brundage, Killanin, and Samaranch presidencies. Most reviewers agreed. In 2013, as the IOC transitioned to new presidential leadership under Thomas Bach, we began to consider how we might address our continuing interest in Olympic television and corporate sponsorship matters. The first thought was to augment *Selling the Five Rings* with a new preface, introduction, and perhaps, three or four chapters to address events that took place after its publication. However, the University of Utah Press was not interested in this proposal, having already published a revised paperback edition in 2004. We subsequently discussed our ideas with Bill Regier, director of the University of Illinois Press. However, he could not envision an effective marketing plan for such a book. How many people would actually be interested in acquiring the new yet merely updated version? Additional text, noted Regier, would drive up the cost of its production. He countered our notion with the thought that a novel manuscript would be much preferred.[3] It was Regier's suggestion that moved us to further expose *Selling the Five Rings* to a critical lens. If we were to move in the direction Regier suggested, what fresh perspectives could we provide?

These conversations left us thinking that while we provided a comprehensive historical treatment of the subject in *Selling the Five Rings*, the depth and detail present made it a dense manuscript, detracted from the book's readability, and likely reduced the size of our audience.[4] In hindsight, our unique opportunity to explore the subject matter in *Selling the Five Rings*, given the wealth of archival material at our disposal, led us to err on the side of providing too much detail, as opposed to too little. Scores of individuals entered and left the storyline. With a few notable exceptions, such as Avery Brundage, Lord Killanin, Juan Antonio Samaranch, longtime IOC director Monique Berlioux, and Dick Pound, Samaranch's right hand in the crafting of the IOC's commercial revenue-generating capacity, they were merely names, underdeveloped historical actors in terms of their personalities. This shortcoming became a relevant consideration for us moving forward. And, of course, there remained a gap in our historical treatment with respect to more contemporary events following Samaranch's retirement that we also sought to fill. When Bill Regier retired, our nascent project was placed in the hands of Senior Acquisitions Editor Danny Nasset.

We set as our two major goals an effort to provide a more focused manuscript by isolating milestone events that illuminate the IOC's financial history in terms of revenue generation, and an enhancement of our literary effort at character development. We focus on the key people and events dealing with the IOC's effort to harness commercialism and its revenue-generation possibilities during the Brundage, Killanin, Samaranch, *and* Rogge presidencies, and the importance of these people and events in shaping the IOC's role as guardian of the Olympic Games in an age of increasing commerce and globalization.

But, in doing so, we knew we would be at an information deficit if we were unable to access primary documents from Lausanne dealing with more recent developments. We reached out to Dick Pound,[5] who in turn contacted IOC director general Christophe De Kepper on our behalf to inquire about current research protocols and the best path for us to have our request for access considered.[6] A noted corporate tax attorney with Montreal's Stikeman Elliott law firm, Pound has been, and continues to be, a seasoned researcher and writer of history in his spare time. He believed then, as he does today, that the IOC gains nothing from sheltering its work from historical examination. De Kepper suggested that we contact Maria Bogner, Head of the IOC Olympic Studies Centre.[7] Ms. Bogner, much like Karel Wendl decades before, shepherded our request through the necessary channels in Lausanne.[8] Ultimately, we learned that IOC president Thomas Bach consented to lifting the embargo on IOC Session, Executive Board, and Marketing Commission minutes for the 2001–2013 period, as well as additional documents requested.

We made a research trip to Lausanne in early March 2016. There we received excellent advice and assistance from Ms. Bogner's team in the Olympic Studies Centre. We are most grateful for Dick Pound's support, Christophe De Kepper's suggestion, Maria Bogner's efforts on our behalf, and President Bach's decision. Second, after learning that the Executive Board minutes produced under President Rogge took the form of discussion summaries, in effect, much less embellished with the detail representative of such minutes produced under Presidents Brundage, Killanin, and Samaranch, Ms. Bogner supported us in our endeavor to supplement our findings on events tied to President Rogge's tenure through personal interviews with key IOC personnel. Thus, we were fortunate in securing personal interviews with Director General Christophe De Kepper, Director of Television and Marketing Services Timo Lumme, (now former) Director of Legal Affairs Howard Stupp, (former) Director of Marketing Services Michael Payne, and (former) Director General François Carrard, each under Samaranch and for a brief period of Rogge's presidency. Subsequently, we sat down with Dick Pound (December 2016) and the United States Olympic Committee's (USOC) now former CEO Scott Blackmun (February 2017). These interviews added significant texture to our narrative, and we appreciate their consent to assist us with the research process. Our journey has confirmed to us that while it is true that human beings create history through their words, deeds, and actions, it is also precisely such folks, through their interest, willingness, and professionalism, who can contribute greatly in assisting those engaged in historical research.

We would like to express our appreciation to Bill Regier for his support and encouragement in pushing us to seek a means of presenting our work in novel fashion, and Danny Nasset for his dedication to this task, as well as his valuable suggestions and guidance. Associate Acquisitions Editor Marika Christofides kept us focused on necessary details. We collaborated effectively with our copyeditor, Julie Gay, who aided us in the production of the manuscript.

One of the important features of the book is the visual imagery we present, and, in this, a number of individuals require recognition: Maria Bogner, Aline Luginbühl (IOC Photos, Strategic Communication Department, Images service); Wayne Wilson (former vice president, Education Services, LA84 Foundation); Shirley Ito (manager, Digital Library, LA84 Foundation); Hilary Dorsch Wong (reference coordinator, Research Services) and Eisha Neely (exhibitions and permissions coordinator and reference specialist), both with the Division of Rare Books and Manuscript Collection, Cornell University. Teri Hedgpeth facilitated our research trip to the USOC's headquarters in Colorado Springs. Dave Deevey assisted us greatly with his transcription of our personal interviews. Greg Sennema, a librarian at Wilfrid Laurier University (WLU), aided us in locating biographical information on some of the key historical actors. Tim Elcombe, Bill McTeer, Jennifer Robertson-Wilson, and Renée MacPhee, four of Stephen Wenn's colleagues at WLU, offered ideas and support, while Roberta and Paul Wenn volunteered their services as proofreaders. Two anonymous reviewers pored over the manuscript and offered meaningful feedback that we hope we have leveraged in delivering a better and tighter finished product. We also benefit from our association with the North American Society for Sports History and the relationships we share with colleagues who value and support our research efforts and for whose work we have much respect, including Ronald Smith, Toby Rider, Thomas Hunt, Austin Duckworth, Matt Llewellyn, John Gleaves, Mark Dyreson, Dave Wiggins, Jan Todd, Adam Berg, Kevin Wamsley, Scott Martyn, Maureen Smith, Larry Gerlach, Dick Crepeau, Doug Booth, Murray Phillips, Jaime Schultz, Allen Guttmann, Kevin Witherspoon, and Bruce Kidd.

This research was supported by WLU and the Social Sciences and Humanities Research Council of Canada. These funds offset expenses associated with the transcription of interviews and travel tied to Stephen Wenn's trip to USOC headquarters in Colorado Springs. WLU's Robert Gordon, provost and vice president academic, and Ken Maly, acting dean, faculty of science, kindly funded the production of the index. Last, our spouses, Martha Wenn and Ashleigh Barney, understand (and accept) our passion for what we do, and keep us grounded.

And, now, a brief word concerning our approach to citations. Our tendency in previously published work has been to provide a large number of endnotes, many of them possessing additional detail. As a means of making the history related in this work more accessible to the reader, we decided in consultation with members of the editorial staff at the University of Illinois Press to use what we dub a hybrid citation model. Any information gleaned from archival sources is cited in endnotes. All direct quotes are cited in endnotes, regardless of whether they appear in an archival or secondary source; however, paraphrased text from secondary source material is not cited in endnotes (with very few exceptions). We have provided a detailed bibliography outlining all books, book chapters, journal articles, and newspaper or magazine articles consulted. And we have policed ourselves to the best of our ability to limit the number of explanatory endnotes. All of this removed us somewhat from our "comfort zone" as historians, but we hope that it translates into a "good read." On that, you will be the judge.

The Gold in the Rings

Introduction

At the International Olympic Committee's (IOC) 112th Session in July 2001, Juan Antonio Samaranch stepped down from the IOC presidency after twenty-one years in office. Jacques Rogge, a Belgian orthopedic surgeon, IOC Executive Board member, and president of the European Olympic Committees, succeeded Samaranch following an electoral victory over Un Yong Kim (South Korea), Dick Pound (Canada), Pal Schmitt (Hungary), and Anita DeFrantz (United States).

Much changed in the Olympic world in the 1980s and 1990s. Dr. Rogge succeeded Samaranch as leader of an organization that little resembled the sport governing body that the Spaniard inherited from his predecessor, Lord Killanin (1972–1980). Cash-strapped and buffeted for years by the intrusion of world geopolitics, most recently witnessed through the Munich tragedy, the African boycott of the 1976 Montreal Olympics, and the U.S.-led boycott of the 1980 Moscow Olympics, the IOC faced a severe challenge. So, too, did its new leader. The IOC still reeled from Montreal's financial debacle and diminished interest on the part of cities to host the Olympics. It demonstrated more "backward than forward" thinking in terms of its lingering ties to the amateur ideal.[1] Pound, a former IOC vice president and Samaranch's right hand in generating billions of dollars of Olympic revenue from the sale of television rights and global sponsorship agreements through The Olympic Programme (TOP, now The Olympic Partners), observed: "In 1980, the Olympic Movement was under sustained attack from political powers and was, indeed, a virtual hostage to world tensions. It was disunited, well short of universal, and had no financial resources to give it the autonomy and independence to resist political pressures."[2] Michael Payne, the IOC's former marketing director, echoed Pound's thoughts: "Everybody was writing the Olympic obituary."[3]

David Miller, Samaranch's biographer, labeled his presidential agenda and developments flowing from it to be "revolutionary."[4] He did not miss the mark. A far-from-exhaustive catalog of changes in the 1980s and 1990s follows: the threat of Olympic boycotts was much diminished due in large measure to Samaranch's skillful application of his diplomatic acumen; far greater numbers of female athletes appeared in the Olympic event program, a number of women were appointed to the IOC, and one (Anita DeFrantz) rose to become an IOC Executive Board member and vice president; professional athletes roamed the Olympic precincts as amateurism and its attendant hypocrisy was consigned to the dustbin of history; the number of National Olympic Committees (NOCs) expanded from 147 to 200; the value of global Olympic television rights exploded, and a worldwide corporate sponsorship program existed, capable of generating more than $550 million on a quadrennial basis; the IOC finally moved from bystander to engaged participant in the battle against doping (resulting from the genesis of the World Anti-Doping Agency); and cities pursued the right to host the Olympic Games with noticeably more enthusiasm and vigor than when Lord Killanin departed as IOC president. Finally, the Olympic Movement under Samaranch survived a serious threat to its autonomy and brand resulting from the Salt Lake City bid scandal of the late 1990s, prompting a drastic reform effort to establish better administrative and ethical practices for its operation in the twenty-first century.

With respect to the IOC's financial health, long gone were the days in 1969 when the Executive Board worried about the IOC's yearly income of 540,000 Swiss francs ($125,470) being outstripped by its expenditures of some 790,000 Swiss francs ($183,241),[5] or when in 1970 Monique Berlioux, the IOC's director from the late 1960s through 1985, appealed directly to Lord Luke, the Finance Commission chairman, for authorization to rent or purchase a new photocopy machine because of the unreliability of the IOC's current machine and accompanying repair costs.[6] Though the situation improved marginally during Killanin's presidency, the IOC's financial situation remained precarious. When Samaranch assumed power, the IOC's cash reserves were less than $200,000, and it possessed perhaps $2 million in total assets.[7] The reserve fund, also referred to as the "survival" fund, first established under Killanin, evolved as a means to safeguard the IOC's finances in the event of the cancellation of the Games for any reason.[8] When Samaranch stepped down, the cash reserves stood at $100 million.[9] At the close of 2013, mere months after Thomas Bach's presidential term commenced, the reserve fund (now known as the Olympic Foundation) stood at 924 million Swiss francs ($1,035,860,000),[10] and this for a nongovernmental, largely volunteer organization.

The overall trajectory of the IOC's financial circumstance in the past fifty years owes much to two critical external developments in the twentieth century: the invention of television and subsequent technological innovations, especially the advent of satellite technology; and globalization.

Television revenue did not immediately alter the IOC's financial situation. IOC president Avery Brundage (1952–1972) limited the IOC's share of the rights fees negotiated by Organizing Committees (OCOGs) in the 1950s and 1960s because he was deeply concerned about the influence that commercial interests and money might have on the image of the IOC and the Olympic Games. IOC members paid yearly dues and covered their own travel expenses to attend IOC Sessions. In 1966 Brundage relented under the weight of pressure from presidents of the NOCs and International Sport Federations (IFs), and some of the IOC's own members, who clamored for shares of the revenue pot. Commencing in 1972, according to the terms of the Rome Formula (the IOC's first allocation plan for television dollars), the IOC, IFs, and NOCs each would pocket a minimum of 11.1 percent of the global television rights fees, with the remaining money transferred to the OCOGs. Satellite technology, first employed in an Olympic context in conjunction with the telecast of the opening ceremony of the 1964 Tokyo Olympics, pushed forward the value of global television rights in the 1970s and 1980s because Olympic broadcasters cherished access to live feeds of Olympic competition. Greater sums of money flowed to the members of the Olympic Tripartite.

Though Lord Killanin recognized the problems inherent in the IOC's annual budget being more than 90 percent dependent on television revenue in the 1970s, he failed in his effort to launch a supplemental revenue stream.[11] Sharing Killanin's concern, Samaranch advanced his own agenda to find a financially rewarding marriage with the corporate world. Samaranch's thoughts sprang from his interaction with Horst Dassler, Adidas's boss and the head of International Sport and Leisure (ISL), an international sports-marketing firm.[12] Dassler's counsel prompted Samaranch to champion TOP. It offered the IOC an avenue to diversify its revenue-generation program by tendering exclusive marketing rights to multinational companies within defined product categories at the Olympic Games and within all Olympic nations for the contracted term. Samaranch and Dassler's collaboration and TOP's resulting financial success were made possible by globalization, or the border flattening in the second half of the twentieth century that birthed multinational companies capable of marketing, selling, and supplying their goods and services globally. These same companies sought global marketing platforms. Michael Payne (through 2004), Timo Lumme, Gerhard Heiberg, Thomas Bach, and Richard Carrión, central members of Jacques Rogge's revenue-generation team, further enhanced the IOC's fiscal status by leveraging the knowledge accrued under Samaranch.

The cachet of the Olympic Games, with their massive worldwide television audience, proved an alluring sports-marketing property. The sums raised from the sale of Olympic television rights and TOP agreements rose steadily. Global television rights fees contracted for Munich (1972), Montreal (1976), Moscow (1980), Los Angeles (1984), and Seoul (1988) totaled $17.8 million, $34.9 million, $100.2 million, $286.9 million, and $402.5 million, respectively. More recently, in May 2014, NBC Universal paid $7.75 billion for the U.S. television rights for six Olympic festivals from 2022 through 2032, while in 2015 Discovery Communications secured European television rights from 2018 through 2024 for $1.45 billion. TOP I (Calgary and Seoul, 1985–1988) generated $96 million, while TOP VIII (Sochi and Rio de Janeiro, 2013–2016) proceeds were slightly more than $1 billion.[13] The energy and commitment of presidents Samaranch and Rogge, the work of individuals in television and corporate sponsorship negotiations who served under them, and the efforts of those tasked with nurturing the Olympic brand explain the human contribution required to effect such staggering results.

With this book we hope to delve deeper into the transformation of the IOC, along with its signature sports property, the Olympic Games, from an illustrious global sport enterprise to an equally illustrious global commercial phenomenon. We remain fascinated by the personal conflict experienced by Avery Brundage, whose dedication to the Coubertin ideal ran headlong into his own business know-how and conservative, capitalist core. Money, thought Brundage, might very well permit the IOC to promote Olympism, but he agonized over how it would alter his (and Coubertin's) vision of the Olympic Movement as an instrument of peace, brotherhood, and youthful health and vigor.[14] Presidents of the NOCs and IFs, who eyed television revenue as a means of expanding the scope of their organizations in the early 1960s, fretted Brundage, could not be trusted to spend the money wisely. He wanted neither competing empires to his or the IOC's authority nor an overt link between the Olympic Movement and commercialism. Ultimately, Brundage's pragmatism trumped his idealism—cash won out over personal conviction.

In 1966 Brundage believed erroneously that he could control the financial aspirations of the NOCs, IFs, and OCOGs. The OCOGs, he thought, would be content with 67 percent of television revenue when he established the Rome Formula for the distribution of television money in collaboration with David Cecil (Marquess of Exeter), an IOC Executive Board member and president of the International Amateur Athletics Federation (IAAF), and Giulio Onesti, an IOC member and the president of the Italian National Olympic Committee. The later years of Brundage's presidency and Lord Killanin's subsequent term of office were awash with inter-organizational arguments concerning how the money should be distributed and challenges to the IOC's authority to set policy in this realm. Under Samaranch, the IFs and NOCs (with one major exception, the United States Olympic Committee

[USOC]) were persuaded to accept the IOC's evolving distribution policies. The tension between the IOC and OCOGs about television revenue also diminished when the global value of television rights skyrocketed, which served to enrich both parties well, and the IOC included the allocation terms for television revenue to the OCOGs in all host city contracts (thus preventing challenge from the OCOGs, as had been the case with the Rome Formula).

The often-fractious relations between the IOC and the USOC on revenue matters dominate the storyline of the IOC's financial history from the mid-1980s through the early 2010s. In the 1980s, USOC leaders, long tired and frustrated by the disparity in sums raised from the sale of television rights in the United States when compared with other global markets, moved to divert U.S. television money to the USOC through rights accorded to it in the Amateur Sports Act (ASA). The USOC also pursued its financial interests aggressively in the context of Samaranch's TOP initiative by invoking the ASA, a piece of U.S. federal legislation passed in 1978, and its exclusive right to the use of the Olympic five-ring logo in U.S. territory.[15] It viewed the TOP concept as a challenge—indeed, an impingement—on its own revenue-generation program, given that the vast majority of envisioned TOP sponsors were destined to be American firms. As events played out, U.S. companies dominated the list of multinationals aligned with TOP at its outset in 1985, a fact permitting the USOC to argue that the prospect of "lost" sponsor opportunities for its own domestic sponsorship program would compromise its bottom line.

The ASA cast a shadow over IOC/USOC relations for thirty years, and its role as a driver of those relations provides a significant thread of analysis for this book. The USOC lobbied for additional concessions from the IOC in the wake of the initial agreements forged between the two bodies on the distribution of U.S.-generated commercial revenue in 1985 (TOP) and 1986 (U.S. television rights via the Broadcast Marketing Agreement). Conversely, the IOC battled to preserve meaningful levels of access to this revenue for the IOC, IFs, and other NOCs. USOC and IOC officials negotiated with a firm level of commitment to the financial interests of their respective organizations. In so doing, however, the resulting fissure in interorganizational trust severely compromised IOC/USOC relations.

In the early years of the twenty-first century, mounting displeasure within the IOC administration and the organization's wider membership concerning the disparity of dollars directed to the USOC, as opposed to the more than two hundred other NOCs, poisoned relations between the two organizations. The city of Chicago, the designated host city of the 1904 Olympics before Pierre de Coubertin transferred them to St. Louis, and a contender for the right to host the 2016 Summer Olympics, paid the price for the frayed relations between the IOC and the USOC. Chicago's bid, despite a sound plan and a supporting personal appearance of U.S. president Barack Obama at the IOC's 2009 Copenhagen Session, was dismissed on the first ballot. The IOC's message was clear. Not wishing to expose other cities to Chicago's embarrassment, the USOC withheld endorsement of U.S. bid cities for the 2018, 2020, and 2022 host-city competitions.

This development marked a turning point that prompted IOC and USOC officials to return to the negotiating table. Both parties accepted that strained relations impeded the pursuit of their individual and collective goals. In 2012, in one of the signature moments of Rogge's presidency, the IOC and the USOC, represented by its (then) president, Larry Probst, and executive director at the time, Scott Blackmun, both of whom invested significant time in relationship-building over the preceding two years, at last found common ground. Setting aside many of their differences, they devised a distribution formula for U.S.-generated television revenue and TOP sponsorship dollars, an agreement extending through 2040.[16]

As a narrative vehicle to drive the analysis of both the IOC's transition from its once financially constrained status to its contemporary position of wealth and corporate might, and the Olympic Games' journey as a sports property of increasing commercial value, we have isolated ten key, transformative events dealing with revenue generation linked to television rights and corporate sponsorship. Some of these events triggered or further established the power of the Coubertin-inspired five-ring logo as a symbol bearing a significant capacity for revenue generation (Helms versus Brundage; Los Angeles, 1984; "Total Olympic Programme"), while others involved policy formulation that heralded meaningful change in the bottom lines of members of the Olympic Tripartite, including the IOC itself (Melbourne, 1956; The Rome Formula; The European Television Market). Challenge to IOC authority with respect to the distribution of commercial revenue (Willi Daume and Munich, 1972's Television Legacy; The Broadcast Marketing Agreement) also reshaped relations between the IOC, OCOGs, IFs, and NOCs. The Salt Lake City scandal (The Salt Lake City Bid Scandal) forced the IOC to confront the ethical failings of some of its members and its own managerial shortcomings to protect both its image and the Olympic brand's revenue-generation capacity. IOC leaders pursued "opportunity out of crisis" as a catalyst for establishing better administrative practices at the turn of the twenty-first century. Last, the Copenhagen Session (The 2009 IOC Copenhagen Session) launched a series of discussions resulting in the resolution of the IOC's differences with the USOC concerning the distribution of commercial revenue, thereby delivering a greater sense of unity within the Olympic Movement. These ten events emerged following significant debate and dialogue. We believe that this approach, in tandem with a focus on the people who propelled developments, provides an effective framework for us as authors who desire to construct this history, and you, the reader, who has chosen to learn more about the Olympics.

CHAPTER 1

Paul Helms versus Avery Brundage

Understanding the Relationship between the Olympics and Money Matters

For a period encompassing the first three decades of modern Olympic history, expanding public interest in the Games was satisfied almost solely by mass communication's fundamental instruments—the printing industry's newspaper and magazine publications. In the late 1920s, radio broadcasts added a further means of mass communication. Commencing in the 1940s, the landmark development of television (some years earlier) substantively altered the landscape, as did the coming of cyberspace later in the century. The financial underpinnings for the existence of mechanisms for print and electronic mass communication depend greatly on what might be called a circulation population, or readers, listeners, and viewers. They form a consumer corpus that in turn attracts the efforts of producers of goods and services to market their goods through advertising.

In exceedingly simplistic terms, for the past 150 years global society has demonstrated overwhelming progress in production of goods and services; distribution of those goods and services until well into the twentieth century (and its relatively contemporary era of globalization) failed to keep pace. The eminent Harvard economist John Kenneth Galbraith, in his classic *The Affluent Society*, informs us that the exercise of consumption/distribution depends on the creation of a need, perceived or real, for a product or service.[1] Enter, then, advertising, the mechanism that drives the need and desire for the fruits of production. Into the world of Olympic matters sprang a fundamental element of market capitalism, the advertisement of goods and services to meet the needs of production and consumption. The greater the attention given to Olympic Games by vehicles of mass communication, the greater the zeal of business and commerce to link with and capitalize on such exposure to the consumer world.

But *exposure* is one thing; *image* is quite another. *Image* is created and perpetuated over time. In order to be attractive to commercial initiatives, the Olympic Movement not only had to demonstrate that it offered the prospect of wide exposure to a consumer marketplace, but it also had to reflect an acceptable image—indeed, one embraced by public norms. When the noble qualities of the Olympic Movement rose in the late nineteenth and early twentieth centuries—peace, brotherhood, altruism, tolerance, goodwill, health and fitness for youth, and virtuous amateur sport participation—all set in a resplendent atmosphere of high ceremony and ritual combined with an ever-expanding international audience through newspapers, magazines, and radio, the die was cast. The "Olympic consumer world" became the target audience. Opportunities for companies to market their products broadened with the arrival of television and the internet. Make no mistake, without the advertising industry, there would be no modern Olympic Games, at least as we have come to know them in our times.

Wedding Rings: A Marriage Made in Heaven

In the euphoria surrounding the closing of the Games of the Vth Olympiad celebrated in Stockholm in 1912, one thing was certain: the Baron Pierre de Coubertin-inspired reincarnation in modern times of Western civilization's ancient Olympic festival had "come of age." Indelibly apparent were many of those qualities that long ago characterized and distinguished the ancient world's most illustrious sporting legacy left to future generations: athletic performance par excellence, ritual ceremonies cast in religious-like tones, resplendent facilities, and onsite spectator masses that gave every indication that a cultural awareness of the Olympic showcase penetrated to more distant environs than simply the stadium.

One prop, however, was missing—the presence of a symbol, a mark, an icon that would identify in bold graphic consequence the Modern Olympic Movement. Coubertin, unwilling to entrust this critical issue to anyone other than himself, took the matter in hand. He already had a model in mind: ironically, "wedding rings." In 1892 he was heavily involved in the merger of two French organizations—his own Comité Jules Simon, and the Union des Sociétés Françaises de Courses à Pied—to form the premier French sports-governing body of the period, the Union des Sociétés Françaises de Sports Athlétiques (USFSA). To mark that historic occasion, a simple logo of two interlocked rings (circles) was established to consummate the marriage and thenceforth identify the organization's athletes in their sporting endeavors. In the year following the 1912 Olympics, a new symbol, five interlocked rings, now recognized in every corner of the modern world, began to appear on Coubertin's personal letterhead. He had no inkling of the power that "his" symbol would attain in a global context. Nevertheless, as he surveyed the some fifty Olympic flags adorned with the five rings at the opening of the Modern Olympic Movement's twentieth anniversary celebrations at the Sorbonne in June 1914, he could not help but be justly satisfied with the results of his labors. Indeed, similar to two rings signaling a marriage in 1892, Coubertin's five rings, created in 1913, consummated another union, one in which the Olympic bride betrothed herself to an international "five parts of the world" groom.

Tentative Steps in Commercial Relationships

Despite a repugnance toward anything commercial tainting his Olympic mission, it was Coubertin himself who constructed one of the first examples of a link to commerce. For the January 1901 issue of *Olympic Review*, the official publication of the IOC largely financed by the baron's personal wealth, he mounted a full-page, inside-cover advertisement for the products of a Parisian sporting-goods firm. He did the same for a Bénédictine liqueur ad in the October 1902 issue. No one has ever been able to document what the baron might have received in compensation for these acts. Coubertin invested most of his personal fortune, inherited from his father, in underwriting costs associated with his Olympic crusade. In fact, he spent much of his wife's considerably greater inheritance on Olympic matters, expenditures which left them both in modest circumstances in declining age and severely compromised their personal relationship as time wore on.

Other modest examples followed. Commensurate with the 1908 London Olympics, organizers pursued a campaign to generate revenue from the placement of ads in "schedules and announcements" print publications. Hence, messages such as those featuring Schweppes Soda Water and Dry Ginger Ale, Vaughton's Medals and Badges, and Wawkphar's Antiseptic Military Foot Powder joined legions of other firms bent on marketing their products and services to an Olympic audience. In Stockholm four years later, ten domestic companies were approved by Swedish organizers to vend their products on the Olympic grounds, including a photographic company and a manufacturer of weighing machines whose products were displayed for the use of patrons. Upon arrival at the first post–World War I Olympic Games, celebrated in Antwerp in 1920, Coubertin was confronted by a miniature World's Fair atmosphere featuring exhibits, booths, kiosks, and shops. In his opening address, Coubertin, who was clearly discomfited by the scene, challenged the assembled spectators and officials to "keep away the opportunities that are advanced [by profit-motivated people] whose only dream is to use someone else's muscles to build upon his own political fortune or to make his own business prosper."[2]

Four years later in Paris for the 1924 Olympics, Coubertin's last as IOC president, it became obvious that his message enunciated in Antwerp had fallen on deaf ears. Of the 320 pages in the *Guide to the Games* published by the Organizing Committee, 256 contained ads for such products as Mercier Champagne, Spalding Sporting Goods, and Grand Marnier liqueurs. More alarming was that athletes performed in the Olympic stadium itself before a backdrop of prominent signboards featuring Cinzano, Dubonnet, Ovalmaltine, and Chevine Niger, *parfum sublime*. The presence in the Paris Olympic stadium of prominently placed advertising signs prompted Olympic officials, led by Coubertin's successor, Belgium's Henri Baillet-Latour, to decree that henceforth Olympic competition venues would not be "disfigured by signs and posters advertising business products."[3] That succinct dictum and its resulting free-from-advertising atmosphere remains in place today.

Be that as it may, the Amsterdam organizers of the 1928 Games awarded "rights packages" to several "concessionaires," including a brewery that operated beer garden restaurants on grounds next to the Olympic stadium. The Amsterdam gathering also presented to the world what would become the longest-standing corporate relationship in Olympic history, the marriage with a popular soft drink known simply as "Coke." The Coca-Cola Company, formed in Atlanta in 1881, first expanded its product into international markets early in the 1920s. In Amsterdam it made its Olympic debut; hundreds of posters outside the stadium announced its presence. By 1929 the company's flagship publication, *Red Barrell*, proudly announced to its employees and shareholders that "Coca-Cola is now found within the bull fight arenas of sunny Spain and Mexico, at the Olympic Games Stadium below the dykes of Holland, atop the Eiffel Tower above 'Gay Paree,' on the holy pagoda in distant Burma, and beside the Coliseum of historic Rome."[4]

In all of the aforementioned agreements between Olympic organizers and commercial firms for "rights," "presence," or "permission," there has never been a scintilla of evidence confirming that these acts demanded a fee paid to the organizers. Rather, the evidence suggests that such arrangements were formed with the purpose of providing needed services for the comfort and convenience of spectators onsite. For organizers, this factor alone was enough.

The First Great Test: Brundage versus Helms— Exploitation versus Protection

As the value of association with the *image* and *exposure* offered by the Olympic Games rose exponentially throughout the 1920s, two conflicting issues resulted: the increasing zeal and initiative of commercial enterprise to capitalize on such an attractive association and, conversely, the determination of Olympic officials to protect their enterprise from unauthorized use. The most important precedent-setting episode in the history of protecting the Modern Olympic Movement's prized assets—*image* and *exposure*—is reflected in the strident confrontation between Paul H. Helms, an American baker who was an exemplar of shrewd business acumen as well as someone supremely committed to Olympic ideals, and Avery Brundage, a former Olympic athlete and self-made, affluent construction magnate, one who ruled American Olympic matters with an iron hand.

Paul Helms has been largely forgotten in Olympic history, while Avery Brundage captured much if not more media attention in his time than any other president of the International Olympic Committee (IOC), including Coubertin, as well as the more contemporary driver of the IOC's "rags to riches" financial story, Juan Antonio Samaranch. In some ways Paul Helms and Avery Brundage were alike. They were born in the Gilded Age; only two years separated their birth in the late 1880s. Both came from families of modest economic circumstance. Each was deprived of a parent early in their lives, Helms his mother, Brundage his father. Both became highly successful businessmen as adults. But there their similarities ended. Helms was diminutive; Brundage was a formidable physical specimen. Helms exuded a pleasing personal demeanor; Brundage was distant, often gruff and abrasive, a man with few close friends, even though he could name legions of acquaintances. Helms displayed qualities of friendliness, compatibility, and compromise on difficult issues; Brundage personified power and uncompromising persuasion in his dealings.

Events surrounding the 1932 Los Angeles Olympics brought Helms and Brundage together. Those events detailed a saga that established a foundation upon which the Modern Olympic Movement and its constituent United States Olympic Committee (USOC) eventually built the superstructure that supports their multibillion dollar endeavors. As the great festival's opening approached in the summer of 1932 (by then, the Olympic Games were just that, a great festival) the city of Los Angeles was transformed into an elaborate party setting. Signs glorifying the competitions were everywhere; banners adorned businesses and public buildings, and pennants hung from street-side lampposts. The economic depression that gripped the world, including California, did not prevent an enormous last-minute rush of ticket buyers from engulfing sales outlets in downtown Los Angeles. On the afternoon of July 30 almost 105,000 spectators, by far a new record, crowded into the Memorial Coliseum to view the opening ceremonies. President Herbert Hoover was not present to officially open the Games; Vice President Charles Curtis represented the White House.[5] For a two-week period almost two thousand athletes representing thirty-nine nations vied in the various competitions. Daily attendance figures ranged from 45,170 on July 31 to 110,410 on August 10. Spectators witnessed sixteen world-record and thirty-three Olympic-record performances, among them the swimming successes of the Japanese men and women and the startling track and field performances of Mildred "Babe" Didrikson, perhaps the most notable hero of the Games in the eyes of Americans. In the face of the economic headwinds, which included a last-minute 10 percent tax (ordered by the U.S. Congress) on Olympic tickets, Los Angeles organizers ultimately reported a $1.5 million surplus.

The 1932 Los Angeles Games introduced a new feature for Olympic athletes: a residential village, at least for men (women competitors were housed at the Chapman Park Hotel in suburban Beverley Hills). Built in Baldwin Hills, a relatively short bus ride from the Coliseum, the Olympic Village was a marvel of planning and execution. A chain-link fence surrounded the premises; twenty-five thousand geraniums, five thousand shrubs, and eight hundred six-foot palm trees beautified the landscape; ten miles of drainage pipe carried waste materials away; refrigeration was provided by ice; cooking fuel arrived in the form of bottled propane gas. Some five hundred pink-and-white two-room bungalows provided accommodation, interspersed lavatories called "comfort stations" took care of toilet needs, and forty kitchen–dining-room facilities satisfied food-service requirements. Delivered to the Olympic Village kitchens each morning were 2,750 pounds of string beans, eighteen hundred pounds of fresh peas, fifty sacks of potatoes, 450 gallons of ice cream, and hundreds of loaves of bread—but not just any bread: rather, Helms Olympic Bread, the flagship product of Helms Bakeries. Its owner, Paul Hoy Helms, was a well-known, well-intentioned, and socially well-connected and public-spirited Los Angeles citizen.

Paul Helms was born in Ottawa, Franklin County, Kansas, on September 19, 1889, to Reverend Elmer Ellsworth Helms, a Methodist minister, and his wife, Ora Ella Hoy Helms. When he was three years old, his mother's premature death split the family. Young Paul was sent to Ohio to be raised on his uncle's dairy farm in the Township of Mount Healthy (near Cincinnati). Paul's "surrogate parents" were his mother's brother, William E. Hoy, and his wife, Anna Marie, each a deaf mute. Together with the Hoys' six natural children, young Helms exhibited a sunny disposition and a bent for the hard work and responsibility demanded by "farm life." He was raised, too, in an atmosphere that encouraged sport. His "Uncle Bill" was a major-league professional baseball player, a centerfielder of distinction. Known as "Dummy" Hoy, he debuted with the Washington Nationals in 1888 and closed his career with the Cincinnati Reds in 1902.[6] Paul Helms was college educated, a graduate of Syracuse University (1912). Of small stature, he was a coxswain on one of the Orangemen's varsity crews. Service in World War I was followed by a stint selling insurance in Pennsylvania and his marriage to Pearl Ellis.

Following a move to New York City in the early 1920s, Helms opened a small bakery with but one home-delivery route. By 1926, at which time chronically poor health forced his temporary retirement, he had built the business to embrace two

Paul Helms (Photo courtesy of
LA84 Foundation.)

hundred delivery routes. In 1928 he shifted his family to the more healthful climate
of southern California. Once settled in Los Angeles and "itching to get back to
work," in 1931 he established Helms Bakeries at the corner of Venice and Washington Streets in Culver City, an area of greater Los Angeles not far from both Baldwin
Hills and the Memorial Coliseum. His products, a variety of breads, rolls, buns,
donuts, and sponge cakes, were sold solely in his own store and to homes along
eleven routes delivered in colorful two-tone blue-and-yellow vans.[7]

A Los Angeles newspaper sketch of the proposed Olympic Village prompted
Paul Helms's original fascination with Olympic matters. An idea evolved in his
mind: athletes required meals, and bread was a universal staple in daily diets the
world over, irrespective of ethnicity and country of residence. Helms's early life,
education, expanding business, and social connections, together with his sales-
manship, all factored into convincing Los Angeles Olympic Organizing Committee
officials to grant him the exclusive bakery-goods supply contract for the Olympic
Village. Providing bread for the Olympic Village's dining tables was one thing;
capitalizing on affiliation with the Olympic Games in marketing his products to
a larger consumer constituency was quite another. Realizing that competitors

lurked in every corner of Los Angeles, Helms moved swiftly to legally register and protect his use of Olympic identity marks.[8] Next, he sought to advertise an official link between his products and the Modern Olympic Movement.[9] Gaining "temporary approval" from the U.S. government's patent office,[10] in rapid fashion Helms Olympic Bread appeared on the market in colorful packaging adorned with the distinctive Olympic five-ring symbol and associated marks. Helms capped his initiative with the proclamation that Helms Bakeries was the Official Olympic Baker. *Olympic Bread*, buttressed by its Olympic brand connections, quickly filled the display cases of Helms's storefront, his home delivery vans, and, even more important, the cupboards and breadboxes in thousands of Los Angeles homes.

Paul Helms was not alone in capitalizing on advertising products in association with Los Angeles' festival. Scores of local firms advertised merchandise festooned with Olympic marks and logos. For instance, the Broadway Hollywood Store maintained an "Olympic booth" outside its main entrance where consumers purchased neckties, handkerchiefs, and stationery embossed with the Olympic rings; Bullocks Department Store on Wilshire Boulevard regularly displayed the five rings in its newspaper advertising for women's apparel; Nisley Shoes extolled the quality of its "Olympic Winners" product line. "Olympic business" was "good business."

Helms Bakeries thrived as its Olympic Bread cut a swath through its competitors. One rival, the huge Weber's Bakery chain, went on the offensive, attempting to muscle in on Helms's exclusive contract to supply bakery products to the Olympic Village. Weber's offered to furnish bread to one of the foreign teams in residence. Like Helms, Weber's *Los Angeles Times* ads appeared with the five-ring symbol, the Latinized motto (*Citius, Altius, Fortius*), the USOC Olympic shield, and a headline challenge: "Have You Changed Yet?"[11] Helms's reaction was swift. Noting Weber's gambit and the veritable avalanche of Olympic-related advertising and marketing of products in the Los Angeles area, he ordered his lawyers to protect his legally acquired copyrights. Weber's Bakery desisted.

The Los Angeles Games came and went. They were judged a huge success. Helms's business underwent steady expansion as it continued to market its products in Los Angeles under the Olympic brand. Then, too, Olympic Bread, having caught the fancy of the German delegation in the Olympic Village, prompted Carl Diem, secretary general of the Berlin Organizing Committee for the 1936 Games in Germany, to forge an agreement with Helms to provide Berlin's Olympic Village bakery needs.

A rapt and increasingly disgusted observer of the Olympic commercial flavor of the Los Angeles Games was Avery Brundage, the American Olympic Association's (AOA) president and one of the most important men in American sport. Born in Detroit, Michigan, on September 28, 1887, to Charles and Minnie Lloyd Brundage, he moved with his family to Chicago in 1892, where his father promptly abandoned his mother, thus consigning young Avery to a youthful life of hard work. From the start he embraced a strong desire to succeed. Raised mainly by his mother and, at times, by "family relatives," he was an inveterate pursuer of part-time jobs. He somehow found time for indulging his passion—competing in sports, especially track and field. A successful high school athlete at Crane Tech in Chicago, Brundage entered the University of Illinois in 1905, graduating four years later with a degree in civil engineering. During his undergraduate years he was an active participant in intramural sports and varsity track and field, as well as various campus societies.

Despite this profile, Brundage was not the type of personality that naturally drew people to him. This trait followed him through his life. He continued his athletic endeavors after leaving the university in 1909 by joining the Chicago Athletic Association. With the possible exception of the discus throw, Brundage could hardly be identified as an outstanding performer in any of the ten disciplines that constituted what was known at the time as the "all-around" event, the forerunner of what became the decathlon. Finishing third in the Amateur Athletic Union's (AAU) all-around championship in 1910, Brundage attempted to qualify for the 1912 Olympic Games in Stockholm. He was successful, barely gaining a place on the 1912 American Olympic Team. His results in Stockholm were disappointing, far behind those of his teammate, the celebrated Jim Thorpe, who won the coveted Olympic gold medal in both the decathlon and pentathlon; Brundage finished a dismal sixteenth in the decathlon, a less dismal sixth in the pentathlon.

Following his Olympic experience, Brundage entered the construction business in Chicago, founding his own company in 1915 (The Avery Brundage Company). He complemented his workdays with volunteer activity in the AAU's Central Association, steadily rising through its administrative ranks to eventually become a powerful member of the AAU's affiliate, the AOA, of which he became president in 1932. After leading the U.S. Olympic delegation to Berlin in 1936 for the infamous Nazi-organized Games, Brundage was co-opted to membership in the IOC. Over much of the same period Brundage navigated the Great Depression of the 1930s in far better circumstances than most Americans. "You didn't have to be a wizard to make a fortune in the Depression," he at one time reminisced. "All you had to do was buy stocks and bonds in depressed corporations for a few cents on the dollar and then wait."[12] By the end of the 1920s Brundage's net worth surpassed $1 million, advancing steadily through the following three decades to reach a reported $25 million by the early 1960s.

It was from Brundage's two lofty platforms of power and responsibility (AOA and IOC) that he confronted Paul Helms. By 1938 Brundage's agitation over Helms's sustained advertising activities finally boiled over. He fired off a letter to William R. Schroeder, managing director of Helms Bakeries, demanding that Helms's "scandalous acts" of advertising using Olympic symbols cease at once. Brundage dispatched a copy of his "Schroeder letter" to fellow American IOC member William May Garland, a Los Angeles resident.[13] Unknown to Brundage, Garland and Helms were good friends—in fact, admirers of each other. Garland responded to Brundage, asking him to soften his demands: "It is always a joy to pass [Helms's] business place for he has illuminated the shield of the IOC on his building. In fact, in a nice dignified way he keeps the thought of Olympism and the Olympic Games alive and before the public in a manner that surely is not objectionable." One can imagine Brundage becoming apoplectic by Garland's "take" on Helms. If not, then surely by Garland's closing thought: "I wish you could have come to Los Angeles, that I might have introduced you to Paul Helms, so that you could have become intimately acquainted with his friendliness to everything that the Olympic Games stand for. He is an immeasurably fine American citizen, highly respected in his own community."[14]

Brundage seethed. Responding to Garland, he railed against commercial efforts to exploit the Olympic Movement. "If manufacturers and dealers . . . use the name Olympic in their advertising," wrote Brundage, "they [the Olympic words and marks] will soon loose [*sic*] their meaning." He went further: "You cannot imagine how many attempts there are to capitalize on the Olympic Games and the difficulty we have in preventing promoters to use the Olympic Movement for their own personal gain. . . . We have strict rules for athletes and so far have excellent cooperation from the public."[15] And there the issue died, at least for the time being. Brundage had little more than bluster in his arsenal of tactics for dealing with commercial infringers on the Olympic Movement. Besides, America faced far more serious dilemmas than a festering problem in the domestic Olympic affairs of the nation: in September 1939 Germany marched on Poland; Europe erupted into full-scale war. The Pearl Harbor tragedy of December 7, 1941, drew the United States into World War II. A moratorium descended on Olympic matters worldwide, including cancellation of the Games of the XIIth and XIIIth Olympiads scheduled for 1940 and 1944.

In the years prior to, during, and immediately following World War II, Helms expanded his marketing portfolio into radio and billboard advertising. By 1950 his eleven original home delivery routes were fast approaching a total numbering one thousand, ranging as far north as Fresno, as far south as San Diego. Baked daily in Culver City, almost a million loaves of Olympic Bread made their way to thousands of California households in individual wrappers and distinctive delivery vans bearing the message: "Olympic Games Bakers—Choice of Olympic Champions." Helms became a well-known benefactor of amateur sport in Los Angeles and southern California, even establishing a charitable foundation for that explicit purpose, the Helms Olympic Athletic Foundation. Well aware of Brundage's reaction if he were to learn of Helms's use of the word Olympic, William May Garland asked his friend to remove the word 'Olympic' from the Foundation's title. Obligingly, Helms complied.[16]

As energetic as Helms was in developing his business, Brundage was even busier in consolidating his power base in the Modern Olympic Movement. Undisputed czar of Olympic matters in the United States since 1928 and a member of the IOC since July 1936, Brundage experienced a meteoric rise in the echelons of the administration of international sport. IOC president Henri Baillet-Latour appointed him to the Executive Committee in 1937. By 1941, stimulated greatly by Brundage's leadership, attempts to organize Pan-American Games commenced, an initiative that reached fruition in 1951. And, following the death of Baillet-Latour in 1942, Brundage's close friend, IOC vice president J. Sigfrid Edström (Sweden), assumed IOC leadership duties, limited though they were in the midst of history's most sweeping and devastating global conflagration. Looking ahead to postwar times, surveying his age (in 1944 he turned seventy-four), and being aware of his noticeable advancing physical infirmity, Edström suggested that a new position, second vice president, be installed in IOC bylaws. A mail vote in 1945 confirmed the idea. Edström appointed "friend Brundage" to the newly created slot. When Edström was confirmed as IOC president at the first postwar meetings in 1946, Brundage immediately "moved up," filling the first vice president position.[17] Speaking publicly, frequently, and loudly on both domestic and international Olympic matters, Brundage was often mistakenly viewed as the leader of the Olympic Movement, years before his eventual election to the presidency in 1952 following Edström's retirement.

Despite his preoccupation with American Olympic matters and his rapidly increasing stature in the IOC, Brundage did not forget about a nagging dilemma occurring in California—the "unauthorized" use of Olympic symbols in selling commercial products, particularly Olympic Bread peddled by Helms Bakeries. Following the end of World War II, the AOA, newly re-minted as the United States Olympic Association (USOA), embarked on an aggressive fundraising campaign to send an Olympic team to the 1948 London Olympics. An important development in protocol for private donations considerably enhanced the campaign—the United States Congress's recognition of the USOA in such a way as to authorize it to issue federal income tax deduction receipts for private contributions made to its program. Such solicited contributions formed the essence of the USOA's financial existence. On several occasions over a period of some twenty years prior to 1947, American Olympic officials tried to gain such a federal judgement. Congress's retort was always the same: the USOA is a sports organization, not an educational organization; therefore, it did not qualify.[18]

Finally, a Detroit group, spurred by the fact that its city (like Los Angeles) envisioned bidding for the 1952 or 1956 Summer Games, volunteered the services of a respected law firm (Cook, Beake, Miller, Wrock, and Cross) to pursue the tax deduction file. In early December 1947 counselor Richard Cross reported that the USOA's quest had finally met with success. The USOA stationery letterhead promptly trumpeted that contributions to the organization were tax deductible.

During the same twenty-year period those advocating the USOA's position also engaged in discussions directed toward taking necessary steps to protect the USOA's interests regarding the Olympic name, motto, and emblems through seeking incorporation status from Congress. No action was ever taken. As in the tax deduction matter, the USOA failed to devote "the time or the expense necessary to do a professional job of protecting the Olympic name."[19]

In late 1947 Helms tendered a bid to supply the American Olympic Team with bread during London's fast-approaching Games. In what Brundage must have considered a gross oversight, the USOA awarded Helms the supply contract, with absolutely no restrictions regarding advertising.[20] After the contract had been duly signed by Helms and USOA officials, Brundage became aware of the agreement. One can imagine his ire. Brundage faced a dilemma—on one hand he castigated Helms for continued misuse of Olympic symbols; on the other he grudgingly

William May Garland, chief organizer of the 1932 Olympics and a U.S. IOC member, hands a check to Herbert Ivey, treasurer of the Los Angeles Olympic Committee for the 1948 American Olympic Teams (LAOCAOT), while Paul Helms, second from left, and John Jewett Garland, president of the LAOCAOT, also submit contributions. (© 1948 / International Olympic Committee (IOC) / United States Olympic Committee. Photo courtesy of the IOC.)

recognized that Helms was fundamentally responsible for raising a great deal of money for the American Olympic Movement. Helms played a central role in furthering the efforts of the Los Angeles Olympic Committee for the 1948 American Olympic Teams, a group of local businessmen, to raise more than $40,000 for the USOA, a sum that nearly outstripped the total forwarded by the other twenty-six municipal committees across the country that engaged in fundraising. Helms supplemented this contribution with $10,000 from the Helms Athletic Foundation, as well as a personal donation of $500.[21]

In typical Brundage fashion, he downplayed the money raised and pressed forward his mission to stop Helms's advertising. Brundage renewed his attack on Helms at a USOA meeting in New York following the 1948 Summer Games. In mid-December he wrote to John Jewett Garland, who had succeeded his father as an IOC member. Railing in his usual abrasive tone whenever Helms's case arose, Brundage argued that the baker's advertising on billboards and radio featured untrue statements, violated Olympic traditions, and reflected poor taste: "I have received many protests from the general public as well as from the Olympic family," he thundered. "As a matter of fact some of Helms's competitors have suggested they might go further than a protest. . . . Cannot something be done to stop this violation of Olympic principles, which has reached the proportions of an international scandal?"[22] Young Garland, like his father, admired Helms. He did nothing to help relieve Brundage's frustration.

Enter John Terence McGovern—The Great Conciliator

Hearing nothing from John Jewett Garland in Los Angeles, Avery Brundage pursued another tack. During the year following the closure of the 1948 Summer Games in London, Helms Bakeries and the commercialization of Olympic symbols became increasingly discussed subjects at the USOA's New York headquarters.[23] One member of the USOA's Executive Council who listened attentively to Brundage's often vitriolic statements against Helms was John Terence (Terry) McGovern, a septuagenarian, accomplished semi-retired New York lawyer. Seeking further information, McGovern met privately with Brundage, agreeing to help in the Helms matter. As it turned out, McGovern became the critical catalyst in its resolution.

Terry McGovern was born in Albany, New York on December 9, 1876, to Irish-born parents, Terence and Catherine (neé Lynch). Eighty-three years later, on the day following his final birthday celebration, New York's *World-Telegram* rhapsodized on McGovern as a "beloved legal-eagle" who has "more titles and non-paying clients than any other lawyer we know" and who, in his lifetime, fostered "the finest ideals in sports."[24] When he died some six months later, on May 26, 1960, the writer of his obituary at the *New York Herald Tribune* proclaimed him "our Sports 'envoy' . . . [who] devoted most of his adult years to the promotion of the highest ideals in the field of national and international sports."[25] Those glowing accolades were rightfully earned. Following a baccalaureate degree in law from Cornell University in 1900, he practiced law in New York City for the next sixty years. A slightly built, former varsity cross-country runner at Cornell, McGovern served in the American Expeditionary Forces in World War I, being honorably discharged in 1918 at the rank of major. In 1921 his distinguished volunteerism in the cause of amateur sport led to his association with the AOA, where he quickly gained a position on the Executive Council as the organization's official nonsalaried lawyer and was, as well, elected as one of the organization's three vice presidents. In 1931 he was elected president of the huge New York City Public Schools Athletic League (PSAL). By the middle of the 1950s McGovern had served on fifty occasions as an official at what was arguably the nation's premier track and field event, the annual IC4A championships (Intercollegiate Association of Amateur Athletics of America). Upon learning of McGovern's death, Philip Noel-Baker, a 1959 Nobel Laureate, wrote to Cornell: "We [Oxford and Cambridge Universities] are grieved to hear of Mr. McGovern's death. The [Oxford and Cambridge] Achilles Club had made him an honorary member in May."[26] Terry McGovern was indeed a sterling servant of American and international sport, including affairs associated with the Modern Olympic Movement.

Once McGovern offered Brundage his help in solving the nettlesome Helms Bakeries file, he became dedicated to the project. Removing "confrontation" from an arena characterized by the emotional battle of wills between the rambunctious Avery Brundage and the convivial but nevertheless determined Paul Helms, McGovern elevated the interchanges to a level of polite civility. "Reporting in" to Brundage in mid-June 1949, McGovern dealt his first card in the poker hand he intended to play:

> Since our last meeting I drafted and redrafted until I thought I had a proper conciliatory form of approach to the attorneys for Helms. . . . [USOA colleagues] think the lapse of time from 1931 to 1949 would ruin our chances. I realize their point but I am never convinced I am going to be licked when I know I have justice on my side. I am trying reconciliation. . . . Failing that course, I may decide it would be better to fight and take a beating, if necessary, than to have the people of the U.S. believe we consent to the outrage. At least a fight would show we did what we could.[27]

Adopting a "soft" approach, McGovern initiated correspondence with Helms's lawyers in Los Angeles. Almost simultaneously, a new twist in the saga emerged. Los Angeles, cheered by its successful staging of the 1932 Summer Games, pressed forward with overtures to bid for and host future Olympic Games, perhaps as early as those scheduled but not yet awarded for 1952 or 1956. Los Angeles formed an exploratory bid committee charged with furthering such a possibility, the chair of which was none other than the well-to-do, well-known, well-connected, philanthropic Paul Helms, impresario of Olympic Bread.

On the afternoon of Sunday, June 19, 1949, Helms convened a meeting at the posh California Club in downtown Los Angeles to lay his committee's plans before American Olympic and amateur sport officials. Representing the interests of two of the three foremost amateur sports organizations in the country (the third was the National Collegiate Athletic Association [NCAA]) was J. Lyman Bingham, assistant to the president of the AAU, and Kenneth "Tug" Wilson, vice president of the USOA. John Jewett Garland represented the IOC. Helms's fellow committee members, Bill Hunter and Wilbur Johns, athletic directors at the University of Southern California (USC) and the University of California at Los Angeles (UCLA), respectively, completed the meeting's attendees. Though most of the discussion focused on Los Angeles' plan to host future Olympic Games, the subject inevitably turned to Helms's perceived abuse of Olympic symbols in advertising his business products. Three weeks later Bingham wrote to Brundage with a full report on his California experience. Bingham was frank:

> There was considerable bad feeling over the use Mr. Helms has made of Olympic insignia. Mr. Helms . . . very graciously explained that it has been in use since the 1932 Olympic Games. He felt that had there been any objections they should have been presented directly to him years ago. He stated that he was familiar with Terry McGovern's correspondence with his attorneys and that he was well pleased with McGovern's attitude. He felt that the attorneys would work out something satisfactory. . . . Incidentally, Mr. Helms voiced considerable displeasure at your having written on the subject to various individuals other than himself rather than taking the matter directly to him. . . . Mr. Helms stated that he had been prevailed upon and was in a position to make use of the Olympic insignia on a national basis; that he was mad enough at one time to actually put some such plan into operation, but now he had definitely decided to confine his activities to Southern California and that he would definitely promise not to take advantage of his copyright in the other states. The weakness in the position of the Olympic Committee at the present time is that they accepted his $10,000 in 1948 with practically no strings attached being fully aware at the time of the manner in which he has capitalized upon Olympic insignia ever since 1932.[28]

Bingham closed his letter with a notable softening shift in tone. "Throughout the meeting the impression kept getting stronger with me that we should work with Mr. Helms on a friendly basis and take advantage of his willingness and the many opportunities he has to be of value to the Olympic Committee. . . . I believe at the earliest opportunity you should have a talk with Mr. Helms. . . . I am sure you will like him and that he will like you," wrote Bingham. "You both have a genuine interest in amateur sport and you cannot be too far apart in your thinking."[29] McGovern received a copy of Bingham's letter. It elicited a rapid response from the counselor, together with a recommendation for Brundage's "next step." McGovern encouraged Brundage to follow Bingham's recommended path: "Lyman [Bingham] believes he [Helms] will ultimately cease to use the circles and otherwise imply our official responsibility for his product, if he is continued to be approached in a friendly spirit. I agree with Lyman that it would be well for you to call on him and talk about the welfare of the Olympic movement."[30]

Brundage did nothing of the sort; in fact, he acted with opposite resolve. First, he wrote to Helms Bakeries' W. R. Schroeder. "Dear Schroeder," he wrote, abandoning the usual courtesies extended in formal correspondence. "The United States Olympic Association, of which I am president, has a long standing grievance against Mr. Helms because of the misappropriation and commercialization of Olympic insignia. The grievance has been growing bitterer throughout the years, and it is shared by the International Olympic Committee."[31] Second, Brundage wrote to Daniel J. Ferris, USOA Executive Board member. The USOA Executive Board amply discussed Lyman Bingham's reflections following his visit to Los Angeles in mid-June and his meeting with Paul Helms. Ferris, too, similar to McGovern and Bingham, held the view that conciliation and compromise should be the approach taken with Helms. Brundage did not agree! "I think Helms hypnotized you fellows," he wrote to Ferris. "He steals our insignia and builds up a fortune, then gives a few dollars to amateur sport and everyone thinks that he is an angel."[32]

The two adversaries in the case, Avery Brundage and Paul Helms, met each other only once prior to 1949, the year that events in the case accelerated to a boil. They were seated beside each other at the head table of the *Los Angeles Times* Sports Awards Dinner in January 1948, an event at which Brundage accepted the Sportsman of the Year Award. Though his differences with Helms were well established by this time, the celebratory setting of the evening deterred Brundage from raising the issue of Helms's "scandalous" advertising. In fact, each resisted getting involved personally with the other. Brundage was content to fire broadsides at Helms from a distance, letting McGovern, Bingham, USOA-appointed lawyers, and other amateur sports officials carry on the legal skirmishes. Helms, on the other hand, listened to envoys sent by Brundage, weighed the views of his own lawyers, and in general maintained a low profile.

Despite the personal impasse, it was Helms who finally broke the stalemate, writing personally to Brundage in late September 1949. Reminding Brundage of "the most satisfactory conference at the California Club" (the Bingham meeting), he related that he would meet with Terry McGovern in New York the following month. Helms recounted some of his own long history pertinent to Olympic matters in California. He ended his missive by raising the prickly "commercialization issue."

Referring to Brundage's strident complaint directed to Helms Bakeries' managing director W. R. Schroeder a decade earlier, Helms simply stated: "Our progress is no different today than in 1939, seven years after the 1932 Games in Los Angeles."[33]

The initiative for a personal meeting between Helms and Terry McGovern came from the venerable New York lawyer. Learning that Helms's business agenda would take him to New York, McGovern sought to capitalize on the fortuitous circumstance by arranging a personal meeting with Helms, a man he knew only by reputation. McGovern, for all his esteem of Brundage, and it was considerable, was well aware of his bristly character. Assessing the personal qualities of Helms, face to face, would be important in weighing his strategy for advancing the commercialization case under his direction.

In early October 1949 Helms, in the cordial atmosphere of McGovern's New York office, sat down with a man whose legal career exemplified wisdom and patience. From the start, McGovern was impressed with Helms, and Helms, likewise, with McGovern. McGovern was quick to send Brundage a report of the meeting. He found the California businessman to be quiet in composure, genuinely friendly and unassuming in his personal demeanor. Helms patiently related to McGovern the history of his firm's involvement in Olympic matters. During his otherwise calm discourse with McGovern, the sole displeasure Helms registered was his umbrage at having been cast by Brundage as a thief of the Olympic symbol, a charge that he considered inflammatory—indeed, a statement that prompted his attorneys to advise him to mount a legal suit against Brundage. Helms wanted an apology,[34] a measure that the American Olympic head owned little history in giving. Much more important for McGovern, however, was Helms's agreement "in principle," rendered near the end of their second meeting, to limit his advertising to the local community of Los Angeles and, even more important, to redesign his advertising emblem to remove identification with the Olympic five-ring symbol and the Olympic motto.[35] Clearly, as persistently recommended by McGovern, events dictated that a meeting between Brundage and Helms take place.

In late December 1949 Avery Brundage, accompanied by Detroit counselors Richard Cross and Arthur Smith, met with Paul Helms, Paul Helms Jr., and their attorneys, G. E. McDowell and Albert Fairies, at a luncheon arranged by the senior Helms at the California Club. Against his doctor's advice he rose from a sickbed to host the meeting. Following a somewhat constrained dialogue between all parties present, mainly concerning trademark issues, they reached an agreement in principle. It called for Helms to henceforth: recognize that pertinent to the United States and its territories the Olympic marks were the property of the USOA; provide no objection to the USOA seeking registration of the Olympic marks; and discontinue use of Olympic marks in his firm's advertising. A concession by the USOA allowed Helms to retain the right to use the word "Olympic" in connection with his bakery products, except that the phrase "Official Olympic Bakers" be exorcised—"Official" went, "Olympic" remained.[36] Following the meeting Brundage quickly conveyed his thanks to Helms "for the enjoyable luncheon that you arranged at the California Club" and closed his letter with the thought that he would be pleased "to report to the United States Olympic Association meeting next month that it can expect full cooperation from you. This will be most helpful in our campaign to protect the Olympic insignia."[37]

Even so, the issue was far from being resolved. Although an "agreement in principle" surfaced, subsequent dialogue delayed the conclusion of the lengthy and troublesome case. A series of communications between Brundage's USOA lawyers and Helms and his legal team occupied the early months of 1950. Helms produced new advertising labels. Gone were the five-ring symbol, the Latinized motto, and the word "official" in juxtaposition with "Olympic." Still, Brundage quibbled about Helms's continued advertising use of the red, white, and blue shield, commonly referred to as the "Olympic shield." The "Olympic shield," emblazoned on the jerseys of American Olympic athletes since 1906 and embossed prominently on official letterhead correspondence had, nevertheless, never been registered by the USOA as a trademark—yet it had been included in the Olympic marks copyrighted by Helms in 1932.[38] A second contentious issue remained: the obliteration of a large sculptured Olympic emblem from the façade of the Helms plant in Culver City, a costly renovation. Through it all Helms's lawyers urged a hard stand; their client had already given up far more than advised. Brundage and USOA lawyers (minus the voice of Terry McGovern) pressed for Helms's complete surrender on all issues.

January, February, and a good part of March 1950 came and went as nitpicking by Brundage and the USOA continued. The more the issue dragged on, the more Terry McGovern became convinced that Helms would concede the main "sticking points" if only Brundage would meet personally with the bakery owner in a manner other than his well-known confrontational demeanor. McGovern attempted to prompt Brundage in this direction:

> I think it advisable for you to see Helms if only as evidence of friendly cooperation for the good of the games. No humans are perfect. Neither you, nor I, nor Helms, nor McDowell [Helms's chief counsel]. . . . Helms has been pretty sick. It would be nice if for that reason alone you greeted his return to health. . . . I have repeatedly stated that neither side is entitled to a 100% victory. We have not a clear and unblemished case; neither has Helms. What concerns me most is that lawyers insist on proving how good lawyers they are, and forgetting that while we do not want to lose face and principle, neither do we want to lose good financial support when we need it. . . . I'm always afraid of lawyers. I succeed because I deceive people into thinking I am a sincere friend of anyone who wants to settle things in a way that human frailties

can be forgiven and forgotten, at the same time having them understand that when I get in a court battle I expect to win it. So you see Helms can be a diplomat. Helms is not trying to dodge, but there are items which he wants to save.[39]

Brundage had no intention of meeting with Helms. Despite McGovern's counsel and plea for a "softer tone," Brundage's intransigence and his busy business schedule stood squarely in the way of a solution.

In the winter and spring of 1950, too, the USOA focused on two objectives. Terry McGovern was in charge of both. The first, aimed at incorporating the USOA through a federal act, McGovern delegated to Cross and Smith. Success in that venture would secure trademark and copyright protection for USOA marks inside the United States and its territories. The second objective focused on consummating a final agreement with Helms. McGovern himself assumed that responsibility.

Since Brundage resisted an amicable negotiation, a stalemate persisted. By mid-June McGovern's well-tried patience reached its limits. He acted, informing Brundage that he "planned to leave for Los Angeles next week to settle the Helms case."[40] Shortly after his arrival in Los Angeles, following meetings with Helms and his counsel, McGovern telegraphed Brundage at 1:42 A.M. on June 27 with a message that set a record for brevity: "Case settled."[41] A second McGovern telegram sent to Brundage some nine hours later was equally succinct: "He [Helms] asks no publicity on settlement."[42] Upon his return to New York a week later McGovern told Brundage that Helms's lawyers had been smug, reinforced by exhibits in the form of Helms's contract with the 1948 Olympic authorities, which bolstered his legal position immensely. Three months later, in early October, McGovern wrote to Brundage revealing the critical factor that made the successful conclusion of the case possible—very simply, the goodwill of Helms himself toward American Olympic fortunes:

> I have never revealed (and do not intend to) the evidence Helms' lawyers had to mousetrap Cross and Smith. But they had it. Not way back; but in 1948. Notice in connection with the $10,000 contribution that Helms would use the insignia exactly as he had been; and he conditioned his contribution upon the privilege so to advertise without any limitation whatsoever. After the settlement his lawyers turned over to me copies of the documents. No wonder they were angry when Helms ordered them to surrender. During my 50 years of practice, in my safe are placed many writings which would embarrass clients and of which they have never been informed. So let it be with the Helms situation.[43]

Parallel to the Brundage-Helms-McGovern dialogue during the first six months of 1950, Cross and Smith's petition in Congress for the formal incorporation of the USOA made headway. In late February Arthur Smith presented a preliminary draft to McGovern. Wrote Smith: "I have considered the tentative draft of the proposed Federal Charter and feel that this matter should be carried forward to a conclusion. . . . I have noted a recent report of a favorable action given on a bill to incorporate the Girl Scouts. Maybe the Girl Scouts have left Congress in the mood to pass necessary legislation for our proposed incorporation so it may well be that the present time is propitious for completing this work."[44] Indeed the time *was* "propitious," and Congress *was* "in the mood." Just short of seven months later, Congress ratified the Act to Incorporate the United States Olympic Association. Among a litany of rights, duties, and responsibilities, the act gave the USOA sweeping jurisdiction on Olympic matters within the United States and its territories, including copyright/trademark ownership of its corporate seal (the Olympic shield), interlocking five-ring symbol, motto, and the words "Olympic" and "Olympiad." The act stated:

> It shall be unlawful for any person within the jurisdiction of the United States to falsely or fraudulently hold himself out as, or represent, or pretend himself to be a member or an agent for the United States Olympic Association or its subordinate organizations for the purpose of soliciting, collecting, or receiving money or material or for any purpose to wear or display the insignia thereof for the fraudulent purpose of inducing the belief that he is at such time a member of or an agent for the United States Olympic Association.[45]

One can imagine Avery Brundage's reaction when he read the opening statement of the act. "Hallelujah" might well have been his exclamation; finally, federal recognition and legal protection for the USOA's name and property. For the future financial health of the USOA, the act contained another critically important passage:

> It shall be unlawful for any person, corporation, or association, other than the United States Olympic Association or its subordinate organizations and its duly authorized employees and agents for the purpose of trades, theatrical exhibition, athletic performance and competition, or for business or charitable purpose to use within the territory of the United States of America and its exterior possessions, the emblems of the United States Olympic Association.[46]

As much as Brundage celebrated the landmark document, his elation was tempered when he read one of the closing paragraphs of the act:

> That any person, corporation, or association that actually used, or whose assignor actually used, the said emblems, sign, insignia, or words for any lawful purpose prior to the effective date of this Act, shall not be deemed forbidden by this Act to continue the use thereof for the same purpose and for the same class or classes of goods to which said emblems, sign, insignia, or words have been used lawfully prior therefore.[47]

Paul Helms's legal position remained secure. Even so, Brundage could not resist describing the results of McGovern's trip to Los Angeles to meet with Helms as a Pyrrhic victory. Writing to Fred Matthei, a member of Detroit's Olympic bid committee, Brundage gloated: "Helms has finally capitulated."[48] Brundage's choice of the word "capitulated" to describe the end of the lengthy Helms affair was, to the Chicago millionaire, an apt expression of victory in the battle to exert his power over the altruistic California citizen and noteworthy contributor to the Olympic Movement in the United States.

The View from Lausanne

In the higher echelons of the IOC, especially at its headquarters in Lausanne, Switzerland, the Helms case was followed closely. The IOC, like the USOA, had never sought to protect its Olympic marks by government legislation in the only jurisdiction possible for its application, Switzerland. For years, the IOC, like the USOA, depended on bluster and, as Brundage put it, "excellent cooperation from the public" in facing commercial encroachment on the Olympic world.

Alarmed at the implications and consequences the Helms case raised, the IOC warned the NOCs to seek protection of Olympic words and symbols in their specific jurisdictions. A strong message for all NOCs to pay close attention to developments unfolding in the United States in the context of the Helms case appeared in the July 1949 issue of the *IOC Bulletin*.[49] Two months later, Sigfrid Edström wrote to his IOC colleague John Jewett Garland to request that Garland lodge an official protest against Helms's use of Olympic marks: "The Olympic circles and the Olympic motto may not be used for commercial purposes. It is against our Olympic rules, and Los Angeles will never get the Olympic Games as long as this outrage continues."[50] A month later Garland responded to Edström, defending Helms and requesting an explanation regarding the use of the five-ring symbol in other nations for advertising purposes.[51] In response to queries sent to NOCs seeking examples of perceived abuse and misuse of Olympic words and symbols, the IOC published a list of reported cases in the November issue of the *IOC Bulletin*. Not surprisingly, this notation appeared: "In the United States of America there is a firm, manufacturing cakes, special breads, and so on, and whose name we will not mention as we do not wish to make for it any additional propaganda . . . our vice-president, Mr. Avery Brundage, has taken the matter up seriously."[52] In fact, though, the IOC had no legal authority over use of the Olympic marks for advertising in the United States or, for that matter, any other country in the world, including Switzerland. Much like the USOA's dilemma, it, too, had failed to register the Olympic marks as Paul Hoy Helms successfully accomplished in 1932.

Closing Thoughts

In the wake of McGovern's return from his meeting in Los Angeles with Helms in June 1950, he was quick to inform his USOA colleagues of successful closure to the Helms case. The tone of McGovern's message clearly departed from what Brundage declared a "capitulation." It cast Helms as a gentleman of the first rank, able and willing to aid the Olympic cause in America:

> Gentlemen: There will be no future devotion to two-thirds of our meeting discussion time to the Helms case. The Helms case is settled. I went to Los Angeles and Mr. Helms agreed with me there to place the integrity, ideals, and hope of the Olympic faith above commercial, legal, and other individual considerations. Mr. Helms conducted himself, at our meetings with his counsel, in a spirit of generosity, cooperation, and quiet dignity. And this in the face of disapproval by his excellent and courteous counsel who were naturally chagrined to give up so much when they, with considerable justification from a legal standpoint, were confident of their position. Mr. Helms agreed to eliminate the circles, the latin [sic], the words "official Olympic bakers," and the word Olympic from the emblem and insignia. All that remains on the shield is "Helms Bread." The above elimination will be carried out on wrappers and trucks and more than 50 other varieties of advertising devices. This work will take much of Mr. Helms' time and a most substantial sum of his money. He also agreed that in any use of the word Olympic external to the shield, he would avoid the use of the word "official" or any other expression which might imply official or interested relation between him and the U.S.O.A. or U.S.O.C. He finally volunteered and signed an agreement to aid, if requested, the U.S.O.A., and U.S.O.C., through his able counsel and at his expense to protect the integrity of my Washington registration of our Olympic shield, as it stands with circles and other insignia. Even before I left California, Mr. Helms had begun black outs on signs and the first of the changed wrappers went out to customers.[53]

Terry McGovern had succeeded in tip-toeing through perilous minefields of strong egos, confrontational tactics, diverse philosophies, and prickly interpersonal relations. It had been an arduous journey, one that left him exasperated at times. In the face of huge commercialization of "things Olympic" in Los Angeles in 1932 and beyond, why had Avery Brundage been especially vexed and consumed by the Helms situation? Perhaps it was the fact that Helms's astute legal registration of Olympic marks clearly demonstrated that Brundage, the highest responsible authority of American Olympic matters, had failed in his oversight responsibilities. For the vain Brundage and his personal psychology, this must have been a bitter pill to swallow.

Following McGovern's triumph, plaudits were quick to come his way. Those from Avery Brundage were among the first to arrive: "My compliments to you again! You have accomplished even more than we expected. In view of the con-sistent success of the McGovern approach perhaps we ought to send you to see Stalin."[54] McGovern lost little time in answering, offering some final counseling on the matter: "Decidedly advise you arrange [to] see Helms. He admires your courage and honesty. He would like now to be your friend and work with you."[55] Despite McGovern's triumph and the new federal act in place, the avalanche of commercial exploitation of Olympic imagery in America, if anything, expanded. McGovern was well aware of the situation, leading to his testy admission to Brundage in the fall of 1950: "I'm tired of this whole silly business!"[56] Citing a 1950 survey, he later told Brundage that more than 22,500 commercial enterprises across America existed that were described in part by the word "Olympic,"[57] 148 of them industrial and mercantile establishments in Los Angeles that assured the public that they provided "Olympic goods, wares, and merchandise."[58]

Despite this disturbing admonition, it was Brundage who sagely pointed out what the new act would mean in the future of the Modern Olympic Movement. In conveying his appreciation to Fred Matthei and the Detroit Olympic bid committee for their role in the saga, he proclaimed: "The International Olympic Committee as well as the United States Olympic Association can never thank you enough for your help in the great victory, which will serve as a precedence for Olympic Committees in all parts of the world in their effort to prevent commercialization of Olympic words and insignia."[59] On this point the soon-to-be IOC president might have added an exclamation point: the "precedence" was indeed Olympian in scope.

CHAPTER 2

Melbourne, 1956

If the personalities and prolonged events surrounding the Helms Bakeries saga of the 1930s and 1940s vexed Avery Brundage, the 1950s produced some of the most trying times in his long association with the Olympic Movement, including, of course, the early years of his term as IOC president (1952–1972). The problems encountered were complex and challenging.

As the Brundage presidency opened, evolving world events impinged on the modern Olympic Games in ways that prompted their transformation into a truly universal, multisport festival. The culmination of World War II produced a Soviet Union and a supporting cast of aligned nations intent on using success at the Games as "soft power" persuasion in advancing the cause of communism world-wide. The resulting East–West Cold War conflict, embodying communist athletes challenging their ideological enemies from the West, provided the Olympics with a recipe for achieving enormous exposure in the form of public spectatorship, television viewership, and media attention. Then, too, the emergence of Third World countries from the embers of European and American imperialism, particularly on the African continent and in Pan-Pacific areas, swelled the size of the Olympic family of nations, the IOC's membership ranks, and, of course, the number of athletes competing in each festival. Over the ensuing years, influential, too, in the web of geopolitics were events that kept the great spectacle in sharp focus before an international audience, including the fracture of Germany, Korea, China, and later the Soviet Union, accompanied by the emergence of the Balkan States into competing spheres of political ideology and economic policy. Deeply embedded and directly linked to the exploding exposure of the Olympic Games to the far corners of the world was the "siren call" of commerce, the result of which spelled a future for the modern Olympics far beyond the imagination of even the shrewdest of pundits.

Of utmost repugnance to Brundage were the IOC's steady steps toward an indelible tie with commercialism, viewed with distaste by Olympic traditionalists of whom Brundage was foremost in reputation. As distasteful as they might have been for Brundage, the overtones of commercialism forecast a turn for the better in the precarious nature of the IOC's financial standing. For the IOC, television served as a promotional platform, a critical source of funds, and the catalyst for its marriage with the world of business.

The explosion of mass media outlets and their fascination with sport contributed more to the rising global popularity of the Olympic endeavor than any other single factor. Though print and radio coverage of the Olympic Games, it must be acknowledged, advanced global awareness and interest, each paled in comparison to television's impact. Between radio's first public appearance in November 1920, when Frank Conrad, a Westinghouse engineer, pioneered public broadcasting by establishing the world's first radio station (KDKA in Pittsburgh, Pennsylvania), to the end of the twelve-year moratorium imposed on the Olympics by World War II, technical improvements in radio equipment and transmissions fell far short of the startling developments in, and the rapid growth of, the television industry. What had once been left to the imaginations of newspaper readers and radio listeners as they consumed sporting events that reporters and commentators described was soon supplanted by the qualities of television's graphic portrayals, at first transmitted on a "delayed" basis and, not long thereafter, beamed "live" via satellite technology.

By the late 1940s, television sport audiences offered enticing consumer targets for the producers and sellers of manufactured goods and professional services. Fledgling television executives quickly recognized the value of sporting events as a major component of entertainment programming. For instance, between 1946 and 1949 the television rights that Major League Baseball sold for its annual autumn showcase, the World Series, increased tenfold, reaching a cumulative figure of $800,000 as the decade closed. In 1950, rights to five editions of the World Series commanded a $6 million contract. The purchase of exclusive broadcast rights to sporting events, and subsequent sales of their associated advertising time to the corporate world, aided immensely in sustaining television as a developing commercial enterprise.

It was in the earliest years of television sport programming that the idea of selling rights to broadcast the Olympic Games surfaced. Oddly, it was Avery Brundage, arch foe of commercial matters linked to the Olympic image, who took some of the first steps toward coupling the Olympic Movement with the cash registers of business. Prior to the 1948 London Summer Games, on behalf of the United States Olympic Association (USOA, renamed United States Olympic Committee [USOC] in 1961) and to its financial benefit, Brundage attempted to negotiate a contract for the sale of television rights to the U.S. Olympic Track and Field trials; he failed. Nevertheless, Brundage, the USOA's president, piloted an organization that depended exclusively on its own fundraising efforts for underwriting its operation. He remained keen on the financial prospects of television rights. In exchange for a share of the proceeds payable to the USOA, Brundage offered to negotiate a U.S. television contract on behalf of the Organizing Committee entrusted with staging the 1952 Helsinki Summer Olympics. Though a contract did not materialize, the soon-to-be IOC president kept a careful eye trained on the burgeoning phenomenon of televised sport and its link to business.

In August 1955 Michael Morris (the Lord Killanin), IOC member in Ireland, wrote to Brundage on the subject of commercial television revenue.[1] Two months earlier (June 1955) Bunny Ahearne, an official with the International Ice Hockey Federation (IIHF), highlighted the issue at a meeting of the IOC Executive Board in Paris.[2] Following up on Killanin's prompt, Brundage dispatched a circular letter to fellow members of the IOC Executive Board in which he referred to the "huge potential value of television rights," a revenue source that could assist the IOC in its efforts to promote Olympic ideals and provide for long overdue and desperately needed expansion of headquarters staff in Lausanne.[3] Brundage was torn between two considerations: the impact that a relationship with the television industry might have on the IOC's image as an organization that purposefully distanced itself from commercialism, and his view expressed in this sentence to his Executive Board colleagues: "I am not sure we should ever get into business, but on the other hand certainly we should not give millions of dollars away."[4]

Lord David Burghley, later the Marquess of Exeter (1956), an IOC Executive Board member and former Olympian, voiced his support of Brundage's message concerning the possibility of pursuing television revenue: "I quite agree with your [Brundage's] comments on television," noted Burghley. "This would seem to be a splendid source of revenue to tap for the IOC and its work."[5] Killanin, gratified that his idea prompted Brundage's initiative in airing the issue with the Executive Board, chimed in with an added thought: "What is important is that this source of high revenue should be diverted to the future of amateur sport, and not to the pockets of commercial enterprise."[6] Despite such assurances, Brundage's internal conflict on this matter remained with him to the end of his two-decade presidency.

Enter Wilfrid S. Kent Hughes

Before businesses could advertise their goods and services through this powerful new medium to members of the consumer marketplace who were also devotees of the Olympics, the IOC needed to develop the concept of television rights and a policy governing their sale. The IOC's effort in that regard, spearheaded by Brundage, focused squarely on the events and aftermath surrounding the Games of the XVIth Olympiad celebrated in Melbourne, Australia, in November and December 1956. The Melbourne Organizing Committee (MOCOG), through its interaction with television and cinema newsreel officials, provided a fundamental precedent on which the IOC drew for establishing both policy and practice toward becoming, in time, an organization whose financial security was no longer a front-of-mind concern for its leaders.

Prior to the 1948 Olympic Games in London—indeed, at the IOC's first post–World War II General Session, Melbourne applied to host the 1956 Summer Olympics. Three years later, at the 43rd IOC General Session in Rome in late April 1949, Melbourne achieved its goal by one vote over Buenos Aires in the fifth and final round of voting.[7] In far off Australia, Wilfrid S. Kent Hughes, Olympic athlete, war hero, cabinet minister, and amateur sport enthusiast, took charge of the organization effort. By the time the Melbourne Games closed in December 1956, he merited inclusion in the pantheon of notable figures who transformed the Games into how the world views them today. Though small sums of money did figure into television broadcasting of the 1948 London Olympics and the 7th Olympic Winter Games in Cortina d'Ampezzo in 1956,[8] it was Kent Hughes's steadfastly argued beliefs on the monetary value of Olympic broadcasts as entertainment programming that proved game changing. Indeed, those beliefs ushered in a new and ultimately financially prosperous era in the IOC's relationship with the television industry.

Kent Hughes, generally called "Billy" by family and close friends, was born in Melbourne on June 12, 1895.[9] By the end of his high school years, his athletic talent, particularly demonstrated in track and field, was a matter of laudable record. His academic accomplishments, too, reflected equal brilliance. In August 1914, at age nineteen, Kent Hughes enlisted in the Anzac Forces engaged in World War I. Before departing for military service abroad, he received word that he had won a Rhodes scholarship to Oxford. Putting Oxford "on hold," he shipped to the Middle East, where he served in Egypt, Palestine, and Syria before taking part in the ill-fated Gallipoli campaign. There at Gallipoli, he was among thousands of wounded Australians evacuated. Following the signing of the Armistice in November 1918, he proceeded to Oxford to embark on his journey as a Rhodes Scholar. Active in athletics at Oxford, he became a celebrated hurdler, competing in the 1920 Antwerp Olympic Games as a member of the Australian Olympic team. Returning to Australia, Kent Hughes entered politics, winning election to the Federal Parliament in 1927 on the Progressive Nationalist ticket.

With the onset of World War II and the Japanese onslaught into Southeast Asia in 1941, Kent Hughes once again joined the country's military, immediately thrust

into the defense of Singapore. The Australian campaign on the Malaysian Penin-
sula ended in a disastrous defeat, the result of which was the Allies' capitulation
on February 17, 1942. He survived three and a half years of debilitating internment
in Japanese POW camps in Singapore, Formosa, and Manchuria. Soviet troops
liberated Kent Hughes and the vastly diminished numbers of his unit in Manchuria in August 1945. In 1947 a grateful United Kingdom awarded him the Order
of the British Empire for "his inspiration to all ranks during his incarceration."[10]
Returning to civilian life and politics, a distinguished record in two World Wars,
together with parliamentary service and proven administrative skills, earned him
the respect of Prime Minister Robert Menzies and an appointment in May 1951 as
interior minister.

Coincident with fulfilling his role as minister, Kent Hughes was offered and
accepted what he considered "a part time job," president of the Melbourne Olympic Games Organizing Committee.[11] Kent Hughes, a vigorous supporter of his
hometown's Olympic host-city candidature and an industrious participant in the
city's subsequent organizational plans, dedicated himself to the task of preparing
for the event—so much so, in fact, that his efforts encroached on his "full time" job
in the Interior Ministry, much to Prime Minister Menzies's consternation. There
was much to accomplish. Government monies had to be procured to help with
providing sport facilities and infrastructure. Disputes between Olympic officials
and local Melbourne municipal representatives had to be resolved. The requirements of International Sports Federations (IFs) for the staging of their sporting
contests placed further demands on his time. Indeed, a plethora of tasks consumed
Kent Hughes in the months, weeks, and days ahead.

Meanwhile, parallel to the later stages of Kent Hughes's and Melbourne's
Olympic preparations, Avery Brundage and the IOC faced one of the most critical crossroads in the entire history of the Olympic Games. The issue concerned
television. Compared with television coverage in Europe and North America, the
technology experienced a tardy arrival in Australia, caused generally by cultural
fears, economic constraints, defense priorities, and, perhaps most tellingly, political machinations aimed at preserving the status of already entrenched competing
media sources (print publishing and radio). In fact, conventional wisdom holds
that the introduction of television to Australia was planned to coincide with the
nation's staging of the Melbourne Games. A conundrum focused on film and television access to cover the Games free of any "rights" charges. Kent Hughes and
his MOCOG colleagues pursued a "hardline" approach when it came to television
and newsreel matters. They demanded remuneration for the rights to televise and/
or film the Melbourne Olympic competitions. Perturbed newsreel and television
executives countered that their medium deserved rights of coverage identical to
those accorded print and photography media—in effect, carte blanche access.

In a spirit of disgruntled solidarity, administrative officers from the Australian Broadcasting Commission, the British Broadcasting Corporation (BBC), Fox-Movietone News, Cinesound Review News, the National Broadcasting Company (NBC), and United Press International (UPI) forwarded a bluntly worded document to MOCOG, claiming their right of access to news coverage of the festival without payment.[12] In an effort to enlist help in supporting his company's view, UPI's Roger Tatarian aimed high. He lobbied the IOC president: "I think you will agree that the whole world would be aghast if the right of newspapers and other older news media to cover the games were ever to be put on the auction block," Tatarian wrote to Brundage, "yet this is apparently being contemplated in the case of television coverage of the Melbourne Games . . . despite the fact that television is only another arm of the press."[13]

Australian government authorities sided with the neophyte Australian television industry, believing that television coverage should be granted gratis because of the advertising that the country would naturally accrue, advertising that would translate into tourist dollars, trade contracts, and foreign investment. In other words: "It pays to advertise." However, Kent Hughes was mindful that Melbourne itself was responsible for paying the final bills, not the Menzies government.

Kent Hughes and his colleagues remained resolute, their stand buttressed by their belief that free and unrestrained filming and live television telecasts would have deleterious effects on MOCOG's chief revenue source—Olympic event ticket sales. If spectator patrons stayed away from the Games to watch the spectacle on television sets in lieu of paying admission to the stadium and other sports venues, the result might well be disastrous. Then, too, Kent Hughes was concerned about the effect that widely viewed television coverage of the Games, even if watched outside Australia in delayed fashion, might have on the economic viability of the Organizing Committee's official Olympic film planned for commercial distribution shortly following the closing of the festival.[14] MOCOG targeted revenue in the form of ticket sales and film subscriptions to offset a goodly portion of its expenses.

Still another consideration factored into Kent Hughes's mission to secure revenues from television. An arrangement between the Organizing Committee and the Menzies government on federal tax money intended for some of the construction costs associated with establishing secondary sports facilities required for the Games depended squarely on the fact that the Melbourne Cricket Grounds, following needed adjustments for track and field events, would serve as the main Olympic stadium. Kent Hughes, a former track athlete and an enthusiastic booster of amateur athletics, envisioned monies from television as the financial means to build a new stadium, one that would serve as the main venue for the Olympic Games—and afterward as a home for amateur athletics (track and field) in the State of Victoria. Australian government authorities would have none of this. The Games would have to proceed using Melbourne's storied cricket venue. But Kent Hughes's vision persisted. If not a stadium for the Games, then a sports edifice built after the Olympic flame had been extinguished, financed by funds gained from televising the Olympics. Kent Hughes thought that a $500,000 (U.S.) bonanza might result from such fees.

How did Kent Hughes arrive at this substantial figure, one that reflects the buying power of $4.63 million in 2019? Shane Cahill offers two possibilities. First, George Moir, a member of MOCOG, informed Kent Hughes that Avery Brundage floated the sum to him during the IOC president's visit to Melbourne in late 1955. Brundage's thinking might have been informed by earlier estimates of $500,000 as the value of U.S. television rights put forth in bid documents by Detroit officials who labored on behalf of their city to win the right to host the 1956 Olympics. Of course, such an estimate offered to Moir ignores a significant issue—the lesser value of television rights for prospective U.S. rights holders resulting from their inability to deliver live coverage to viewers of an event staged in Melbourne. Second, Lewis Luxton, MOCOG's deputy chairman, pursued a contract for exclusive film rights for Great Britain with Associated Re-Diffusion (AR) for £25,000, with an additional rider that AR would act as MOCOG's agent in discussions with U.S. television networks, with $500,000 serving as the base figure for any rights package. However, dreams of a massive deal with Westinghouse, one of America's notable sponsors of the nation's emerging television industry, faded in no small measure due to Westinghouse's standing as one of NBC's major shareholders, just one of the U.S. media giants alienated by MOCOG's overall approach.[15]

Olympic News versus Olympic Entertainment

Kent Hughes and his MOCOG colleagues were adamant that television networks worldwide should be granted rights to broadcast the Games as part of their programming only if they paid for that privilege. Television networks claimed that the broadcasting of Olympic events was identical to newspaper reporting of them—in effect, *news* reporting. Kent Hughes, however, thought differently. To him, extended television coverage of Olympic events was not *news* at all, but rather *entertainment*.

What was the difference with regard to television programming? In Kent Hughes's eyes, Olympic *news* reporting was television programming that did not exceed three one-minute *news* segments of Olympic coverage per day as elements of broadcast programming, for which Melbourne organizers were willing to grant on a royalty-free basis. No fees would be required. And, Olympic *entertainment*? Kent Hughes labeled *entertainment* as any time span greater than the prescribed three one-minute *news* segments. International networks spurned Melbourne's royalty-free offer, countering with a demand for no less than three three-minute segments for a total of nine minutes daily. Melbourne rejected this demand. Borrowing from a well-defined axiom already apparent in American television embodying payment of rights fees to televise sporting contests, Kent Hughes argued, "Sporting and athletic groups which stage contests with a wide appeal to spectators are entitled to expect fees for the TV and film rights."[16]

Rebuffed by Kent Hughes's repeated denials of the request for nine minutes of free newsreel Olympic Games coverage per day, corporate titans of international television and film abandoned further discussion, announced angrily that filming of athletics was not *entertainment* but rather *news* reporting, and they resisted any interpretation that such coverage merited payment. They, like Kent Hughes, did not yield. An angry and consolidated media coalition subsequently implemented an almost universal boycott of Melbourne Olympic Games coverage outside Australia.[17]

Following the closing of the Melbourne Games, Kent Hughes's reflections on the television matter offer further insight: "Sport is probably T.V.'s greatest asset and they want to get it free. The issue is not 3 or 9 minutes of free film . . . the fight in the future will be for as much film as they like to decide is *news*."[18] Instructive, too, is the perspective of Paul Talbot, an Australian by birth and citizenship, owner of Fremantle Overseas Radio, who served as chief negotiator for MOCOG on the subject of American film and television rights to the Melbourne Games. "It was not the 3 minutes in each of the three daily broadcasts to which we objected," offered Talbot on the parties' failure to bridge the divide, "but, rather, to the fact that the networks insisted that each of the three minute segments would be different and that they could then combine them for a total of 9 minutes, which with their wraparound and commercials, would make a daily sponsorship program. At that time, 15 minute programs, including the national news, were common on network TV."[19]

Censure of Kent Hughes within the media fraternity was rapid and at times vitriolic. Neither was such censure limited solely to angry international media firms. An avalanche of criticism descended on him from Australian government authorities and media representatives. They roundly criticized him for sacrificing worldwide publicity for Australia in a shortsighted attempt to squeeze revenue from television and newsreel companies. In Australia, where the birth of television was almost simultaneous to the staging of Melbourne's Olympic Games, John Williams, managing director of the *Herald and Weekly Times*, Melbourne's major newspaper (owned by Keith Murdoch, father of present-day media industry mogul Rupert Murdoch), scored the Melbourne Olympics chief as an unfaithful Australian. If the Olympic Games could not be seen on all Australian television networks—indeed, networks the world over—argued Williams, then Kent Hughes had ill-served his fellow citizens. "If you sell exclusive rights . . . I shall have to write you down in the paper," threatened Williams in a telephone conversation with Kent Hughes some eleven months prior to the opening of the Games.[20]

If confrontation and bluster in the end generally removed Melbourne's Games from international viewing, a greater degree of sanity prevailed among local Melbourne parties with respect to televising the Games in Australia. On the eve of the opening of the Games in early November 1956, it was estimated that at best there might be five thousand television sets in the Melbourne area. Under pressure from Melbourne television stations, Kent Hughes and his committee made a last-minute decision with regard to the local market. Television would be granted free access to events that were "sold out." A virtually "sold out" program of track and field events staged in the Melbourne Cricket Grounds translated into thorough telecasting of those events. In effect, Melbourne saw a great deal of the 1956 Olympic Games on live television. As the Games progressed, sales of television sets spiked dramatically. In an era when transmissions could hardly penetrate beyond the city's immediate environs, viewers in Sydney had to be satisfied with watching Australia's first Olympic Games in delayed fashion, by dint of film flown overnight from Melbourne. In a last-minute agreement, too, Kent Hughes and his colleagues attempted to recoup at least some financial consideration from commercial forces by selling contracted rights to Melbourne's Channel 9. The amount acquired by the Organizing Committee was £1,000 (Australian). Channel 9 immediately sold advertising rights to the oil conglomerate Ampol for £8,000. Ampol's sales manager was circumspect: "In the end, I suppose we got it for peanuts."[21]

The irony of Channel 9's £7,000 profit, to which Kent Hughes was painful witness, bore out the wisdom of his stubborn resistance over allowing television free access to the Games. That aside, Lewis Luxton admitted belatedly that the generally restricted television coverage, internationally and domestically, reflected poorly on both MOCOG and television and newsreel negotiators.[22] *New York Times* writer Jack Gould offered a far blunter view: "The Olympic Games as an institution, Australia as a nation and television as a medium of the free world all have suffered as a result of the consequences of the extensive blackout."[23]

Despite the negativity aroused in the television industry relative to the broadcasting standoff in Australia, the IOC had some cause for celebration. Four years following the Melbourne Games, after television rights to the 1960 Olympic Games in Rome were consummated, Paul Talbot wrote to Kent Hughes in Rome in July 1960, observing what the television issue precedent in 1956 meant to the Olympic Movement of the future: "There is no question but that if you had submitted to the very considerable pressure placed upon you in 1956 to allow the Games to be covered with no reimbursement to the Australian Committee, the Italian Committee would not now be enjoying financial support from television."[24] There resides little doubt, in view of subsequent television rights sales the world over, that Talbot's remarks were both prophetic and on the mark.

Sir Wilfrid Selwyn Kent Hughes passed away on July 31, 1970. Accorded a state funeral, he was eulogized as a man who "walked alone, neither seeking nor attracting a following among the back-bench conservatives or malcontents. Looking and sounding like the surviv[or] of an earlier age, when Melbourne Grammar boys rushed to serve King and country, he sat erect on his mount on Anzac Day 1968 wearing the uniform of the Light Horse. Friends and political opponents recognized in the man a dignity, integrity, vitality and kindliness. Those closest also knew that behind the formal exterior was a devotion to family, a capacity to talk to anyone, and a dry sense of humor."[25] Kent Hughes witnessed television pass into the startling age of satellite transmission, with all its ramifications for the prospective financial health of the Olympic Movement. At the end of his 1956 television rights ordeal in Melbourne, though he could count "nothing in hand," Kent Hughes could be satisfied, as future events would prove, with the fact that he had provided the basis for "billions in precedent."[26]

Wilfrid S. Kent Hughes accompanies HRH Prince Philip, Duke of Edinburgh, during the Opening Ceremony for the 1956 Olympics at the storied Melbourne Cricket Grounds. (© 1956 / International Olympic Committee (IOC). Photo courtesy of the IOC.)

Avery Brundage and the Re-crafting of Rule 49

Despite attempts by newsreel and television networks to draw Avery Brundage into support of their stance against that of Kent Hughes's Melbourne Committee, in general the IOC's neophyte president, elected in 1952, trod a careful path in the run-up years, months, and weeks surrounding Melbourne's preparations—yet, nevertheless, not quite careful enough in Kent Hughes's opinion. Most folks with whom Brundage interacted in the context of Olympic affairs since his participation in the 1912 Stockholm Olympics were well familiar with the qualities of the opinionated and often pugnacious Chicagoan. In Kent Hughes, Brundage met his match in obstinacy. In late 1954, during a visit to Melbourne less than two years before the Games opened in November 1956, Brundage weighed in on the progress of preparations under Kent Hughes. "Not impressive," he exclaimed. Kent Hughes rebutted Brundage, stating that Melbourne's seemingly "casual gait" should be weighed against the typical Australian trait of a slow start and a fast finishing sprint when the final challenge came into focus. Besides, an already difficult task was not made any easier, quipped Kent Hughes, in one of his few outwardly testy moments, when "Chicago blow-ins come out here and blow their tops over nothing in particular and everything in general."[27]

There were lessons with respect to Melbourne's troubles for Brundage to heed in crafting his approach to television matters. Brundage was determined to prevent a reoccurrence of the problems Melbourne organizers had faced, problems he largely attributed to a lack of any established policy. In proactive fashion, he launched an investigation of the television industry that eventually resulted in an expansion of the IOC's *Olympic Charter* rule on publicity (Rule 49). In 1958 Brundage orchestrated the organization's first official policy governing the sale of Olympic television rights. The journey toward that achievement was not effortless. Whenever the subject of money associated with sport was raised, Brundage's uneasiness over exposing the Olympic Movement to the taint of commercialism was never far behind. He also believed, prophetically as it turned out, that large sums of money placed at the disposal of the Olympic Movement would promote conflict among Olympic officials, and Brundage was convinced that television rights would generate "large sums of money." Beyond revenue prospects, however, Brundage envisioned another beneficial outcome for the Olympic Movement from the IOC's marriage with the television industry. He appreciated an opportunity for the consumption of Olympic messaging in terms of the IOC's promoted values by a captive, engaged, worldwide audience.[28] Television, in effect, might well act as an electronic missionary of the Olympic Movement's fundamental principles.

Some nine months prior to the opening of the Melbourne Games, Brundage met with his IOC colleagues at their General Session meetings held in conjunction with the Olympic Winter Games in Cortina d'Ampezzo, Italy. There, in the idyllic winter splendor of the Italian Alps, Brundage pledged to embark on an information-gathering and consultation process with respect to television and the Olympic Games.[29] IOC colleague Prince Axel of Denmark counseled Brundage that the IOC should adopt a friendly attitude with broadcast executives because the Olympics as a television spectacle held financial promise for both the IOC and the networks. "We must . . . explain to them our difficulties and our everlasting lack of funds required to achieve the vast and heavy tasks assigned to us," he observed. Prince Axel envisioned that a beneficial partnership between the IOC and television might provide the means to "stir worldwide interest [and] bring them a great number of new subscribers and publicity contracts."[30] Indeed, there was both money and positive exposure for both sides through a partnership. In broaching such thoughts, Prince Axel's vision prefigured by forty years the thinking of Dick Pound and NBC's Dick Ebersol, who in 1995 made headlines with the consummation of two separate television rights agreement packages for the 2000/2002 and 2004/2006/2008 Games for $3.5 billion, in the process ensuring a measure of financial security for the IOC and further burnishing NBC's image and promotional opportunities as America's Olympic network.

The crux of the matter, to establish a policy that distinguished between "Olympic television rights"—the right purchased by a network granting the buyer the exclusive privilege of televising extended coverage of an Olympic festival—and the extent of access for royalty-free *news* purposes to television and newsreel companies, occupied Brundage's thoughts as the 1960 Olympic Winter and Summer Games neared. With Prince Axel's counsel in mind, combined with the lessons of Kent Hughes's difficulties in Melbourne, Brundage launched efforts to fulfill his pledge made in Cortina d'Ampezzo. By 1958, he was well along toward completing a carefully planned, deliberate consultation process aimed at establishing IOC television policy through modification of the *Olympic Charter*'s Rule 49. Consultation with a number of representatives of U.S. commercial television networks and the European Broadcasting Union (EBU)[31] resulted in the modification to Rule 49 (that in its original form addressed publicity matters). The *Olympic Charter* now firmly outlined the IOC's ownership and procedures for the sale of Olympic television rights.

Rule 49 set out the IOC's exclusive ownership of the Olympic Games, its relationship with negotiations for the sale of Olympic television rights, and its autonomy with respect to the distribution of revenue accruing from those negotiations. Prompted primarily by Brundage's desire to protect the IOC from what Pierre de Coubertin long ago denigrated as the "slough of commercialism,"[32] Rule 49 licensed Organizing Committees to negotiate the television rights fees with the purchasing networks. The IOC in turn reserved the authority to render final approval of the contracts negotiated. Thus, the IOC stood at "arms-length" from a direct association with what Brundage viewed as the sleaziness of the commercial marketplace. Borrowing from the counterproposal media executives generated and offered to Wilfrid Kent Hughes (who rejected it), Rule 49 spelled out the distinction between *news* and *entertainment*. Television and cinema news agencies were granted access to nine minutes of royalty-free daily coverage; however, television networks seeking exclusive rights to more extensive coverage would have to pay for any enhanced level of programing.[33] The IOC reserved the right to distribute the money raised from the sale of television rights.

The Implementation of Rule 49

If Avery Brundage thought that the *Olympic Charter*'s reconfigured Rule 49 was his salvation in arresting his unease with the specter of Olympic commercialism, he could not have been further from the mark. Events surrounding the award of and preparations for the 1960 Winter and Summer festivals raised a Pandora's box of problems destined to aggravate the IOC president.

Of immediate concern was Brundage's imposition of Rule 49 on the Organizing Committees of the 1960 Winter Games awarded to Squaw Valley, California, and the Summer Games granted to Rome. The chief argument advanced by both Squaw Valley and Rome was that at the time they were awarded the Games (1955) and accepted the conditions of hosting them, no policy on the IOC's ownership and sale of television rights existed. Both Squaw Valley and Rome harbored their own visions for selling rights and accruing the benefits thereof; each argued vehemently that the IOC could not impose Rule 49 retroactively.[34]

Squaw Valley, a relatively undeveloped winter resort community in Northern California's Sierra Nevada range, denigrated by Brundage as hardly "a picnic ground," nevertheless won the hosting distinction over Innsbruck, Austria, by mounting a "superb, high pressure publicity campaign" carried forward by Alexander Cushing, president of the Squaw Valley Bid Committee.[35] An early Cushing endeavor, once the Games had been awarded, was a quest to secure a $1 million grant from the State of California to help launch the project. Prompted by ridicule from Brundage that $1 million was ridiculously inadequate, Cushing asked for increased funding from the state legislature.

By mid-1957 the legislature committed $7,990,000 to the Squaw Valley Organizing Committee.[36] There was a caveat, however: the Organizing Committee pledged partial reimbursement from monies raised via gate receipts, concessions sales, and the sale of television rights.[37] Try as he might, Brundage was unable to overturn the "pledge" made by the Squaw Valley authorities to the California legislature.[38] By September 1957 Brundage was reconciled to the fact that there was little chance to secure control of Squaw Valley television money. Freed from the bonds of IOC control, the organizers pressed ahead with selling television rights for the 1960 Olympic Winter Games. The sole contract negotiated for Olympic entertainment programming entailed a $50,000 payment from the Columbia Broadcasting System (CBS).

If Avery Brundage bristled at length over his relationship with Squaw Valley officials on the matter of television rights fees, his interaction with Rome's Summer Games Organizing Committee authorities was even more prickly. His chief correspondent with regard to Rome's Olympic matters was Giulio Onesti, president of Rome's Organizing Committee. Onesti proved to be a willing and able combatant against the autocratic and usually dominating Brundage.

Similar to Squaw Valley's organizers, Onesti rejected Brundage's assertion that "the Rome Organizing Committee . . . understands that the disposition of [all television money] rests in the hands of the International Olympic Committee."[39] Onesti did not "understand." Rome, he protested, accepted the challenge of staging the 1960 Olympics in accord with the rules in place when the city had been awarded the Games in 1955, the identical argument advanced by Squaw Valley. To this defense, however, Onesti added an equally salient counterpoint. With regard to disposition of any television rights fees accruing to the IOC, Rule 49 applied only, Onesti stated, to the sale of "live" television rights. Strict interpretation of Rule 49, noted Onesti, precluded any IOC claim to any television revenues extracted from the U.S., Canadian, and Japanese markets because contemporary technology did not permit live transoceanic transmissions.[40] All Olympic footage to be shown in those countries would have to be flown there and aired in the form of delayed telecasts. Avery Brundage, largely stymied in his mission to secure a healthy share of the television rights to the 1960 Rome Games, grudgingly acceded to Onesti's placating offer of 5 percent of the net proceeds from the sale of television rights, with a guaranteed minimum payment of $50,000.[41]

In the end, the Olympic Winter and Summer Games of 1960 occurred without mishap—indeed, with much glamour. Squaw Valley's winter festival opened with a dazzling ceremony showcased by a glorious fireworks display orchestrated by Walt Disney Productions. While CBS aired a mere fifteen hours of coverage, two of them in prime time, the February spectacle marked the first time that the Olympics were seen live on American television. A combination of new sport facilities built specifically for Rome's Summer Games, together with the archaeological remains of buildings once resplendent in antiquity, provided the backdrop to the Games of the XVIIth Olympiad. Described by one journalist in attendance as "the loveliest Games of the modern era," the Rome Olympics successfully blended the aura of the ancient with the demands of modern sport.[42] The Rome Olympics were the first Summer Games to be televised live in Europe; eighteen countries received the broadcast. The Games were also televised on a delayed basis in the United States, Canada, and Japan, continuing a trend that would forever change the manner in which the public watched the Olympics.[43] EBU paid $667,967 for the live European transmission rights; CBS spent $394,940 for the U.S. television rights.[44] In the end, after factoring foreign exchange elements, Onesti and his Rome colleagues reaped a total of $1,178,257 from gross television rights sales.[45] More than a year after the close of the Rome Games, Otto Mayer, the IOC chancellor, was still trying to exact from Onesti what he believed to be the full and fair payment to the IOC.[46]

The 1960 Winter and Summer Olympic festivals also featured the beginnings of confrontational negotiations between the IOC and OCOGs, leading the IOC to become painfully aware of the overtones attached to how its entry into commercial circumstances impinged on its relationships with Olympic partners, especially those partners who felt that their financial needs were greatest, of whom successive OCOG leaders were the most vociferous in their arguments. The correspondence of Brundage, Otto Mayer, and Squaw Valley and Rome organizers belabored the question as to which organizational body controlled the revenues created by the sale of television rights and provides an early indication of how television policy influenced IOC/OCOG relations. Avery Brundage, in particular, correctly forecast the potential friction between the IOC and Organizing Committees as a result of the appearance of television revenue. His paradoxical combination of Olympic idealism and desire for the pragmatic benefits of commercialism was never clearer than reflected in his concept of "sharing." On one hand he wanted the IOC, IFs, and OCOGs to share the fruits from the sale of television rights; on the other hand he wanted to control how much each received.

In hindsight, a review of the Melbourne media rights negotiations and their immediate aftereffects provides a foundation for understanding the evolution of the IOC's relationship with the television industry and helps place much of the contemporary debate in historical context. It is to the mid-twentieth-century Olympic Games host city Melbourne and the instructive resolve of its steadfast leader Wilfrid Kent Hughes that the concept of Olympic television rights—payment in exchange for the privilege of covering the Games beyond the rights granted to news agencies—entered the financial hallmark that surrounds the Olympic Movement today.

CHAPTER 3

The Rome Formula

Avery Brundage and Television Money

During his twenty-year IOC presidency (1952–1972), Avery Brundage twice approached a crossroads in his thinking concerning the wisdom of leveraging the television industry for commercial revenue for the IOC and its affiliated bodies. He encountered the first in the aftermath of the Melbourne Olympics, when he had to decide whether the IOC should accept any commercial revenue from the sale of Olympic television rights. Later, in the 1960s, he agonized over how to protect the IOC's image when Organizing Committees (OCOGs), International Sport Federations (IFs), and National Olympic Committees (NOCs) jockeyed for shares of burgeoning Olympic television revenue facilitated by the advent of satellite technology. On both occasions his corporate head conflicted with his Olympism-infused heart. Twice, his head won out. His decisions forever altered the IOC's and the Olympic Movement's financial foundations—yet, ultimately, in Brundage's mind, not for the better.

Driven by his passion for Coubertin's Olympic idealism, an unwavering commitment to amateurism, and a firm belief in the need to maintain clear separation between sport and politics, Brundage's strong will and autocratic leadership piloted the IOC through the challenges of the Cold War years when the splintering of the Olympic Movement remained a distinct possibility. Dick Pound linked this feat to "the sheer force of [Brundage's] personality."[1] However, for Brundage, the marriage of sport and television and the enhanced sums available for sport properties resulting from satellite technology and live, transoceanic broadcasts invited conflict within the Olympic Movement. OCOGs sought maximum revenue to offset escalating costs of hosting the Olympics, while NOC and IF leaders lobbied vociferously for meaningful shares to advance their respective enterprises.

"One should be suspicious of any amateur organization that has money," wrote Brundage in 1965. "The minute this occurs its complexion changes and not for the better."[2] The thought of a commercialized Olympic Games troubled him greatly. In drafting Rule 49, despite the protections afforded by granting the IOC final approval rights for all television contracts and subsequently establishing a distribution plan (Rome Formula) in 1966 to channel television money to the OCOGs, NOCs, and IFs, one that encouraged the OCOGs to seek maximum return from television negotiations, Brundage was largely responsible for setting the Olympic Games on this very path.

Admittedly, Brundage found himself in a difficult situation. OCOG officials, those entrusted with delivering the Games, looked out for their own financial interests and, in doing so—beginning with Rome and Squaw Valley and their manner of interpreting Rule 49—frustrated Brundage greatly. Wishing to divest himself of further aggravation with OCOGs, he negotiated lump-sum payments from Innsbruck ($20,000), Tokyo ($130,000), Grenoble ($60,000), and Mexico City ($200,000) to the IOC that could be shared with the IFs. NOCs, who did not receive a share of Olympic television money in 1960, 1964, or 1968, clamored for some of the revenue, and the IFs, who received meager portions of the revenue pie in 1964 and 1968, argued vociferously for a bigger piece. Satellite technology's influence on the value of "live" television rights to major sport events, including the Olympic Games, fueled their arguments.

In Brundage's mind, television money served as a viable source of funds for those tasked to organize and stage the Olympic Games but was much less desirable if placed in the hands of amateur sport organizations. He sought to protect the IOC's image, but in shutting the NOCs out of television money from Innsbruck, Tokyo, Grenoble, and Mexico City, and meting out only tiny sums to the IFs, he was squarely at odds with those in the IF and NOC communities who considered this revenue as manna from heaven in support of their respective mandates. Pressure exerted by both parties on Brundage, as well as by some of his own members who believed the IOC should move to secure its own financial future through a meaningful share of television rights fees, pushed him toward the second crossroads. In 1966 this process resulted in the development of the Rome Formula, an allocation plan that provided the IOC, IFs, and NOCs each with a minimum share of 11.1 percent of global television revenue, commencing in 1972. It is this event that provides the central focus for this chapter.

For Brundage, both the realities of the emerging broadcast medium and his desire to preserve his personal power governed his decision to craft the Rome

Formula. Brundage recognized, albeit with a healthy measure of angst, that addressing the financial demands of the IFs and NOCs was unavoidable due to changes in the sport television marketplace. However, in giving some ground on revenue matters, Brundage calculated that the NOCs and IFs might shelve their increasingly voiced aspirations for greater influence in Olympic decision-making, leaving the IOC (and, by extension, himself) unchallenged as the sole leader of Olympic affairs. Power sharing was not on Brundage's agenda. However, in the end, the NOCs and IFs took the money offered through the Rome Formula and continued their respective campaigns for more say in the corridors of Olympic power. The eventual establishment of the General Assembly of International Federations (GAIF) and the Permanent General Assembly of National Olympic Committees (PGA) in 1967 and 1968, respectively, both enhanced their lobbying capacities and impinged on Brundage's power base.

Even some IOC members, especially those most familiar with the IOC's financial condition, viewed television money as a blessing and a vital revenue stream. The Soviet Union's Konstantin Adrianov, an IOC vice president, viewed television money as fuel to fulfill the IOC's mandate as a "force for peace and social improvement."[3] Denmark's Ivar Vind and Britain's Marquess of Exeter believed such money would lend much greater sophistication to the management of Olympic affairs.[4] West Germany's Georg von Opel was even more bullish: "I am of the opinion that one person in the Lausanne office should do nothing but secure money for the IOC."[5] In 1967 Brundage supported the establishment of the Finance Commission to manage the IOC's financial affairs and monitor television rights negotiations but fussed at its inability to control spending at the IOC's Lausanne headquarters.[6] "Distressed and disillusioned," wrote Brundage's biographer, Allen Guttmann, "[he] watched as the IOC adopted first the financial procedures and then the fiscal attitudes of a modern corporation."[7]

By the close of his presidency, it was all too much for Brundage. He demanded reform with respect to revenue generation from television. The IOC "should have nothing to do with money," he railed at members of the IOC Executive Board mere months before the 1972 Munich Olympics.[8] The IOC, he stated, should no longer feel compelled to bankroll the IFs and NOCs through shares of television rights fees and would be wise to relinquish all authority over television to the OCOGs that would be responsible for the IOC's four-year budgetary needs.

Brundage, now eighty-five years old, pleaded with members of the Executive Board for this remedial action to safeguard the reputation of the Olympic Movement that was carefully nurtured during the preceding seventy-five years.[9] "Brundage long warned that money fostered conflict, bold ambition, and financial self-interest among amateur organizations," concluded Matthew Llewellyn and John Gleaves in their 2016 comprehensive historical examination of the amateur ideal.[10] The arguments over television money within the Olympic Movement and the longing for more and more of it by amateur sport officials shocked and dismayed him. His Executive Board colleagues listened. France's Count Jean de Beaumont fretted about the effect on the NOCs resulting from such a shift in policy and predicted a stiff reaction from the IFs. Lord Killanin offered politely that Brundage's words deserved "some consideration" but that nothing could be altered in terms of the IOC's approach before the 1980 Olympic festivals.[11] But most were likely looking at their shoes, knowing that ship had sailed. They no doubt concurred with Kenya's Reginald Alexander's three-year-old assessment that "[television money] in the final analysis is the lifeblood of the [IOC's] administrative existence."[12] Indeed, the old man's time had come and gone.

Television Money and the IFs

Two issues drove the interests of leaders of the IFs such as Berge Phillips (Swimming), Thomas Keller (Rowing), Roger Coulon (Wrestling), and J. Francis "Bunny" Ahearne (Ice Hockey) concerning the distribution of Olympic television money in the 1960s. First, Brundage's policy of claiming a nominal sum from the 1964 and 1968 OCOGs, subsequently shared with the IFs, irritated them greatly. In the early 1960s, satellite technology changed the calculus concerning the value of the television medium for the IFs who concluded in 1957 that tying their financial futures to television was too speculative.[13] Brundage's practice stunted their opportunities to grow and develop their sports. For them, Brundage ignored the realities of the newly evolving sport economy. Ahearne, a travel agent and long-time executive with the British Ice Hockey Association, profited handsomely for years by handling travel needs for touring North American ice hockey teams in Europe. He and his colleagues called for the transfer of one-third of all television revenue to the IFs.[14] "Let us once and for all recognise the fact that our amateur sports are a colossal business," he claimed. "And no one," continued the Irishman, "no one should deny us the right of making an honourable and justifiable and reasonable commercial approach, when we are talking millions of dollars."[15] Second, Brundage's willingness to support International Amateur Athletics Federation (IAAF) president and fellow IOC Executive Board member, David Cecil, the Marquess of Exeter, in his efforts to maintain the IOC's control over the distribution of the IFs' money to the individual federations bothered the IF members. Exeter's influence with the process represented a clear case of conflict of interest.[16] "Despite my amateur heart," stated Ahearne, "[the IOC's policy for television money distribution] insults my financial brain."[17] Ahearne even issued a claim on a portion of the proceeds of the Innsbruck television money and threatened to cancel the ice hockey competition if the money was not forthcoming.[18]

Phillips, Keller, Coulon, and Ahearne chafed under Brundage's autocratic rule, resented his dismissive attitude toward their concerns, and criticized his perceived failure as a consensus builder and his intractable position on amateurism. Their campaign for more television money meshed with their overall campaign to push Brundage and the IOC to "consider the international sport federations as partners rather than minions."[19] Though Ahearne was the most vociferous and prone to rhetorical flourish in pressing the IFs' case, Phillips, Keller, and Coulon were the IFs' most diligent and persistent advocates.

Phillips, a lawyer by profession, served on the executive boards of the Australian Swimming Union (1940–1973) and swimming's international governing body, the Fédération Internationale de Natation Amateur (FINA, 1948–1976), holding (in the case of FINA) the posts of vice president (1952–1964) and president (1964–1968). He served as an Olympic referee for swimming at five Olympic festivals and as chief judge at three others. Phillips managed the Olympic swim facility at the 1956 Melbourne Olympics and was a member of Wilfrid Kent Hughes's Melbourne OCOG. He worked as an official at ten Commonwealth Games extending from 1938 through 1990 and served on the Executive Board of the Australian Commonwealth Games Association from 1946 to 1976. He was no lightweight, and a stickler for the enforcement of rules, perhaps most effectively illustrated by his extended feud with Australian swimming legend, Dawn Fraser. In 1976 Queen Elizabeth II conferred upon him the Order of the British Empire (O.B.E.) in recognition of his contributions to the sport of swimming. "No Australian," asserts Brian Oliver, "[exerted] more influence in the Commonwealth Games, the Olympics, and world swimming during the second half of the twentieth century."[20]

Keller, a chemical engineer and president of Swiss Timing (1972–1989) was a five-time Swiss sculling champion and bronze medallist at the 1950 European Rowing Championships who qualified for the 1956 Melbourne Olympics—only to lose his opportunity to compete as a result of his country's decision to boycott the Melbourne Games in light of the Hungarian crisis. He served as president of the Fédération Internationale des Sociétés d'Aviron (FISA), rowing's international governing body, commencing at age thirty-four in 1958 while still an active participant in the sport, through to his passing in 1989.

Keller stepped into the role of GAIF president for seventeen years (1969–1986) following Phillips's two-year tenure as its founding president (1967–1969), eventually establishing GAIF's base of operations in Monaco. He campaigned relentlessly on behalf of the IFs for more authority and input to the Olympic Games as Brundage prepared to step aside, throughout Killanin's presidency, and in the early years of Samaranch's tenure. "A ruggedly handsome Swiss with soft brown eyes, a ready smile and a steely determination," wrote *The Times*'s John Hennessy in the early 1970s, Keller believed this position justified "since [the IFs] govern their sports for 52 weeks a year, compared (as he maintain[ed]) with the two weeks every four years of the IOC."[21] "Keller had no regard for the IOC or for the NOCs," wrote Dick Pound, "and thought that the Olympic movement would be much better off in the hands of the IFs, who controlled the sports and without whom the Games would not be possible."[22] Monique Berlioux concurred with this assessment of Keller's view of the place of the IFs in the Olympic world: "As President [of GAIF] he wanted to give it too much importance."[23] Juan Antonio Samaranch, ever the wily, crafty, and calculating leader, outfoxed Keller when he established the Association of Summer Olympic International Federations (ASOIF) and the Association of Winter Olympic International Federations (AWOIF) and delegated their leadership to Primo Nebiolo and Marc Hodler, respectively, such that any generated Olympic revenue flowed from the IOC through these organizations to the IFs, not GAIF. Keller's voice was thenceforth largely muted.

France's Roger Coulon was elected president of the International Amateur Wrestling Federation in 1952 and soon changed its name to the Fédération Internationale des Luttes Amateurs and then shifted its headquarters to Lausanne, Switzerland, the first of many IFs to do so over the ensuing decades. Born in France's Auvergne region shortly after World War I, Coulon led an eclectic life as an iron worker, art locksmith, amateur painter, rally driver, and skilled wrestler, whose career on the mat was cut short due to an accident. He served as the mayor of Pont-du-Château, a small village near Clermont-Ferrand, and presided over France's amateur wrestling federation from 1944 through 1959. He made his mark in the French Resistance when he parachuted into France and assisted in the preparations for the D-Day landings in Normandy. For his efforts he received the U.S. military's Silver Star, France's Croix de Guerre, and the rosette of the Medal of Resistance. "Of medium height, with broad shoulders," wrote Monique Berlioux, "[Coulon's] generous forehead shone a blue metallic gaze of intelligence and charm. He sported a thick moustache, the ends of which he liked to twist."[24]

The Marquess of Exeter, who considered an association of IFs as a distinct threat to the power and influence of the IAAF, identified Coulon as the driving force behind the push to enhance the influence of the IFs governing minor sports on the Olympic program, the quest for enhanced revenue from Olympic television, and, once GAIF was established, its search for official IOC recognition.[25] Coulon emerged as GAIF's founding secretary general and fulfilled those duties until his passing in 1971. Collectively, in the mid- and late 1960s, Phillips, Keller, Ahearne, and Coulon represented a formidable quartet in challenging Brundage's long-held views concerning the IOC's (and his own) sweeping authority over Olympic affairs.

Given his office and disposition, Brundage was the principal roadblock to their financial aims and hopes for reform in the relationship between the IFs and the IOC, but close behind in his opposition to their activities was Exeter. Born in Stamford, England, in 1905, David George Brownlow Cecil, Lord Burghley, became the 6th Marquess of Exeter in 1956. Educated at Eton and Magdalene College, Cambridge, Burghley captured a gold medal in the 400-meter hurdles at the 1928 Amsterdam Olympics, a silver medal in the 4 x 400-meter relay four years later in Los Angeles, and three gold medals at the inaugural Commonwealth Games (known as the British Empire Games at the time) in 1930. A resident of Burghley House, a sprawling estate in Lincolnshire, he, it was once written, was the "only athlete who [could] look at 35 Rembrandts in his own home, then jog through 40,000 acres without leaving his own domain."[26] As a hurdler, Burghley employed a unique training technique by placing matchboxes on the top of the hurdles to train his lead leg by clipping them off while running, though this regimen was portrayed inaccurately in *Chariots of Fire*, the well-known film that depicts events at the 1924 Paris Olympics. Hollywood deemed that Burghley, portrayed as Lord Lindsay by Nigel Havers, used glasses of champagne. Impossible, noted one of Burghley's daughters, who stated that her father "had far too high a regard for champagne to risk wasting it if he brushed a hurdle."[27]

Part of Cambridge sporting lore as a result of his successful completion of the Trinity College Great Court run in 1927 in less time, a little over forty-two seconds, than it took for the Trinity clock to peal twelve times, Burghley entered the IOC in 1933, became IAAF president in 1946, and chaired the 1948 London OCOG and the British Olympic Association (BOA, 1936–1976). He served a twelve-year term as a Member of Parliament for Peterborough (1931–1943), representing the Conservative Party before resigning his seat to assume the Governorship of Bermuda until 1945. Fellow British hurdler Bob Tisdall observed, "He always seemed to have complete control of his nerves and ha[d] the happy gift of being able to talk about any subject under the sun, the farther removed from Athletics the better."[28] Exeter sought to curtail the plans of Coulon, Keller, Ahearne, and Phillips to preserve the influence of the IAAF (whose power would be diminished by any organization modeled after the United Nations, where all constituents enjoyed one vote) as much as he did to safeguard the IOC's position of authority.

Exeter and Brundage shared a background in track and field, and a passionate commitment to the amateur ideal (though both were willing to turn a blind eye to state amateurism behind the Iron Curtain in their quest for the expansion of the Olympic Movement's global footprint), but Exeter's two challenges to Brundage for the IOC presidency in 1952 and 1964 complicated their relationship. Brundage even signaled to one IOC member his willingness to stand down in 1964 if Exeter did not run. Exeter's "charm [and] popularity among the members," as well his perceived status as IOC president-in-waiting, Allen Guttmann asserts, might have sparked jealousy. Exeter's backers convinced him to seek the presidency, and the final voting result in Tokyo was not publicized but was reportedly close. "Elegant, witty, vivacious, affable, [and] gauntly handsome," noted Guttmann, "Exeter must have seemed unfairly to have plucked without effort the fruits for which Brundage had labored."[29] They became more distant in the later years of Brundage's presidency but maintained very close communication on matters pertaining to the IFs throughout the 1960s.

In early 1961, when Brundage mused that the IOC might relieve itself of a major headache if it permitted the IFs to determine the distribution of their shares of the Innsbruck and Tokyo television revenue,[30] Exeter pushed back hard: "Heaven forfend that the International Federations should have to decide on how to divide the donation from the I.O.C. The result would make the Congo [the scene of a contemporary civil war] look like a kindergarten."[31] Brundage's waffling threatened the extensive work Exeter completed in establishing a distribution scheme for the IFs' money based on the relative contributions of the bodies governing sports on the Olympic program.

By the end of May, Exeter produced a draft formula for the allocation of television revenue to the IFs tied to a rolling average of attendance at events sponsored by the IFs in the previous three Olympic festivals, one that ensured a minimum payment to minor IFs due to the sacrifice of some of the larger IFs, including his own.[32] Though the IAAF was due 54 percent of the money, Exeter proposed that its share be reduced to 26 percent and that other larger IFs such as Swimming, Equestrian, Boxing, and Basketball should also cede money to the minor sports. The rolling average, stated Exeter, controlled for the fluctuations in popularity of the various sports in the different host sites.[33] They divulged little in a circular letter to the IFs in July, but it was noted that eligibility for television revenue depended on the individual IFs declaring the Olympics to be its World Championships for the year and that the sums transferred would vary based on the "contribution" of the IFs to the Games.[34] At this time, neither opposition to the minimal sum granted to the IFs nor Exeter's formula coalesced.[35] The IOC Executive Board's control of the distribution of the money from Innsbruck and Tokyo—or, more accurately, Exeter's and Brundage's plan for doing so—was a fait accompli.

Satellite Technology: A Catalyst for Confrontation with the IFs

At the same time Brundage and Exeter finessed a path forward with respect to the distribution of the Tokyo/Innsbruck money, groundbreaking work was occurring within the communications industry.

Though Sir Isaac Newton pondered the possibilities for placing an object in Earth's orbit in the seventeenth century based on his knowledge of gravitational forces, it would be centuries before advances in rocketry made such an idea feasible. With respect to satellite communications, British scientist and author Arthur C. Clarke offered his thoughts on the possibility of worldwide, instantaneous, satellite communication through the placement of "three space stations" in a high-level (35,870 km) geosynchronous orbit in a letter to colleagues in June 1945, followed by what is now considered a landmark article in *Wireless World*.[36] He specifically cited the evolution of Nazi Germany's V-2 rocket and thought in a "few more years"[37] further scientific leaps would result in rockets powerful enough to place satellites in orbit. In 1945, in the absence of the invention of transistors, Clarke believed the satellites would have to be manned, such that these technicians could replace malfunctioning equipment and "burned out radio tubes."[38] Clearly, he did not have everything figured out, and for this reason he believed the evolution of such space stations would be a good deal distant. He did not even take out a patent on the notion of a communications satellite.

More than a decade passed, but in October 1957, with the successful placement of the Sputnik 1 satellite into a low Earth orbit for three months, the "space race" was enjoined. The U.S. Army Ballistic Missile Agency responded three months later with the launch of the Jupiter C rocket that delivered Explorer 1, the first active U.S. satellite, designed by James van Allen, into Earth's orbit for the next twelve years, although it was not a communications satellite. In the United States, through the National Aeronautics and Space Administration's (NASA) leadership, numerous companies, including Hughes Aircraft, AT&T, RCA, and Bell Laboratories, pressed forward with various initiatives aimed at establishing communications satellites. By 1964, Telstar 1 and 2 (AT&T/Bell), Relay 1 and 2 (RCA), and Syncom II and III (Hughes Aircraft) were placed in low-, medium-, and high-altitude orbits, respectively, with Syncom III even displaying images from the opening ceremonies of the 1964 Tokyo Olympics to the United States. The Intelsat I, II, and III satellites, products of the International Telecommunications Satellite Consortium, managed by the Comsat Corporation (a U.S. entity), appeared over the next five years, a process resulting in far wider dissemination of live coverage from the 1968 Olympics and a global telecast to an estimated five hundred million viewers of U.S. astronaut Neil Armstrong's historic moonwalk in July 1969.

In the Olympic world, the value of television rights grew markedly as a result of the prospect of live broadcasts. While Tokyo organizers secured $1,577,778 from the sale of global television rights ($1.5 million from NBC in the United States alone), Mexico City ($9.75 million) and Munich ($17,792,000)[39] officials benefited greatly from the new broadcast landscape. Innsbruck's television receipts totaled slightly less than $1 million ($936,667), but successor OCOGs in Grenoble ($2,612,822) and Sapporo ($8,475,269) witnessed noticeable gains, too.[40] IF leaders took note of the new economics of sport television and soon pressed for redress regarding the amounts transferred to them and the manner in which those shares were determined.

Television and the NOCs

At its 1959 Session in San Francisco, the IOC approved granting the IFs half of the lump sums transferred from Tokyo and Innsbruck, but the decision did not sit well with some IOC members whose ties were primarily to the NOC community. At the IOC's Athens Session in June 1961, Armand Massard, France's Olympic fencing champion (individual épée) in Antwerp and a bronze and silver medallist in the men's épée team competitions in Antwerp and Amsterdam, respectively, and the president of the French Olympic Committee from 1933 through 1967, objected to handing money to the IFs. They could and did raise revenues from their World Championships. The IOC's policy left the NOCs, often dependent on government funds, frozen out.[41] Massard was also an IOC vice president (1952–1968) who served the majority of his IOC tenure (1946–1971) on its Executive Board. His comments followed upon his letter to Brundage penned some nine months earlier in which he asserted the IFs were without "real needs," and that the reliance of some NOCs on government funds threatened their independence.[42] Brundage conceded that such financial dependence "too often means governmental interference which, of course, is quite contrary to the Olympic Movement,"[43] but the sums available did not permit distribution to the NOCs.[44]

India's Guru Dutt Sondhi, an IOC member since 1932, the founder of the Asian Games Federation, and manager of three Indian Olympic teams (Amsterdam, Los Angeles, and Berlin), sided with Massard. Sondhi believed the NOCs possessed a superior claim to a portion of the television money than the IFs. The IOC grants money "to the IFs, who are merely the rule-makers of their sports," stated Sondhi, "[while] it does nothing for the NOCs," who bear the "heavy financial burdens of sending teams to the Games. This is surely unfair."[45] Sondhi grew tired of the IFs' posturing and pursuit of more power, influence, and money. "As it is," wrote Sondhi, "the IFs have assumed too much power and dignity to themselves and covertly, if not overtly, try to overawe the I.O.C."[46] Sondhi's view that the IFs were superfluous or redundant in the administration of Olympic affairs surely would have made the likes of Coulon, Keller, Phillips, and even Exeter, bristle. "Regulation, no doubt," concluded Sondhi, "is important, but the NOCs could have done it by themselves too, under the direction of the I.O.C."[47] Though both Massard and Sondhi lobbied Brundage, the most energetic and calculating individual in pursuit of television money for the NOCs was Italy's Giulio Onesti.

In Rome's northern Parioli district sits the Centro di Preparazione Olimpica Giulio Onesti, the Italian Olympic Committee's (CONI) high-performance training center, built in 1954, but re-dedicated in 1982 in honor of the long-time CONI president (1946–1978). Born in Turin in 1912, Onesti was a lawyer, a member of Italy's Socialist Party, and a participant in Italy's Partisan resistance in World War II, tasked with dismantling CONI following World War II. The assignment lined up with the new Socialist government's directive necessitating the dismantling of the Fascist Party and the shuttering of organizations tainted with ideology. But, in this undertaking, Onesti soon understood the prospect for a massive vacuum at the center of Italian sport, and he convinced government officials that CONI could be reformed. After being named its new president, he went on to establish a funding model for CONI based on a lottery (Totocalcio) tied to weekly professional football scores. Onesti was "utterly tireless, . . . brilliant and charming," writes Carl Posey, "with a shark-sized smile and a quick eye for useful innovation."[48] He played a central role in securing for Cortina and Rome the right to host the 1956 Olympic Winter Games and 1960 Olympics and served as the president of the Executive Boards of the respective cities' OCOGs. When combined with his leadership of CONI, Onesti's appointment to the IOC in 1964, when countryman Count Paolo Thaon di Revel retired, surprised few.

Onesti championed the interests of the NOCs and aggravated Brundage in his efforts to empower them through the establishment of a permanent umbrella organization for the world's NOCs. He wasted little time in doing so. Onesti issued an invitation for representatives of the NOCs to meet in Tokyo prior to the IOC's Session in 1964, though definitive advances in his agenda did not occur until the officials from sixty-eight NOCs gathered in Rome in early October 1965, once again at Onesti's invitation. Delegates birthed a Co-ordinating and Study Committee to examine the matter and Onesti's stated goal.[49] In an effort to project the collaborative spirit within the NOCs as well as their power, Onesti, at CONI's expense, chartered a plane to fly the NOC representatives who convened in Rome to their scheduled meeting with the IOC Executive Board two days later in Madrid. Clearly, Totocalcio was delivering significant funds to CONI, and Onesti leveraged that money to press forward. In Madrid, Onesti and his colleagues pushed for 25 percent of future Olympic television revenue for recently established NOCs and those in financial need, as even Onesti did not see the wisdom in dividing the money among the existing 118 NOCs.[50] None of this startled Brundage given Onesti shared his personal views on the distribution of television money with him in June.[51]

Something had to give. The IFs wanted 33 percent of the money, while the NOCs desired 25 percent—combined, nearly 60 percent of the available money—but it was the OCOGs who shouldered the cost of infrastructure required to host the Games; and then there were the IOC's own budgetary requirements. "They all seem to forget," lamented Brundage to his IOC colleague Ivar Vind, "that the Olympic Movement has reached its present exalted position without any money."[52] How would Brundage tackle this environment of competing interests? "It was impossible to satisfy everybody," Brundage told Onesti and his colleagues. "The IOC can only conclude that the International Federations, the NOCs and the IOC all generally lack funds."[53] To those in attendance at the IOC's Session in Madrid a few days later, Brundage pledged that the IOC would establish a distribution formula for 1972 and beyond to assign shares to the IOC, IFs, NOCs, and OCOGs.[54]

Onesti was battling on two fronts in search of respect, influence, and television money for the NOCs. Much of his lobbying focused on Brundage[55] as the situation demanded, but he was also seeking similar consideration from the IFs. In this effort, he sought a meeting of the Study and Co-ordinating Committee with the IFs before the IOC's 64th Session scheduled for Rome in April 1966 through an approach to Rudyard Russell, president of the Association Internationale de Boxe Amateur (AIBA). But Russell balked.[56] The IFs had little interest in advancing Onesti's cause and believed his interests served to diminish their possible gains in any new allocation formula for television money. Russell's eyebrows likely arched when Onesti suggested the IOC and the IFs needed to bring much greater consistency to amateur regulations across all sports.[57] Even though sound advice, this hardly seemed any of Onesti's business, and Russell likely asked himself why he was sticking his nose there. Onesti reported to his colleagues that the "International Sport Federations consider themselves on the same level as the International Olympic Committee, whilst the NOCs, in their opinion are on a level with the National Federations, and it seemed unlikely that they would change their opinion."[58] He informed Russell that he did not agree with his opinion of the NOCs' status within the Olympic Movement and judged such a meeting premature.

Onesti was also unsettled by the efforts of Donald Pain, the IAAF's honorary secretary general, to derail his pursuit of a share of television money for the NOCs. Pain sent a circular letter to the National Federations around the world, the bodies responsible for electing NOC members, to withhold support for the IOC's plan to make any increase in the IFs' share of television money contingent on the NOCs receiving consideration in a revised distribution plan.[59] But Onesti's resolve was steadfast.

Giulio Onesti, an IOC member (1964–1981) who also headed the Italian Olympic Committee (1944–1978), advocated strongly for the NOCs' access to Olympic television revenue. He played a key role in the genesis of the Rome Formula. (© 1964 / International Olympic Committee (IOC). Photo courtesy of the IOC.)

The Road to the Rome Formula

The voices calling for one-third of future Olympic television revenues for the IFs were not silent following Brundage's and Exeter's collaboration on dealing with Tokyo and Innsbruck's television proceeds. In 1963, in no small measure due to the advent of satellite technology and its prospects for live television broadcasts, the IFs renewed their campaign. And, while Brundage gave the IFs some encouragement that their concerns would be addressed,[60] he spent the better part of the next two years backing away from this pledge. In 1964 he quietly reserved $200,000 from the Mexico City organizers for distribution to the IOC and the Summer IFs.[61]

USOC vice president (1953–1965) and later president (1965–1968) Douglas Roby, who also served on the IOC from 1952 through 1984, recalled Brundage's modus operandi in dealing with IF and NOC leaders on controversial matters: "[The IOC would] have meetings with the national Olympic committees or the international federations and [Brundage would] say, 'We'll take it under advisement.' It was a brush-off. . . . He just wouldn't listen. . . . Let them talk, and then forget it."[62] Clearly, in the case of the IFs, Brundage sought to rein in their financial ambitions.

They pressed their case once again in 1965 coincident with Onesti's campaigning on behalf of the NOCs.[63] In April, Exeter reported that the wolves were baying. "The wildest proposals," he wrote, "were put forward that they wanted to refuse to have any television unless they got their share." He worked with a few "reasonable people" to get the IFs to back down from this threat.[64] When the Summer IFs were informed by IOC treasurer Marc Hodler that they would share $100,000, Brundage fended off their rebuke by stating that their appeal in 1963 slipped his mind! Brundage spun a wonderful tale to a personal delegation of IF leaders, headed by Rudyard Russell, about his embarrassment at having overlooked their call for one-third of television revenue two years earlier, but that the terms for Mexico City were finalized.[65] His fingers and toes must have been crossed. Even though Brundage was unmoved by the criticism, the Executive Board did discuss in preliminary fashion the possible merits of a move away from the lump-sum policy to a distribution based on established percentages commencing in 1972 at its July 1965 meeting in Lausanne.[66] It marked a first, tentative step toward a new policy direction that ultimately opened the floodgates of television revenue to the IFs and the NOCs.

In early 1966 Brundage called on Giulio Onesti to chair an IOC subcommittee to try to accomplish what Brundage himself believed could not be done—satisfy everyone. Onesti and fellow committee members Ryotaro Azuma (Japan), Gabriel Gemayel (Lebanon), Vladimir Stoytchev (Bulgaria), Mario Negri (Argentina), Reginald Alexander, and Guru Dutt Sondhi were informed that the interests of the IOC, IFs, NOCs, and OCOGs needed to be considered in any distribution plan.[67]

Brundage's selections revealed his clear intent to give a voice to those with leanings toward the interests of the NOCs. Stoytchev, Alexander, Gemayel, and Sondhi (who was also a past vice president of the Federation Internationale du Hockey) were NOC presidents; Azuma was a former NOC president, while Negri was a past president of FINA.

Exeter surely took note and expressed his disappointment to Brundage that he had not been placed on Onesti's committee.[68] Brundage replied that Exeter's status as an IOC vice president afforded him ex-officio status on all subcommittees and duly informed Onesti that Exeter's experience with this portfolio necessitated consultation with him before any plan was forwarded.[69] Exeter thanked Brundage for reminding him of his ex-officio status and stated he believed it critical that the IOC determine the distribution of funds to the IFs and NOCs as opposed to groups representative of them. "Decentralizing such power," believed Exeter, "would be extremely harmful to the IOC."[70] Without question, Exeter's self-interest showed as the size of the IAAF's share was threatened.

Onesti, who questioned the needs of the IFs for television money, and Exeter, who felt money for the NOCs would make a meager dent in their budgetary requirements,[71] exchanged correspondence that Onesti characterized as "ample and intense" before finding a path forward. Onesti offered Exeter an olive branch: "I know that the [IFs] find in you their greatest defender of their rights, but I am sorry that the controversy has been brought to levels of such exaggerated tension that do not conform to the reality and the nature of our conduct."[72] A plan surfaced soon thereafter.[73] Onesti might not have been aware of Exeter's complicated relationship with his Federation colleagues on the matter of television money. Still, Brundage's stratagem became clear. Onesti and Exeter, admittedly big personalities, were forced to compromise.

Onesti, Exeter, and their fellow subcommittee members assumed 1972 global television revenues to be $5 million and $1 million for the Summer and Winter Games, respectively. In the case of the Summer Olympics, the first million was the IOC's, to be shared equally with the NOCs and IFs. Half of the second million was the IOC's, while the other half went to the OCOG. Of the third million, one-quarter went to Lausanne, while three-quarters went to the OCOG. Any money in excess of $3 million was 100 percent transferrable to the OCOG. In short, if the $5 million target were reached, the IOC's share would be capped at $1.75 million, but the IFs and NOCs were only guaranteed $333,333 equal shares of this sum, or 6.67 percent of the estimated $5 million. Any other payments were at the discretion of the IOC. The same system was employed in the context of the Winter Games, but the percentages were applied to successive $200,000 portions.[74]

Phillips and Ahearne fulminated when the IFs met in Rome on April 22 to study the proposal.[75] Within the previous week, ABC signed a $4.5 million deal for U.S.

television rights to the 1968 Mexico City Olympics. The IFs were due to receive a mere $100,000, or 2.2 percent of the money, a proportion that would only drop when the contracts in other markets were signed. Feelings were running high. Rudyard Russell, the meeting's chairman, read the terms of Onesti's proposal aloud while delegates scrambled to commit the plan to note paper.[76] Ahearne's jaw dropped. "We are the bosses," he charged in decrying the IOC's refusal to address the IFs' claim for one-third of all television revenue. "We are not talking of chicken feed . . . we are not talking of pennies. . . . We are talking of millions of dollars. Millions."[77] With regard to amateurism, it was time for the IFs to "divorce sentiment from finance." "Don't let us put the amateur mask over our brains," he urged.[78] "We are not dealing, gentlemen, with sport now," he continued, "we are dealing with hard facts."[79] And if the IOC and Brundage, whom he labeled the "High Priest of Amateurism,"[80] did not yield to their demand, the IFs should stay home.[81] Phillips, too, believed the IOC needed to stay the course and press for one-third of the money in any formula. "Our friend, Mr. Brundage," remarked Phillips derisively, failed them in not attending to their proposals issued in 1963 and 1965. He said that Ahearne's call for a possible boycott, deserved consideration.[82]

With temperatures rising in the hall, others joined the chorus. Oscar State, secretary general of the International Weightlifting Federation, advised his colleagues to inform Onesti's committee "which has put forward this very inviting formula before us that we reject it completely."[83] Nikolai Nikoforov-Denisov, AIBA's vice president and Russell's successor in 1974, countered Onesti's plan with his own: 35 percent to the IFs; 25 percent to the NOCs; and 20 percent to each of the OCOGs and the IOC.[84] The sums flowing to the IFs from Mexico City, stated the IAAF's honorary secretary general Donald Pain, were "nothing less [than] derisory." He called for revisiting discussions concerning the IFs' share as "there may be a contract, but it is not a good contract for any sporting point of view."[85] Buoyed by the level of agitation in the room, Ahearne stated that what emerged from the Onesti committee was "so utterly stupid . . . I think they must believe we have no brain."[86]

State, Ahearne, William Jones (president of the Fédération International de Basketball Association), and Paul Bonet-Maury (secretary general of the International Judo Federation) debated over who exactly owned the Olympic Games. Jones said the IFs should engage lawyers to study the question to clarify what demands the IFs could reasonably lodge. State and Ahearne countered that they owned their world championships, and in declaring the Olympic Games to be their world championships, they were not sacrificing ownership of anything. Bonet-Maury was puzzled by the discussion: "*Mais si nous n'avons aucun droits, je nevois pas trés bien ce que nous faisons ici?*"[87] Of course they had a right to demand television money. Without the IFs there could be no Games, he concluded. By issuing any form of offer on a share of television rights, the IOC, said Ahearne, was conceding partial ownership of the Games to the IFs. Ahearne was firing in all directions, even delivering a subtle dig to Donald Pain and the IAAF during the proceedings for not supporting the equal distribution of the IFs' money across the Summer federations regardless of the size and popularity of the events they staged, as he consented to in the allocation of the Winter IFs' money.[88] If Brundage had stood with his ear cupped to the door, he would have been sorely tempted to barge in.

The IOC Executive Board caucused at Rome's Hotel Excelsior to consider the Onesti proposal. Marc Hodler spearheaded revisions, ultimately accepted by the Executive Board, which granted the IOC, IFs, and NOCs each one-third of the first million, two-ninths of the second million, and one-ninth of any further millions.[89] The remainder belonged to the OCOG. OCOG officials, the negotiators of the contracts, were now motivated to pursue maximum revenue, given that their percentage share of the sum rose in lockstep with the size of the agreements, but those with an eye for money within the IOC, IFs, and NOCs would be cheering them on, too, as they benefited from not the first few millions but the gross value of each contract. Working with the $5 million estimate, though a woeful underestimate of the likely returns for 1972, the Summer IFs and NOCs were now guaranteed $888,888 or 17.78 percent of such a sum. Despite the tangible shift in the fortunes of the IFs resulting from the Hodler revisions, Coulon and Phillips were far from satisfied when the formula was presented at the IOC Session. It was not one-third. William Jones convinced his colleagues that the elevated percentages and the removal of the caps were acceptable for 1972, as long as a "common committee" was tasked to further consider the distribution formula in the future.[90] It proved a fragile peace.

The Fallout from Rome

With the ink barely dry on the Rome Formula, Brundage and Exeter discussed how the IOC might monitor the manner in which the IFs spent their newfound money. The conduct of some IF officials in Rome rattled Brundage. "The commercial attitude of some of the International Federations is deplorable," he concluded.[91] His interaction with them in Rome, Brundage told Exeter, "horrified" him.[92] "Should we not ask the Federations to report on the use of [the television] money," Brundage queried Exeter? He thought the money might provide leverage to demand and receive greater cooperation from the IFs with matters of IOC interest.[93]

"Professionalism continued to flood the Olympic arena in the 1960s," reported Llewellyn and Gleaves, and Brundage became increasingly outraged to the point he said the Winter Games should be canceled if the willful flouting of amateur regulations by skaters and skiers continued.[94] Exeter noted the amateur issue required greater collaboration between the parties. He suggested a small IOC delegation might meet with the IF leaders on an individual basis "and try by co-operation to bring them into line. The background threat of not getting their whack of the money," offered Exeter, "can be known but not openly used! This for ethical reasons!" And while Exeter thought the IOC had "the right to see their balance sheets," he dismissed the feasibility of controlling the IFs' spending, which would result "in the most terrific row and also be impractical."[95] Brundage held fast that "we should have certain requirements and know something about the application of the money," even if, as Exeter correctly noted, the IOC had "no right nor do we want to interfere with their domestic affairs."[96] "If we are not careful," Brundage warned Albert Mayer, "this television money can lead to disaster."[97] Brundage and Exeter were seeking means of putting the genie back in the bottle when it came to the prospect of the IFs' expanding wealth.

In early 1967 Roger Coulon sought Exeter's opinion on the advisability of a meeting of the IFs with the IOC Executive Board. Coulon's approach puzzled Exeter, given Rudyard Russell was the principal liaison between the IFs and the Executive Board.[98] Exeter was suspicious of Coulon's motives and advised Brundage to stay away from any meeting the FILA Secretary General organized. "We would be putting a sword in the hands of those who wish to have an association of NOCs," observed Exeter, "for they would then argue that if the officers of the IOC meet not fully representative gatherings of the International Federations, why should they not do the same at similar meetings of the NOCs?"[99] Brundage agreed with Exeter's assessment.[100]

Exeter sensed a "power grab" within the IFs. Coulon and a number of his like-minded colleagues were maneuvering for the formation of an association of IFs.[101] The IAAF will not affiliate itself with such a body, stated Exeter.[102] He had no interest in such a body where the IAAF's influence would be severely diminished by a one-IF–one-vote system. Coulon understood that an attempt to "scuttle" a fledgling General Assembly of International Federations (GAIF) was active and that Exeter was centrally involved. He was unwilling to relent and informed Brundage that three-quarters of the IFs planned to meet at Lausanne's Continental Hotel in April: "The majority of IFs cannot admit the fact that the [IAAF], whose President is also a member of the [Executive Board] of the IOC considers to have the right to oppose our decisions."[103] Coulon was, like Onesti, a bit of a bulldozer.

When Coulon and his colleagues discussed the vexing matter of television money at GAIF's inaugural meeting in Lausanne, the Summer IFs called for the immediate elimination of Exeter's plan for distribution of television money based on the relative contribution of the individual IFs in favor of equal payments to all (as was the practice among the Winter IFs). They also renewed their demand for one-third of all television revenue.[104] Peace with respect to television money had been fleeting.

One of the challenges Exeter faced amid the protracted discussions with Coulon and his allies concerning the distribution of television money was his rather unique standing as an IOC Executive Board member, IAAF president, and BOA chairman. He had a foot in all camps scrambling for shares of television revenue not transferred to the OCOGs and could even well recall the fiscal demands of staging an Olympic festival. It provided him a 360° view of the landscape but left him open to accusations of bias from all sides. When he offered his services to Brundage a year earlier to craft the distribution formula for the IFs, there was no illusion concerning the possible blowback. "I am preparing my 'head for the block' in the distribution of the monies," he wrote.[105]

Exeter was unmoved by protests concerning his role in distributing the Summer IFs' portion of Olympic television revenue. He advised Brundage to proceed immediately with the distribution of monies to the IFs in connection with the 1968 Olympic Games, as "an attack is so often the best form of defense."[106] There was some good news as the Mexico City OCOG, in light of the better-than-expected returns from television rights negotiations, consented to send an additional $100,000 to Lausanne to be shared with the IFs.[107] Included with the check to the IFs should be a full explanation of distribution plan and its rationale, Exeter said, "as I think it is very healthy that all should know what a small contribution most of the noisiest are making towards the Games and how generously they are treated!"[108] Exeter sought to derail any momentum toward the establishment of an association of IFs.

It is fair to conclude that in trying to resolve his own approach to television revenue and its disbursement, Exeter's allegiance to the IAAF and IOC prevailed, while that of the BOA and other NOCs took a backseat. He labored to deliver money to the IFs, dating back to his failed attempt in the 1950s to convince Brundage of the need for a tax on Olympic tickets to accomplish this aim. When television money became available, he actively protected the IAAF's interests through his efforts concerning the distribution of television money transferred to the IFs while taking no steps to include the NOCs in any overall distribution plan until Onesti's activities—and Brundage's decree that the NOCs had a right to some of the money—forced it upon him. If one views the distribution of the Summer IFs objectively, it is difficult to dispute Exeter's call for an allocation based on the contribution of IFs, and his effort to scale back the returns for the likes of the IAAF and other major sports in favor of the minor sports was commendable. Of course, it all looked much different to Coulon and Keller, who sought parity with the IAAF. Keller, for instance, held that rowing's problem in drawing spectators did not reflect a lack of popularity but was tied to the remote locations where rowing basins were often situated that made it more challenging for spectators to attend.[109]

In July 1967 Brundage met one on one with Roger Coulon in Winnipeg, Canada, the day before the opening of the 5th Pan-American Games. Charles Palmer, the

The Marquess of Exeter (standing in the foreground), who had Avery Brundage's ear on matters concerning Olympic television revenue in the 1960s, appears next to Tommie Smith, Peter Norman, and John Carlos during the historic medal ceremony following the 200m race at the 1968 Mexico City Olympics. (© International Olympic Committee (IOC) / United Archives. Photo courtesy of the IOC.)

International Judo Federation's president, sat down with the men to facilitate the discussion as an interpreter. Coulon said the IOC did not give the IFs a "fair hearing" on television, and he called for two IOC members and two GAIF leaders to form a joint commission to examine the issues further. Brundage dismissed the notion of a "joint commission" but did indicate a committee could discuss the matter;

however, he was not committed to a timeline. He also reiterated that Exeter's plan would not be phased out at this date in favor of an alternative distribution plan.[110]

But, oddly, within two weeks IOC secretary general Johann Westerhoff informed Exeter that Brundage was willing to grant the IFs the right to determine their own distribution plan.[111] Exeter could hardly believe what he read! In Exeter's view, no reversal of policy was possible, as the method of distribution of the Mexico City money was approved by the IOC Executive Board and the Session. The minor IFs, stated Exeter, were receiving "several times as much as they are entitled to upon any logical basis." For Exeter, the time for mincing words with Brundage was over. The transfer of television money to the IFs resolved the difficulties the IOC faced years earlier when the IFs demanded gate money. If some of the IFs wanted more money, they needed to attract more spectators. He reminded Brundage that the "smooth running of the games depended on a good relationship between IAAF and IOC, [and] it would be jeopardised" by the equal allocation of shares as advocated by the minor sports. Any change at this time represented a "breach of faith." A "disaster" loomed, warned Exeter: "There is no possibility of any agreement at all in the present mood of the avaricious views of the small IFs," he offered, "and the question would come back to the IOC for arbitration."[112] Ceding authority in this matter to the IFs was untenable.

Did Westerhoff have his facts straight? Had Brundage wobbled in his commitment to Exeter's plan? If so, Exeter's words stiffened his spine. Brundage informed Coulon that the IOC's authority over matters pertaining to the sports on the program, the selection of host cities, its rules including those dealing with eligibility, and television money and its distribution, were "under the sole and exclusive control of the IOC." "Personally, I have deplored on more than one occasion, the idea of financial considerations being introduced into Olympic affairs. For the first time," he continued, "serious arguments have been provoked and I do not like it!" Brundage asserted that the majority of gate receipts flowed from Athletics, Football, and Boxing, and none of them attended GAIF's first meeting. Exeter completed a "very careful" study, Brundage noted: "He has tried, I think, to be fair." Coulon and Phillips continued to press for the allocation of equal shares to the federations.[113] Though entitled to $68,430 of the available $150,450 based on having provided 45.6 percent of the gate receipts on average for the last three Olympic Games, the IAAF received $35,000, or 23.3 percent. Exeter showed that Keller's rowing federation was due a measly $315 if strict use of the average gate receipts determined the percentage payments, but his plan elevated the payout to $5,700.[114]

Coulon, Phillips, and Keller were relentless. The Executive Board met with IF officials in January 1968. The Executive Board traversed familiar ground with their guests. Phillips indicated the IFs wanted one-third of all future television revenue distributed in equal shares to the Summer and Winter federations, including those who staged world championships in the same year. Exeter reviewed his past efforts and emphasized that "his Federation made enormous sacrifices. . . . As it is, certain federations entitled to very little were granted considerable amounts." He would give no ground. Keller pleaded rowing's case again, as he stated any plan centered on gate receipts was not "fair" because it compromised his federation due to the remote location of rowing basins. Coulon wanted "all" of the 1968 Olympic television money transferred to the IFs immediately; however, the record is unclear exactly what he meant by "all"—one-third or the $150,450 due to the IFs that it could duly apportion? "Bunny" Ahearne, not missing an opportunity to stir the pot, suggested that the global receipts from the Winter and Summer Games be lumped together and divided equally amongst all of the IFs.[115] The waters remained roiled, but in the end Exeter's plan prevailed.

Coulon, Phillips, and Keller, along with a number of other IF leaders, convened with the IOC Finance Commission in Mexico City prior to the 1968 Olympic Games to address matters pertaining to 1972 Olympic television money. Members of the Finance Commission present for this gathering were its chairman, Lord Luke, Count Jean de Beaumont, Marc Hodler, Gunnar Ericsson, and Reginald Alexander. Phillips held that the money should be sent to the IFs, who could decide its distribution based on the needs of the individual IFs. Not acceptable, said Donald Pain, who, as Exeter's proxy, knew that such a decision was a death knell for the IAAF. Its share would plummet in size. When Lord Luke requested a definitive formula from Phillips, he responded that the distribution should simply fall to the IFs. Reginald Alexander asked what process was in place if an IF disputed the sum granted to it: in other words, what was the nature of an appeal process? Phillips responded weakly that "it was not the time to raise this question as this occasion has never arisen."[116] For Phillips it was simply the IFs' money to do with what they desired.

Count Jean de Beaumont, his mind perhaps drifting to his challenge to Brundage for the IOC presidency (ultimately unsuccessful) in four days, called for two proposals from the federations, as two points of view existed. Coulon said only one proposal was forthcoming, and it simply was that the money should be transferred to the federations, "who would distribute it according to their own wishes." Pain refused to participate in any meeting organized by Coulon to develop one plan acceptable to all. Again, Beaumont, whose patience waned, asked for two plans, but William Jones responded bluntly "that there would not be two propositions as 21 federations were on one side and the IAAF on the other." Charles Palmer convinced Pain that the search for a unanimously supported proposal was worthwhile, and Pain committed to that process, one that Keller indicated could be concluded by April 1969.[117] The search proved fruitless.

GAIF leaders met in Lausanne in late May and early June 1969 to reach agreement on a proposal that they could place before the IOC Finance Commission. How best to knock down the IAAF's share and elevate those of the minor sports? If

$2 million was a reasonable estimate of the Summer IFs' share, in the mind of the GAIF leaders, $500,000 was to be divided equally among all twenty-one IFs, while the remainder was subject to percentage payouts based on "contribution." However, what emerged from their discussions was a different method of calculating "contribution." Instead of using a rolling average of gate receipts exclusively, GAIF officials mixed in with these attendance figures the number of sessions for each sport and each IF's number of affiliated countries. Using Tokyo data to calculate contribution (even though only Munich data would ultimately be employed and the three-year rolling-average concept was shelved) and apply the results to an expected $2 million from Munich for purposes of discussion yielded interesting and predictable results. The formula downgraded the IAAF's contribution because its event sessions numbered only fifteen, while sports such as Basketball, Volleyball, and Boxing scheduled twenty-nine, twenty-four, and twenty-four, respectively. It also compromised FIFA's figures because while it boasted the highest attendance figures from Tokyo (616,400) and number of affiliated countries (135), it had only nine sessions. Still, FIFA fared better under GAIF's proposal than it did under the IAAF's plan. The gulf between GAIF and the IAAF was never wider, as GAIF's plan resulted in the IAAF's planned receipt of $257,177, while the IAAF's own proposal resulted in its receipt of $420,000. Attendees at the GAIF meeting were resolved to pursue "unanimity from all federations against the IAAF formula."[118]

A solution eluded the parties for three more years. In Munich, four days before the global television community was transfixed by the infiltration of the Black September terrorist cell into the Munich Olympic Village and the unfolding tragedy and loss of life of eleven Israeli athletes and team officials, three IOC vice presidents, Lord Killanin (then serving as president-elect), Jean de Beaumont (whom Killanin defeated in the election a week earlier to succeed Brundage), and Herman van Karnebeek met with a number of IF officials, including FIFA's president, Sir Stanley Rous; Marc Hodler, president of the Fédération Internationale de Ski; and Thomas Keller, GAIF's president of some three years' standing. With respect to the IFs' campaign for television money in the previous decade, events were filled with much bickering, bravado, infighting, and spasms of righteous indignation, but the meeting on this day reflected a sense of calm and serenity rarely witnessed in earlier discussions. The Summer IFs had indeed reached a classic compromise in settling their differences. Keller observed that the Summer IFs wished to divide the first half of money due to them into equal shares, approximately $38,000 per IF, while allocating the second half of the money on the basis of gate receipts from Munich. The six Winter IFs would share their portion of global television revenue from Sapporo equally. What if some Summer IFs complained that their stadia were not large enough and that their gate receipts were suppressed? asked Beaumont. Keller replied that "it was up to each Federation to ascertain that their facilities and installations were large enough." Besides, he noted, this was the decision and will of the Summer IFs. Killanin expressed his own thought "that once the money was given to the IFs, it was theirs to do [with] what they wished."[119] Brundage possessed this thought, too, at least in terms of their determining their own distribution method, but he could never pull himself to put that thought into action in the 1960s. Ceding authority did not come naturally to the man. When his knees buckled, Exeter was there to steady him, lobbying on behalf of the IAAF's interests.

And, with that, it was done. The IOC vice presidents Keller, Rous, and Hodler moved on to the next item on their agenda.

Closing Thoughts

There were numerous issues that confounded and perplexed Brundage in the 1960s, highlighted by the controversy over South Africa's place within the Olympic Movement, the discriminatory attitudes of those running the Mediterranean Games and the IVth Asian Games, who denied access to Israeli athletes in the former and Israeli and Nationalist Chinese competitors in the latter, the emergence of the Games of the New Emerging Forces (GANEFO), and the rearguard action he constantly fought with regard to maintaining his vision of the amateur ideal.[120] The long, slow, tortured march to the Rome Formula revealed that many within the IOC, despite Brundage's success in fending off Jean de Beaumont's challenge for the presidency in 1968, and those within the NOC and IF communities believed his philosophy concerning commercial revenue and his perception of the roles of the NOCs and IFs passed their "best before" dates.

In the waning weeks before the IOC adopted the Rome Formula at its 64th Session in April 1966, Giorgio de Stefani, an Italian IOC member and one of the Session's organizers, asked Brundage for a copy of his speech for the opening session to expedite its translation into three languages.[121] Brundage duly responded that he had not drafted anything yet given competing demands on his time, but he pledged to get started and follow through on Stefani's request. He confessed that it was not "easy to compose speeches for the IOC after talking to the same people, on the same subject, for fifty years."[122] While Brundage struggled to pen the speeches, more and more folks within the Olympic community found it increasingly difficult to listen to them, too. Reginald Alexander appealed to Brundage that the time for him to stand aside had come as the 1968 IOC Session in Mexico City approached: "Avery, you're eighty; you're on top. You've been at it now sixty years and when you're on top, there's only one way to go, and that's down." If he stepped aside now, his legacy was secure, said Alexander.[123] Brundage would hear none of it. When Lord Killanin could not be convinced to run against Brundage in 1968, and Brundage refused to step aside, Jean de Beaumont stood as Brundage's sole challenger. Brundage prevailed, despite Beaumont's belief that a decision to reelect him represented "a challenge to common sense in the eyes of the world."[124]

Satellite technology changed the landscape of sport television, offering sport organizations the prospect of new and appreciated revenue. Within the Olympic realm, doubts about the commitment to Olympism and the amateur ideal within the NOCs, IFs, and certain quarters of the IOC itself plagued Brundage throughout the 1960s, even though he understood the financial challenges all three bodies faced and the possible benefits of television money in facilitating their work. He grew restless with the overspending in the IOC's Lausanne headquarters, a result of the newly leveraged money from television, and demanded controls on that spending through the auspices of the Finance Commission. For Brundage, the accord reached in Rome proved a Pyrrhic victory. GAIF continued to grow and exert its power, Onesti did not retreat from his mission to establish the PGA, which he accomplished in 1968, and the rising tide of television money continued to challenge his ideals of pure amateurism and Olympism.

Brundage expressed sympathies for the financial needs of the NOCs in the 1960s, if not the ambitions of Giulio Onesti, and this was not startling in the context of television revenue. Years earlier, he offered his services in his capacity as USOA president to broker the sale of U.S. television rights to the 1952 Helsinki Olympics on behalf of the Helsinki OCOG and its president, Erik von Frenckell. Brundage proposed transferring the first $100,000 and one-third of any additional money to Helsinki; the USOC would retain the remainder. Von Frenckell eventually abandoned his personal negotiations with U.S. television executives and accepted Brundage's offer, but he was unable to entice the networks to purchase the rights. Even before this, Brundage pondered the sale of television and radio rights to the 1948 U.S. Olympic track and field trials as a means of offsetting the USOC's costs in sending athletes to London, and he considered $25,000 to be a reasonable target. Nothing materialized.

In empowering Giulio Onesti as chairman of the subcommittee tasked to find a distribution formula in early 1966 and in loading the group with individuals whose sympathies rested primarily with the NOCs, Brundage clearly valued the NOCs' work and accepted their need for some financial support. What he could never tolerate was Onesti's reach for increased authority and influence for them through the PGA. And when rumors abounded that Onesti sought the IOC presidency in 1968, Brundage's views hardened further. In August 1971 Brundage dismissed summarily Onesti's ongoing effort in seeking the IOC's official recognition of the PGA: "Since it exists, the IOC is aware of that fact—but, this does not signify that the IOC has recognized it as a legitimate organization . . . and I doubt that it ever will. There is nothing whatsoever," he continued, "that the PGA does that cannot be done better by the IOC itself, so it is a completely useless organization, as I have explained to you on several occasions."[125] Onesti's unrelenting beavering to elevate the status and influence of the PGA likely prompted Brundage's suggestion to the IOC Executive Board as he stepped down that the IOC was not compelled any longer to transfer large sums of television money to the NOCs. Soon enough, Onesti, the NOCs, and a path forward in managing the IOC's relations with them fell to Lord Killanin.

Brundage's and Exeter's efforts to control the IFs' access to television money in 1964 and 1968, while privileging the IAAF in its allocation (though based on sound logic when one considered the respective IF's contribution to the Games themselves), contributed to a breach in relations between the IOC and the IFs and within the IF community itself. Coulon, Phillips, and Keller, exploited these strained relations in establishing GAIF. Their persistent demand for one-third of television revenue irritated Brundage immensely and distressed him, too. Their maneuverings and machinations, judged Brundage, threatened the foundation that Coubertin built and that which Brundage sought to preserve. "You will remember how obnoxious some of the Federation representatives were in Rome and I can assure you," Brundage informed Exeter, "that in their private meetings with me they were even worse. You would have been horrified, as I was—I have never heard such blatant commercialism from amateur sport officials."[126] Their bulldog mentality, and what he perceived as their abandonment of Olympic ideals, flummoxed him and prompted Brundage's call to greatly curtail financial support for the IFs from television revenues by the close of his presidency.

The passing of the Rome Formula represents a transformational event in Olympic history, as it forever altered the level of access for the IOC, NOCs, and IFs to television revenue, thereby changing the ways in which they could pursue their mandates. The path to this agreement informs us greatly on the people central to this development, individuals who tried to navigate their own feelings toward Olympism, amateurism, and sport in what was a rapidly changing economic environment. Competing beliefs within this assemblage of historical actors contributed greatly to what ultimately proved to be seismic change in how the IOC managed its interaction with the IFs and NOCs. As the decade closed, the IFs and NOCs commanded and relished a measure of enhanced respect, and their concerns could no longer be batted away as easily by IOC officials, including Brundage or anyone who sought to succeed him. Television money weakened relations among the IOC, IFs, and NOCs in the 1960s: the evolution of GAIF and the PGA tells us that much, but, in time, Lord Killanin claimed this revenue served as the "glue"[127] to keep the Olympic Movement together in the 1970s. What he meant was that while the IFs and NOCs still experienced frustrations in their dealings with the IOC at times, increasingly lucrative television payouts proved a useful salve for any perceived wounds.

The genesis of the Rome Formula, the role of the Brundage, Exeter, the IFs, and the NOCs in establishing it, as well as the fallout for the IOC's relations with the IFs and NOCs, provide a fascinating tale but so, too, does the way in which the 1972 Munich and Sapporo OCOGs set their financial goals in negotiations with television executives. In short, the Rome Formula, in light of elevated costs of broadcast infrastructure required to provide television transmissions in the satellite age and, by virtue of its terms, the reduced percentage of television money accruing to the OCOGs, did not work for them.

CHAPTER 4

Willi Daume and Munich, 1972's Television Legacy

Willi Daume on the Rome Formula

The IOC's 64th Session in Rome in April 1966 resonates within the history of IOC policy-making concerning television revenue. One day following the passage of the Rome Formula, the General Session bestowed upon the cities of Sapporo, Japan, and Munich, West Germany, the right to host the 11th Olympic Winter Games and the Games of the XXth Olympiad, respectively. During the formal presentation of their candidatures before the final vote, among a series of assurances, representatives of all the competing delegations pledged to abide by the terms of the IOC's newly passed legislation governing the allocation of television money.[1] For Willi Daume, an IOC member, president of the West German Olympic Committee, and head of Munich's bid, the IOC's decision in favor of Munich marked the end of a whirlwind six months.

In late October 1965 Daume entered the office of Munich's mayor, Hans-Jochen Vogel, to sound him out on his thoughts concerning a prospective bid to host the 1972 Olympics. Stunned by Daume's proposal, Vogel envisioned numerous roadblocks to Munich's success, yet he did not dismiss the idea out of hand. Following a series of consultations with city officials, close advisors, West Berlin's mayor (and future West German chancellor) Willy Brandt, and even those who might oppose such an initiative, Vogel embraced the concept.

Daume and Vogel charged forward to place a bid in the hands of Lausanne officials, complete with infrastructure plans, budget details, and a vision, by the deadline of December 31. Having cleared that hurdle, they forged ahead in preparation for the Rome IOC Session four months later. Munich prevailed. This six-month odyssey, from the moment of conception to ultimate victory, is unimaginable to anyone with recent experience seeking the right to host the Games. Cities often commence their early planning ten years before the hosting date and have seven years to prepare for the arrival of the athletes once they have secured the right to host the Games.[2] Bottom line, Daume and Vogel put together a bid in two months, and Munich welcomed the Olympic world a little over six years after their triumph at the 1966 IOC Session in Rome.

Yet, between Munich's moment of triumph in Rome and the signing of the Munich Organizing Committee's first television contract with the American Broadcasting Company (ABC) three years later, Daume's thoughts on the Rome Formula changed. His successful effort to maximize Munich's share of the $13.5 million contract by circumventing its terms had far-reaching effects on the IOC's attempts to implement the Rome Formula for more than a decade. And IOC officials were none too pleased.

Willi Daume's Olympic Dream

"Willi Daume," wrote biographer Jan Rode, was "one of the most important personalities of German and international sport in the second half of the 20th century."[3] Prior to World War II, Daume, an attendee of the 1928 Amsterdam and 1932 Los Angeles Olympics and a member of Germany's basketball team in Berlin, was also an official with his local sport club, Eintracht Dortmund. As Europe recovered from the conflict, Daume's rise within West Germany's sport community was swift. He became chairman of the Deutscher Sportbund (German Sport Association) in 1950, was appointed to the International Olympic Committee in 1956, and was elected president of the West German National Olympic Committee in 1961. His leadership of the 1972 Munich Organizing Committee served as a springboard for him to become the first German member of the IOC Executive Board (1972–1976). Given his administrative roles, he figured prominently in events tied to the IOC's handling of the existence of West and East Germany. His unwavering support of Avery Brundage's designs for a unified German Olympic team in the 1950s left him on good terms with the American, but the construction of the Berlin Wall in 1961 eventually diminished his thinking that this approach, used in 1956, 1960, and 1964, had much of a future.

Munich was not Daume's first choice for the site of a West German–hosted Olympic Games. In dealing with the immediate fallout of the Berlin Wall, Daume believed that an Olympic festival staged in West *and* East Berlin could bridge the divide, if temporarily, that the wall created. When he pitched the idea to Brundage in 1963, the IOC president was soon won over, as was Willy Brandt. However, fierce opposition from the federal governments in Bonn (Federal Republic of Germany [FRG]) and East Berlin (German Democratic Republic [GDR]) scuttled further planning. The ruling Conservatives in Bonn lacked any interest in advancing Brandt's political profile (he was a Social Democrat) and considered such a project as one that might lead to Berlin's being declared a free city (a Soviet goal), thereby preventing West Berlin's full integration into West Germany. East Germany viewed Daume's initiative as "a great provocation," one that served West German interests, and its politicians cried foul at the absence of any consultative process before Daume launched his proposal. How could West Germany be serious about any collaborative venture when its government routinely denied visas to East German athletes? Brundage understood from a visiting delegation of East German officials that Daume's dream for the 1968 Olympics had no chance. It was abandoned. Daume regrouped, and Munich emerged as his new focus.[4]

Daume and Vogel felt they possessed some valuable leverage in the bid competition for the 1972 Summer Olympics. At the IOC's Madrid Session in October 1965, where Giulio Onesti marshaled those seeking to form the Permanent General Assembly of NOCs (PGA), the IOC admitted the unworkable nature of the practice of German athletes competing on a unified team. In Grenoble and Mexico City, East and West Germany fielded separate teams, a long-sought goal of East Germany. Daume believed that the IOC and Brundage would look for means to similarly satisfy West German aspirations.

With his West Berlin–East Berlin plan mothballed for two years, Daume thought the time was right to move aggressively on behalf of Munich's candidacy and, if successful, to showcase the new West Germany. A rapidly growing city, known for its yearly Oktoberfest celebrations, Munich boasted an industrial base featuring BMW, Siemens, and MAN (a builder of diesel vehicles), a number of well-respected institutions of higher learning, as well as its newly achieved status as one of West Germany's film-making centers. Jealousies in Hanover and Hamburg, where some officials viewed Munich's bid as brazen and without merit, were overcome, as were concerns about projected costs at various layers of government and the vestiges of the city's links to Hitler's National Socialist Party.[5] They finessed the needed messaging from officials in Bonn so that the IOC believed that the FRG would accord East German athletes the rights and privileges the global contingent of competitors enjoyed, even if the politicians' real posture was less clear cut.

Daume correctly anticipated that Cold War dynamics fueled opposition to Munich's bid in the Soviet Union and East Germany, but he confronted it, at least internally, by pledging to nominate Konstantin Adrianov for one of the IOC vice

Willi Daume, president of the 1972 Munich Organizing Committee (left) and Avery Brundage. (© 1972 / International Olympic Committee (IOC). Photo courtesy of the IOC.)

president slots and promising to put forward Heinz Schöbel, a well-known East German sport official, for IOC membership. The Communist critique continued, but these two prominent voices fell silent. Meanwhile, Vogel traveled to Chicago to meet personally with Brundage in extolling Munich's features. The compact planned footprint for athletic venues proved popular with IOC members; that, combined with well-conceived presentation in Rome, meant Munich cruised to an easy second-ballot win over Madrid and Montreal, with Detroit having been eliminated on the first round. For Daume and Munich, it was time to convert the dream and vision to reality.

The Rome Formula Revisited

It started with a somewhat innocuous exchange of correspondence between Avery Brundage and Herbert Kunze, one of the vice presidents of the Munich Organizing Committee, in April 1969. After what Kunze characterized as an "intensive" three days of negotiations with ABC officials, Munich reached a deal on American television rights. Brundage duly responded that the Finance Commission would review the contract and provide an opinion at the IOC's Warsaw Session in June.[6] Upon review, members of the Finance Commission were startled by two elements of the agreement: its terms, which categorized $6 million of the $13.5 million as a technical services fee transferred directly to Munich to pay for broadcast infrastructure; and its timing, given the expert opinion it had solicited, indicated a higher return would be achieved closer to the date of the Olympics.[7]

In Warsaw, Kunze informed Lord Luke, chairman of the IOC Finance Commission, and his colleagues that ABC's original offer was $6.5 million but moved to $13.5 million. Columbia Broadcasting System (CBS) showed interest, but its best offer was $10 million. The National Broadcasting Company (NBC) declined to enter the bidding. Kunze confirmed that the ABC deal was not binding, but he believed it was the best offer available.[8] Before departing Warsaw, Kunze and Vogel discussed the merits of a consultative process with industry experts, as desired by Luke, which might yield a higher sale price. Vogel consented, but Kunze indicated that it must be billed as an IOC initiative to avoid any ill feelings with ABC. And, regardless of this dialogue's track, Munich owed ABC a response before the end of the year.[9] Nothing materialized from these discussions that topped ABC's offer, so Kunze's read on the situation was accurate, but all of this bought the IOC time to address Munich's effort to sidestep the terms of the Rome Formula.

In the intervening months, Tomoo Sato, Sapporo's secretary general, informed Lord Luke that his team reached a U.S. television rights contract with NBC. The contract value was $6,401,000, with a minimum of $5 million sent to Lausanne for division, according to the terms of the Rome Formula.[10] Sato pivoted to his discussions with European and Canadian television executives and explained that the technical services fee from the NBC deal provided needed funds for the provision of broadcast facilities for the world's telecasters.[11] Machinations in Munich and Sapporo drew the rebuke of the Executive Board. In late October it concluded that broadcast facilities remained the responsibility of the Organizing Committees (OCOG), and that this fact would be included in any instructions given to future bid cities.[12]

The Marquess of Exeter was particularly aggrieved. He believed IOC approval of the Munich/ABC contract invited "a tremendous hammering from the International Sport Federations [IFs] and NOCs," who accepted the Rome Formula knowing that the gross television receipts were subject to division among the parties. "These rights belong to us," asserted Exeter, "and the position of the Organizing Committee is that of our agent. I do not think that any of us have ever visualized that they would not pay the proceeds gross to us, and in fact help themselves to 2 million dollars of IOC, International Federation and NOC money."[13] His calculations revealed Munich would receive approximately $10 million from the ABC contract, something that was quite unreasonable and might provoke hard feelings in Montreal, Madrid, and Detroit, cities that contested Munich for the right to host the 1972 Olympics under a far different understanding of the conditions governing television contracts.[14] Brundage concurred.[15] By February 1970, Exeter faced questions from the IFs about the Munich contract and why such a deduction might be possible while leaving the OCOG a full sharing partner of the rights portion of the contract.[16] That same month, Daume and his colleagues submitted a fifteen-page defense of their approach to the U.S. television contract to the Finance Commission.[17] It duly accepted the $6 million fee for technical services,[18] but the Executive Board balked.[19]

Lord Luke pressed Sapporo and Munich to abide by the letter and spirit of the Rome Formula.[20] At the IOC's 69th Session in Amsterdam in May 1970 he could report little progress.[21] Two months later, a clearly frustrated Luke conveyed to Daume that the IOC believed Munich was committed "to see[ing] that the IOC should get as little as possible," and this was not "conducive to the best of goodwill between us."[22] Daume remained steadfast. He viewed Luke's "reproach" to have been "unjustified" and asked for Luke's "goodwill a little longer" in order to find a solution.[23] Though Sato reduced the deduction from the NBC contract to $1 million,[24] he, too, was holding firm to the concept of a technical services fee.

However, Luke's diligent lobbying paid dividends in September when he received notice that Sapporo would transfer the gross value of the NBC contract to Lausanne for distribution.[25] Sato's reversal was likely tied to Sapporo's financial need, as no money flowed from NBC to any of the parties until the IOC approved the contract, and the Winter Games were only seventeen months away.

Thinking Sato's decision to blink afforded him leverage with Munich officials, Luke duly reported this development to Daume, as well as the Executive Board's directive to him, once again, to seek Munich's consent to the IOC's interpretation of the Rome Formula.[26] Daume looked to resolve the matter "without any feelings of ill will on any side" and stated his OCOG had "no intention of demanding anything that is not realistic."[27] Simply put, Daume believed that the U.S. rights fee, which had climbed $3 million from that paid by ABC for Mexico City, and the cost of installations borne by ABC at that time, $3.5 million, were being rolled into the Munich contract in the form of the $6 million technical services fee. Daume knew the Finance Commission recommended approval of the contract months earlier, but the Executive Board did not accept that advice, so a split existed in the IOC ranks. He requested another meeting with the Finance Commission in the new year.[28] Daume needed the money, but so, too, did the IOC, whose revenue situation was bleak. Its expenses were being covered by money ($274,200, or DM 1 million) borrowed from the Munich Organizing Committee. In this standoff, Daume held the better hand.

The IOC's Financial Situation

In September 1969 IOC director Monique Berlioux updated Lord Luke on the IOC's dire financial circumstances. The IOC's fiscal status had concerned Luke and his colleagues since the establishment of the Finance Commission in 1967; however, they struggled to control spending in Lausanne.[29] The IOC had SF 30,000 to cover the remaining three months of 1969, wrote Berlioux, but its salary costs for that period were SF 88,000. The upcoming Executive Board meetings in Dubrovnik were slated to incur expenses of SF 28,000. Office expenses to close out 1969 would be SF 20,000, and this did not include the anticipated SF 17,000 to cover production of the *Olympic Newsletter*. An "urgent solution," said Berlioux, was needed.[30] Luke replied that the IOC's financial picture was "very grave," concluding that the IOC had exceeded its available revenues by SF 1,354,000 in the previous twenty-one months. Henceforth, Luke decreed, spending requests required approval of the Finance Commission.[31]

Brundage, too, had concerns. He placed responsibility on the desk of former secretary general Johann Westerhoff, who "with the encouragement of some members . . . ran wild and as a result, we are in a very precarious situation."[32] Brundage also called for an overhaul of the IOC's accounting procedures, which he found far too expensive.[33] In this campaign he enlisted the support of Jean de Beaumont, who also wished to streamline the accounting policies.[34] Access, or rather lack thereof, to the IOC's financial records also rankled him: "I must say," Brundage told members of the Finance Commission, "that I do not understand this situation at all. It has always been a mystery with no justification about the IOC accounts. Count de Beaumont tried to obtain an analysis, later General Clark attempted to get information. My assistant, Mr. Ruegsegger was asked to make a report, was ignored, my own attempts had no success. Lord Luke has been waiting for our 1968 report ever since the end of the year. Why there should be this lack of cooperation and delay in handling the accounts for a small, simple operation like ours at Château de Vidy is beyond me."[35]

Luke dispatched Reginald Alexander, a fellow member of the Finance Commission, to Lausanne to examine the accounting procedures, and Berlioux viewed the visit as undue meddling in her affairs. She was particularly miffed that Alexander approached the IOC's fiduciary officers directly for documents without requesting them from her. Berlioux complained to Brundage that Alexander's actions undercut her authority,[36] and she chastised Alexander in personal correspondence: "As long as I am in charge of the administration, I kindly ask you not to go over my head."[37] Alexander was unmoved. He was acting on Lord Luke's request to use his background as a Chartered Accountant to examine the IOC's financial situation and find ways to reduce the costs of its "bookkeeping and accounting procedures." "This and nothing more," Alexander told Berlioux, "is exactly what I have been trying to do, and will continue to do so, until these functions are entirely satisfactory, and I hope inexpensive."[38] Berlioux shot back that she thought Alexander blamed her for the troubling issues with the IOC's bookkeeping, and she reminded him that these policies existed before her arrival.[39]

Meanwhile, Beaumont saw little progress in the reduction of the IOC's bookkeeping expenses and told Brundage, "We are still paddling in the pond."[40] Brundage's patience dissipated. In July 1970 he was unwilling to "condone" the situation any longer and reported to members of the Finance Commission that Beaumont and Berlioux had prepared new procedures such that the IOC would not continue to spend SF 60,000 for the auditing of a SF 800,000 budget. If no one took issue, stated Brundage, these policies would be enacted.[41]

Within weeks Arthur Young and Company, the IOC's auditors, were released from their contract. Luke viewed Brundage's actions dimly: "I am greatly surprised at this unilateral action by yourself, which makes one wonder whether it is worth having a Finance Committee at all, if this is the way you treat it."[42] However, it was not Brundage who canceled the Arthur Young contract; it was Berlioux. Brundage informed Luke that she took independent action, but he supported the decision.[43] Though only a few months into her new role as IOC director, Berlioux was battling gamely for respect and authority in a man's world.

Willi Daume may have lacked a detailed picture of the clashes among those managing the IOC's finances, but they, along with the anxiety over the IOC's cash flow that all of them felt, benefited him in the protracted discussions concerning the Rome Formula and pushed the IOC to the table. At the Finance Commission's meeting in late January 1971, Luke and his colleagues yielded (a second time) to Daume's interpretation of the Rome Formula, specifically that the broadcast installations costs should not be borne by an Organizing Committee from its share of the gross value of global television rights. The IOC's consent hinged on Munich's forgiving its DM 1 million loan to the IOC and the approval of the IOC Executive Board. Herbert Kunze hesitated briefly, but he signaled Munich's willingness to waive the loan.[44] The Executive Board signed off on ABC's contract six weeks later.[45]

Daume played the long game and won. He waited the IOC out, knowing its strained financial state, and secured valuable revenue for Munich in its efforts to accommodate the needs of the world's television networks in the still-nascent satellite age. His success had far-reaching effects over the next decade on IOC relations with OCOGs concerning television money.

After two years of haggling with Munich, Beaumont conceded to Brundage that the IOC's financial situation forced its hand. On the positive side of the ledger, the forgiven loan assisted the IOC in meeting its operational costs through 1976.[46] The decision was necessary and could not be delayed any longer, offered Beaumont, "as the situation was somewhat critical."[47] "We cannot always entrench ourselves behind a wall of indecision," he added.[48] Luke echoed this thought as the two sides had been "deadlock[ed]."[49] Brundage thanked both men for their efforts and considered the agreed-upon terms beneficial to the IOC's fiscal status.[50] They closed the loophole in Rule 49, such that the gross value of each television contract was transferrable to Lausanne, and extracted a pledge from both Montreal and Denver, the hosts of the upcoming 1976 Summer and Winter Olympic Games, that Daume's approach would not be replicated[51]—or so they thought. The burden of managing the matter fell to Brundage's successor, Lord Killanin.

Lord Killanin

"He was a man of majestic roundness, with pink skin, and curling silver hair," wrote Monique Berlioux in describing Lord Killanin at the time of their first meeting in 1967. "White side whiskers cut across his plump cheeks," she continued; of course, the ever-present pipe was there, too.[52] His eight-year term (1972–1980) as IOC president followed Avery Brundage's tumultuous tenure. Killanin's presidency was marked by difficulties such as Denver's withdrawal as host city of the 1976

Avery Brundage prepares to transfer presidential authority to Lord Killanin in Lausanne in 1972. The two men are accompanied by Juan Antonio Samaranch. (© 1972 / International Olympic Committee (IOC). Photo courtesy of the IOC.)

Olympic Winter Games, resulting from its citizenry's concerns over finances and environmental impact, the massive cost overruns in Montreal that left few cities with a burning ambition to host what was proving to be a much larger and more expensive exercise than in years past, the intrusion of world geopolitics in the form of the African boycott of the 1976 Montreal Olympics and Canada's refusal to admit Taiwanese athletes to the country under the banner of the Republic of China, as well as the Jimmy Carter–inspired boycott of the 1980 Moscow Olympics. The stress of the job—particularly (in his wife's mind) the challenging prelude to the Montreal Olympics—resulted in a heart attack in 1977 and also left Killanin fifty-five pounds lighter than when he took office.

Schooled at Eton, the Sorbonne, and Magdalene College (Cambridge), Killanin, an Irish peer at age thirteen and a member of the House of Lords at twenty-one, launched his professional career as a journalist in the 1930s, covering major events of the decade, such as Edward VIII's abdication and the Sino-Japanese War. While not an elite athlete, Killanin enjoyed boxing, rugby, swimming, and rowing in his formative years, and had a lifelong love of horse racing.

He volunteered for military service in World War II and participated in the D-Day landings as a brigade major with the 79th Armoured Division (30th Armoured Brigade). Killanin arrived in Normandy following the initial military engagement and after the beachheads were secured. And, while his service with the 30th Armoured Brigade in the European campaign earned him a Member of the British Empire designation,[53] at the time of the fiftieth anniversary of the Normandy landings he confessed that his place in history might have been much more infamous. Astride a new motorcycle issued to him, Killanin was enjoying simply "swanning around" the coastal roads before a push inland. One day, a number of jeeps pulled up beside him, with one of those vehicles bearing a rather "fierce" looking Field Marshal Bernard Montgomery ("Monty"), commander of Allied ground forces in Normandy. An adjutant queried Killanin for directions to British headquarters. Killanin, not knowing its location, but not wishing to appear "foolish," pointed Montgomery and his entourage "over there." Montgomery's convoy drove off with sirens sounding so as to clear the road. Only later did he learn he risked Montgomery's capture or death by actually sending him in the direction of the German lines. Once he discovered his error, he "laid low for a few days." When he knew that nothing disastrous had resulted, he "got on the [motorcycle] again, and motored on into France."[54]

An author, Killanin published his first book, *Sir Godfrey Kneller and His Times, 1646–1723*, in 1948, though he edited and contributed to *Four Days* (1938), a book detailing events surrounding the Munich crisis before the war. A number of other books, including *The Shell Guide to Ireland* (co-authored with Michael Duignan in 1975), *My Olympic Years* (1983), a personal reflection on his involvement with the Olympic Movement, and *My Ireland* (1987) followed in later life. After resigning his military commission, he became a film producer and worked with director John Ford on a number of projects, including *The Quiet Man* (1952) starring John Wayne and Maureen O'Hara. Killanin's varied life path intersected with the Olympic Movement in 1950 when he became president of the Olympic Council of Ireland (a post that he held until 1973), and he was soon thereafter co-opted by the IOC (1952) at the suggestion of Britain's Lord Burghley (the Marquess of Exeter).

Following his election to the Executive Board in 1968, Killanin defeated Jean de Beaumont for the presidency in 1972. Killanin's road to the presidency mirrored Samaranch's in two respects, as both served as the IOC's head of protocol, an important position in that the officeholder acts as the key communications point person for the organization with its membership, and it was a useful way to get oneself known among those who ultimately vote. Both also burnished their reputations and bona fides by serving on the Executive Board, the powerful decision-making body sitting just under the president in the IOC's organizational structure. The affable and jovial Irishman was a desirable personage for members who chafed under Brundage's extended period of autocratic rule. One of his more interesting initiatives as president, one that did not gain traction, was an effort to eliminate national team uniforms, flags, and anthems. Propaganda wars, mused Killanin, would cease. At the time of his election in Munich, Killanin stated pointedly: "We have the big shots, America and Russia, trying to prove their way of life is better because of the number of medals they win. It proves nothing of the sort."[55]

Killanin's departure and Juan Antonio Samaranch's arrival marked a major change in the way the officeholder viewed the connection of the Olympic Games to the "outside" political world. Killanin did not intervene aggressively with American and Soviet political leaders during the prelude to the 1980 Moscow Olympics. "I am one of those who still believe," commented Australia's long-serving IOC member (1977–2013) Kevan Gosper, "the IOC moved too slowly to meet with presidents (Leonid) Brezhnev and (Jimmy) Carter on the 1980 boycott crisis. Killanin's argument that politics should keep out of sport," he concluded, "ignored the reality of international governments."[56] In fending off pressure to cancel, postpone, or transfer the Games, Killanin, in keeping with Brundagian tradition, lamented that politics intruded in Olympic affairs. With reference to the Soviet military action in Afghanistan, he stated: "That does not mean that I or the International Olympic Committee are condoning the political action taken by the host country, but if we started making political judgments, it would be the end of the games."[57] It harked back to Brundage's pronouncement concerning the Soviets' decision to suppress student dissent in Budapest in 1956 in the months prior to the Melbourne Olympics: "Every civilized person recoils in horror at the savage slaughter in Hungary, but that is no reason for destroying the nucleus of international cooperation. . . . the Olympics are contests between individuals and not nations. In an imperfect world, if participation in sports is to be stopped every time the politicians violate the laws of humanity, there will never be any international contests."[58]

Juan Antonio Samaranch's approach to interaction with world political leaders stood in stark contrast to that displayed by Brundage and Killanin and was no better exemplified than through his efforts at shuttle diplomacy prior to the 1984 Los Angeles Olympics, his thorough, calculated dialogue with South Korean and North Korean officials in 1986 and 1987 that averted a large-scale boycott of the 1988 Seoul Olympic Games, and his ambitious travel schedule that put him in contact with the vast majority of the world's leaders in the first twelve years of his presidency.

Dick Pound likely pinpointed the prevailing future view of Killanin's contribution to the IOC in terms of its dealing with money and finances. "I think history will regard Killanin as a transitional president, as the IOC and the Olympic movement moved off the kitchen table and into the boardroom."[59] When Killanin was a mere two years into the job, he viewed an overhaul of the IOC's operations in Lausanne his most pressing concern: "My biggest job as I see it is overhauling the administration. Mr. Brundage ran a one-man show. I'm a corporation man. I've had management consultants in, trying to smooth procedures. I'd like to turn over an efficient, overhauled machine to my successor."[60] While the Finance Commission emerged under Brundage's leadership, its mandate broadened through Killanin's initiative. Jean de Beaumont, the chairman of the Finance Commission under Lord Killanin, took a major role in monitoring the IOC's interests in negotiations, and Killanin himself intervened in European television negotiations for the 1976 Montreal Olympics, the first time an IOC president played a hands-on role in the negotiations of such a contract. In many respects, Killanin prepared the ground for Samaranch's approach that further elevated the IOC's role in television negotiations.

Killanin, too, facilitated changes in athlete eligibility regulations, specifically the advent of the trust-fund system and the removal of the term "amateur" from the *Olympic Charter*, which set the stage for the transition of the Olympic Games to a sport competition that welcomed "professional" athletes under his successor. Samaranch achieved this goal by assigning IFs the opportunity to set eligibility regulations for their respective sports, knowing that they wished to have the best athletes present, "amateur" or "professional," as a means of promoting their sports through the emerging global television spectacle. Despite these significant changes tied to finances and Olympic eligibility, Killanin most prized his ability to facilitate the reentry of China into the Olympic Movement, such that athletes from the People's Republic of China competed in Lake Placid.

When Samaranch stepped down after twenty-one years in office, he did so through a carefully orchestrated, showy series of gatherings at the IOC's Session in

Moscow in 2001. This was not Killanin's style. On the eve of Samaranch's election at the IOC's Moscow Session in 1980, Killanin spent a quiet evening in his hotel room, sharing a drink and conversation with two junior IOC members, Dick Pound and David McKenzie. They all agreed that Samaranch had coalesced sufficient support for his election the following day, and Killanin offered, with a healthy measure of prescience, that Samaranch would be effective in the role. If Killanin's aide had not searched out Pound and McKenzie at the hotel's restaurant and requested that they spend a little time with Killanin, he would have spent the evening in solitude. It was a vote of confidence Brundage had been unwilling to give Killanin. "In [Brundage's] eyes," wrote Allen Guttmann, "Killanin was an intellectual lightweight, a former journalist and filmmaker without the depth of character necessary for the office held by Coubertin, [Henri] Baillet-Latour, [Sigfrid] Edström, and [Avery] Brundage." Brundage told Willi Daume at the time of Killanin's ascendance, "We need a leader, and Michael isn't a leader."[61] Guttmann speculates, not without justification, that Brundage may not have considered anyone sufficiently qualified to follow him.

Killanin preferred to share a "jar" with journalists at the end of IOC Sessions;[62] he was, at heart, a friendly man who was not caught up in the trappings of the office. His exit from the IOC office was a quiet one, and though marred by the U.S.-led boycott of the Moscow Games, it stood in stark contrast to the charged atmosphere in Munich, where he assumed the presidency in the wake of the blackening of Olympic history by Palestinian terrorists.

Jean Drapeau and Preparations for the 1976 Olympics

Jean Drapeau's "vaulting ambition," wrote Jack Todd, a long-time *Montreal Gazette* sports columnist, made possible the 1976 Montreal Olympics.[63] For Drapeau, winning the right to host the 1976 Summer Olympics furthered his aim to transform Montreal into the Paris of North America on the heels of championing the construction of Montreal's subway system, hosting the World Expo '67, and welcoming a Major League Baseball team to the city in 1969. He latched on to the idea of bidding for the Games while touring Lausanne in 1963 and drew inspiration from the IOC's contemporary museum, a facility far less grandiose than the Olympic Museum opened in the early 1990s that rests on the shores of Lake Geneva today. Drapeau was a commanding, industrious presence who exuded personal modesty but possessed a grand vision for his city. He knew only how to dream big. The Olympics and the infrastructure resulting from hosting the games, thought Drapeau, could leverage the transfer of the United Nations to his city. In the pursuit of his dreams, he had little time for Montreal's other elected officials and pursued a "go-it-alone style of governance." Nick Auf der Maur, a city councillor, while attesting to Drapeau's reputation as a "master builder," stated disdainfully that he and his colleagues on Montreal City Council earned their Can$22,000 salaries by coming "down once every two or three months [to] approve two or three hundred resolutions the mayor had put together."[64]

Drapeau, after a failed attempt to secure the right to host the 1972 Olympics, eventually sold IOC members on the concept of a self-financing project, but it fell badly off the rails, in large measure due to his unceasing willingness to spend money. "Diminutive, autocratic, [and] mustachioed," Drapeau dismissed growing concerns about the financial plans and their execution: "The Olympics can no more run a deficit than a man can have a baby," he stated haughtily.[65] Initial estimates at the time of the award of the 1976 Olympics in 1970 pegged the cost at Can$120 million, a number that climbed to Can$300 within three years. In the end the final invoice read Can$1.6 billion, and Montreal was saddled with debt that required thirty years to close.

Parisian architect Roger Taillibert, Drapeau's controversial and expensive selection (many Canadians were aghast at his reported Can$50 million fee and Drapeau's refusal to hire a Canadian) as the individual responsible for designing Montreal's facilities, including the Olympic Stadium and the athletes' village, charged that corruption and lack of oversight compromised his efforts. "The construction of the Olympic Park and stadium showed me a level of organised corruption, theft, mediocrity, sabotage and indifference," stated Taillibert, "that I had never witnessed before and have never witnessed since. The system failed completely and every civil engineering firm involved knew they could just open this veritable cash register and serve themselves."[66] If Drapeau left him in charge, rather than have him operate at a distance from Paris, Taillibert maintained there would have been a different and better outcome. Known for his design of Paris's Parc des Princes, he delivered that budgeted $12 million stadium project at a cost of $18 million in 1972. Construction delays plagued progress in Montreal, and the Quebec Federation of Labour and the Confederation of National Trade Unions used strikes to extract maximum salaries for construction workers by shutting down construction sites for 155 days out of the 530 working days between December 1974 and April 1976. All of this did little for Lord Killanin (or his health), who pondered the need to shift the festival to an alternative site.

A three-year investigation of the entire debacle, headed by Quebec Superior Court Judge Albert Malouf, fingered Drapeau as the "principal culprit" behind the mess, even though he was not accused of personally profiting from the staging of the mega-event.[67] Malouf and his fellow commissioners concluded that Drapeau was "not only . . . entirely lacking in the aptitudes and knowledge required for this role but also, as a politician and first magistrate of the city, he should have avoided placing himself in this position."[68] Drapeau labeled the Malouf Inquiry and its final report an exercise in scapegoating. None of this dissuaded Montreal voters from reelecting him in 1978 and 1982 (he retired in 1986). Some twenty years after the Montreal Olympics, despite lingering criticism of the heaps of money he threw at his Olympic dream, no apologies were forthcoming: "You have to think about the future all the time," argued Drapeau, "and thinking about the future costs money."[69]

Montreal's Contract with ABC

Jean Drapeau pledged to respect the IOC's policy concerning the distribution of television money; however, this pledge was made in 1970, eight months before Willi Daume successfully squeezed the IOC for $6 million in technical services fees. He saw an opening and, with Montreal's costs spiraling upward, he exploited it. In May 1970 Lord Luke confirmed in correspondence with Drapeau and his fellow mayor in Denver, William McNichols, "complete cooperation" was required between the IOC and the OCOGs on television matters, including agreement on the documents sent to the television networks outlining bidding procedures.[70] During a visit to Montreal in early November 1972 Killanin caught wind that television negotiations for U.S. rights were in an advanced stage and the Montreal Organizing Committee (COJO) planned to follow Daume's path in deducting a technical services fee from the gross value of the contract. In detailing his discussions, Killanin wrote, "I personally believe that 'hardware' is as much part of the installations as Press Boxes or Running Tracks. This point will have to be fought hard by the Finance Committee."[71]

Later in the month, Paul Desrochers, president of COJO's Finance Commission, met with the IOC's Finance Commission in London. COJO, he said, was nearing a deal with ABC for $25 million. With an expected additional $25 million from the rest of the world, Desrochers, in dismissing the terms of the Rome Formula, reported that COJO would send $7 million of the $50 million to Lausanne.[72] Even though Killanin reminded Montreal officials earlier in the month that "gross television receipts" were subject to the Rome Formula,[73] Gerry Snyder, vice president of COJO's Finance Commission, disputed the notion, and Desrochers indicated as a special counselor to Quebec premier Robert Bourassa that the IOC's interpretation of its rules "was unacceptable" to the provincial government.[74] Rather than declaring Desrochers's plan offside, and fighting hard as had been Killanin's directive, Beaumont floated his own proposal.

Beaumont noted that the Rome Formula, if applied to the projected $50 million in television revenue, yielded $18 million for the IOC. He asked Desrochers and Snyder to meet the IOC halfway at $12.5 million. No decision was reached.[75] Killanin was startled by Beaumont's proposal, which had not been vetted by the

Executive Board and did not conform to the IOC's rules. He understood the IOC's fiduciary responsibility to the IFs and NOCs.[76] Killanin stewed for a few days and then contacted COJO's president, Roger Rousseau. Killanin reminded him of Drapeau's pledge at the time of the award of the 1976 Olympic Games to his city and cited Rule 21 of the *Olympic Charter*: "All payments for TV rights and financial contributions in connection with television belong to the IOC, who will dispose of certain portions to International Federations, National Olympic Committees and Organizing Committees." COJO's approach was "not justifiable."[77] Not only was he irritated by COJO's activities and Beaumont's counterproposal, he was unsettled by NBC's charge that COJO gave it no opportunity to bid for the U.S. rights.

Roone Arledge

Roone Arledge, head of ABC Sports, dismissed NBC's whining. He observed that ABC's $25 million U.S. rights payment troubled his own network's board of directors, as the gross value of the contract leapt from Munich's $13.5 million. It was a "ridiculously high," "exorbitant," and "unbelievable" payment, stated Arledge, an assessment designed for public consumption to protect ABC's position and comfort IOC and COJO officials that the deal reached was a good one for them. "When NBC found it had come in too late to negotiate, they tried to destroy our relationship with [COJO] by creating a smokescreen to the effect that competitive bidding was the rule." Nothing could be further from the truth, said Arledge. NBC's sport properties had not been secured by competitive bidding, he noted in taunting his rivals: "This was a case of the public relations stance you take when you're a disappointed suitor, and NBC often takes that stance."[78]

In the early 1970s Roone Arledge was well on his way to establishing himself as the undisputed king of U.S. sports television, a visionary whose leadership, drive, and creativity would later pull ABC's underperforming News Division to the upper echelons of the industry in the 1980s. Arledge received the first-ever lifetime achievement Emmy Award, the thirty-seventh of his illustrious career, mere months before his passing in 2002.

Born in Forest Hills, New York, on July 8, 1931, Roone Pinckney Arledge parlayed his journalism degree from Columbia College into work with the DuMont Network and NBC in the 1950s but caught his big break when ABC recruited him to produce its college football telecasts in 1960. He launched enduring American sport programming such as "Wide World of Sports" and "Monday Night Football" over the next decade while also carving out ABC's reputation as America's Olympic network through his role in the acquisition of U.S. rights to the Innsbruck, Grenoble, Mexico City, Sapporo, and Munich Olympics.

In 1994, as his career wound down, *Sports Illustrated* ranked Arledge third, behind only Muhammad Ali (whose career Arledge supported and advanced by pairing him with Howard Cosell for on-air interviews in the 1960s and 1970s) and Michael Jordan in terms of impact on the sporting world in the previous four decades. His operating style confounded and frustrated some of his colleagues in the sports industry, and perceptions of his arrogance rankled others. Jim Spence, a former ABC Sports senior vice president under Arledge, stated, "For as long as I've known him . . . [Arledge] listened only to the sound of his own voice." The late Frank Deford noted that Arledge "could be gregarious and charming, political, a man fond of the creature comforts who reigned, felicitously, at a time when expense accounts generously covered a multitude of desires, as befitted network royalty." He motored around Manhattan in a chauffeur-driven Jaguar. Yet, frequently, he was difficult to find, attended few staff meetings, often delivered messages to staff through others, and did not excel at returning phone calls. His shadowy presence at ABC Sports, observed Deford, earned him the nickname the "Wizard." ABC's wise-cracking college-football analyst, the late Beano Cook, deadpanned upon news of Arledge's acceptance of a second portfolio, the presidency of ABC News, that "now Roone'll have two offices where you can't find him." But Barry Frank, former president of CBS Sports and an executive with International Management Group, who himself became involved in Olympic television rights negotiations as a consultant in the 1980s, neatly summarized Arledge's game-changing work and legacy: "The bottom line on Roone is . . . without him we'd all be making $50,000 a year selling suits at Barneys."[79]

In the end, Arledge served as president of ABC Sports from 1968 through 1990, the latter thirteen years while also president of ABC News, and became America's Olympic storyteller through the production of ten Olympic broadcasts, including Montreal. His efforts, along with the on-camera performance of Jim McKay, amid the tension and horror in Munich resulting from the infiltration of the Olympic Village by Arab terrorists and the subsequent failed hostage rescue attempt, were revered within the industry. He had a knack for drawing viewers in to understand the stories and lives behind the performances they were watching, and in so doing he made instant celebrities of people such as Peggy Fleming, Olga Korbut, Mark Spitz, Franz Klammer, and Nadia Comaneci. It was a formula employed with much success in the American market by Dick Ebersol, former president of NBC Sports and one of Arledge's protégés, in more recent years.

COJO's Sleight of Hand

Roone Arledge was heavily invested in the Olympic Games. He viewed it as a pillar within ABC's sports programming mix. In his acquisition of the U.S. rights to the Montreal Olympics, Arledge's first priority was not the division of the money in terms of who got what but rather the bottom line figure of $25 million. The decision to siphon away $12.5 million for technical services had been COJO's.[80] In future discussions with Killanin and Berlioux, he understood their frustration with Montreal officials and advised the IOC to manage television rights negotiations in the future, given the OCOGs themselves did not possess the knowledge to do so.[81] He, too, found his dealings with COJO difficult: "I've dealt with some banana republics before, but never have I encountered a nest like the people up there."[82] The IOC's strained dialogue concerning the proposed terms of ABC's contract with Roger Rousseau and his Montreal colleagues continued.

The IOC's frustration was on full display at a series of meetings between COJO and members of the IOC's Finance Commission and Executive Board in early February 1973. At the Finance Commission session Roger Rousseau asked how much television money the IOC received from Munich. The answer: $5.5 million. Montreal was prepared to "give" the IOC $5,166,000 from the ABC contract. Marc Hodler took exception to Montreal's posture, as the money was not Montreal's to "give"—it was the IOC's to distribute according to the accepted distribution policy. Monique Berlioux added that the IFs stood in lockstep with the IOC. "[COJO] will have no Olympic Games without the athletes who belong to the IFs."[83] The Executive Board was miffed that Rousseau ignored the Rome Formula, and Killanin was irritated that the IOC learned of the ABC contract via press reports.

The IOC found itself in a difficult position. If the IOC and COJO failed to reach an agreement, Hodler noted, Rousseau "was prepared to tell the press that the IOC wanted too much money."[84] Killanin, the three IOC vice presidents, and the Finance Commission huddled with Rousseau and Snyder. Killanin indicated that the IOC would accept COJO's contract with ABC if it was the only contract including a technical services fee.[85] Even though Beaumont was keen to see a signed agreement as the IOC was sacrificing valuable interest income,[86] discussions continued in the weeks ahead given Rousseau held out for a 50 percent for technical services from all contracts.[87]

The turning point in this strained dialogue occurred on May 12, when an IOC lawyer, in Lord Killanin's absence but on his authority, signed an agreement with COJO setting out the protocol for the negotiation of future television contracts. Unfortunately for the IOC, the lawyer did not notice that an annex to the agreement, added by COJO, authorized Montreal officials to deduct 50 percent of the gross value of all future television contracts.[88] Killanin and the IOC were now on the back foot in any future discussions.

When the IOC Finance Commission convened in Varna in October, Beaumont, Hodler, Lord Luke, and Berlioux grilled Rousseau on television matters. Rousseau estimated hardware costs at $56 million. Beaumont reminded Rousseau that Drapeau pledged not to seek technical services fees, while Lord Luke stated the Rome Formula already favored the OCOGs. Rousseau replied that the IOC must accept the financial realities of what it took to establish the broadcast infrastructure. Beaumont excused Rousseau from the room, and the Finance Commission deliberated. While Beaumont thought the IOC should request $9 million from Rousseau and leave him to sign remaining deals in whatever fashion he might choose, Berlioux advised against any compromise offer, noting that Rousseau and his colleagues would interpret it as a sign of weakness. She said that the IOC should examine future contracts on a case-by-case basis and prolong the review period for contracts to compromise COJO's financial status. She reasoned that a more desperate Rousseau would be more inclined to accept the IOC's interpretation of the Rome Formula.[89] Her advice won out. Summoned back to the meeting, Rousseau received this news without reaction.

Within three months, the IOC Finance Commission's resolve weakened. It was prepared to concede to Rousseau's demands.[90] Killanin, too, grew weary of the lack of progress. Though Berlioux's strategy sought to starve COJO of needed funds, it did the same to the IOC, IFs, and NOCs. Part of the IOC's calculation involved the Canadian government's reluctance to assist Drapeau to realize his grand plans. Prime Minister Pierre Trudeau's minority Liberal government, with much of its standing in Parliament tied to the French-speaking province of Quebec, understood the political risk of a blank check. Prevailing French/English tensions in Canada precluded such a move, as many English-speaking Canadians in the country's other provinces already thought the federal government pandered to Quebec's interests. The government financially supported Vancouver's (unsuccessful) bid for the 1976 Olympic Winter Games but had not provided funds for Montreal's bid. In 1973, only after the province of Quebec accepted responsibility for any debt incurred, did the federal government establish funding streams in the form of a national lottery and coin-and-stamp programs.

To assist Montreal, Killanin and the Executive Board informed Rousseau that the 50:50 provision in all contracts was accepted but could not be included in the European Broadcasting Union (EBU) deal. EBU was a collective of government-funded television networks. Such an action set a difficult precedent, as EBU nations did not pay host broadcasters of sport events in other European countries any sum for broadcast installations. Rousseau replied that a gross value for EBU rights would be negotiated and simply split in half. Killanin consented to this plan but asked that it be kept secret. He wanted neither EBU nor Innsbruck officials aware of the IOC's concession.[91]

Innsbruck

In 1970 Innsbruck officials did not celebrate the award of the 1976 Olympic Winter Games to their city. They were not in attendance at the IOC's Session in Amsterdam. The IOC voted in favor of Denver, Colorado, only to have the western U.S. city reject the Games two years later. Left scrambling, the IOC settled on Innsbruck, the host city of the 1964 Olympic Winter Games as Denver's replacement. In March 1973 Killanin delegated oversight responsibilities to Hodler and Berlioux to head off any problems with the Austrians as had been foisted upon the IOC by Daume and Rousseau.[92] In June, Innsbruck's secretary general Karl Heinz Klee reported on initial talks with ABC, CBS, and NBC, and his hope for $10 million to $15 million in global television rights.[93] At this time Innsbruck's Mayor, Alois Lugger, agreed to the IOC's interpretation of the Rome Formula, but over the next few months, amid the negotiation of a $10 million contract with ABC, Innsbruck's position shifted. The contract assigned $2.2 million to technical services for "special facilities" requested by ABC. While bothered by this development, it was but a pinprick compared to the discomfort IOC officials suffered in their dealings with COJO. Klee agreed that the ABC contract was the only contract subject to a deduction for broadcast infrastructure, so he shifted the rights fee to $8 million and reduced the technical services payment to $2 million.[94] Going forward, Klee and his colleagues kept their word.

More Machinations in Montreal

Lord Luke summarized the prevailing view in Lausanne in the wake of the Executive Board's agreement with Rousseau on the ABC and other television contracts. "Munich O.C. were bad enough in their time," offered Luke, "but Montreal O.C. are far worse and have deliberately shaped the whole operation in their favour."[95] The IOC's hopes for no further aggravations in its dealings with COJO on television matters were soon dashed. Rousseau parceled off Canadian television rights to the Canadian Broadcasting Corporation (CBC) for $1. COJO argued that the Canadian government was providing $25 million toward the broadcast facility costs, and as a taxpayer-funded entity, the CBC should not be asked to shoulder any additional financial burden.

Of course, this initiative precluded the receipt of any money by the IOC, IFs, and NOCs from the host market and generated howls of protest from IOC officials. Lord Luke commented that "COJO's attitude in this affair was not in the spirit of a partnership."[96] Marc Hodler stated that the acceptance of such a contract threatened the possible returns from the European market.[97] The Executive Board refused to accept the CBC contract. Even though Montreal officials claimed the $1 figure appeared in the contract left for review and IOC approval in Lausanne in February 1974, Berlioux brought the contract to the Executive Board meeting in October and observed that the dollar figure had been left blank. The $1 scheme was shared with the IOC in September.

Answering outrage with outrage, the Executive Board (on the recommendation of the Finance Commission) told Rousseau that the Canadian television rights were valued at $12 million, such that the IOC should receive $2 million. There was no basis for this estimate. The IOC's own television adviser, Walter Schätz, previously informed IOC officials that the Canadian television rights possessed a maximum projected value of $1.82 million. Canadian IOC member Jim Worrall, who also served on COJO, acted as mediator in discussions the following day. Rousseau refused to proceed with COJO's report to the Executive Board until the Canadian television situation was resolved. The two sides settled their argument. COJO agreed to pay the IOC $300,000, a sum in line with the IOC's receipts if the Canadian rights had yielded $1.8 million. If global television revenue exceeded $37 million, the IOC was owed an additional $100,000.[98]

COJO battled with EBU for 2½ years before reaching an agreement for the European territory. The Europeans deeply resented COJO's efforts to circumvent protocol by attempting to sell television rights to individual EBU-member networks.[99] The prospect of a television blackout in Europe loomed. The IOC's priority remained global coverage of the Games, and this reality brought Killanin and Drapeau to a face-to-face private meeting in London on September 7. For the IOC president, a European television blackout was anathema. Drapeau yielded ground. Two days later, Killanin shared the results of his separate discussions with

Lord Killanin and Monique Berlioux are shown during a meeting of the IOC Executive Board in Lausanne in February 1974. (© 1974 / International Olympic Committee (IOC) / Jean-Paul Maeder. Photo courtesy of the IOC.)

Drapeau and EBU officials: the broadcast unions in Western and Eastern Europe, Asia, South America, the Arab States, and Africa agreed to pay $9.5 million for rights and technical services, with EBU's total contribution resting at $4.55 million.[100] COJO's board of directors approved the results of Killanin's intervention that took place at the eleventh hour.[101] All parties drew a deep breath.

Closing Thoughts

It is left for us to wonder how much shifting in his seat Willi Daume did in his role as a member of the Finance Commission and Executive Board during the throes of the IOC's conflict with COJO concerning television contracts and the distribution of broadcast revenue. After all, it was his initiative, as head of the Munich OCOG, in signing a U.S. television deal with ABC that included a deduction from the gross value of the contract for technical services that translated into a blueprint Montreal and Innsbruck organizers followed. Though Innsbruck limited this deduction to the U.S. contract, as had Daume, Canadian officials were aggressive and obstinate in their dealings with Killanin and other members of the IOC's leadership. They resolutely pursued 50 percent of each television contract for technical services, thereby acquiring 50 percent of each deal plus two-thirds of the remaining 50 percent. In doing so, they proved not averse to a little skulduggery in their preparation of documents for IOC signature guaranteeing that eventuality. Daume's enterprise and inventiveness with respect to Munich's U.S. television contract set off a cascade of events over the ensuing eight years that greatly propelled the IOC's transformation to a corporate entity.

Killanin's mounting displeasure regarding the IOC's interaction with OCOG officials on commercial revenue, particularly COJO executives, pushed him to seek means of elevating the IOC's knowledge base concerning the television industry. In March 1973 he shared with Monique Berlioux that the IOC might be well advised to manage television negotiations in the future.[102] Other key players were like-minded. Reginald Alexander pressed the IOC to access the "best possible international advice" on television contracts and establish a committee to manage the IOC's affairs pertaining to television. Beaumont and Luke advised that "specialist knowledge" would prove valuable.[103] Roone Arledge, now a fixture on the Olympic scene, advised the IOC that it was best placed to manage direct negotiations with television companies in the years ahead to lend continuity to the process.[104]

The IOC Executive Board addressed these needs by dividing its Information and Culture Commission into a number of subcommittees, including, Publications, Culture, Press, and Television.[105] The Television Subcommittee boasted a diverse membership, replete with Berlioux (whose profile was steadily expanding in the early 1970s as chair), representatives of the television industry and the

IFs, as well as IOC legal advisers.[106] Killanin understood the need for such a body given the IOC's reliance on television revenue for over 98 percent of its budgetary needs. It was tasked with expanding the IOC's understanding of television matters, including negotiating practices, generating a host-city questionnaire on television issues, and through the "television expert," Schätz, maintaining involvement in the negotiations process and working to improve IOC/OCOG relations. Schätz's mandate did not involve constantly driving the value of television contracts to the maximum available for fear of killing "the hen that lays the golden eggs."[107]

The genesis of the Television Subcommittee foreshadowed much greater involvement of the IOC in television negotiations in the future and marked a clear break with Brundage's philosophy concerning commercial revenue. Killanin viewed this initiative as a means of protecting the IOC's financial interests, dealing with the new realities of the television medium, and fulfilling its role as partner of the NOCs and IFs, which also relied on Olympic television revenue to fund their operations. However, it took yet another round of frustration with the 1980 Organizing Committees in Lake Placid and Moscow to push Killanin to declare a need for the IOC to be represented formally at all meetings with television network executives and OCOG officials. In 1977 the IOC approved "joint negotiation" of all television contracts with the OCOGs, commencing with the 1984 host cities of Sarajevo and Los Angeles.[108] Much as had been the case with the IOC's efforts to implement the Rome Formula, there was little that was smooth about this transition either.

CHAPTER 5

Los Angeles, 1984

Peter Ueberroth's Vision ·

In 1948 Avery Brundage, czar of American Olympic matters, proclaimed, "Business is business and sport is sport. It is impossible to mix them."[1] This theme was echoed repeatedly throughout his two-decade IOC presidency. Flying in the face of Brundage's observation was the commercial legacy of the 1984 Olympic Games, one conferred on the Olympic Movement by Peter Ueberroth, president of the Los Angeles Olympic Organizing Committee (LAOOC). In his aggressive pursuit of a business model to underwrite the cost of putting on the great festival, Ueberroth, a West Coast entrepreneur and surprise choice to lead Los Angeles' Olympic project, "punctured" the Brundage dictum uttered regularly by the IOC's former president.[2] Harnessing the private sector to fund the city's Olympic project, together with a clear focus on a plan to maximize the use of preexisting sport facilities as a means of limiting capital costs, Ueberroth produced a staggering profit of some $232.5 million.

Ueberroth's success stimulated renewed interest in the civic chambers of metropolitan centers around the world to pursue the right to host the Olympics, interest stifled by the infusion of geopolitics into the Olympic Movement and the burgeoning costs of staging festivals in the 1960s and 1970s. For Ueberroth's critics the Los Angeles Olympics marked a watershed in the commercialization of the Olympic Games and accelerated their descent into the abyss of commodification. The lumbering history of the amateur ideal, highlighted by controversies involving Jim

Thorpe, Babe Didrikson, Paavo Nurmi, Jesse Owens, Barbara Ann Scott, the Puma/
Adidas shoe wars, and Karl Schranz, supported a long-held claim by some that the
Olympics had been all about money. Despite this, the Los Angeles Games proved a
valuable and timely tonic for the Olympic Movement, saddled as it was by Denver's
withdrawal as host of the 1976 Olympic Winter Games due to environmental and
financial concerns, the Munich massacre, Montreal's massive fiscal missteps and
the boycott there by some twenty African nations, and the U.S.-led boycott of the
1980 Moscow Olympics. Allen Guttmann observed that "the organizers were able
to crow about the glories of capitalism, and the critics of the games were free to
sermonize about the horrors of capitalism."[3]

Ueberroth's modus operandi reflected both his personal beliefs and the environment in which he operated. In his autobiography, published a year after the
Games, he noted, "I believed then—as I do now—that there are many important
programs much more deserving of government support than a sports event, even
one as special as the Olympic Games."[4] Ueberroth sought to limit taxpayer money,
which had not been the case in Montreal amid the grandiosity fostered by the city's
mayor, Jean Drapeau. Ueberroth's vision, shared by the United States Olympic
Committee's (USOC) president William E. Simon, also meshed with the thoughts
of a majority of Angelenos who refused to countenance the use of public dollars
on the enterprise. They forbade such expense by means of a referendum enacted
shortly after Los Angeles was named host city in late 1978. Though Ueberroth, to
some extent, patterned his approach after those who delivered the 1948 London
Olympics in the wake of World War II when a need for austerity prevailed, he also
tailored his thinking to the contemporary milieu marked by an intensification of
the connections between sport and commerce. He targeted television networks
around the globe as entities required to expend greater numbers of dollars for the
platform and publicity that Olympic coverage provided them, and he leveraged the
Olympic brand and American patriotism to squeeze U.S. corporations for substantial sums of money for sponsorship rights.

When Ueberroth assumed the mantle of LAOOC's leadership in March 1979,
the International Olympic Committee (IOC) had already been forced to abandon
past practice by ceding responsibility for the organization of the Games to a private,
nonprofit corporation—the LAOOC (indemnified by the USOC)—as opposed to
the city of Los Angeles. The IOC had no option. Though Tehran debated the merits
of a bid, the IOC was bereft of serious interest from any other city in hosting the
1984 Summer Olympics. Aside from the financial risks, Los Angeles, for some
cities, looked unbeatable, given it was putting forth a bid for the 1984 Summer
Olympics following bids for 1976 and 1980. Would the IOC say no to Los Angeles
three times? Given the USOC's assumption of the financial risk with the LAOOC,
William Simon and his colleagues hammered out terms favorable to them in the

event that the Games made money—namely, 40 percent of any profit. The remaining 60 percent would be shared by U.S. national sport federations (20 percent) and the LAOOC (40 percent) for the advancement of youth sport in Southern California. It was into this cauldron of problems that Peter Ueberroth stepped. Deftly, he translated his financial plan and vision into reality despite the intrusion of world geopolitics in the form of the Soviet-led boycott.

Los Angeles' Olympic Past

"Los Angeles is, from its own vantage," wrote Mark Dyreson and Matthew Llewellyn, "*the* Olympic city. No city has bid more frequently or more furiously for the Olympics. No city has made the Olympics as central to its core identity."[5] William May Garland, a Los Angeles–area real estate developer and IOC member (1922–1948), championed Los Angeles' successful bid for the 1932 Summer Olympics, though the city's earliest pursuit of the Games dated back to 1915. Garland was an energetic, industrious, and determined booster of Los Angeles. He took six junkets to Europe between 1919 and 1923 as means of fostering support for the city's aspirations. The Olympic venture wedded nicely with the urban boom in Los Angeles in the early 1900s, and the bid benefited from the impending opening of the Los Angeles Memorial Coliseum mere weeks following the IOC's 1923 Rome Session, where Pierre de Coubertin delivered Garland the good news.

Subsequent bids by Los Angeles submitted to the IOC for the 1948, 1952, 1956, 1976, and 1980 Olympics failed before the city was awarded the 1984 Olympics. As the calendar rolls on through 2020, Angelenos know their community is tabbed as an Olympic host city for the third time (2028), a status otherwise held only by London (1908, 1948, and 2012).[6] In a unique deal brokered by IOC president Thomas Bach and approved by the Executive Board and General Session, Paris, too, will soon be a three-time host city (2024). Bach injected a measure of stability into the site-selection environment in light of an increasing number of cities withdrawing from the host-city bidding process or not engaging at all due to concerns about costs. Instead of a winner and a loser from the two finalists in the contest to host the 2024 Olympics, he crafted a path for two winners.

Ueberroth Takes Charge of L.A.'s Olympic Project

In the face of the Los Angeles referendum refusing to sustain public debt in order to finance the Games awarded to the city by the IOC, together with the IOC's reluctant but necessary agreement for a private group (the LAOOC) to finance and organize the 1984 Olympic festival, it was obviously necessary to identify a leader of the enterprise. An entrepreneur and successful executive within the travel industry,

Ueberroth drew the attention of Korn Ferry International, the executive search firm tasked by the LAOOC to generate a collection of candidates. As a California resident, one versed in the ways of global commerce and who also possessed a sport background (as a water polo player at San Jose State University who unsuccessfully tried out for the 1956 U.S. Olympic team), Ueberroth's qualifications seemed apparent. Ultimately, the search committee established a pool of candidates, including the likes of high-profile individuals such as Chrysler's chairman Lee Iacocca; National Football League chairman Pete Rozelle; Alexander Haig, a former White House chief of staff, and at the time, NATO's supreme commander; and, prominent sportscaster Curt Gowdy. Ueberroth remained unconvinced about whether he was a good fit for the position. "I thought they needed a household name, like Pete Rozelle or Alexander Haig, to put the public's mind at ease," Ueberroth observed.[7] However, his wife counseled him that there was nothing to lose from engaging in the process. In the face of persistent lobbying from search committee officials and his emergence as one of six on the short list, his competitive juices kicked in.

Ueberroth's early professional experience related to the airline industry in Oakland and Honolulu produced in a relatively short time an invitation from financier Kirk Kerkorian to run the Honolulu office of Los Angeles Air Service (Los Angeles Air Service soon became Trans International Airlines). In less than a year in Hawaii, Kerkorian promoted Ueberroth, only twenty-two years old, to vice president and a 3 percent shareholder in the company, and, further, he transferred Ueberroth to Los Angeles. This course of events proved critical relative to future Olympic matters in the City of Angels. An energetic and restless Ueberroth soon set his sights on "moving on." Together with partner Dick Sargent, a pal from college days, Ueberroth formed Travel Consultants Inc., which, within a decade, boasted fifteen hundred employees and $300 million in yearly revenue, second in size only to American Express as a travel organization. This, then, was the state of Ueberroth's professional life at the time representatives of Korn Ferry approached him concerning the Los Angeles Olympics.[8]

Entertainment mogul David Wolper, a member of the LAOOC search committee, ultimately supported Ueberroth's candidacy despite their less-than-pleasant first meeting six years earlier. In 1973 Wolper and a group of associates were seeking franchise owners for a new sport venture—a professional volleyball league. During a meeting at Wolper's home, Ueberroth listened to their business plan, then proceeded to dissect its shortcomings and predicted the league's downfall as a result of lavish and unwise spending. Lending support for Ueberroth's appointment were industrialist Justin Dart and the USOC's William Simon. Wolper, too, thought he could do the job: "[Ueberroth's] the guy who tried to tell us how to run our damn volleyball league. And he was right. We went broke. That's the guy we need. If anyone can run a Spartan Olympics, the cheap sonofabitch can."[9] Ultimately, following an extensive vetting process of all candidates, Ueberroth received the support of the twenty-plus members of the LAOOC board by one vote over department-store magnate Ed Steidle, chairman of the May Company. A study completed by Arthur Young and Company and Peat, Marwick, and Mitchell on revenue streams established by Munich, Montreal, and Moscow set out the scale of Ueberroth's task in stark terms. The bean counters concluded that, in the absence of government funding available to each of those Organizing Committees (OCOGs), Los Angeles needed to elevate nonpublic revenue sources (primarily television rights, sponsorship agreements, and ticket sales) sixfold to fulfill its mission.

Ueberroth's Three Pillars

TELEVISION MONEY

Ueberroth's overall financial plan, one adopted through necessity and personal inclination, departed from those his predecessors had pursued, but he differed little from them in terms of seeking an optimum figure in negotiations for a U.S. television contract. The result of those negotiations served as a bellwether for OCOGs in their fundraising efforts and established a bar for them to pursue increased yields in other global broadcast markets.

In his management of negotiations in the U.S. market, two things stand out. First, prior to Ueberroth's appointment the LAOOC sought exclusive authority over television rights negotiations, contrary to the IOC's intent to transition to "joint negotiation" with the OCOGs of all television contracts, beginning with the 1984 Olympic Winter Games and Summer Olympics.[10] Lessons learned from their dealings with Willi Daume, Jean Drapeau, and Roger Rousseau, and the Lake Placid and Moscow OCOGs motivated Lord Killanin and his IOC colleagues to establish this approach as a means of protecting the financial interests of the IOC, International Sport Federations (IFs) and National Olympic Committees (NOCs). With this intent, the IOC resisted the LAOOC's overtures, but within three months of his arrival Ueberroth obtained an agreement that made the LAOOC the senior partner in negotiations with television executives.[11] The sums from television rights were too critical to LAOOC's bottom line for Ueberroth to consent to the constraints of "joint negotiation." With respect to the IOC's goal to assert itself more dramatically in television negotiations, time stood still in its dealings with Ueberroth. Second, in search of operating capital, Ueberroth and LAOOC's board of directors devised a means of securing funds from the negotiations protocol. U.S. television executives soon learned that in order to enter the bidding, a refundable $500,000 deposit was required. All interest from the deposits accrued to the LAOOC. Once a date for the launch of negotiations was determined, a supplemental deposit of

$250,000 was required. The scheme delivered $1,000 a day in interest to LAOOC for its operations.[12]

When word of these events reached Lausanne, Monique Berlioux queried Ueberroth immediately. Such an arrangement required the IOC's approval, she noted, and marked a violation of the *Olympic Charter*. Contracts, Berlioux informed Ueberroth, were not to be finalized without IOC consent (Rule 49) and one was not permitted to publicize an Olympic festival before the Games preceding it had concluded (Rule 60).[13] Killanin made the same assertion concerning Rule 49 to Paul Ziffren, the chairman of LAOOC's board of directors,[14] but Ziffren downplayed Killanin's concerns and indicated that no actual contract negotiations took place.[15] Killanin dismissed Ziffren's explanation. In noting that five entities—ABC, CBS, NBC, ESPN, and Tandem Productions—each delivered $500,000 to the LAOOC, he intoned that the initiative was "quite unacceptable to the International Olympic Committee."[16] Ueberroth's explanation to Berlioux that any talks thus far with the interested parties were merely "fact finding sessions" drew a similar rebuke.[17]

Monique Berlioux, in executing her role as the IOC's liaison with OCOGs on television matters, visited Los Angeles in early June 1979. Wolper, who headed LAOOC's negotiations, explained to her the efforts to secure operating capital. She was unmoved. Berlioux countered that the IOC deserved a one-third share of any money accruing to LAOOC. Nothing materialized. At the same time, Wolper forewarned her that LAOOC would be pushing European executives to contribute more and that it "would not accept to give away the television rights to Europe at the ridiculous level they were actually."[18] On the heels of Montreal's showdown with EBU, as well as the brinksmanship on the part of Montreal officials and EBU executives that risked a blackout in Europe, this could hardly have brought a smile to her face. In that instance, Killanin's eleventh-hour intervention had been required to avert disaster. Wolper pledged to give the IOC a one-month notice before commencing formal U.S. television negotiations, but LAOOC's financial needs dictated that he move forward sooner rather than later. There was no mistaking LAOOC's senior-partner status in television negotiations.

Los Angeles Times writers Kenneth Reich and Lee Margulies understood the need for Ueberroth and the LAOOC to sign a lucrative U.S. contract. They believed that a $150 million deal might be possible, one that included both television rights and the contribution required for the winning network to establish the broadcast infrastructure necessary to fulfill its role as host broadcaster. The talks between the LAOOC and bidding networks due to unfold in September were critical to LAOOC's aspirations. "The stakes of the talks are immense," wrote Reich and Margulies. "For Los Angeles organizers, the U.S. television contract will be the largest single agreement they sign and, depending on the terms, could go a long way toward establishing the financial viability of the 1984 games."[19]

Meanwhile, Ueberroth and Wolper told skittish members of LAOOC's television advisory committee, who viewed a $150 million projection as unrealistic, that the floor price in negotiations in a package deal for rights and host-broadcaster contribution would be $200 million. Wolper's Bel Air home was the venue for negotiations that yielded ABC's eye-popping $225 million bid, with $100 million reserved as the rights portion of the deal. However, Ueberroth tempered his enthusiasm until the IOC signed off. He left nothing to chance in advance of Monique Berlioux's second trip to Los Angeles to consider the agreement.

Ueberroth delegated responsibility for Berlioux's stay and itinerary to Joel Rubenstein, LAOOC's vice president, who he knew could provide the attention needed to encourage Berlioux's approval on behalf of the IOC. Despite Ueberroth's thought that the $33.5 million due to the IOC from the ABC deal would satisfy Berlioux and other Lausanne officials given the IOC's less-than-robust financial situation, Rubenstein rolled out the red carpet for their visitor: "The checklist for her impending visit was encyclopedic. We had to make sure the swimming pool was available, that Evian water was supplied, that there were exquisite flower arrangements, that the room met her French tastes, that restaurant arrangements were made at the finest eateries, that appointments were not scheduled either early in the morning or late at night, and that her travelling staff received equally impeccable treatment."[20] The $33.5 million more than satisfied Berlioux and the IOC. LAOOC announced the deal at a news conference in late September, and the IOC Executive Board gave its formal support a month later in Nagoya, Japan, where Killanin concluded that the terms of the agreement "were most satisfactory."[21]

Ueberroth's commitment to driving up the yield from European television came into full view when officials from the LAOOC, the IOC (including Berlioux), and EBU executives (including the organization's future, long-time president, Albert Scharf) convened at New York's Park Lane Hotel in May 1981. In the wake of the ABC contract, television negotiations in the global marketplace were deferred as a result of the disruption caused by the U.S.-led boycott of the Moscow Olympics. The gulf between EBU and the LAOOC was wide. Ueberroth observed that EBU's region, Western Europe, boasted one hundred million television sets; with $1 per set as a reasonable means of opening discussions, $100 million would satisfy the LAOOC.[22] Scharf's jaw dropped. He knew full well that EBU paid $4.55 million and $5.65 million, respectively, for rights and technical services for the Montreal and Moscow Olympics.[23]

Scharf said that Ueberroth's figure—given that EBU relied on government contributions and lacked the ability to generate revenue through advertising, as was the case with the big three U.S. networks—was "out of consideration."[24] Ueberroth, seeking not to offend anyone with his position, indicated that "as long as both parties were well meaning, there was nothing wrong with disagreeing." In his opinion, the "Olympic Movement had been undervalued." Scharf countered with an approximate 40 percent increase on EBU's Moscow contract, for a total of $8.33 million. Soccer's World Cup television rights, observed Scharf, totaled a mere $16.5 million, with EBU's contribution representing $5.27 million.[25] Berlioux, playing the role of good partner, questioned whether Scharf's counterproposal was realistic, further asserting that the value of television rights was "never where they should be regarding the Olympic Games."[26]

Nervous EBU officials caucused outside the conference room. On returning, Ueberroth underwhelmed them with his idea to subtract two times EBU's $8 million offer from his proposed $100 million, leaving for consideration $84 million. "The year of the Games," offered Ueberroth. Scharf, perceiving that Berlioux was more sympathetic to EBU's cause than Ueberroth, asked her whether she understood the full ramifications of such a position and the manner in which it imperiled future negotiations. Berlioux nodded affirmatively. Though Scharf retorted that he would take the $84 million figure to the EBU's Administrative Council, he and his team knew it was dead on arrival. Ueberroth relayed the following to LAOOC's board of directors: "We found this group (EBU) to be very well informed, very sincere, and very professional. Financially, we are far apart."[27] Ueberroth, Scharf, and Berlioux agreed that the discussions would remain confidential.[28]

Within a month EBU's secretary general Regis de Kalbermatten expressed his displeasure at a report in the *Stuttgarter Zeitung* that outlined the LAOOC's strategy to elevate the value of television contracts in Europe and Japan. While the figures mentioned did not match those discussed in New York, the report revealed EBU might consider $65 million. Ueberroth offered that compromise was possible[29] and dismissed Kalbermatten's insinuation that he had violated their agreement. Although the quotes attributed to him were accurate, Ueberroth assured him that he mentioned no prospective contract terms. Ueberroth doubted that $65 million was a figure that EBU would seriously consider: "So, in conclusion," he informed Kalbermatten, "let's continue to work in good faith and see if we can bring the parties together."[30]

At this time, emerging Italian media baron Silvio Berlusconi inserted himself into the Olympic narrative. Berlusconi's politics, life, and scandalous behavior became fodder for tabloids in the years ahead, but at this time he was committed to challenging the grip on Italian broadcast media exerted by RAI, Radiotelevisione Italiana, the nation's government-supported station and a member-network of EBU. Berlusconi's Canale 5, a private network, bid $10 million for the Italian rights alone, a figure exceeding by almost $1.7 million EBU's offer on behalf of thirty-three nations.[31]

The IOC's new president, Juan Antonio Samaranch, was reluctant to deal with Canale 5 because it could not ensure coverage for all Italians.[32] As another round of scheduled talks with EBU officials loomed, Ueberroth pressed LAOOC's case: "A panel of some of the most important television executives in our country which comprise our television advisory commission are insisting [we proceed with negotiations with Canale 5] and we agree with their opinion." Ueberroth also urged Samaranch to consider the financial benefits for the IOC, IFs, NOCs, and future OCOGs.[33] However, as Samaranch prized complete coverage in Europe provided by EBU more than the additional revenue possible through a set of fledgling private networks stitched together whose collective broadcast reach left some Europeans without access to Olympic telecasts,[34] he denied Ueberroth the opportunity to conclude a deal with Berlusconi. Even though the LAOOC managed negotiations, Samaranch and the IOC still reserved the right to sign off on all agreements.

Ueberroth adopted a hard line with respect to the structure of the EBU contract. EBU countered LAOOC's demand for $30 million with a $12 million offer. During the course of discussions, EBU moved to $19.8 million, but Ueberroth placed a $7.8 million technical services component in the contract. Berlioux protested. She reminded Ueberroth that the IOC accepted the significant deduction for technical services from the ABC contract with the understanding it was the only such deduction included in the total of deals negotiated. Such a deduction limited the IOC/IF/NOC share of the contract to $4 million.[35] Ueberroth dug his heels in: the IOC was protecting the EBU and limiting the LAOOC's ability to maximize revenue from Europe, and the LAOOC's bills needed to be paid. "If the IOC wants more it must get it directly from the EBU," he wrote Samaranch at the close of negotiations.[36] Samaranch's maneuvering room was limited. Ueberroth said this was likely EBU's best offer.[37] Knowing that the NOCs and IFs consented to receiving their shares in 1984, Samaranch achieved one meaningful concession from Ueberroth: the IOC would receive its $4 million "up front" at the time of the LAOOC's receipt of EBU's first $12 million installment in February 1982. Samaranch convinced the Executive Board to approve the EBU contract in light of the possible $1.1 million that could be reaped through investing the $4 million over the intervening months.[38]

With the EBU contract settled, Ueberroth and his team tackled Japan, the third targeted market that was projected to drive the television revenue stream. Originally set to commence in January 1980, negotiations were deferred at the request of Japanese executives because of the uncertainty of the country's participation in the Moscow Olympics; later the same year, talks were further postponed due to a national election spurred by a nonconfidence vote in Japan's parliament.[39] Months passed.

Fruitless negotiations dragged throughout 1982,[40] in part because Japanese television executives, acting on behalf of a pool of networks, found Ueberroth's demands simply unrealistic.[41] Katsuji Shibata, president of the Japanese Olympic Committee, in an appeal to Samaranch, conveyed the state of alarm in the Japanese television industry.[42] Samaranch and Berlioux's subsequent "back-room" discussions with Japanese officials revealed the possibility of an agreement in the vicinity of $18 million.[43] By December the sides were getting closer to returning to the table, but preconditions existed. The Japanese needed to affirm that $16 million was the lowest figure for opening negotiations, while Los Angeles had to accept that its maximum at this stage of discussions was $21 million. Ueberroth sought contracted terms somewhere between the two figures.[44]

In late January 1983 the LAOOC and the Japanese networks found common ground. Oddly, Berlioux and her IOC team left the talks in Los Angeles thinking no deal had been reached.[45] The final terms perturbed her: the $19 million contract set aside $2.5 million for technical services and $5 million of the $16.5 million rights portion of the deal for the IOC.[46]

When Berlioux departed, she advised LAOOC officials that the IOC would reduce its share from $5.5 million to $5 million, but only if the LAOOC reduced its expectations as well. In short, by not altering the global sum of $19 million, the LAOOC simply pulled $500,000 from the IOC/IFs/NOC share of the contract for its own coffers in consummating the agreement. Danny Russell, a member of Berlioux's support staff, was still at the Biltmore Hotel but had not been called back to the renewed discussions with Japanese negotiators after Berlioux had left. Berlioux expressed her disappointment to Ueberroth. "Based on the relationship we have established, I fail to understand how these events could have been allowed to occur and I would appreciate hearing from you with an explanation as to the handling of this matter by the LAOOC," she wrote.[47] Ueberroth, who did not attend the negotiations, turned aside Berlioux's concerns. He attributed the flow of events to the erratic behavior of the Japanese, who repeatedly left the table calling for an end to discussions—only to reach out within hours for further talks. While "not pleased" with the value of the contract, even though it marked a vast increase on the $4.5 million price tag for Japanese rights to the Moscow Olympics, Ueberroth did not question the best efforts of LAOOC personnel to secure a contract.[48] Again, LAOOC's senior-partner status in television rights negotiations, as well as Ueberroth's hard-nosed and sometimes bruising tactics in meeting Los Angeles' financial goals, were evident.

In the end, Los Angeles' television contracts totaled in excess of $286 million, a near-threefold increase on the television money accrued by Moscow's organizers. Their efforts yielded 37 percent of LAOOC's generated revenue. Critical gains in the United States, Western European, and Japanese markets were the result of tough bargaining, sometimes prompting frayed relations between IOC and LAOOC officials. Rupert Murdoch's aggressive, eye-catching $10.6 million bid for Australian television rights through his property, Channel 10, was a pleasant surprise. Rival Channel 7 acquired the Moscow rights in Australia for $1.36 million. Still, in the final analysis Roone Arledge and ABC's continuing belief in the value of the Olympics as a sports property and a centerpiece of the network's sport programming mix served as the principal revenue driver and greatly assisted Ueberroth's enterprise.

CORPORATE SPONSORSHIP

"The 1984 [Los Angeles] Games were a watershed where the LAOOC simultaneously rewrote the economic framework for staging an Olympics and sparked an era where North American capital would come to dominate the macro-economics of the Olympics,"[49] Josh Lieser observed. No truer words have ever been written about the influence of Ueberroth's financial planning on the narrative of Olympic hosting and the IOC's own approach to mining the global corporate communities for revenue. While Ueberroth executed Los Angeles' financial blueprint, Samaranch committed himself to fashioning a worldwide corporate sponsorship program, with money shared by the IOC, NOCs, and OCOGs, known as The Olympic Programme (TOP). American multinationals have consistently fueled the program, first launched in 1985 in connection with the 1988 Calgary Olympic Winter Games and Seoul Summer Olympics. As time passed, however, a greater diversification in the sites of the participant companies' corporate home headquarters can be noted.

With respect to revenue generation, Ueberroth dispatched Joel Rubenstein to Lake Placid to investigate the approach to corporate sponsorship that organizers of the 1980 Olympic Winter Games had adopted. His report was discouraging. While Lake Placid secured more than three hundred corporate sponsors, their efforts translated into less than $10 million (in cash). Rubenstein believed the "clutter and duplication"[50] within the cohort of sponsors suppressed possible revenue. He advocated limiting each sponsor category to one company, thereby enhancing its overall value. Ueberroth accepted the advice and set out a $4 million floor price for any corporate sponsor, but he kept his own counsel on the matter, with the exception of a few LAOOC officials. Sensing the opportunity to lock up the soft-drink category and seize headlines by playing off Coca-Cola against Pepsi, Ueberroth pursued discussions with their respective chairmen, Don Keough and Don Kendall. Coca-Cola's $12.6 million deal served as a springboard for Ueberroth, Rubenstein, and their colleagues, who raised $126.7 million from a three-tiered corporate sponsorship and licensing scheme (with thirty-four sponsors, sixty-four suppliers, and sixty-five licensees).

While Coca-Cola saw its long-time affiliation with the Olympics, dating back to 1928, as valuable and meriting protection from its rivals, not all paladins of U.S. consumerism understood Ueberroth's determination to maximize LAOOC's haul from the corporate sector. U.S.-based (Rochester, New York) Eastman Kodak, which claimed a link to the original Olympic Games in Athens, thinking its place

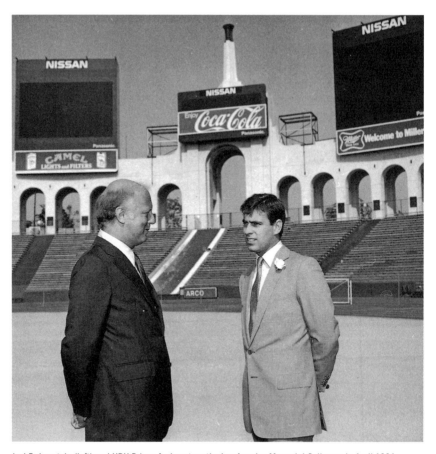

Joel Rubenstein (left) and HRH Prince Andrew tour the Los Angeles Memorial Coliseum in April 1984. Rubenstein's analysis of Lake Placid's sponsorship program prompted Peter Ueberroth to seek a different model based on exclusivity for product sponsors which ultimately triggered handsome financial dividends and established a template for future Organizing Committees. Naturally, organizers removed all sponsor advertising (visible in this picture) from the venue before the Olympics in accordance with the IOC's clean-venue policy. (Photo courtesy of LA84 Foundation.)

secure as a sponsor, delayed signing an agreement as a means of saving interest. It maintained a lowball strategy in not meeting Ueberroth's floor price, content to wait him out. Ueberroth declined to play Kodak's game. He pivoted and signed a $7 million deal with Fuji Film through the auspices of Dentsu, a Japanese advertising company. Kodak executives raged, and heads rolled at their corporate headquarters. Though Kodak returned to the Olympic fold as one of the inaugural sponsors of the TOP program, it permitted Fuji an opportunity to establish a foothold in the U.S. advertising market, a decision that had long-term ramifications for Kodak's corporate health.

REFURBISHED FACILITIES

Restraining capital costs was central in the planning process vital to LAOOC's bottom line. A review of Olympic construction spending, adjusted to 1984 U.S. dollars, demonstrates Ueberroth's commitment to construction-cost containment. Wayne Wilson highlighted that construction in Los Angeles (on the scale seen four years later in Seoul) would have consumed much of Los Angeles' surplus, leaving LAOOC with a much-reduced profit of $36.4 million. Costs reached $1,708,596,472, $92,973,000, $289,037,442, $358,455,155, and $327,465,633 in Moscow, Los Angeles, Seoul, Barcelona, and Atlanta, respectively.[51] The city's vast array of usable facilities, such as the Los Angeles Memorial Coliseum, the Los Angeles Sports Arena, the Anaheim Convention Center, Santa Anita Park, and venues at East Los Angeles College, Loyola Marymount University, and California State University, Fullerton, contributed to Ueberroth's mission, since they merely required upgrades and renovations. The use of dormitories at three area universities for athletes' accommodation, in lieu of a costly Olympic Village, also figured prominently in his formula.

Ueberroth's vision on corporate sponsorship extended to LAOOC's responsibility to provide the required venue inventory. Los Angeles lacked viable facilities for three Olympic sports—aquatics, indoor cycling, and shooting. Navigating the local politics entailed in establishing these and other venues provided its own set of challenges. For financing, Ueberroth targeted the corporate sector. Some three hundred thousand spectators viewed Olympic swimming events at USC's swim stadium, which was built at a cost of $3 million with money supplied by McDonald's. Don Gerth, president of California State University, Dominguez Hills, did not want his school left out of the Olympic media spotlight dominated by USC and UCLA (along with USC and University of California, Santa Barbara, one of the three sites chosen for athletes' accommodation) and reached an agreement to provide the parcel of land necessary for the Olympic Velodrome. The Southland Corporation, parent company of the 7-Eleven chain of variety stores, provided the $3.5 million in necessary funding. Ueberroth convinced company executives that a velodrome, in light of 7-Eleven's "bike-in clientele," and the "fast-paced, fast-growing sport"[52] of cycling, offered their company a useful marketing tool. After abandoning a number of possible sites, Ueberroth settled on the Prado Recreation Area in San Bernardino County as the location for shooting, in a facility ultimately funded by Fuji Film.

Ueberroth was fond of quoting Britain's wartime prime minister and statesman, Winston Churchill, who once stated: "Some see private enterprise as a predatory target to be shot, others as a cow to be milked, but few are those who see it as a sturdy horse pulling the wagon."[53] Without question Ueberroth harnessed the corporate sector as a means of "pulling" Los Angeles' wagon.

Berlioux, Ueberroth, and the Post–L.A. Years

Monique Berlioux and Peter Ueberroth are perhaps the most influential Olympic personalities of the late twentieth century who never became members of the IOC. Their careers took divergent paths in the years following the Los Angeles Games.

During her years as IOC director, Berlioux exerted more influence on Olympic affairs than 95 percent of those who served as IOC members. As Dick Pound noted shortly after her passing in August 2015, "[Berlioux] was the most powerful woman in sport on the face of the planet."[54] But the preparatory years for the Los Angeles Olympics marked a tipping point in her career as Samaranch asserted more influence in the IOC's operations than had his predecessors, Brundage and Killanin. She did not adjust to the dynamics of her new workplace; her relationship with Samaranch soured, and he orchestrated her dismissal in 1985. "Her wish to control the IOC collided with [Samaranch's]," confirmed Pound.[55] Though Samaranch's overhaul of the IOC's administrative practices was already well underway, Berlioux's departure was a strong indicator that he was confident and resolved in moving beyond the IOC's old guard and old ways. Berlioux retreated to Paris to work in the office of then-mayor Jacques Chirac.

Howard Stupp, the IOC's former long-time director of legal affairs who arrived at the same time Berlioux's exit was fast approaching, noted that at the peak of her power in the 1970s, she read every piece of mail coming into the Château de Vidy and signed everything that was mailed out.[56] It is a hard circumstance to imagine, notes Stupp, but it reflected her place at the hub of the Olympic Movement. Berlioux set agendas for IOC meetings and ensured that decisions rendered at IOC Sessions resulted in action. She managed correspondence flowing to and from Lausanne, played a major role in the budgeting process, spearheaded the organization's involvement in the negotiation of television contracts in the 1970s and early 1980s, provided a public face for the organization, and delivered press conferences with a degree of aplomb that earned the praise of journalists. Samaranch's biographer, David Miller, observed that Berlioux "not only had her feet effectively under the President's table, but could and did lay her hand on every doorknob, every appointment, every contract, every single decision that was made."[57] She was a tough workplace supervisor and taskmaster who demanded from others the long hours of service that she provided. Her managerial style resulted in IOC staff turnover exceeding 25 percent each year. Berlioux could be difficult.

For a time, she did not make the mistakes committed by her predecessors, Johann Westerhoff and Eric Jonas, each of whom took actions destined to irritate their boss, Brundage, who relieved them of their duties. She ensured that Brundage, and later Killanin, set policy; she simply found ways to enact it.[58] Samaranch, who drew support from Berlioux in his quest for the presidency, moved to Lausanne after his election in 1980. At that time, she was at the height of her influence and clout.

In their early days of interaction, all seemed well. "We are lucky to have Madame Berlioux as Director," observed Samaranch. She managed a staff of seventy and earned a yearly salary exceeding $100,000.[59] However, the two soon clashed when Samaranch began to chip away at the scope of her duties. Trust between them dissipated, and Samaranch began holding meetings with individuals in the gardens of the Château de Vidy to avoid any snooping. "The most delicious rumour that circulated," reports Dick Pound (then a rising star within the IOC's ranks), "was that Samaranch and Berlioux had each bugged the other's office." In 1983 Berlioux, while not removed from television negotiations, was forced to cede her lead role on behalf of the IOC to Pound. Samaranch was well aware that Pound and Berlioux disliked each other, and while he knew the Canadian was a good match for the job, it was convenient that his appointment of Pound was sure to aggravate Berlioux even further than her mere loss of authority.[60] Samaranch's suspicions were aroused (as were Pound's)[61] that Berlioux had been leaking information to ABC in past negotiations for television rights in the United States. Samaranch's demand for bona fide competition going forward was so earnest that in January 1984, when the IOC negotiators, Calgary officials, and representatives of the U.S. networks convened in Lausanne for bidding on the rights to Calgary 1988—the first U.S. deal Pound brokered—all IOC personnel, including Berlioux, were escorted to the washrooms at the Palace Hotel to "prevent secret messages from being passed."[62] Berlioux's frustration was compounded in 1985 when Pound, at Samaranch's insistence, took over her duties in sealing final contractual arrangements with ISL and Horst Dassler to bring the TOP global sponsorship program to fruition.

As the 1984 Sarajevo Olympic Winter Games approached, "[Berlioux] was not even listening to Samaranch," stated Ashwini Kumar, a member of the IOC Executive Board, "and I had said that if a paid employee would not listen to the boss, they must go." "She would not accept that she was a servant of the IOC," he concluded. Though members of the Executive Board grew weary of Berlioux's overbearing personality and misplaced understanding of her station in the IOC hierarchy, they were not alone in that regard. An annoyed Walter Tröger, the IOC's sports director, resented Berlioux's meddling in his sphere of operations. She was "efficient and knowledgeable, but she was a dictator," stated Tröger.[63] It became an untenable situation. Samaranch, confirms Payne, decided "Lausanne was not big enough for the two of them."[64] Pound, in retrospect, complimented Berlioux on her demonstrated abilities in Lausanne. "In many ways, it was a pity that she was so abrasive. She was possessed of much ability and was an efficient and tireless worker. She was the top female sports administrator in the world and could, no doubt, have continued in her position had she not offended so many people and, most importantly, had she been able to adjust to the fact that the new IOC president was a horse of a different color."[65]

Samaranch approached Pound, whose "uneasy" relationship with Berlioux dated back to the time of his co-optation to the IOC in 1978,[66] about how the IOC could dismiss Berlioux, as well as what legal repercussions might follow. Once Pound convinced Samaranch that the IOC could proceed unfettered with her dismissal, after balking on following through with this action when the IOC met in Sarajevo the previous year, Samaranch secured her resignation in 1985.[67] "You couldn't have two crocodiles in the same pond, and Samaranch as the boss didn't want another one behind him," observed Jean de Beaumont, who knew Berlioux well through his service as chairman of the IOC Finance Commission in the 1970s. "Until [Samaranch] arrived," said Beaumont, "she was the only man in the IOC."[68]

As for Ueberroth, David Miller asserts Samaranch failed to convince the IOC Executive Board of the merits of Ueberroth's nomination for IOC membership, but Ueberroth questioned just how hard Samaranch had pushed. Some IOC members

Peter Ueberroth (Photo courtesy of LA84 Foundation.)

viewed Ueberroth with suspicion, doubting his ability to serve as a team player. "He's too commercial, too much of a shark," offered those Executive Board members more amenable to the nominations of Anita DeFrantz and Robert Helmick.[69] Former USOC president Robert Kane viewed Ueberroth as "competent [and] hard working" but struggled with Ueberroth's arrogance, feelings fueled, in part, by his thoughts concerning Ueberroth's unwillingness to regard (and promote) the USOC as a true partner in the staging of the Olympics. Privately, however, Kane also conceded that a "large ego" was required to "pull off" the Los Angeles Olympics.[70]

Ueberroth's post–Los Angeles 1984 life was anything but dull. Named Man of the Year by *Time* in 1984, he served nearly five years as commissioner of Major League Baseball (1984–1989), sat on Coca-Cola's board of directors for twenty-nine years (1986–2015), co-chaired the Rebuild Los Angeles project for two years (an effort to spur the private sector in restoring and revitalizing areas of the city damaged by the Rodney King riots), purchased the iconic Pebble Beach Golf Links in partnership with Clint Eastwood and Arnold Palmer, made a run at California's governorship, spearheaded a number of corporate turnarounds, and served four years as USOC president (2004–2008).

Closing Thoughts

Though Ueberroth anticipated a surplus of only $18 million as late as March 1984, the number climbed substantially due to higher than anticipated coin and ticket sales, the dissolution of a reserve fund from ABC's contract resulting from better-than-expected television ratings, and the savings of an additional $64 million in anticipated spending due to "contingency planning."[71] On behalf of his leadership team, Ueberroth made "no apology for generating in excess of $200 million for youth and amateur sports . . . or good, sound financial management."[72] His success in generating a surplus (ultimately $232.5 million) altered the trajectory of the Olympic Movement in both the short term and long term. Cautious civic officials, who viewed an Olympic bid as a risky financial enterprise, stood on the sidelines in the 1970s. But, in view of climbing television revenue combined with the newly configured TOP sponsorship program, they saw a way forward. The IOC no longer went hat in hand in its efforts to secure Olympic host-city bids. Samaranch's successful campaign to open the Olympics to professional athletes also spurred added media interest. "Shown the alluring path to possible profits," writes Andrew Zimbalist, "cities and countries now lined up for the honor of hosting the games."[73] What might be dubbed "The Ueberroth Effect" is clear when one examines the number of declared Olympic-bid cities in the pre– and post–Los Angeles

Table 1: Number of Declared Olympic Bid Cities, 1972–2012

Olympic Year	Date of Award	Winter	Summer
1972	1964	4	4
1976	1970	4	3
1980	1974	1	2
1984	1978	3	1
1988	1981	3	2
1992	1986	6	6
1994	1988	4	—
1996	1990	—	6
1998	1991	5	—
2000	1993	—	5
2002	1995	9	—
2004	1997	—	11
2006	1999	6	—
2008	2001	—	10
2010	2003	8	—
2012	2005	—	9

Source: Wenn, "Peter Ueberroth's Legacy," 162.

periods (see table 1). Ueberroth's lesson for prospective organizers influenced bid competitions for the 1992 Summer Olympics and beyond. The post–Los Angeles years were heady days for Samaranch and the IOC. The reinvigorated Olympic bid environment stands as a major element of Peter Ueberroth's legacy.

But Samaranch, complacent in the post–Los Angeles atmosphere, ignored that the increasingly competitive bid process factored into spiraling "added costs" of hosting the Games, a ramification that contributed immeasurably to an already risky and potentially disabling financial endeavor. Then, too, Samaranch failed to meaningfully confront the encroachment of unflattering, and in some cases corrupt, practices and conduct of bid committee officials and, as well, members the IOC, who sidestepped existing IOC regulations in efforts to "buy" or "sell" votes for treasured host-city distinction. The conflagration otherwise referred to as the Salt Lake City Scandal was the result.

The intensity and competitiveness of Olympic bidding increased in the aftermath of the Los Angeles Olympics. Douglas Booth states that Ueberroth's success "alerted cities to the Olympics as a potential vehicle for economic gain and a source of prestige."[74] But Booth also asserts that Samaranch encouraged bid committees, beginning with those championing Barcelona's aspirations for 1992, to invite IOC members for bid-city visits, establish friendships, and become part of the "Olympic Family." In the effort to elevate the profile of the IOC, its mission, and its membership, and to capitalize on the increased attractiveness of hosting the Games, candidate cities were further encouraged to establish a presence at international sport meetings where IOC members would be present and to visit IOC members in their home countries. Lobbyists offering their services to bid committees soon followed, as did increasingly lavish hospitality for events around the globe tied to IOC Sessions sponsored by bid committees. "Competition," states Booth, "obliged candidates not only to follow suit but to upstage their rivals with more luxurious gifts and bigger parties at more exotic locations. . . . Pandering to IOC members became the recipe for winning hosting rights."[75]

Marc Hodler, a veteran IOC member, expressed concern about the new dynamics of Olympic bid competitions in the post–Los Angeles era, but Samaranch and the IOC Executive Board brushed aside his concerns, expressed as early as 1986. Six years later, the IOC did pass limits on the value of gifts that could be provided to IOC members by bid committees, scaled back the number of bid-city visits IOC members were permitted, and proscribed lavish entertainment. However, in the absence of any monitoring or oversight process, bid committees were little constrained, and those IOC members who had in the past exploited their status for personal benefit and enrichment did not alter their behavior. It was a textbook example of a simmering crisis, festering beneath the surface of the IOC's operations. When Samaranch eschewed any investigation of rumored misconduct by IOC members in the absence of unsuccessful bid committees "naming names," the powder keg for a crisis existed. In the context of the Salt Lake City crisis, the IOC paid a heavy price in terms of its image and reputation.

The growth of the Games in the post–Los Angeles years, characterized by the need to cater to larger numbers of sports, athletes, and media personnel, the new reality and economics of security planning in the post–9/11 era, and the increasing tendency of host cities to see the Olympics as a catalyst for major infrastructure spending that could remake their civic landscapes for the next generation, prompted a drift from Ueberroth's blueprint. The increased costs, when combined with the global economic crisis of 2007–2008, curbed interest toward hosting the Olympics. Sochi's final expense line in excess of $50 billion also had a chilling effect on bidding. Beijing and Almaty (Kazakhstan) stood as the only options for host of the 2022 Olympic Winter Games, given the withdrawal of Oslo, Stockholm, Lviv, and Krakow. This problematic bid environment was a powerful signal to IOC President Thomas Bach for the IOC to seek means of reducing the cost of hosting the Games. Such an imperative was a central element of Bach's *Olympic Agenda 2020*, a "strategic roadmap"[76] for the future of the Olympic Games, adopted by the IOC in 2014. How could costs be contained? One answer within *Olympic Agenda 2020* was to prioritize bid cities with preexisting facilities such that new facility spending was reduced. Somewhere, Peter Ueberroth smiled knowingly.

CHAPTER 6

"Total Olympic Programme"

November 25, 1985

Before an assemblage of journalists at New York's Pierre Hotel in late November 1985, Don Keough, the Coca-Cola Company's chairman and COO, stated, "As businessmen, we know that the Olympic Movement has unparalleled appeal to all peoples of the world. The Olympic Games, both Summer and Winter, are unmatched spectacles, watched by rapt audiences in every corner of the world. Association with such an event is every marketer's dream."[1] Keough, Juan Antonio Samaranch, and Robert Helmick and George Miller, the United States Olympic Committee's (USOC) chairman and executive director, convened the press conference to announce the launch of the IOC's worldwide corporate sponsorship program, TOP, referred to by Samaranch in his prepared remarks as the "Total Olympic Programme" (later, The Olympic Programme, now The Olympic Partners).[2] With Keough's more than thirty years of service to Coca-Cola,[3] the press conference to announce his firm's status as the first multinational company to align itself with the IOC's initiative was surely a career highlight. Dick Pound, chairman of the IOC Marketing Commission, and Michael Payne, Olympic project director for International Sport and Leisure Marketing (ISL), the IOC's partner agency regarding TOP, also attended.[4] Coca Cola's discussions with Samaranch concerning ISL and TOP, based in Lucerne, Switzerland, extended back more than two years.[5]

In citing the "example and success of the Los Angeles Olympic marketing programme," Samaranch said the IOC was "definitely convinced" to move forward with the program that had been in the planning stages for "a few years."[6] The concept was simple. TOP was conceived in collaboration with Horst Dassler and ISL, a sports marketing company that Dassler, Adidas's kingpin, founded in 1982 (co-owned by a Japanese advertising firm, Dentsu) and was designed to reduce the complexity of a company's efforts to link with the Olympic Movement. At the time, marketing officials within the corporate world were required to negotiate individual agreements with NOCs in each of the targeted territories. It was a messy, complex, and unnecessarily convoluted task. TOP created a "one-stop shopping" system. "The benefit of [the] new program is that you can make one deal and sew up the whole package of marketing rights without going around the world," stated Dick Pound, whom Samaranch tasked to push the program from concept to reality when his confidence in Monique Berlioux's fitness for the job waned.[7] A four-year TOP deal offered companies exclusive marketing rights within a designated product category, including advertising linkage to Olympic marks and emblems, hospitality and promotional opportunities at Olympic Games, and preferred access to Olympic tickets. In Coca-Cola's case, the TOP deal facilitated by ISL eliminated the need for the more than twenty-five deals the giant beverage firm signed with host cities or NOCs in the 1984 cycle.

Samaranch believed money amassed through the IOC's link with ISL would "counter balance," its "virtual, total dependence on television revenue."[8] It also offered smaller NOCs, which lacked a marketing environment conducive to raising significant dollars from corporate sponsorship, an allocation of funds from the program. "With this new programme," said Samaranch, "each member of the Olympic family will have a greater—and more equal—stake in the Olympic activities. From now on, each National Olympic Committee will be able to utilize its part of this sponsorship funding in order to further develop its Olympic efforts."[9] Greater, yes; more equal? Well, not exactly.

The Amateur Sports Act (ASA) passed by the U.S. Congress in 1978 awarded the USOC exclusive rights to the use of the Olympic five-ring logo and other marks and emblems in the United States. USOC officials well understood the critical nature of the U.S. market to the success of TOP, and so did Dassler and Samaranch. Some in USOC leadership circles, appalled by what they believed would serve as a conduit for U.S. corporate dollars to NOCs to fund the development of rival athletes in Communist nations, denigrated TOP. Additionally, they held that the USOC's fundraising efforts would have to be ramped up to compensate for a perceived loss of prospective revenue and a challenge to the U.S. medal count. Larry Huff, a member of the USOC's Executive Committee, even advocated the exclusion of Communist nations from any sharing formula. "Total Cold War mindset," recalled Payne.[10]

In exchange for permitting its activation in the United States, the USOC exacted a price—15 percent of the TOP money, though there was some fluidity to this percentage relative to individual sponsor categories.[11] The remainder would be divided among the Organizing Committees, specifically in TOP's first cycle, those in Calgary and Seoul, the other NOCs, and the IOC. The press conference, in hindsight, marked the close of two years of discussion with the USOC culminating in its consent to ISL and the IOC to operate TOP in the United States. The IOC/USOC accord green-lighted the program on a global basis. Without the USOC's consent, it would have been stillborn. As well, it reflected a further demonstration of the Coca-Cola Company's long-standing commitment to the Olympic Games, first seen in Amsterdam in 1928 as a beverage supplier for the U.S. Olympic team. His company, remarked Keough, was no "Johnny-come-lately to the Olympics," and it relished the opportunity to deepen its association with the Olympic Movement.[12]

But once the journalists filed their stories, there was much heavy lifting for ISL and the IOC ahead. While the concept was simple, TOP's execution was far more delicate and complex: it required buy-in from the world's NOCs, especially those in strong commercial markets, as they would have to sacrifice domestic ownership of product categories designated for use within TOP. Domestic sponsor contracts in support of NOCs could not be in competition with a product category awarded to a TOP sponsor. Though known as The Olympic Programme, those on the inside dubbed it "The Olympic Puzzle," a testimony to the glut of issues to deal with in bringing sponsors and the NOCs together.[13] NOC leaders in major markets lacked confidence in the IOC's ability to spearhead this marketing enterprise on a global basis given its earlier failed effort under Killanin to generate sponsor dollars in collaboration with Intelicense, a marketing company based in Switzerland and owned by Canadian Stan Shefler.[14] And, of course, interested parties other than Coca-Cola would have to be recruited. Could other multinationals be attracted to the concept underpinning TOP, and what value did they place on membership within the program? Time was short. The 1988 Calgary Olympic Winter Games were only a little more than two years away.

The Amateur Sports Act

Though ISL approached Samaranch and the IOC in 1982 and reached a preliminary agreement on the program the following year, it was the USOC and its use of the ASA that posed the barrier against commencing the program well before its eventual launch in November 1985. To understand the challenge faced by the IOC and ISL in inaugurating TOP, especially with regard to vigorous American resistance, we briefly examine the nature of the legislation, the underlying reasons for its genesis, and an early test case that amply demonstrated its legal "weight" within the U.S. court system.

The ASA drastically reorganized amateur sports in the United States and resolved a near-century of conflict among amateur sport governing bodies that degenerated over time into untenable working relationships, relationships that prevented the United States from fielding its best possible international amateur sports teams, particularly with respect to its Olympic mission. Their interaction featured internecine distrust and quest for power, further exacerbated by the entrance of the Soviet Union into the Olympic Games in 1952, an appearance that led rapidly to an erosion of the once-dominant position of the United States at the top of the quadrennial festival's medal tally. Superimposed on the shadow of Cold War politics was America's deteriorating performance, climaxed by an especially poor showing at the 1972 Summer Olympics in Munich, attributed to a malfunctioning administrative structure that needed major surgery if the nation was to do well at the 1976 Summer Olympics and beyond. Then, too, the celebration of America's bicentennial in the year coincident with the Montreal Games (1976) added urgency to the quest to restore America's Olympic luster.

Control of amateur athletics in the United States reflected a long and tumultuous history. At the heart of the problem rested sustained conflict between the National Collegiate Athletic Association (NCAA) and the Amateur Athletic Union of the United States (AAU). The NCAA termed the struggle between the two as "The Problem That Won't Go Away."[15] The AAU, formed in 1888, existed as the supreme authority for certifying an athlete's amateur standing, thus qualifying the athlete for domestic, international, and Olympic participation. The AAU's control over amateur sport remained unchecked until the founding of the NCAA in 1906. The NCAA's jurisdiction encompassed the regulation and supervision of college athletics. Because college athletes competed in various domestic and international sporting competitions, many of which the AAU governed, disputes over "ownership" of athletes rapidly became an issue, but more especially when intercollegiate sports in America mushroomed in intensity and national popularity.[16]

In the face of rising public criticism of the poor U.S. Olympic performance in Munich, together with reciprocal finger-pointing as a means of apportioning blame by AAU and NCAA officials, a call was made for the federal government to step in and bring resolution to the fundamental problem—the shortcomings of the American Olympic effort. A frustrated Cecil Coleman, president of the National Association of Collegiate Directors of Athletics (NACDA), wrote to Vice President Gerald Ford on November 9, 1972 complaining that "only through a White House Congress on Amateur Athletics," whereby a new "super-structure" might emerge to coordinate all international athletics, could the inherent differences between the sports bodies be settled. If Ford agreed with this principle, wrote Coleman, "make this known to President Nixon."[17]

Between 1972 and 1974 the White House quietly undertook "first steps" in a journey aimed at providing a solution.[18] "First steps" came in late September 1973 in the shape of a President Nixon–approved process by which a President's Commission on Olympic Sports (PCOS) might be formed.[19] With Richard Nixon's resignation in August 1974, Gerald Ford assumed the duties of the Oval Office. On December 28, 1974, Ford signed Executive Order 11868 authorizing the creation of PCOS.[20] Its most prominent recommendation empowered the USOC as the central coordinating body for amateur sports that compete internationally. The work of the PCOS was the crucial factor leading to the ASA, which, in finality, codified and implemented its recommendations.[21] After a lengthy and belabored process in Congress, the ASA became law on November 8, 1978, with President Jimmy Carter's signature. It permanently altered the amateur sporting landscape in the United States as a new parental authority existed for amateur sport, including Olympic sport—the USOC.

Lord Killanin has been criticized for not monitoring events in Washington closely. The absence of a timely response to the clauses tied to the legislation granting the USOC exclusive rights to the use of Olympic marks and emblems in the United States proved exceedingly problematic for the IOC, leading Dick Pound to assert: "Killanin dropped the ball. When the U.S. Amateur Sports Act started to come along there [with Congress] . . . taking the view that the [USOC] was given authority over the five rings in the United States even though it amounted effectively to an expropriation of the IOC's property rights of the five rings . . . the [IOC] should have right then and there said 'no.' 'No, no, no, no, we own the five rings. You're allowed to use them in the United States but you cannot exclude us from using them.'"[22]

Intelicense

"The [Intelicense] contracts signed by the IOC turned out to be a fool's bargain," stated IOC Executive Board member Kéba Mbaye in 1985. "Unfortunately, in my opinion, it is too late to do anything about it now."[23] Six years after IOC director Monique Berlioux, with the approval of the Finance Commission and Executive Board, committed the IOC to a seventy-year contractual relationship with Swiss-based Intelicense S.A. Corporation for the marketing of Olympic Winter and Summer pictograms, Mbaye could not have been more succinct and accurate in his appraisal. Pictograms are the small, stylized athlete figures that appear on signage at Olympic venues and on Olympic telecasts. Intelicense's president and CEO, Montreal native Stan Shefler, intended to affix the pictograms to various companies' products in exchange for payment. Shefler's failure to secure access to the U.S. market gutted the value of Intelicense's deal and prompted an extended legal dispute in the United States and Switzerland between the IOC and Intelicense.[24] It would be another five years after Mbaye offered his verdict before the IOC fully extricated itself from the legal entanglements stemming from this ill-conceived sponsorship program.

The Intelicense saga provided a lesson to IOC officials about the strength of the ASA and the willingness of the USOC to employ it as a means of defending its "turf" from those seeking to generate Olympic-related revenue in the United States, the need for access to the U.S. market as a means of better ensuring the success of any global Olympic-marketing exercise, and the need for careful contract writing. While we cannot label the Intelicense episode transformative, it is informative for a number of reasons: it was a significant prelude event within the history of TOP; it marked one of the key events that brought François Carrard, the IOC's director general (1989–2003) and an influential figure during Samaranch's presidency, into full-time employment with the IOC; and, when the deal was signed in 1979, its consummation also reflected the zenith of Monique Berlioux's power in Lausanne. Lord Killanin, who neared the end of his presidential tenure in the late 1970s, exerted little authority over the development of the IOC's contractual relationship with Intelicense.[25] Rather, the IOC's interests were represented by Berlioux and the IOC's legal adviser, Georges Straschnov.

Enter Stan Shefler and Intelicense

Born in 1930, Stan Shefler graduated from Montreal's Sir George Williams College. His early focus in business was in real estate. In 1959 Shefler and his brother-in-law, Irwin Feldman, unveiled Designs for Business Canada Ltd., a subsidiary of New York–based Designs for Business Inc., a company that provided office planning and interior design work for corporations. His business interests were diversified. He and his wife, Roni, opened a number of Swiss fondue (Swisspot) restaurants in Vermont. His ties to Vermont were significant, evidenced by a secondary residence in Stowe and Governor Richard Snelling's decision to appoint him as Vermont's ambassador to Europe in 1977.

Shefler, who founded Intelicense (headquartered in Fribourg, Switzerland) in 1971, was part of the Montreal Organizing Committee's (COJO) sponsorship team. In the wake of the financially troubled 1976 Summer Olympics, COJO sought to recoup some money from the marketing of pictograms it had purchased from the 1972 Munich Organizing Committee,[26] plans that fell far short of expectations. COJO transferred the rights to the pictograms to the Olympic Installations Board, a provincial (Quebec) government agency.[27] Shefler believed that Intelicense could use the pictograms without the IOC's permission. His pursuit of this activity irritated Monique Berlioux,[28] drawing the two organizations into conflict.

As a means of avoiding a legal impasse,[29] Berlioux shifted course and authorized Shefler, at his suggestion,[30] to redesign the Munich/Montreal pictograms, while also moving to secure control over Winter pictograms designed by Alfred Kunzenmann and employed by the 1976 Innsbruck Organizing Committee.[31] Berlioux believed that the IOC and Intelicense, once adversaries, could establish a mutually beneficial, long-term relationship. Shefler, seizing the possibility for financial gain, moved swiftly on both fronts.[32] In 1979 the IOC and Intelicense drafted two separate contracts granting Intelicense a seventy-year term as the IOC's exclusive agent for the marketing of Kunzenmann's Winter pictograms and the Munich/Montreal pictograms, redesigned by Julien van der Wal. Revenue deriving from the program was apportioned 40 percent to the IOC, and 60 percent to Intelicense, with the latter responsible for any royalties needed to obtain consent from participating NOCs.[33] Success hinged on the cooperation of the NOCs and their granting to Intelicense access to their respective territories.

Berlioux alerted all NOCs to Shefler's IOC-authorized project and encouraged the NOCs to work with Intelicense.[34] It is on this front that the program ultimately collapsed and exposed both parties to nearly a decade of litigation. While a number of NOCs, including China, Greece, and Mexico, signed cooperation agreements with Intelicense, the USOC was not at all interested in undercutting its control of the use of the Olympic rings, marks, and emblems in the United States granted to it through the ASA, passed into law in Washington the previous year. The USOC, asserted Shefler, needed to be made to heel. The IOC countered that Intelicense knew the contracts were governed by the *Olympic Charter* and that the IOC did not possess the authority to force any NOC into a relationship.[35]

The USOC's Shot across Stan Shefler's Bow

In late May 1981 F. Don Miller, the USOC's executive director, told Shefler that the USOC opposed his efforts to capitalize on a contractual relationship that Intelicense established with Sport Graphics Inc. that permitted Sport Graphics to "distribute sports bags bearing copyrighted Olympic pictograms and the Olympic rings on a worldwide basis" in the United States. He noted the USOC's rights accorded to it through the ASA and that Shefler's activities were not welcome.[36] Though it is not clear whether the pictograms alone would have triggered this response, van der Wal's use of the Olympic rings in the redesign of the Summer pictograms surely did.[37] None of this should have startled Shefler, who had tried for more than a year, without success, to secure Miller's consent to conduct business in the United States.[38] Less than a year into his new role as IOC president, Samaranch weighed in. He noted that the *Olympic Charter* governed the agreements and that Intelicense was compelled to obtain the permission of NOCs to operate in their respective territories.[39]

In November 1982 the USOC filed a civil suit in the District of Columbia against Sport Graphics, Millsports (the marketing agent for International Sports Marketing, a sublicensee of Intelicense in the United States), and Intelicense. The USOC sought an end to the use of the Winter and Summer pictograms in the United States. The court ruled in the USOC's favor in March 1983, but a final judgement was delayed. Additional hearings were held on October 6 and 7 before Judge James Oakes of Vermont's Second Circuit.[40] In their pretrial preparations, the USOC's lawyers interviewed Georges Straschnov, who maintained adamantly that Shefler was warned about the need to obtain consent from the NOCs, including the USOC. Straschnov also offered that the Olympic rings were part of Julien van der Wal's redesign of the Summer pictograms, but that Shefler added the rings to the Kunzenmann Winter pictograms at some point following the IOC's acquisition of their copyright and without the IOC's consent.[41] His words regarding the caveat issued to Shefler reassured members of the USOC's legal team given the absence of declarative text in the agreements covering the matter.

In November Judge Oakes delivered a resounding victory to the USOC in its efforts to protect its rights.[42] Intelicense appealed the decision. With the appeal still in process, Shefler devised yet another version of the pictograms in March 1984, using "colored parallelograms" instead of rings and the word "Olympic" in block, capital letters. He attempted to activate the new version's use in the United States, but Vermont's Second Circuit expanded the reach of Oakes's decision, stymieing Shefler. The U.S. Court of Appeals backed Oakes's judgement,[43] and Shefler subsequently faced a $212,000 damage award (to the USOC).[44]

Meanwhile . . . in Switzerland

The IOC's outside legal counsel, François Carrard, correctly anticipated that this loss would spur Shefler to accelerate and intensify ongoing legal proceedings that Intelicense brought against the IOC in Switzerland, with an accompanying claim for significant damages because the IOC did not back Intelicense in its showdown with the USOC.[45] In March 1983 Shefler secured a temporary injunction that stopped the IOC from granting any third party, anywhere in the world, the right to use pictograms other than the Kunzenmann or van der Wal pictograms.[46] Carrard advised the IOC not to terminate the 1979 agreements in the Swiss or U.S. court systems in light of Shefler's actions, as this exposed the IOC to exorbitant damage claims from Intelicense.[47]

Over time, this is exactly what Carrard determined to be an element of Shefler's legal strategy in Switzerland. Either the IOC would seek to terminate the agreements, paving the way for Intelicense to issue a damage claim, or the repeated legal thrusts on Shefler's part would wear out IOC officials to the point when they would move to purchase Intelicense from him to eliminate the problem.[48] Shefler's activities signal he determined Intelicense's financial prospects were dim in light of the likely loss of the U.S. market. Thus, he explored ways to extricate himself from the situation.

Intelicense's lawsuit in Geneva proceeded with hearings in May 1984, presided over by Judge Francis Strub.[49] Carrard again concluded that the IOC needed to stay the course and not surrender its position by canceling the 1979 agreements as a result of Shefler's tactics. Such a cancellation would leave the IOC open to a substantial damage claim.[50] The parties convened at Carrard's office on June 7, 1984, to review the status of their dispute. Nothing materialized.[51] In two further meetings, Strub's efforts to effect a "conciliation" process failed.[52] The affair dragged on through 1985. Two more meetings between Samaranch and Shefler on July 11 and September 5, 1985, yielded nothing tangible toward a settlement.[53]

In early 1986 Shefler upped the ante. He pressed forward with his earlier-promised claim for damages. In a seventy-four-page submission, Shefler sought damages for SF 65 million, with nearly SF 56 million of this sum estimated as Intelicense's lost profits. Judge Strub met with IOC officials and Shefler and lawyers representing both parties on May 20, 1986, to explore a possible settlement. Strub offered, without any prejudice toward the pending case, that Shefler deserved a measure of compensation for his time, energy, and financial investment in the project, and the number Strub contemplated was between SF 1 million and 2 million. Shefler's lawyers found this sum not even worth discussing.[54]

Shefler's Passing Changes the Dynamics of the Legal Process

Stan Shefler died suddenly in Palm Springs, California, on October 16, 1986, at age fifty-six. His second wife, Sara, and two sons from his first marriage, Charles and Marc, survived him (as did his first wife, Roni). Perhaps, mused Carrard, an opening existed to bring the troubling saga to a close. "If these heirs are more reasonable than Stanley Shefler," he stated, "they might see an interest in receiving some money and bringing an end to all pending litigation."[55] What Carrard and other IOC officials did not know in these early days following Shefler's passing was that Sara Shefler and Stan Shefler's sons were not on good terms. The sons and their stepmother, a young, haute couture model who wore the designs of Christian Dior, Yves St. Laurent, and Givenchy and was familiar with the runways of Milan and Paris,[56] jockeyed for control of the situation through their respective legal teams. While Charles and Marc inherited the bulk of the estate, Sara Shefler had been named Intelicense's director. Navigating these negotiations with the two parties who were embroiled in a feud provided additional challenges. Even though the IOC Executive Board set aside SF 2 million in September 1987 for a prospective settlement,[57] matters percolated for another three years, until the three sides reached a deal for the sum of $1.4 million[58]—interestingly, a figure at the top end of the range initially suggested by Judge Strub in 1986.

In 1990, more than a decade after Monique Berlioux's initial correspondence with Stan Shefler, the IOC closed the Intelicense file. This was none too soon for

Samaranch, who "could not understand how the IOC ever signed such a contract," while noting that "the signatories had demonstrated a high level of incompetence."[59] In this assertion, he squarely trained his focus on Monique Berlioux and Georges Straschnov, yet Carrard cautioned that assigning personal blame to anyone was "a rather delicate subject" as the Executive Board and Finance Commission signed off on both October 1979 agreements with Shefler.[60]

The Lessons of Intelicense

The Intelicense initiative offered a lesson in the hazards of contract writing when those developing the contracts are not well enough informed on details concerning IOC marks and emblems, or cognizant of the need to avoid multiple interpretations of those contracts by including definitive links to conditions within the *Olympic Charter*. For his part, Lord Killanin did not exercise sufficient due diligence as president, explained possibly, in part, by health problems during the late stages of his term. Clearly, the entire exercise offered a cautionary tale for the likes of Pound, Payne, and the IOC's director of legal affairs at the time, Howard Stupp, as they pressed forward with the TOP program and contracts with the inaugural set of multinational firms seeking linkage with the program. In retrospect, Pound likened the Intelicense affair to a "carbuncle,"[61] an irritation of sorts. However, the length and number of "Intelicense" reports Carrard penned in his role as outside legal counsel in the 1980s (which reside today in the IOC's archives) suggest that it was a more pressing matter for those walking the halls of the Château de Vidy on a daily basis.

Though the Intelicense case did not mark Carrard's baptism in legal work on behalf of the IOC, work that later translated into his appointment as the IOC's director general after the 1988 Seoul Olympics (he stepped down in 2003), it consumed a good deal of his professional time following his entry into the Intelicense narrative in April 1981.[62] In far understated fashion, he labeled the Intelicense affair "a hard fight."[63] In managing the legal side of the IOC's interests in the Intelicense case, Carrard performed admirably. There's little doubt he impressed Samaranch with his work on the file. While it is far from the solitary reason why Samaranch selected him in 1988 to assume the duties that Raymond Gafner fulfilled following Berlioux's departure from the IOC, it contributed greatly to the impression Samaranch formed about his work capacity, unflappable bearing, self-confidence, attention to detail, and professionalism. These were all qualities he sought in the IOC's new director general.

The USOC's dogged defense of its rights at the outset of the Intelicense case, rights granted to it by the passage of the ASA, is also noteworthy and foreshadowed the long narrative of IOC/USOC debates over matters tied to Olympic revenue distribution for the ensuing thirty years, revenue generated by the TOP program on a global basis and in the United States via television broadcast rights. Shefler's activities further alerted the USOC to the breadth of its authority over the use of Olympic marks and emblems in its territory.[64] Well before the last gavel sounded on the IOC/Intelicense case, the USOC actively asserted those rights to establish lucrative revenue streams from the TOP program and U.S. Olympic television rights.

Why did Killanin permit Berlioux such latitude in dealing with Shefler and Intelicense? The answer rests in the power and authority over the IOC's operations she achieved during the absentee presidencies of Avery Brundage (1952–1972) and Killanin (1972–1980), neither of whom established their principal residence in Lausanne. During her era of service to the IOC (1967–1985) Berlioux's status as a woman with decision-making authority was unique. While many women have populated the IOC's staff since 1985, her sweeping authority over numerous aspects of Olympic affairs, largely as a result of her iron grip on the staff in Lausanne, remains unprecedented. Women were not permitted to serve on the IOC until 1973, with the first female appointees not commencing service until 1981. Berlioux occupied a place at the epicenter of Olympic affairs under Brundage and Killanin, but her inability to coexist with Samaranch resulted in her dismissal in 1985.

Horst Dassler and TOP

As Christmas approached in 1982, a courier entered the IOC's headquarters bearing a limited-edition lithograph by the noted Italian artist Franz Borghese. Titled "The Case against the Bourgeoisie," it was a gift for Juan Antonio Samaranch from Horst Dassler's colleague and ISL's president, Klaus Hempel. A letter from Hempel accompanying the gift provided some background on Borghese's emergence as his country's "most creative satirical artist." The letter also noted the relationship ISL forged with FIFA earlier in the year as the machinery underpinning international football's worldwide marketing program. Hempel, tellingly, also noted that ISL's ambition extended beyond FIFA to other sport organizations.[65] Clearly, Horst Dassler hoped to explore such a relationship with the IOC. Having established the IOC's New Sources of Financing Commission in 1981, Samaranch sought means to offset the IOC's almost sole dependence on television money. And the relationship between Samaranch and Dassler was deep, given Dassler's assistance in advancing Samaranch's candidacy for the IOC presidency two years earlier. Dassler, a master manipulator of personal relations, was calling in the favor.

Juan Antonio Samaranch (left) awards the Olympic Order to Horst Dassler in 1984. (© 1984 / International Olympic Committee (IOC) / Albert Riethausen. Photo courtesy of the IOC.)

Seldom in the history of international sport business and politics has there existed an individual with the power and influence of Horst Dassler, associated in his entire lifetime with the giant sports equipment and apparel firm known as Adidas. His unparalleled energy and ubiquitous presence in international sport over three decades reached deeply into the power structures of national and international sports federations and the organizing committees of the world's largest and most glamorous mega events, including the Olympic Games. Horst Dassler, more than most, rapidly came to understand and employ the "mechanics of power." To Dassler, the fundamental element in the pursuit of power was the element of forging human relationships with the powerful.

To fully understand Horst Dassler's place in history one has to know of the intricate family web of his forebears, particularly his father, Adolf (known affectionately as Adi), and his father's older brother, Rudolf (Rudi).[66] Together, Adi and Rudi Dassler formed Gebrüder Dassler, a shoe manufacturing firm located in the small town of Herzogenaurach in northern Bavaria. Established in the early 1920s, Gebrüder Dassler brought an end to the family's generation-long tradition in the weaving industry. Adi, quiet and plodding, was a true tinker, germinating ideas and inventing techniques and machines to produce sturdy workingmen's shoes. Rudi, on the other hand, was a born salesman, a loud, glib talker. Both were sports enthusiasts. Their contrasting demeanors coalesced to make their firm a domestic leader in the manufacture and sales of soccer boots and, later, track and field shoes. Among their mainstay products were the first sports footwear with leather spiked soles, an invention of Adi's genius. At the Berlin Olympic Games in 1936 the Dasslers were successful in their quest to supply German track and field athletes with their shoes. A similar quest to adorn the feet of the most famous athlete at those Games, Jesse Owens, also met with success. The Owens case marked the birth of a sports clothing and equipment firm extending its brand through association with an iconic sports figure.

World War II and its aftermath brought an end to an already strained, indeed precarious relationship between Adi and Rudi Dassler. Driven apart by their differing personalities and fervor for Adolf Hitler's National Socialist regime, Rudi being far more attracted to Hitler's aims than Adi, at odds with each other's managerial philosophy, together with warring wives, Gebrüder Dassler met its demise in April 1948. Adolf filed for registration of a new company, Germany Adidas. Rudolf countered, registering his company as Puma. In the years following, the competition in the sports shoe market between the two brands was waged with angry vengeance and intense rivalry, often crossing the boundaries of questionable ethical behavior, perhaps best illustrated by the celebrated "Shoe Wars" of the 1968 Mexico City Olympics.

Born on March 12, 1936, Horst, the first child of Adi and Käthe Dassler, grew up amid the increasing rancor and alienation between his father and uncle. Sent to Melbourne for the 1956 Olympic Games, twenty-year old Horst cut his teeth on pursuit of what he later announced as his underlying principle leading to business success: "Everything is a matter of relationships."[67] To athletes, officials, sports federation leaders—indeed, to most with whom he came in contact—Horst Dassler's intelligent, quiet, self-effacing, courteous, generous, oftentimes compassionate manner made him a person whose company was sought and enjoyed. Those qualities factored relentlessly as Horst Dassler immersed himself into sports politics at their highest level.

As the Olympic Games' marriage with television intensified as a result of the advent of satellite technology in the 1960s, the global market for athletic shoes expanded greatly. Following the Tokyo Games in 1964, severe demands on Adidas's production output dictated expansion. Young Horst, scarcely thirty years old, was sent by his parents to the Alsace, there to establish Adidas France and join with Adidas Germany in an effort to capture greater European and global market share of athletic shoes over its rivals, chief of which was Puma. There in the Alsace, from his bastion of power, Dassler built a colossal business enterprise. Seemingly indefatigable, he traveled incessantly, appearing at major sports championships, shaking hands and rubbing shoulders with international sport's power brokers. In all places he left behind a legacy of close personal relationships, built upon the cultural practice of wining and dining by personal invitation, a hospitality touch rarely equaled by any in the greater world of sport politics. His company guest-house, states Michael Payne, boasted "one of the largest wine cellars in France and Michelin star level cuisine."[68] Dassler's tendency in these meetings was to lovingly finger a large Cuban cigar. His guests sometimes did the same.

Given Dassler's wide-ranging and influential activities through the 1960s and 1970s, together with the staggering television-prompted global popularity of the Olympic Games and Samaranch's calculated pursuit of the IOC presidency, it was inevitable that their paths intersect. Their first meeting occurred in September 1973 in Barcelona, where Samaranch fêted Dassler with a black-tie dinner in the "grandest Catalan style."

In the late 1970s, when the IOC turned its attention to means of raising revenues other than from the sale of television rights, Dassler's friendship with Samaranch, together with his demonstrated ability to bridge sport performance and business enterprise, eventually resulted in handsome dividends for each.[69] TOP, the revenue-producing scheme ultimately hatched, had nothing to do with marketing and selling athletic shoes or apparel. Rather, it had everything to do with an agent (ISL, Dassler's marketing company) entering into a contract agreement with a sports organization (IOC) for the sale of its product (Olympic Games) to a commercial sponsor (in other words, Coca-Cola, Visa) for the privilege of showcasing its product advertising before a mass television audience.

Though the basic idea and earliest examples of their practical application originated in the early 1970s with Patrick Nally, Dassler's business partner with the English firm West Nally, it was Dassler who rapidly and forcefully implemented the scheme in its most energetic and sophisticated circumstances through ISL, which he formed following his falling out with Nally. Sponsorship rights gained to soccer's World Cup, explicitly bestowed on him by FIFA boss João Havelange, underscored Dassler's business dictum—relationships mattered most. Through the benevolent relationships established with Samaranch and Primo Nebiolo, the czar of international track and field, Dassler's new undertaking continued in the 1980s with alliances between ISL, the Olympic Games, and the International Amateur Athletics Federation (IAAF).

When Horst Dassler died on April 10, 1987, he was fifty-one years old, at the height of his power in the world of sports apparel and equipment manufacturing and commercial sponsorship. His Adidas firm employed more than twelve thousand people worldwide, generating an annual turnover in excess of $2.2 billion, manufactured more than four hundred sporting items, including 250,000 pairs of shoes per week. About Horst Dassler's legacy in world sport matters, Nally, his former partner, may have said it best: "Horst became the puppet master of the sporting world, pulling the strings to create massive changes, the pinnacle of which is his legacy of control of the modern Olympic Games. . . . Behind the scenes he would know whatever had happened it had happened entirely to plan."[70]

TOP's Wobbly Foundations and the Chase for the TOP I Sponsors

Soon after Hempel sent his Christmas greetings and the Borghese lithograph to Samaranch, Peter Ueberroth, president of the 1984 Los Angeles Organizing Committee, and Gary Hite, Coca-Cola's manager of International Sports/Consumer Promotions, consulted Dick Pound about how such an ISL-inspired program might be structured for the IOC. In light of its collaboration with Dassler on the FIFA deal, Coca-Cola's vast global sport sponsorship program was increasingly tied to ISL. Pound, now on the Executive Board, and in charge of television rights negotiations seemed an appropriate sounding board for the two men. He saw promise in the idea, especially if Adidas's worldwide contacts and infrastructure were leveraged. Though Pound knew FIFA could muscle its national federations to "toe the line," the IOC had no such hold on the NOCs, especially those in the few countries able to generate significant sponsorship revenue. In short, the TOP concept would be seen as a threat to their financial bottom lines. But, with little to lose Pound saw no danger in letting Dassler explore the idea. This was the substance of his counsel for Samaranch, who subsequently authorized Dassler to press forward. Monique Berlioux was delegated as the IOC's contact person.

The IOC Session's approval of ISL's proposed project on the recommendation of the New Sources of Financing Commission and the Executive Board in March 1983 marked a major coup for Dassler. The decision, in the absence of a tender process, did little to endear the IOC to trailblazers in sports marketing, such as Dassler's former partner, and now rival, Patrick Nally, founder of West Nally, and Mark McCormack, founder and chairman of International Management Group. Both were closed out from discussions on how their firms might have approached such a venture. The IOC and ISL signed a preliminary agreement on June 2, 1983.[71]

In the face of a number of challenges, it would be another two years before a final agreement between the IOC and ISL was inked. First, if the Intelicense debacle taught the IOC anything, it was the need for access to the U.S. market as a fundamental element of any global sponsorship program tied to the Olympics.

The USOC, relying on its rights enshrined in the ASA, leveraged them with vigor and authority. It would receive 15 percent of the revenue accrued by the program after ISL's broker's fee had been paid out. Second, there was a steep learning curve for all those IOC and ISL officials engaged in launching the program: "People look back now at the TOP program, and you look at [its] phenomenal success, and what sort of business analysis and everything that must have gone into it at the beginning," stated Michael Payne, whom Dassler hired from West Nally to serve as ISL's Olympic project director. But no such business analysis existed. "We were making it up," he laughed.[72] Third, Monique Berlioux was less than enthusiastic about the concept, or ceding power, and was unwilling to permit ISL the authority to reach deals on the IOC's behalf. Everything required her approval, a caveat that was hardly conducive to blazing a path forward.

Pound voiced deep concerns about Berlioux's shortcomings as the IOC's point person on the ISL file: the constraints she placed on ISL's negotiators and her tendency not to deliver updated TOP-related contracts to the IOC Executive Board for consideration. As well, he expressed his doubts about the program's chances for success. Samaranch told him bluntly at the Executive Board meeting in Calgary in early 1985 that the task to see TOP across the finish line was his. Wait a minute, thought Pound, that's not a job I want—I'm just trying to identify challenges we face! Samaranch, unmoved, declared it was Pound's assignment to remove any obstacles. Pound soon empowered ISL to make handshake deals with sponsors that could be later finalized in face-to-face meetings between company executives and members of the IOC's leadership team. This afforded the likes of Jürgen Lenz, ISL's deputy CEO, and his energetic salesman and principal foot soldier in the U.S. market, Rob Prazmark, a more secure and credible foundation for discussions with interested executives.[73] The final agreement between the IOC and ISL was signed on May 28, 1985, an event triggered by the (long-elusive) resolution of negotiations with USOC officials. Within the week, Samaranch relieved Berlioux of her duties as IOC director.

Michael Payne

We met with Michael Payne at his Lausanne home office in March 2016. Our interview was wide ranging, covering the rise of the TOP program, past strategy in television negotiations, the efforts of Juan Antonio Samaranch, Jacques Rogge, and Thomas Bach in overseeing the IOC's revenue-generation efforts, and the morass that was the Salt Lake City bid scandal.[74] His service as ISL's point person in establishing TOP predated his tenure as IOC marketing director. He and Pound functioned well in tandem to effect Samaranch's vision to develop a second meaningful revenue stream to lessen the organization's near-complete dependence on television rights fees.

Payne is chairman and CEO of Payne Sports Media Strategies and advises various organizations, including a number of International Sport Federations (IFs) and even a few bid committees seeking the right to host the Olympic Games (notably London 2012, Rio 2016, and Los Angeles 2028). For fourteen years following his departure from the IOC, he was in the employ of Formula One Group but stepped aside in early 2017 when Bernie Ecclestone's run as CEO ended. He has served as an adviser to Sir Martin Sorrell, the former CEO of WPP, a major player in marketing communications around the globe.[75] In January 2017 he concluded a year's work in association with Shankai Sports in bringing e-commerce giant Alibaba and the IOC together through the former's TOP sponsorship running through 2028,[76] and he aided in brokering existing Olympic television contracts in Brazil and Australia. He has found time also to serve as an industry columnist for *CNN*, *BBC World*, *Fortune*, *FT*, and *Japan Yomiuri Shimbun*.[77]

Payne spent many days in his young adult life as an aspirant for the British Ski team and, in the mid-1970s, as a professional in the fledgling sport of freestyle skiing, or, as he termed it, the "hot dogging" circuit. He was Britain's professional freestyle king for two years. As an avid collector of books on the subject of mountains, and as a recreational skier, Payne still has an affinity for alpine settings. In fact, as he settled in behind his desk on the day of our interview, his weathered face showed the effect of snow-reflected sun rays after eight hours in the Alps the day before.

Payne readily admits that his professional path was somewhat unusual in that he never attended university. As he entered adulthood, a measure of good fortune and timing tied to the emergence of the sport sponsorship industry galvanized his energy and initiative. Prompted by his recognition that he was far more adept at generating personal sponsorships for himself and his fellow "hot doggers" than at championship skiing, he gravitated toward the business side of sport. This led him to join West Nally, a pioneering leader of sports-event marketing. Now firmly embedded in the business of sport, Payne joined ISL to help develop TOP.[78] It was from his association with ISL that Payne's expertise came to the attention of Juan Antonio Samaranch and the Olympic Movement. In 1989 he joined the IOC headquarters staff at the Château de Vidy as marketing director.

In considering Payne's tenure in Lausanne, *The Times*'s Steven Downes offered that his leadership helped grow "the Olympic brand from what was essentially an amateur, Chariots of Fire–style operation, to become a business with a multibillion annual turnover."[79] His skill as a salesman underpinned his reputation: "[Payne] could sell sand to the Saudis," observed one colleague.[80] Those skills were sorely put to the test in the earliest days of his work on the TOP venture.

Visa Lends Stability to the Enterprise

In June 2010 a cadre of IOC and marketing community officials descended on Lausanne to reminisce and swap stories about TOP's humble beginnings twenty-five years earlier. Though Coca-Cola's commitment gave some visibility and heft to the IOC/ISL collaborative effort, those selling the sponsorship deals in forty-four prospective product categories[81] struggled to get CEOs to sign on the dotted line. Rob Prazmark, formerly a member of ABC's sales force, encountered resistance to what were perceived as ISL's exorbitant demands. Samaranch's missives to executives affiliated with the likes of Motorola, Campbell Soup, AT&T, and Merrill Lynch yielded nothing.[82] Kodak's decision to join Coca-Cola impressed few observers. The sponsor community judged it as simply an effort to swiftly counter competitor Fuji Film's gains made in the context of the Los Angeles Olympics, as opposed to Kodak's faith in TOP's merits and future. Federal Express joined, but any momentum achieved soon dissipated. Dentsu was striking out in Japan, and none of the quartet of manufacturing giants in South Korea—Hyundai, Daewoo, Goldstar, and Samsung—stepped up.

American Express (Amex), the prized jewel and major target within the credit card category, dismissed Prazmark's approach, though it did ask for the right of first refusal if a competitor expressed interest.[83] ISL declined the request, and Amex walked away from a chance to lock up the credit card category for $9 million. "They told us to get lost," offered Pound.[84] "They were so arrogant about their brand," recounted Prazmark.[85] Amex, planning to wait things out for a price drop, harbored doubts about TOP's global financial prospects. Its executives believed Amex could leverage the few major markets of real value to the company when the IOC and ISL conceded TOP's failure as a global concept.[86]

Progress was bleak, but Lenz, undeterred, stubbornly pressed forward. "Many a weaker soul would have folded his cards,"[87] concedes Payne. Prazmark, too, stayed the course. He kept knocking on doors. Blessed with a "pitchman's gift," Prazmark, a graduate of Buffalo's Canisius College and now president (and founder) of 21 Sports and Entertainment Marketing Group and a recognized leader in global sport sponsorship, displayed determination. In terms of his approach to sales, "They don't mean 'no' until they tell you 'no' four times," says Prazmark. "The first time they must not have understood what you were presenting. The second time they say 'no' is usually a request for information. The third time, they are negotiating with you and really mean 'yes.' But if they still say 'no' by the fourth time, they don't see the value in your proposition."[88] Citibank–Diners Club, following Amex's lead, sent Prazmark out the door. Then the tide turned. Having scratched Amex and Citibank–Diners Club from his list, Prazmark called Jan Soderstrom, Visa's vice president of marketing.

Soderstrom had recently moved to Visa from Atari Corporation, a maker of entertainment electronics products and, interestingly, a sponsor of the 1984 Los Angeles Olympics. Soderstrom believed her former employer drew little benefit from its financial outlay in Los Angeles, but she was with Visa now, and her new company was intent on making major inroads against Amex, the industry king. John Bennett, Visa's senior vice president of marketing, saw a means of edging Visa forward in the international marketplace, but the company's board of directors thought the price too steep. Bennett laid his cards on the table. A TOP sponsorship, he said, presented Visa an opportunity to "stick the blade into the ribs of American Express." With Visa's board, Bennett's line "was brutal, but persuasive," recalled Payne.[89]

Visa and ISL officials convened in New York to discuss a deal. Much to ISL's surprise (and delight), Visa lobbied ISL's executives on the merits of bringing Visa on board. ISL's representatives had anticipated a need to sell Visa officials on the attractiveness of a TOP contract. By April 1986, the basis for an agreement existed.[90] The two teams hammered out a final deal for $14.5 million, signed on July 21, 1986.[91] It proved a game changer for Visa. Worldwide sales ballooned 18 percent in three years, exceeding company forecasts by 6 percent. Visa jumped from third to first in the credit card market.

There were many long faces in the executive suites at Amex. In 1996 James Robinson III, retired chairman and CEO of Amex, ruefully conceded that the decision to spurn ISL's approach "was one of the worst, if not the worst mistake that he made [during his career] at Amex."[92] Though clearly not entirely attributable to its TOP-sponsor status, Visa's affiliation with the Olympic Movement aided its thirty-year journey of growth within the credit card market. From 148 million credit cards in 1986, it boasted 3.2 billion in 2017. Over the same time period, its global market share jumped from 20 percent to 68 percent (based on sales volume) and its number of merchant locations climbed from 5.4 million to more than 40 million.[93]

Visa's deal, on the heels of ISL's failed discussions with Amex, offered a powerful and timely "signal" to the marketplace.[94] Agreements with 3M, Time (later Time/Sports Illustrated), Brother, Philips, and Matsushita followed over the next two years and, together with the previously signed contracts, generated a total of $96 million. Calgary, Seoul, 159 NOCs, and the IOC shared the money. It wasn't the $200 million that ISL officials targeted, but it was a tidy sum, and something to build on. Successive TOP cycles, featuring charter members of the program, Coca-Cola, Visa, and Panasonic (formerly Matsushita), together with a host of other companies seeking an international marketing platform at various junctures over the previous three decades, such as John Hancock (TOP III–V), Samsung (IV–), and Kodak (I–VI), delivered $172 million (II, 1989–1992), $279 million (III,

Pictured from left in 1997, VISA executives John Bennett and Jan Soderstrom, IOC president Juan Antonio Samaranch, Dick Pound, and Michael Payne. Bennett and Soderstrom were instrumental in seizing the credit card category for VISA in the fledgling TOP program in the mid-1980s when American Express passed on the opportunity. (© 1997 / International Olympic Committee (IOC) / Giulio Locatelli. Photo courtesy of the IOC.)

1993–1996), $579 million (IV, 1997–2000), $663 million (V, 2001–2004), $866 million (VI, 2005–2008), $950 million (VII, 2009–2012), and slightly more than $1 billion in conjunction with the 2014 Sochi Olympic Winter Games and 2016 Rio Olympics (VIII, 2013–2016).[95] Recent megadeals with Toyota (2015) and Alibaba (2017) are in place, and with some other sponsors now paying $200 million for four years,[96] it is clear TOP commands valuable traction for today's multinationals.

Closing Thoughts

Horst Dassler and TOP transformed the financial underpinnings of the IOC and the wider Olympic Movement and forever altered the flow of Olympic-related revenue to Organizing Committees. Many have questioned, challenged, or excoriated his methods, but there is little question that Dassler understood international sport and its value as a marketing vehicle to multinational corporations in an increasingly global marketplace. By the 1980s, wrote Deborah Philips and Garry Whannel, "[he became] the central figure in a web of mutually linked interests; his power was considerable."[97]

An examination of his character and historical legacy reveals that Dassler's cutthroat competitive nature, bred by years of battling chief rival Puma (owned by his uncle and father's older brother, Rudolf), was further underscored by his preference for working in the shadows. With ISL he exploited his vast knowledge of the sport industry acquired over the years as part of his father Adolf's Adidas operations and his past collaboration with Patrick Nally, as well as the personal relationships he pursued with leaders in international sport and those he viewed as future allies whose careers and standing he advanced. Nally was blunt: "From the very beginning, Horst has bought people." Monique Berlioux considered him "the real boss of world sports."[98] "There was a lot of controversy as to what his power was and what he could and couldn't do," offered Ollan Cassell, former executive director of the Athletics Congress (now USA Track & Field), the national federation for track and field in the U.S. "He did so many things people didn't know about that it is impossible to judge what the impact of his death will be." Cassell held that Dassler was a stabilizing force for an Olympic world beset by recent boycotts, and Dassler's absence invited uncertainty. "Without Adidas' money or Horst's influence, there could be big trouble if another Olympic boycott occurs," stated Cassell at the time of Dassler's passing. "He had the ability to pull everything together."[99]

Following Dassler's death, the caliber of leadership at ISL slipped. Both Pound and Payne lost confidence in ISL's fitness to drive TOP forward. In the mid-1990s they met with Samaranch and informed him of their concerns. "The leadership of ISL doesn't understand the business," they told him. They recommended parting ways. Samaranch was uneasy and reluctant. "You realize this is going to cause me all kinds of problems," he said. "I'm going to get all kinds of pressure from the Dassler family, [Horst's] sisters and all that. Are you sure about that?"[100] Though unaware of the festering crisis encompassing ISL's connections with FIFA, or predicting ISL's bankruptcy a few years later, Pound and Payne knew a different course was needed for the IOC. Samaranch accepted their advice, and the IOC moved on. Years later, in the wake of ISL's bankruptcy in 2001, a grateful Samaranch expressed much appreciation for the advice.[101]

As a means of softening the blow for ISL and facilitating the divorce, Pound and Payne "engineered it so that it looked like ISL was firing us, rather than vice versa." IOC and ISL negotiators finalized the terms of the high profile split on the sidelines of the IOC Executive Board meetings in Nagano, Japan in 1995. Huddled around a table on small barstools, ISL officials Jean-Marie Weber and Christophe Malms accepted the terms forwarded by Pound, Payne, and François Carrard because they feared the possible fallout for ISL on the renewal of its contract with FIFA. Payne believes that the spending spree ISL engaged in following the IOC's action, meant to prop up its image as a global leader in the industry, did little for its longer-term financial picture and contributed to its eventual demise.[102]

Meridian Management S.A., a U.S.– and Swiss-based agency headed by Laurent Scharapan and Chris Welton, managed the TOP program from 1996 through 2004, but by 2004 the IOC believed it best to manage its own marketing program and placed its operations in-house. Pound, who stepped aside from leading the IOC's Marketing Commission following his loss to Jacques Rogge for the IOC presidency (2001), had moved on with his role as the founding president of the World Anti-Doping Agency. In 2005 Meridian, partly owned by the IOC, morphed into IOC Television & Marketing Services S.A., a wholly owned subsidiary of the IOC, under the direction of Timo Lumme. The process was not a smooth one. Earlier, Payne offered three options to Rogge regarding the IOC's marketing operations and its ties to Meridian: "You can maintain the status quo, you can evolve, or you can decide you want to bring it all in-house." Rogge opted for the latter. Payne supported the decision but warned Rogge and Marketing Commission chairman Gerhard Heiberg that Meridian would not greet such news favorably, which would naturally stir up its allies within the sponsor community. The IOC's action needed to be decisive, counseled Payne, but Heiberg expressed second thoughts after the plan was initiated, which resulted in added complications.[103] This matter, along with a desire for new challenges, contributed to Payne's decision to depart the IOC, which in turn triggered Lumme's hiring.

The clear effort to link the Olympics with "big business" through the development of the TOP program troubled those who longed for an era in Olympic history long past. Federal governments were no longer willing to bankroll the staging of Olympic festivals. The IOC's near-total dependence on television rights fees in an era charged with the prospect of boycotts inspired by world geopolitics invited much risk. Other sources of revenue had to be mined. Dassler showed the IOC the way to do just that. At the close of TOP VIII following the 2016 Rio Olympics, the total revenue raised for the Olympic Movement since TOP's inception in 1985 sat at $4.6 billion and counting.

CHAPTER 7

The Broadcast Marketing Agreement

The BMA: An Overview

In March 1986, six months after the USOC insisted that the IOC cede it a 20 percent share of U.S. television revenue if broadcast rights holders and commercial advertisers continued the practice of employing the Olympic rings as part of a network composite logo or in commercials on Olympic telecasts, the two sides signed the Broadcast Marketing Agreement (BMA). The Amateur Sports Act (ASA) served as the lever for the USOC's demands, as it had in guiding the USOC's approach in relation to the evolution of TOP. While the IOC rationalized its decision to grant 15 percent of the TOP revenue to the USOC (this share was later elevated to 18.5 percent and then 20 percent) because of the preponderance of U.S.-based multinational companies that made up TOP's cohort of sponsors, the USOC's action in wielding the ASA in connection with U.S. television broadcasts irked them.

However, the IOC realized it had little chance of successfully challenging the USOC's rights in a U.S. court. The U.S. legal system had spoken with respect to the USOC's firm grasp on its rights in accordance with the terms of the ASA. The Intelicense case represented a recent example. In signing the BMA, the IOC agreed to transfer 10 percent of the U.S. Olympic television contract to the USOC in perpetuity. The initial (10 percent) USOC share was activated for the rights fees paid for the 1992 Olympic Winter and Summer Games. For 1988 the IOC and the Seoul and Calgary OCOGs shelled out $5 million each, so as not to unduly pull larger amounts of previously negotiated television revenue from the operations in South Korea and Canada. In the years ahead, this share grew to 12.75 percent. As the twenty-first century opened, many within the world's National Olympic Committee (NOC) community were at odds with the USOC over its share of Olympic commercial revenue, revenue that far exceeded anything received by any of the other NOCs.

European IOC members, in particular, grew to resent the enormous sums transferred to Colorado Springs. Whispers for change in the 1990s soon became full-throated calls for redress. However, USOC officials were unflinching, stout defenders of the USOC's share of Olympic commercial revenue. Numerous attempts to bridge the divide on the revenue issue failed. It took more than twenty-five years before the IOC and the USOC found common ground in establishing a revised distribution formula for television and corporate sponsorship dollars in 2012.

This chapter examines the early days in the IOC and USOC's fractious relations concerning television money that resulted in the genesis of the BMA and the BMA's subsequent influence on IOC/USOC relations over the ensuing decade. Its initial focus falls on the teamwork exhibited by Robert Kane, the USOC's former president (1977–1981), and his fellow Cornell University alumnus, and long-time U.S. Representative from New York's 30th District, Barber B. Conable Jr.[1] Their efforts on Capitol Hill advanced discussions concerning the USOC's claim for a share of television money based on its interpretation of the ASA and started the flow of U.S. television dollars directly to the USOC. Kane and Conable collaborated to bring federal legislation before Congress that would have granted the USOC a 10 percent excise tax on all U.S. Olympic television contracts.[2] An excise tax was not an enticing prospect for the IOC. Congress retained the right to increase that tax in future years. In the end, Kane and Conable pushed the IOC to the negotiating table to reach an agreement with USOC officials for the USOC's receipt of 10 percent of the U.S. television contract.[3]

The USOC's efforts to further enhance its share of U.S. television revenue through outreach efforts to members of U.S. Congress in the 1990s—and the IOC's response, primarily managed by Canada's Dick Pound, then an IOC vice president and chairman of the IOC Marketing Commission—provides a window to the splintered interorganizational dynamics. IOC president Juan Antonio Samaranch viewed Pound, a North American, as one well-equipped to deal with the American mindset in discussions concerning the USOC's financial aspirations and the IOC's revenue interests. Samaranch once conceded to the IOC's director general, François Carrard, "I'll never understand the Americans, but Dick Pound knows them, so I let him do it."[4] As we will see, the Samaranch/Pound tandem resembled a good-cop–bad-cop pairing, with Samaranch more conciliatory toward the USOC's financial aspirations than Pound.

Robert Kane, the USOC, and Revenue Goals

Robert Kane's tenure as USOC president is best remembered for his need to navigate the USOC's interests during the tumultuous times surrounding the American Olympic team's withdrawal from the 1980 Moscow Olympic Games and his work involved in pressing forward the USOC's priorities when Congress established the ASA. Kane was a Cornell man through and through, having earned his bachelor of science degree in 1934, followed by service as the school's director of athletics (1944–1971) and later its dean of athletics (1971–1976). He also served on Cornell's board of trustees. A three-year member of Cornell's track and field team, he once held its 200m and 400m records (the former until 1977). Kane began his career in U.S. Olympic administration in 1951, culminating in his assumption of presidential duties in 1977.

As USOC president, Kane firmly believed that too much U.S.-generated Olympic revenue departed American shores, compromising the execution of the USOC's mandate. Particularly, the amount of U.S. money flowing to the Soviet Union in advance of the 1980 Olympics deeply bothered him, while the USOC and American

Robert Kane, third from left, appears with his Cornell University 880-yard relay teammates, R. E. Linders, J. L. Messersmith, and R. A. Scallan, who won at the prestigious Penn Relays in 1934 in Philadelphia, Pennsylvania, USA, in a time of 1:27.8. (Archives picture collection, #13–6–2497, APC# 10722. Photo courtesy of the Division of Rare and Manuscript Collections, Cornell University Library.)

athletes received "nothing."[5] In this assertion, Kane was shading the truth: the USOC did, at the time, receive a portion of the minimum 11.1 percent of global television revenue distributed to the NOCs. But in real terms, the sum was admittedly small.

Kane set aside his pursuit of a share of U.S. television money for a few years because of the USOC's unique revenue sharing agreement with Peter Ueberroth's 1984 Los Angeles Organizing Committee. In the aftermath of the 1984 Los Angeles Olympics, Kane pressed U.S. television companies to funnel 10 percent of the value of their contracts for the 1988 Olympics to the USOC. The networks, fearing the negative effect of such action on their relationship with the IOC, declined to act.[6] Undeterred, Kane contacted his local congressman, Sam Stratton, "but failed to get a hearing." Admittedly desperate, Kane approached Barber Conable to seek his aid and counsel in enticing Congress to take action on the USOC's behalf.[7] Conable had been sympathetic to the USOC's and Los Angeles' efforts to establish a coin program in association with the U.S. Mint in advance of the Los Angeles Olympics.[8] Could Kane count on his support of the USOC's financial goals tied to U.S. Olympic television contracts?

Enter Barber Conable

Robert Kane easily fits into anyone's popular narrative dealing with U.S. Olympic affairs in the late 1970s and early 1980s given his role as the USOC's president from 1977 through January 1981. The contributions of Kane's friend Barber Conable, a World War II Marine, veteran of the Battle of Iwo Jima, a distinguished veteran of Washington politics, and ranking Republican on the House Ways and Means Committee at the time of his retirement in 1985, are less well known.

Born in Warsaw, New York, in 1922, Barber Benjamin Conable Jr. was named after his father. A product of "small town, rural values of western New York,"[9] "Bunt," as his parents nicknamed him, spent his teenage years living on a farm that his father, the county judge, purchased because he believed Franklin D. Roosevelt was bent on destroying the country. The farm served as the elder Conable's insurance policy for his family during the grim years of the Great Depression.

An A student in high school, the junior- and senior-class president, and captain of the football team, Conable earned a bachelor's degree in medieval history from Cornell in 1942 and his law degree six years later, following his military service. He entered the U.S. House of Representatives in 1965, applying himself to the role with much energy. Conable made a special commitment to maintaining communication with his constituents through well-crafted newsletters detailing legislative developments. A strong supporter of Richard Nixon's policies, Conable was dismayed by the president's handling of Watergate. In fact, Conable is credited

Barber Conable, pictured in 1992, ably assisted Robert Kane in advancing the USOC's financial claim to a share of U.S. Olympic television revenue through congressional channels in the 1980s. The threat of an excise tax on U.S. Olympic television deals via federal legislation payable to the USOC ultimately resulted in the establishment of the Broadcast Marketing Agreement between the IOC and USOC. (Cornell University Public Affairs Records Deceased Alumni Files, Collection 41-2-877, box 450. Photo courtesy of the Division of Rare and Manuscript Collections, Cornell University Library.)

with being the creator of the term "smoking gun," an addition to the political lexicon that has come to describe the taped conversations of June 23, 1972, that set Nixon on a path to resignation.[10] A highly respected legislator on both sides of the aisle, he was voted "most respected member" of the House of Representatives in 1984 as he prepared to step down after twenty years of service. Political commentator George Will, never one to dispense gratuitous praise, said, "There will never be a better congressman."[11]

In 1985, in the months before he took up his appointment as president of the World Bank, Conable entered the Olympic storyline by heeding Kane's call for assistance in navigating the Capitol's corridors. Conable suggested that Kane reach out to two of his former colleagues on the House Ways and Means Committee, Sam Gibbons (D-Florida) and William Frenzel (R-Minnesota), but they turned aside Kane's pleadings that the USOC deserved revenue from an excise tax on U.S. Olympic television contracts.[12] Temporarily stalled, Conable found a more engaged advocate on the Ways and Means Committee, Michigan's Guy Vander Jagt. Vander Jagt's willingness to usher legislation through Washington's political labyrinth gave Kane "a great lift."[13] Vander Jagt created H.R. 3770, designed "to amend the Internal Revenue Code of 1954 to provide funding for the United States Olympic Committee by imposing an excise tax on amounts paid for United States television and radio broadcast rights for Olympic events."[14] However, momentum stalled.

The USOC's executive director, George Miller, was well informed on Kane's collaboration with Conable, as well as the difficulties encountered. With Kane's consent, he launched his own strategy to secure a share of U.S. Olympic television revenue for the USOC in September 1985.[15] Mere months removed from the USOC's financial gains tied to the fledgling TOP global corporate sponsorship program, Miller informed the IOC that the USOC required compensation if U.S. Olympic broadcasters wished to make use of a composite logo (a composite logo blends the five Olympic rings with the broadcast network's logo) on their telecasts, and/or if the networks continued to sell advertising time complete with the privilege for advertisers to employ the Olympic rings in their commercials.[16]

George Miller had big shoes to fill when he took over as the USOC's executive director in early 1985. A former combat pilot who served in Vietnam, he retired from the U.S. Air Force in September 1984, holding the post of deputy commander of Strategic Air Command at the close his military tenure. He was sworn in as executive director in February 1985, along with USOC president Jack Kelly,[17] whose term lasted mere weeks before a tragic heart attack resulted in his passing. Miller, a native of McKeesport, Pennsylvania, was chosen over Baaron Pittenger to succeed F. Don Miller (no relation), whose service as executive director spanned the USOC presidencies of Phillip Krumm, Robert Kane, and William E. Simon. Don Miller's efforts were well regarded by many, even revered by some, in terms of their positive effect on the USOC's prominence in the wake of its headquarters move to Colorado Springs, which occurred on his watch.

George Miller's time in Colorado Springs was brief but coincided with a period in which the USOC prospered financially by harnessing the ASA in pursuit of U.S. television money and global sponsorship revenue. He resigned for "personal reasons" after eighteen months on the job, largely because his administrative pairing with Robert Helmick, who replaced Jack Kelly, proved dysfunctional, due in great measure to policy differences. Miller's lack of sport administrative experience was a concern for some. "Being inexperienced in amateur sports," stated Todd Smith, executive director of U.S. Diving, "he had a lot of catching up to do. It's not a good situation," he added, "when you have Bob Helmick and George Miller publicly expressing differences on policy. You should work those out beforehand and have a unified front."[18] "George was a military man, and that's how he wanted to run things," noted another observer. "He was not very flexible. It is easy to see where he and Helmick wouldn't get along."[19]

Miller's brief tenure in the role, especially in the aftermath of the steady hand Don Miller had provided, was not a positive circumstance and touched off a period of instability as Baaron Pittenger (interim on two occasions), Harvey Schiller (who resigned after three weeks on the job in his first casting in the role, but who later served a five-year stint), John Krimsky (interim), Dick Schultz, Norm Blake, Scott Blackmun (interim), and Lloyd Ward all held the office between 1987 and 2003.

Yet there's no denying George Miller's impact on the USOC's financial fortunes. In May 1985, after protracted negotiations, the USOC opened up the U.S. territory to International Sport and Leisure (ISL), the Swiss firm that created TOP. Without the USOC's consent permitting TOP sponsors access to the U.S. market, the program's financial promise (TOP yields more than $1 billion on a quadrennial basis today) would have crumbled. Stan Shefler well understood the American market's importance in the context of his pictogram project. The USOC's posture vis à vis Intelicense and its refusal to grant access to the U.S. market doomed Shefler's initiative.

While IOC officials could justify sharing prospective global sponsorship money with the USOC because of the importance of the U.S. market to TOP, Miller's claim for a portion of U.S. television revenue was another matter.[20] Howard Stupp, the IOC's director of legal affairs (who concluded a thirty-three-year career in the position in January 2018 and now serves as a special legal adviser to the IOC), questioned the USOC's timing and motives: "Why is the USOC now making the claim? Are they genuinely concerned with the well-being of their marketing program and are they trying to protect what is rightfully theirs? Or, are they just being greedy?"[21] Looking back at the USOC's use of the ASA to leverage commercial revenue from the IOC in the 1980s and 1990s, while also confirming the improved state of interorganizational relations today, Stupp stated, "I was always happy with the Amateur Sports Act because it gave [the USOC] great power to protect the Olympic properties . . . but the USOC was not supposed to use that against us. And, I can't say they ever really did, but sometimes they would pull it out and rub it in our face" to advance their negotiating position.[22]

As the years drifted by, Pound, Payne, and others within the IOC, even Stupp, rationalized the terms of the BMA, and the direct payment of 10 percent of the value of U.S. television contracts to the USOC because the U.S. market is the only one in which the IOC sells both the broadcast rights and the rights to the broadcast network to create a composite logo. This second element of the contract package certainly exceeded 10 percent, insists Payne, and given the USOC's rights within the ASA, it made the USOC "a legitimate shareholder." Still, Payne bristles at the manner in which the USOC extracted the BMA through the use of politicians in the U.S. Congress.[23]

In 1985, though, the IOC was not inclined to accommodate the USOC's demand for a share of U.S. Olympic television revenue with or without the ASA's weight behind its argument.[24] However, the IOC's ability to stall in responding to Miller's direct approach took a decided turn when the thrust of Vander Jagt's bill became part of the Tax Reform Act of 1985. Vander Jagt's search for a co-sponsor of H.R. 3770 became unnecessary when Conable informed Kane, "My friends were able to get the specific language of the bill [added to the Tax Reform Act]."[25] With the specter of an excise tax circulating on Capitol Hill, the IOC's position was weakened, and a deal with Miller for a set amount was preferable to a tax measure that might well rise in the future.[26]

A Two-Pronged Approach Pays Dividends for the USOC

Howard Stupp and other IOC officials, most notably Samaranch, were irritated by the USOC's political maneuvering. The situation compounded ill feelings between the two sides arising from the USOC's refusal to share a portion of the surplus from the 1984 Los Angeles Olympics to offset costs of the participating NOCs that delivered additional athletes to compensate for the absence of competitors from the boycotting Communist bloc. Ueberroth, who commenced duties as commissioner of Major League Baseball in October 1984, favored setting aside $6.8 million to reimburse the NOCs for "room, board, and certain services."[27] The LAOOC board of directors approved Ueberroth's plan, but the USOC balked.[28] Ueberroth did not hide his disappointment: "I'm just disappointed. I wanted each country to be able to say it was our guest at the Games. They helped us so much in our time of crisis (with the Soviet boycott) that to refund their payments to us would be the right thing to do.... I still feel this is right. I feel it very strongly. But it's up to the LAOOC and USOC boards."[29] Instead, the USOC parked $4.2 million in a "Friendship Fund," a grant program open to applications from NOCs to aid in the training of their athletes (it was wound down in 1988).

William Simon and Don Miller used the USOC's $110 million share of LAOOC's surplus to establish the U.S. Olympic Foundation (now the U.S. Olympic Endowment), a nonprofit funding agency. Samaranch asserted that such a surplus would not have been possible without the support of the Olympic teams that expended greater revenue in delivering more athletes to Los Angeles. He forcefully questioned USOC officials on this matter.[30] Still, Samaranch believed that Stupp's thought on the necessity for negotiations concerning the distribution of U.S. television money well considered. He tasked Pound to seek a resolution. Samaranch wrote to Pound, "My personal point of view is that we should try to reach an agreement with [the] USOC [on television money] before the respective postures become tougher. I believe you are the right person to propose a project of agreement for which I rely completely upon you."[31]

Pound was unwilling to accede to the USOC's demand for 20 percent of the value of the U.S. television contracts for Calgary, Seoul, and beyond.[32] Ultimately, he, along with fellow IOC members Julian Roosevelt (United States) and James Worrall (Canada), who assisted in the negotiations with USOC officials, recommended to the IOC Executive Board that a 10 percent share on all future contracts be transferred to the USOC, but with the caveat that the USOC lobby congressional authorities to remove the excise tax from the Tax Reform Act of 1985.[33] Pound and IOC officials wished to preempt any excise tax increases by Congress in the future. The USOC Executive Committee, at the urging of George Miller, who cited the need to foster good relations with the IOC, complied. The USOC's wish was communicated to federal legislators.[34]

Pound's delay in moving forward with his recommendation was tied to the nettlesome U.S. television negotiations for the Seoul Olympics. A depressed negotiating environment provided a deep blow to Seoul organizers, who, with much reluctance, settled for the $300 million coaxed out of NBC through Pound's diligent work; they had expected much more. Pound wanted to shelter Calgary and Seoul from significant financial concessions. He devised a means of absenting them from the loss of 10 percent of their U.S. television contracts. The USOC accepted $5 million from each of the IOC, Seoul, and Calgary in lieu of the 10 percent share assigned to the USOC in future years.

Robert Kane and George Miller concluded that the USOC's two-pronged approach, whether by design or good fortune, shifted the leverage in negotiations in its favor, once the excise tax's inclusion in the Tax Reform Act of 1985 occurred. Kane believed the strategy brought the IOC to the negotiating table: "We had strived unavailingly to convince [the IOC]. . . . to grant the USOC a 10 percent share of US TV rights fees [Miller initially asked for 20 percent], but it steadfastly demurred. When the Tax Reform Act of 1985 appeared ripe for passage," wrote Kane, "blockage was suddenly and unexpectedly released."[35] George Miller shared Kane's view.[36]

George Miller, in extending thanks to Barber Conable, noted that the IOC's concession "would never have happened were it not for the Excise Tax." Miller subsequently lauded Kane for his "outstanding work." For his part, Kane understood Conable's key role, writing years later that he "made long distance calls, wrote numerous letters in the USOC cause, but refused to submit a bill. 'My contribution to the Olympic cause,' [Conable told me]."[37] And some contribution it was. In the remaining years of Conable's life alone (he passed away in 2003), the USOC's share of Olympic television revenue from the U.S. Winter and Summer television contracts totaled more than $300 million. In 2004, a year after Conable's death, the share moved to 12.75 percent, with the most recent deal consummated by the IOC and USOC in 2012 shifting the USOC's share beginning in 2020 to a slightly lesser percentage by virtue of a complicated formula.

To judge by the exchange of thoughts between Samaranch, Pound, and Stupp, the IOC was committed to a negotiated agreement with the USOC in late September and early October 1985, weeks before the introduction of Vander Jagt's H.R. 3770. It was not a matter of "if" an agreement with the USOC would be pursued, given the IOC's understanding that the USOC's claim rested on a solid but admittedly frustrating legal foundation, one that would be difficult for a Swiss organization to contest in a U.S. court, but rather "when" and "how much" should be conceded to the USOC. Pound confirmed that the prospect of the excise tax was a "relevant factor" and likely expedited an agreement. However, the USOC, too, was motivated to reach an agreement without the ultimate involvement of U.S. federal politicians. If money flowed from Congress to the USOC, perhaps the levers of congressional control over certain elements of the USOC's operations would also be extended.[38] A concern with protecting its autonomy provided the USOC with excellent reasons to bargain and reach an amicable solution with the IOC.

Kane and Conable's lobbying efforts in Washington, when combined with Miller's use of the ASA, yielded the desired result.[39] The BMA further augmented the USOC's revenue-generating capacity that had been given a recent boost through the launch of TOP. For an organization struggling to attain a measure of financial stability in the 1970s, these events greatly enhanced the USOC's financial outlook. IOC officials came to terms with these concessions in consideration of the overall growth of commercial revenue available with the advent of TOP and the continuing escalation in the value of television contracts, not to mention the percentage of this money emanating from U.S. corporate sources; however, if IOC officials believed that the USOC's financial ambitions were completely fulfilled, they were mistaken.

Dick Pound's Central Role in the 1980s and 1990s

Blessed with a sharp mind and prodigious capacity for work, Richard "Dick" Pound invested much time in effecting Juan Antonio Samaranch's financial vision for the Olympic Games during his presidency by running television rights negotiations (1983–2001) and the IOC's Marketing Commission (1988–2001). Pound was a central figure in IOC affairs beyond those simply tied to finance in the Samaranch era. He served on the Executive Board (1983–1991, 1992–2000) and completed two terms as a vice president (1987–1991, 1996–2000). In the wake of the seismic events at the 1998 Tour de France, when the IOC and wider sporting world acknowledged the need to tackle doping in sport, Pound was tasked to lead the fledgling World Anti-Doping Agency (WADA) and did so as its chairman from 1999 through 2007. He spearheaded the launch of WADA at exactly the same time that he was one of the lynchpin members of the IOC's crisis management team amid the Salt Lake City bid scandal.

A tax lawyer with Stikeman Elliott in Montreal, Pound served as chancellor of storied McGill University from 1999 through 2009, holds honorary degrees from seven Canadian universities, as well as others from institutions in England and China, and was elevated to Companion of the Order of Canada in 2014, the highest level of the Order of Canada that "recognizes outstanding achievement, dedication to the community and service to the country."[40] He sits on the IOC Marketing

(2005–) and Communications (2018–) Commissions, and the WADA Foundation Board (1999–). He also wielded control in 2015 of the first phase of WADA's investigation of systematic state-sponsored doping of Russian athletes.

Born in St. Catharines, Ontario, Pound spent the bulk of his childhood in Ocean Falls, British Columbia, when his father's work (an engineer in the paper industry) took him to Canada's western-most province. There he fished, played baseball, and emerged as an age-group swimmer. Ocean Falls, a small, isolated (now former) pulp- and paper-mill town, sits 480 kilometers north of Vancouver as the crow flies, but traveling there was no easy feat: it took thirty-six hours by car during Pound's childhood and still requires a fifteen-hour-drive (1,004 km) from British Columbia's largest city today. Ocean Falls, in part due to its location next to water and parents' expectations that all children needed to learn to swim for their own safety, boasted a swimming culture. With perhaps a population of three thousand in its boom years, the town placed at least one swimmer on each Canadian Olympic team from 1948 to 1976.[41]

When Pound was fifteen, his father's job necessitated a move to Montreal. He continued to hone his swimming talent at the Montreal Amateur Athletic Association[42] and surged forward in Canada's competitive swimming community, reaching the finals of two Olympic events in Rome (1960), while later winning a gold, two silver, and a bronze medal at the 1962 Commonwealth Games. He earned a bachelor's degree in commerce from McGill in 1962, his law degree from the same institution in 1967. His service to the Olympic Movement began in earnest with his fourteen years of executive duties with the Canadian Olympic Committee, first as secretary general (1968–1977) and then as president (1977–1982). He was co-opted to the IOC in 1978. After his election in 1980, Samaranch soon deduced that Pound's abilities and energy deserved a place within his administration. Despite Pound's mere five years as an IOC member, Samaranch ushered him onto the Executive Board through the personal support of his candidacy. With respect to the IOC's revenue generation portfolio in the early 1980s, Monique Berlioux's star plummeted as a result of Samaranch's growing loss of confidence in her ability to manage the IOC's affairs. In that regard, Pound swiftly shouldered Berlioux's significant former duties.

Ed Waitzer, a colleague at Pound's law firm, marveled at Pound's ability to juggle his heavy daily professional workload with the extensive service to the IOC, as well as his writing of history books. "He's one of the most varied guys I know," commented Waitzer. "He's in a part of law that changes from day to day. . . . Then he has this Olympic hat, and he writes books. Something that most people see as a major event in their lives, he just tosses off on airplanes. . . . Does time, in some Einsteinian way, slow down for him as it does not for the rest of us?" wondered Waitzer.[43] When given a chance to respond to Waitzer's musings, Pound smiled: "The time's there. It's just a matter of not pissing it away."[44] John Cleghorn, former chairman and CEO of the Royal Bank of Canada, paid tribute to Pound's "intelligence and photographic memory." "He is extremely well-organized and can compartmentalize his time. He never shows stress," observed Cleghorn, "and his self-deprecating wit and natural humour seem to keep him in balance."[45]

With Pound as his point man on financial matters, Samaranch effected a deliberate good-cop–bad-cop strategy with Pound. On occasion, in floating policy initiatives to the IOC membership, "Samaranch would ask me to try something out," Pound said, "to test the reaction, to stretch responses." If there was blowback, "then [Samaranch] could retreat behind a defensive excuse that I was young and impulsive. I didn't mind, I could ride with that, and we were pursuing the same objectives."[46] Samaranch respected Pound's abilities and forthright expression of his views, even when he differed with Samaranch's own approach to certain matters. But having too many independent thinkers on the Executive Board was deliberately avoided. Samaranch needed to know he had a majority that would follow his lead at all times.

Though Samaranch was more amenable to pursuing accommodation with the Americans, Pound sparred repeatedly with USOC officials such as Harvey Schiller,

Juan Antonio Samaranch and Dick Pound chat during a break in a meeting of the IOC Executive Board in Seoul in 1986. (© 1986 / International Olympic Committee (IOC) / Albert Riethausen. Photo courtesy of the IOC.)

Dick Schultz, and John Krimsky over revenue distribution. For the IOC, and the wider Olympic Movement, the Samaranch/Pound partnership was one that forever altered the financial foundation of the IOC and, in turn, reaped much revenue for the NOCs, International Sport Federations (IFs), and local Organizing Committees (OCOGs).

Though a strong candidate to succeed Samaranch, Pound lacked a European birth certificate, a virtual necessity for the position. Eight of history's nine IOC presidents, including incumbent Thomas Bach, have been Europeans. In 1995 Pound opposed Samaranch's effort (ultimately successful) to extend the IOC member age limit to eighty. This translated into Samaranch's serving through the 2000 Sydney Olympics. Pound struggled to accept Samaranch's support of Rogge in the presidential campaign, especially following the yeoman efforts he made to salvage the IOC's tarnished reputation and to shield Samaranch from calls for his resignation in the wake of revelations concerning the Salt Lake City bid scandal. Yet he maintained a healthy admiration for the Spaniard's commitment to the Olympic Movement: "He took a very badly fragmented, disorganized and impecunious organization and built it into a universal, united and financially and politically independent organization that has credibility, not only in the world of sport, but also in political circles. That's an enormous achievement to accomplish in 20 years."[47]

The McMillen Bill

In the 1990s, the USOC initiated two major efforts in Washington to enhance the financial terms of the BMA. Dick Pound stood in the way. In both cases, the appeal to congressional allies for assistance followed failed attempts by USOC officials to negotiate an improvement on its 10 percent share. Though the USOC lobbied for 30 percent of global TOP revenue, it eventually settled for 15 percent. With ensuing TOP cycles, the USOC argued that its continued participation necessitated the transfer of an enhanced percentage of the generated revenue to Colorado Springs. While IOC/USOC discussions on these matters were not tension free, and the USOC's share grew to 18.5 percent and then topped out at 20 percent of total TOP revenues,[48] the IOC understood that without the USOC's participation the TOP program, and the money that it produced for the world's other NOCs, would not exist.[49] The USOC's share of U.S. television revenue prompted far more contentious discussions.

USOC officials pressed for 20 percent of U.S. television contracts in 1989 and 1990, but Pound dismissed their entreaties. A strong signal that Congress might take renewed interest in the subject emerged when the Brookings Institution published an article focusing on the disparity between television rights fees paid by U.S. broadcasters and those in other regions, especially heavily populated Western Europe.[50] For instance, the 1988 Calgary negotiations for U.S. television rights, managed by Pound and Barry Frank, a former CBS Sports executive, proved wildly successful. The utilization of a sealed-bid process secured ABC's eye-popping $309 million offer. However, Samaranch, committed to blanket television coverage in Europe, was unwilling to explore the possibilities offered by emerging private television companies. He did not transfer control of European negotiations to Pound, whom he knew would introduce such rival bidders to the process as a means of lessening the disparity that angered USOC officials and U.S. television executives. Samaranch personally retained control over European negotiations, assisted by Marc Hodler, a member of the IOC Executive Board. EBU acquired the Western European rights to the 1988 Calgary Olympics for $5.7 million.

A well-rehearsed approach unfolded in EBU's discussions with Hodler and Samaranch. The EBU argued that it operated as a public broadcaster solely on money provided by federal governments within its territory and therefore did not have the revenue resources available to U.S. networks through the sale of commercial advertising. EBU's head of sports programming, Richard Bunn, matter-of-factly informed Robert Lawrence and Jeffrey Pellegrom (authors of the aforementioned Brookings Institution article, "Fool's Gold: How America Pays to Lose in the Olympics") that "unlike the Americans, we don't bid for the rights to the games; we negotiate."[51] CBS shelled out $243 million for U.S. rights to the 1992 Albertville Games, while EBU paid a mere $18 million. The USOC denied any involvement in the production of Lawrence and Pellegrom's article, but Lausanne officials were suspicious. Within the IOC's Executive Board chambers, Pound lamented EBU's "sweetheart deals."[52] Before the close of 1989, additional U.S. and Western European Olympic contracts further eroded his ability to deal with the USOC. What is more, the contracts provided additional cause for Congress, with prodding from USOC and U.S. television executives, to take action.[53]

However, as bidding to stage the 1996 Summer Olympics entered its late phases in 1990, the USOC retreated from applying further pressure on the IOC. Officials in Lausanne realized that the USOC did not wish to poison the atmosphere with financial demands while Atlanta's bid was under consideration. Within weeks of the IOC's decision in September 1990 to award Atlanta the right to host the 1996 Centennial Games, the effects of lobbying on Capitol Hill by representatives of the U.S. television industry and the USOC burst forth in the House of Representatives. Tom McMillen (D-Maryland), a former basketball Olympian, introduced the Olympic Television Broadcast Act.

From an IOC perspective, three troubling elements formed the foundation for the McMillen bill: U.S. television broadcasters could not interrupt live coverage of an Olympic event with a commercial; the responsibility for negotiating U.S. Olympic television contracts would be transferred from the IOC to the USOC; and U.S. television networks would be granted an exemption from the Sherman Anti-trust Act, thereby permitting them to submit a pooled bid. Any limitations placed on advertising would exert considerable drag on offers from U.S. television networks because of the restraint placed on their ability to recoup their rights fee from the sale of commercial time. Second, if the USOC controlled negotiations, it could set its share of the contract, and it surely would be greater than 10 percent. Finally, a pooled bid from the U.S. networks, effectively absent of a competitive process, would have a deleterious effect on the amount of money from the U.S. market.[54]

Following a trip to Washington for a face-to-face meeting with McMillen in January 1991, Pound pointed to rough waters ahead and counseled Samaranch on the need to push the value of European television contracts.[55] Pound knew that the McMillen bill resulted from Samaranch's unwillingness to tackle the alarming disparity between sums paid by the U.S. networks and those in other television markets, especially Europe. "If the networks are really involved in this," wrote Pound in reference to the call for an exemption to the Sherman Anti-trust Act, "then our problem will be exacerbated [and] until we show that other parts of the world are approaching U.S. levels on a per capita or other appropriate measure, we can expect little sympathy from within the U.S."[56] McMillen argued that the United States, in any number of global ventures, including military actions such as the one (Operation Desert Storm) pending in the Middle East to dislodge Saddam Hussein's forces from Kuwait, accepted a disproportionate financial load. His bill, he believed, would have a trickle-down effect for U.S. consumers in that prices charged for products sold by companies who were required to pay immense sums for advertising time on Olympic telecasts (in light of the needs of the broadcasters paying large rights fees) would be constrained.

Pound framed his hour-long session with McMillen as "cordial" and "worthwhile." Their discussion, he recounted, "without the filter of the USOC," proved useful. Pound told McMillen of the USOC's current share of Olympic commercial revenue and its unique position in this regard compared to the world's other NOCs. He floated the possible negative reaction of IOC members resulting from his bill as they prepared to vote on the host city for the 1998 Olympic Winter Games, specifically in regard to Salt Lake City's candidacy. Reflecting later, Pound mused that it might be time to hire someone to monitor developments in Washington with an eye to providing advice as to how best to protect the IOC's interests. The USOC's conniving with Washington politicians, he asserted, demonstrated that "our interests at this time are not/not the same as those of the USOC."[57]

USOC president (and IOC Executive Board member) Robert Helmick[58] offered a conciliatory tone concerning the U.S. television market and the McMillen bill. Helmick and Pound agreed on one thing: the sums demanded from the U.S. market stood in stark contrast to those in Europe. This reality played a significant role in fostering McMillen's initiative. Helmick believed that changes in the European television market offered a corrective effect on this disparity in the future. However, his statement that "it was always a concern to everyone within the Olympic

Movement when a government tried to intervene in sport in any way"[59] belied the USOC's contribution toward crafting the bill, confirmed by McMillen in his meeting with Pound in January. To Pound's suggestion that the IOC employ a lobbyist in Washington to safeguard the IOC's interests, Helmick issued a warning: "To seek separate representation in order to attempt to lobby against this bill would produce very negative effects, as it would in any country if an international organization attempted to become involved in internal politics without calling upon the cooperation of the domestic organization." Helmick concluded that "it was the USOC's considered judgement that this could be controlled."[60] His comments reflected that Helmick perhaps realized, albeit late in the process, just how much the McMillen bill would have suppressed the value of U.S. Olympic television rights and, ultimately, the USOC's own net receipts. In 1991 the McMillen bill dropped off Washington's legislative docket.

Events did little to quell the USOC's desire to move beyond the share of U.S. television revenue dictated by the BMA. Discussions concerning the USOC's share of U.S. Olympic television revenue continued through 1991 and 1992. A meeting between Michael Payne and the USOC's John Krimsky in February 1991 failed to bring the parties to an agreement.[61] Talks percolated for another eighteen months. Pound thought that the two sides arrived at a solution prior to the USOC Olympic Congress in Miami in October 1992, but Harvey Schiller, the USOC's executive director, informed Pound that the USOC would not sign the agreement. He was adamant that revisions to the BMA include increases in the shares of the U.S. television contracts for the 1998 Nagano Olympic Winter Games and the 2000 Summer Olympics. Pound replied that the USOC's refusal to conclude an agreement in timely fashion prevented any new provisions concerning revenue distribution from being included in the host-city contracts, which had already been signed by Nagano, and circulated to the bid cities for the 2000 Summer Games. Schiller's demand for a 20 percent share of U.S. television revenue beginning in 2004 also perplexed Pound. He responded that the IOC might be willing to consider 15 percent.[62]

To Schiller's counterproposal for additional revenue from the 1998 and 2000 U.S. television contracts, which involved paying the USOC an additional fee for acting as a television negotiations consultant in the U.S. market, Pound offered a shell game. It was not possible to deduct anything from the pool of money assigned to the OCOGs, IFs, NOCs, or the IOC, he stated. However, it might be possible to pull money from the USOC's share of TOP revenues because it was difficult to retain the current method of distributing corporate sponsorship monies which granted the USOC more money than received by all of the other NOCs combined.[63] Pound's response agitated USOC officials and could be interpreted as his method of tweaking the noses of Schiller and his colleagues. He had long tired of the badgering.

Pound Says "No" to Schiller, Presses Samaranch

Pound's interaction with Harvey Schiller typified the difficult days in the relations between the IOC and USOC marketing teams in the early 1990s. Relations between the parties were "cantankerous," recalled Payne.[64] Not satisfied with Pound's approach and his unwillingness to capitulate to USOC demands for modifications to the BMA, Schiller pulled an end run, sending a letter directly to Samaranch outlining the USOC's proposal. Pound took him to task for going over his head. A reading of the memorandum leaves little to one's imagination concerning Pound's dwindling patience.[65]

The USOC's demand for a larger share of U.S. television revenue troubled Pound. When the IOC and USOC signed the BMA, the IOC accepted the USOC's claim that its sponsorship program was adversely affected by the U.S. Olympic network's ability to sublicense the use of the IOC-approved composite logo to Olympic broadcast advertisers. "You persuaded us," Pound wrote to Schiller, "that the broadcasters were, in effect, thus able to offer competing sponsorships and that there was a diversion of sponsorship funds which might otherwise go to the USOC." It was the sole basis of the USOC's claim, Pound said, noting also that the IOC was now willing to accept the USOC's request that third party use of the composite logo be prohibited. "In the circumstances," he wrote, "I am sure you can appreciate the difficulty which I have in understanding why the USOC should have *any* share of U.S. television revenues, when the only basis for requesting a share has now been removed as a problem for the USOC in its sponsorship efforts."[66]

Pound understood that the designation of the USOC's 10 percent share of U.S. Olympic television revenue bore a limited shelf life. Though the BMA was a legal and binding agreement, privately Pound realized that the USOC would have to be accommodated in time. But not on Schiller's terms. Pound and Schiller came to loggerheads as a result of Pound's refusal to grant to the USOC 20 percent of the revenue from future U.S. Olympic television contracts and acquiesce to Schiller's insistence that this percentage be established as the benchmark in any agreement. Talks bogged down as the working relationship between the IOC Marketing Department and the USOC deteriorated further in 1993, 1994, and 1995. While Samaranch and USOC president LeRoy Walker enjoyed a good relationship, Pound, Payne, and USOC officials such as Schiller and Krimsky were uneasy lunch companions as marketing issues provided the grist for conflict.

Knowing some of his frustrations with Schiller and his USOC colleagues stemmed from the IOC's approach to the European television market, Pound persistently lobbied Samaranch for a new approach. He hammered home his central argument, primarily for Samaranch's benefit: "The IOC could no longer have all its eggs in one basket and depend almost entirely on U.S. rights. It was also not right for the U.S. to pay a disproportionate price for the rights. The IOC had to broaden its base." The IOC's past approach, voiced Pound, lay at the root of its troubles with the USOC concerning television money.[67] He pushed Samaranch and Hodler hard. The campaign resulted in $247 million contract with EBU for the entire European market for the 1996 Atlanta Olympics, a contract that was still below market value, but not embarrassingly so.[68] EBU acquired the Western European rights (minus Spain, whose TVE paid $15 million) for the 1992 Barcelona Olympics for $75 million. Samaranch still favored EBU and harbored no thoughts of abandoning the decades-long relationship. Still, he moved toward acceptance that the emergence of private networks in Europe would alter the telecommunications landscape and would present the IOC with an opportunity to use the new conditions as a means of enhancing the value of its television rights in the region.

Pound could only hope his efforts to harangue Samaranch and Hodler—a mission based on sound logic and in the IOC's best interests in light of the prolonged, difficult dialogue with the USOC—would pay dividends. He stayed the course, to good effect. However, Pound did not limit his attention to driving the value of Olympic television rights in the European market. The value of Latin American television rights moved from the $2.92 million contracted for Seoul (1988) to $11 million for Sydney (2000) and $17 million for Athens (2004), a 582 percent increase (despite dealing with a broadcast union that had a direct channel to Samaranch). These festivals yielded $7.37 million, $45 million, and $50.5 million in a competitive Australian market, a 685 percent jump. The Japanese market, where Un Yong Kim managed negotiations, moved from $50 million for Seoul to $135 million for Sydney and $150 million for Athens.[69] Prior to the 1992 Barcelona Olympics, Pound invested significant time in a (failed) effort to greatly improve the financial return for television rights in sub-Saharan Africa. Though his eyes were firmly fixed on the U.S./EBU situation, Pound's vision to enhance the Olympic Movement's revenue base via television rights fees was a global one.

Dick Ebersol: Olympic Impresario

In the mid-1990s the IOC explored the possible benefits of negotiating multifestival rights agreements with networks in the world's television markets. The IOC might sacrifice dollars by not taking advantage of the market closer to the date of actually staging an individual festival, but longer-term deals offered financial security for the IOC and better information for bid cities to generate their budget proposals. The pros outweighed the cons. In early 1995, Rupert Murdoch's Channel 7 (Australia) acquired the rights to the Atlanta ($30 million) and Sydney ($45 million) Olympic festivals for $75 million. However, the NBC contract for the Sydney ($705 million) and Salt Lake City ($545 million) festivals and a follow-up set of negotiations that yielded a $2.3 billion deal covering the 2004, 2006, and 2008 festivals cemented the IOC's strategy of negotiating multigames agreements with other global partners.

The roots for long-term television contracts reach back to a discussion in a bar in Monaco between Michael Payne and Gary Fenton, the head of Sports with Australia's Channel 7, when they attended the 1995 Sportel Convention, a gathering of sport industry leaders. Fenton and Payne discussed the prospective value of Australian television rights for the 1996 Atlanta Olympics. Fenton struggled to see how Channel 7 could make it work. "We just can't meet your numbers on Atlanta," he said. Channel 7 was keen on the rights but saw a roadblock. "Well, think out of the box," replied Payne. "Yeah, great, what does that mean?" queried Fenton. "I don't know," Payne recalled, "what [about] bidding for two, no one's ever done that before." "Are you serious?" asked Fenton. They resolved to discuss the matter with Dick Pound, who managed all negotiations aside from Europe and Japan. "A week later," said Payne, Channel 7 officials "were on a plane for Montreal, and the deal was done."[70]

In 1995, changes to the economic foundation of American television and Channel 7's deal triggered NBC's negotiations with the IOC on multifestival contracts. In the late summer months Westinghouse announced its purchase of CBS, and Disney merged with ABC and its parent company, Capital Cities Communications. NBC's march to the hallowed status of "America's Olympic Network," which started with the acquisition of rights to the Seoul (1988), Barcelona (1992) and Atlanta (1996) Olympics, was threatened. CBS already possessed the U.S. rights to the 1998 Olympic Winter Games. The infusion of capital to NBC's rivals changed the dynamics of impending negotiations for the rights to the 2000 Sydney Olympics. In order to make a splash in the U.S. sports television market, media baron Rupert Murdoch signaled FOX's willingness to spend $700 million on rights for Sydney. NBC officials, whose discussions with their ABC counterparts to develop a joint bid for the Sydney Olympics stalled, pivoted and looked for a means to outmaneuver their competitors. Dick Ebersol, NBC's president of its Sports Division, called Gary Fenton and quizzed him on how he'd secured the Atlanta/Sydney deal.[71]

In describing his attitude toward life and work, Ebersol once commented, "I like to win, I like to have fun, and I don't like to wear a coat and tie." *Sports Illustrated*'s Sally Jenkins argued that this approach was central to Ebersol's success in marshaling internal support at NBC to pursue and acquire U.S. Olympic television rights for five Olympic festivals at a cost of $3.5 billion.

NBC CEO Bob Wright, Ebersol, and fellow NBC executives Randy Falco and Ed Swindler considered the financial implications and possibilities of pursuing the rights to the 2000 Sydney Olympics and 2002 Salt Lake City Olympic Winter Games. Jack Welch, CEO of NBC's parent company, General Electric, dispatched Ebersol's team to Göteborg, Sweden, on a private jet to meet with Pound, who they believed was there attending the 1995 World Track and Field Championships. Upon their arrival they learned that Pound was not in Sweden, but Samaranch was en route. Ebersol and his colleagues hid in their hotel room until they were able to contact Samaranch. A hastily and secretly convened discussion resulted in Samaranch setting up a meeting between Ebersol and Pound. Wright's Gulfstream jet ferried the NBC delegation to Montreal the next day for a conference with Pound at his law office. He, too, saw the merits of the proposal and immediately communicated his thoughts to Samaranch. A few hours later, the third draft of a contract formulated on Pound's laptop computer satisfied both parties.

Ebersol was on a roll. Even though 1995 witnessed the demise of The Baseball Network, NBC's joint venture with ABC and Major League Baseball (MLB),[72] which was a matter of great consternation for Ebersol, the 1995–96 television season marked the first time that one U.S. network, NBC, covered the Olympics (Atlanta), the NBA Finals, the World Series, and the Super Bowl. Ebersol was much aggrieved by MLB's role in the collapse of The Baseball Network, charging angrily, when NBC and ABC walked away in June 1995, "I can't imagine being involved in baseball at least for the rest of this century." But those feelings subsided rapidly, and by November he committed NBC ($400 million) to a joint rights contract with FOX ($575 million) for the next five baseball seasons.[73] In 1996 Ebersol topped *Sporting News*'s list of the one hundred most powerful people in sports.

Much as Roone Arledge did in piloting ABC Sports' coverage of the Olympics in the 1970s and 1980s, Dick Ebersol, as the head of NBC Sports, shaped Americans' viewing of the Games as well as the Olympic brand's appeal in the United States in the 1990s and the early twenty-first century. "For all of the problems of the IOC/USOC relationships," under Samaranch and later Rogge, recounted Michael Payne, "the Olympic brand, per say, enjoys a very special status in America." Ebersol, he continued, must be accorded "tremendous credit" for this situation "because he was the window, the producer, under which the American population experienced the Olympics." Illustrative of Ebersol's commitment to the Olympic Movement and the image of the Games was his decision to squelch coverage of the 1996 Atlanta Olympics outside the competitive venues where he found the unrestrained commercial scene repugnant. To his producers and directors, observed Payne, Ebersol said, "Anybody who shows me a shot outside the stadium is fired." The IOC was discomfited by the commercial squalor, but Ebersol's actions confirmed he "understood what made the Olympics special, and different from any other sports event."[74] Ebersol's status as a long-term partner by virtue of the multigames agreements made him especially sensitive to the need to nurture the Olympic brand.

His involvement with the Olympics dated back to his work as a researcher for ABC Sports while on a two-year hiatus from his studies at Yale during the lead-up to the 1968 Grenoble Olympic Winter Games. Of this opportunity to work for

Roone Arledge and establish what evolved into a lifelong connection to the Olympics, Ebersol observed, "I was touched by an angel."[75] It helped feed his passion for sport, given he had little athletic potential himself: "I had the hand-eye coordination of a giraffe," concluded Ebersol.[76]

While perhaps best known for his work in sports television, Ebersol, a native of Connecticut whose father Charles once served as the chairman of the American Cancer Society, spent his early years at NBC developing weekend programming. In 1975, a year after his arrival at NBC, Ebersol collaborated with Lorne Michaels to launch *Saturday Night Live*, a staple in Saturday night programming in the United States for more than forty years. As a result of Susan Saint James's appearance on SNL, Ebersol met the actress, perhaps best known for her roles in two television series, *McMillan and Wife* and *Kate and Allie*, to whom he's been married since 1981 (following a six-week whirlwind romance).

His stint as head of NBC Sports from 1989 through 2011 saw him deliver a wide range of sport events to NBC's viewers, including MLB, National Football League, National Hockey League games, Triple Crown horse races, and NASCAR events, and launch channels such as Versus and the Golf Channel. He also conceived the program "Sunday Night Football." While he enjoyed a healthy measure of success, there were downturns. NBC lost more than $200 million on its coverage of the 2010 Vancouver Olympic Winter Games and 2012 Summer Olympics, due chiefly to the network's overbid for those rights in 2003.[77] The XFL football league, his collaborative venture with professional wresting kingpin Vince McMahon, failed.

Ebersol reveled in the media spotlight in the wake of the Sydney/Salt Lake City negotiations, but he did not rest, with the five-year joint baseball agreement with FOX and MLB merely one indication of energetic endeavors. Sensing Samaranch's comfort with the NBC/IOC partnership, he thought a second deal possible. He received Wright's authorization to pursue the concept. In September, Ebersol met with Samaranch and Pound in Lausanne. Ebersol's plan aimed at the purchase of the 2004 and 2006 Olympic festivals. Pound set to work on crafting a brief, code-named "Sunset Project." It examined ways of structuring such an agreement given both sites were yet to be named. When IOC and NBC negotiators re-convened on November 7, Ebersol learned that the IOC wished to add the rights to the 2008 Olympics to the "Sunset" contract. Pound considered it prudent to link the NBC deal to the TOP cycles.[78] Two weeks later, they concluded a $2.3 billion contract.

Ebersol's deal-making firmly established NBC's ascendance to the status of America's Olympic network.[79] Reflecting later, he concluded that the two agreements "represent to me the great innovative deals of my career."[80] For the IOC, the financial security was simply too appealing. In addition, future bid committees could more effectively structure their proposals if they understood the extent of available revenue from the U.S. television market.

Dick Ebersol and Juan Antonio Samaranch (seated from left) sign the IOC/NBC deal (Sunset Project) for the 2004 and 2008 Summer Olympics and 2006 Olympic Winter Games in March 1997 in Lausanne as the IOC's director of legal affairs, Howard Stupp, guides Samaranch through the documents. Dick Pound, lawyer Don Petroni, and USOC president William Hybl are standing from left in the background. (© 1997 / International Olympic Committee (IOC) / Giulio Locatelli. Photo courtesy of the IOC.)

USOC Officials Respond to the Sunset Project

The IOC's long-term strategy angered CBS, ABC, and FOX executives, who were shut out of the discussions, and infuriated USOC leaders, who correctly understood that part of Pound's motivation for going forward with the NBC project was his knowledge that the deals locked the USOC into 10 percent of $3.5 million. In 1992 Harvey Schiller's attempt to secure an elevated percentage of U.S. television revenue was unsuccessful when he sought a more advanced timetable for the receipt of that elevated percentage than Pound offered, and he insisted on a 20 percent share.[81] Schiller's successor, USOC executive director Dick Schultz, too, lobbied Pound for 20 percent (the USOC's position when it first invoked the ASA in September 1985).[82] Pound grew increasingly frustrated with those who harangued him. For Pound, Ebersol's vision, spurred by the results of Payne's discussion with Gary Fenton in a Monaco bar, happily coincided with his efforts to stem the USOC's financial ambitions and safeguard money for the IOC, IFs, and NOCs.

The Sunset Project, negotiated without the USOC's knowledge, prompted a firestorm of protest from American Olympic officials. The USOC refused to approve the contract and once again pushed forward the terms of the ASA in its rationale for doing so. Pound, who occasionally consulted USOC officials concerning past negotiations for U.S. Olympic television rights, kept them on the sidelines for discussions of the 2004/2006/2008 contract. Through his interaction with the likes of Schiller and Schultz, he was only too aware of the USOC's unceasing campaign to increase its 10 percent share. He knew that some accommodation with the USOC was necessary but resisted its demand for 20 percent of future U.S. television money. Once again, the USOC turned to Capitol Hill for leverage in discussions.

Leaning on his diplomatic skills, fancying himself a peacemaker, Samaranch, at Schultz's invitation for direct discussions, sought to bring resolution to the dispute over the second deal with NBC. Schultz indicated the USOC's willingness to scale back its demand to 15 percent. However, before Samaranch signed off on such an arrangement, he and Pound learned that Schultz's face-to-face negotiations represented only one element of the USOC's approach to securing its future wealth and control over the U.S. market. Schultz employed the same strategy devised by George Miller to achieve the USOC's financial aims through the BMA. Miller married his negotiations with the IOC to Kane's and Conable's efforts on Capitol Hill to push the IOC towards an agreement in 1986. Now, ten years later, Schultz resurrected the USOC's connections in Washington, but did so in clandestine fashion while concurrently dealing personally with Samaranch. The USOC pursued the central element of its interest in the McMillen bill—the transfer of the right to negotiate U.S. Olympic television contracts to the USOC from the IOC—lobbying Congress for assistance. This planned change to the ASA was buried in an unrelated Senate bill under discussion in Washington.

It took six months for this breach to be repaired when the two sides agreed on a shift of the USOC's share to 12.75 percent. The IOC Executive Board previously determined that commencing in 2004, the Olympic Movement would receive 51 percent of global television revenue (an increase from its previously enjoyed 40 percent). Samaranch and a majority of IOC Executive Board members believed this elevation in the IOC's share was possible because of the increasing sums available to OCOGs through TOP. Thus, following Pound's suggestion, Samaranch proposed that the USOC, IOC, IFs and NOCs receive 12.75 percent each, with the remaining 49 percent transferable to the OCOG. The USOC was content with 12.75 percent. Because of the move to a 51 percent share for the Olympic Movement, upping the USOC's percentage imposed no financial hurt on the IOC, IFs, and remaining NOCs. It was a relief for the USOC, reported Anita DeFrantz, an IOC Executive Board member who also had a seat on the USOC Executive Committee.[83]

Closing Thoughts

Robert Kane's entreaty to his friend Barber Conable, and Conable's astute decision to enlist Guy Vander Jagt in support of the USOC's goals in maneuvers on Capitol Hill, led to the crafting of the Tax Reform Act of 1985, legislation that empowered the USOC in such a way that its argument for a share of U.S. television contracts could not be dismissed by the IOC. Kane and Conable did not intend to poison relations between the two bodies; they simply sought financial support, rightful support in their minds, for America's Olympic efforts. Generations of U.S. Olympians owe a measure of gratitude for their diligence and commitment to that cause.

The ASA gave the USOC a tool to push forward its financial aspirations, and it did so with success in the 1980s. The BMA further entrenched the newfound wealth of the USOC. However, for more than twenty-five years the BMA stood at the center of the IOC's prickly relations with the USOC on revenue matters. Sums transferred to U.S. Olympic coffers became a source of frustration and anxiety for some IOC officials and NOC leaders, as did the USOC's future efforts to employ the threat of congressional action as a means of enhancing its share of U.S. television revenue.

In the aftermath of the signing of the BMA, driven by a desire to increase its revenue base and authority, the USOC pursued its legislative agenda in Washington. The McMillen bill served as one example of this tactic; however, Pound headed off this congressional threat. USOC officials were disturbed by the amount of money U.S. television networks paid relative to the sums negotiated by the IOC in Europe and a number of other large markets, including Japan. They were unwilling to accept the extent to which U.S. networks were bankrolling the development of competitors to U.S. Olympians through the IOC's distribution of television money to the global contingent of NOCs. USOC executives argued that, in order to compensate the USOC for the IOC's unwillingness to extract fair market value from major non-U.S. regions, and as a result of its rights enshrined in the ASA, the USOC was entitled to 20 percent of the U.S. television revenue. Pound disagreed.

In the 1990s, escalating friction between Pound, who acted as the IOC's point person in negotiations with the USOC concerning television issues, and former USOC officials Harvey Schiller, John Krimsky, and Dick Schultz can be attributed, in part, to a clash of egos. These individuals, representing the two most powerful organizations in the Olympic Movement, carried out discussions that centered on the distribution of hundreds of millions of dollars. Their skirmishes also concerned the USOC's concept of its role in television negotiations, which it steadfastly sought to expand. The USOC was interested in centralizing administration of all Olympic matters in the United States, especially finance, in its Colorado Springs headquarters. In the minds of IOC executives, USOC officials lacked a global vision and viewed the IOC's Lausanne operation with disdain. Pound understood the Americans' motives and methods. "The basic position of the USOC is that, in the United States, the IOC has no role and that it is the USOC which controls and runs all things Olympic," he wrote to his fellow IOC Executive Board members in 1996. "The fundamental attitude of the USOC toward the IOC," he added, "is that the IOC knows nothing about the Olympic Movement in the United States and that the IOC should not be carrying on any activity in the United States, including the sale of television rights."[84] Pound, for his part, labored mightily to maintain the IOC's right to "do business" in the United States. The Sunset Project was one means of controlling the ambition of USOC officials, especially pertaining to television revenue and television negotiations policy in the medium term.

The Sunset Project confirmed the collective wisdom of Pound and Samaranch, who explored the possibility, and Pound's acumen as the chief negotiator representing the IOC's interests in discussions with television networks. First, the collection of contract signings it prompted improved the IOC's relationship with television networks because both parties (the IOC and the individual network in each region) shared a long-term commitment to the Olympic Movement. The networks also relished the enhanced opportunities for cost recovery. Second, advancing the timeline for the negotiation of television deals permitted the IOC to provide much helpful financial data to prospective host cities, an important tool for the individuals responsible for constructing budget forecasts. Cities that competed for the 2004 Olympics (Athens), 2006 Olympic Winter Games (Turin), and those such as Beijing, Paris, and Toronto, each of which bid for the right to host the 2008 Summer Olympics, factored this information into their planning. Third, these deals also provided financial security for the IOC and the Olympic Movement. No doubt Salt Lake City officials caught in a maelstrom of controversy in 1999 were relieved that all major television contracts were in place. Last, Pound's decision, approved by Samaranch and the Executive Board, to conclude negotiations with NBC in 1995 for U.S. television rights to the three festivals before the debate concerning the USOC's share was resolved, proved astute. The BMA outlined a payment of 10 percent of the U.S. television contract to the USOC commencing in 1992 and extending beyond in perpetuity. Pound improved the IOC's negotiating position with the USOC, which was still hungering for 20 percent. With respect to television rights negotiations, Pound served the IOC well in his efforts to establish a position of financial security for the organization in the 1990s.

In 1996, Dick Schultz's push to finesse changes to the ASA by subverting the terms of the BMA without the IOC's knowledge, a step taken largely in response to the results of the Pound/Ebersol negotiations, was a gamble of sorts. If Schultz had been successful in obtaining the right to negotiate U.S. television contracts (for the USOC), the IOC would have been drawn into a public confrontation with the USOC. IOC officials lacked confidence in the prospect for a favorable verdict in a court action carried out in the United States despite the seemingly valid argument that the IOC's intellectual property rights (the television rights) would have been usurped. Schultz's decision to pursue amendments to the ASA while at the same time discussing changes to the BMA with Samaranch backfired when an NBC employee discovered the bill moving through the Senate. Any hope for 15 percent of future U.S. television contracts or control of negotiations was dashed; however, the realities of the U.S. market's place in the Olympic economy moved the parties toward a solution (12.75 percent). The process involved, and the path taken in search of this agreement, reflected both the massive breach in terms of interorganizational trust and the unique and important nature of the U.S. market concerning Olympic revenue generation.

When Michael Payne stepped aside from his position as IOC marketing director in 2004, he sat down with IOC president Jacques Rogge and director general Urs Lacotte (François Carrard's successor) to brief them on a variety of marketing issues. The status of IOC/USOC relations was front and center in this discussion. "Of all of the complexities of everything we're dealing with," stated Payne, "this actually is probably the most difficult file. It's exceedingly complex, it's very political, and has the risk of pulling everything down," he warned. "So if there's one thing a new team of leadership needs to get their head around, it's this."[85] Payne was unconvinced that Rogge grasped the gravity of the problem. Rogge believed that the issues devolved largely to a personality clash between Payne and John Krimsky.[86] As for attempts on his watch to put things on a better footing, Payne concluded, "We tried, and failed." He characterized the state of play in 2004 as an "uncomfortable truce" between the parties.[87] As time marched on, events obliged President Rogge to invest significant time and energy in improving IOC/USOC relations.

In 2009, USOC officials viewed Chicago's shocking first ballot dismissal in the vote for the 2016 Summer Olympics as a signal that it had "some big problems" and amounted to "a wake-up call" for the need to address its relationship with the IOC and its image in the greater Olympic world. The spotlight had been placed squarely on the USOC's shares of marketing revenue. Payne credited the outreach efforts of USOC president Larry Probst, who bore the scars from Chicago's loss, and Executive Director Scott Blackmun, who arrived on the scene in 2010. They clearly prioritized building a "better rapport and relationships" with IOC officials in effecting positive change in the dynamics of IOC/USOC relations in recent years.[88]

Avery Brundage, who served as USOA president and later headed the IOC (1952–1972), warned those who might listen to him about commercial revenue and the threat from the flow of money from television rights fees to members of the Olympic family. Even though the television industry afforded the possibility of promoting the Olympic Movement on a global basis, when it came to money, Brundage doubted that his fellow Olympic administrators could avoid conflict over who got what. He witnessed in his lifetime such arguments in the context of events linked to the adoption of the Rome Formula in 1966 and Willi Daume's calculated approach to U.S. television rights negotiations for the 1972 Munich Olympics. What horror might he have felt in witnessing the process involved in the generation of the BMA or the rise of the TOP program? A glimpse at IOC/USOC relations during Samaranch's presidency and the arguments engendered confirms that decades after his passing, Brundage's thinking was sound.

CHAPTER 8

The Salt Lake City Bid Scandal

"None of us in the IOC could have predicted, let alone 'scripted,' the aftershock of events surrounding the Salt Lake City scandal," observed IOC Executive Board member Kevan Gosper in 2000, "as we travelled through the first half of the last year of the twentieth century—the 105th year of our existence as the supreme international sporting organization."[1] Michael Payne, the IOC's former marketing director, concurred with Gosper on the challenge the IOC faced in managing fallout from revelations revealed by Salt Lake City's local media in late November 1998 that the Salt Lake City bid committee funded the tuition of the late René Essomba's daughter, Sonia, to attend Washington's American University in the early 1990s (René Essomba had been an IOC member from Cameroon). It soon became clear that this news story and its implications could not be contained solely to Salt Lake City. When Marc Hodler, a member of the IOC Executive Board, chairman of the Coordination Commission for the Salt Lake City Olympic Winter Games, and president of the International Ski Federation for forty-seven years, insinuated that Essomba's alleged behavior in accepting such a sizable gift as possible inducement for support of an Olympic host-city bid was likely common to 5–7 percent of the IOC membership, the world's media pounced.

The IOC's internal investigation, headed by Dick Pound, an IOC vice president and chairman of the Marketing Commission, unearthed other payments to a number of IOC members by Salt Lake City bidders. In the end, six IOC members were expelled, another four were resigned, and a number of others received varying degrees of censure. The sales pitch that Samaranch, Pound, and other key IOC officials such as Payne and Director General François Carrard, projected in 1999, especially to their television partners and major corporate sponsors, was that the IOC recognized the gravity of the Salt Lake City problem, accepted the need for serious reform, and had a plan for delivering the necessary changes. If television partners or TOP sponsors abandoned their relationships with the IOC, the tarnish of the Olympic brand, already a matter of grave concern, would be compounded. Though sponsors could have been replaced, the overall revenue yield would have been reduced markedly as the value of the sponsorships would have dropped.

In reflecting on those early days of the crisis when the IOC encountered intense global scrutiny from journalists, fielded some three hundred media inquiries each day at its headquarters,[2] and grappled with repeated outcries for Samaranch's resignation, Payne confessed that he and his Lausanne colleagues were "beaten down" in every sense of the term. "You literally came to work not knowing if the IOC would survive the day," observed Payne.[3] It was a tough, relentless, wearying slog as the senior IOC members and executives tried to navigate the organization through turbulent waters. "A ghastly time," echoed Carrard.[4] But why did the IOC find itself in this difficult circumstance, how did Samaranch and his staff manage the crisis, and in what ways did the trying experience prove transformational for the IOC and the Olympic Movement?

The roots of the Salt Lake City crisis lay in the generally acknowledged success of the 1984 Los Angeles Olympics delivered by Peter Ueberroth and his energetic team of executives who were committed to staging the Olympics without taxing the public purse. Increasing costs associated with hosting the Olympic Games diminished enthusiasm in the world's major cities toward bidding for an Olympic festival. The nearly $1 billion cost overrun witnessed in Montreal only added to the trepidation felt by civic leaders who previously eyed the Olympics as a mega-event capable of advancing their city's global image and leveraging the money necessary to upgrade municipal infrastructure. Los Angeles was the IOC's only viable host-city candidate for the 1984 Olympics. But a nervous citizenry was unwilling to authorize the expenditure of public funds for the great enterprise. Faced with this dilemma, Ueberroth, his senior aides Harry Usher and Joel Rubenstein, and Los Angeles Organizing Committee (LAOOC) chairman, Paul Ziffren, charted a path for staging the Games with a budget notable for the near absence of public funds and a much-reduced emphasis on the construction of new facilities. Security costs were partially offset by a hotel tax and a tax on tickets applied by the city. In effecting this plan, in the end they delivered an eyebrow-raising profit of $232.5 million.

The grand success of Los Angeles does not fully explain the emergence of conduct witnessed in Salt Lake City and, in truth, conduct evident in earlier bid cycles. Ueberroth's success did, however, spark interest in bidding for the Olympic Games.

Newly created TOP revenue also contributed to the renewed bullishness among prospective bidders. Steadily increasing television rights fees, too, especially in the U.S. market, fostered more enthusiasm on the part of civic leaders and property/ land developers who had historically often combined forces to plan and present Olympic host-city bids. The escalating cachet of the Olympics and its attractive- ness to broadcast executives as a television property was driven, in part, by Sama- ranch's quest to open the Olympics to professional athletes.

The availability of increasing commercial revenue altered the dynamics of the bidding process, but so, too, did a policy change effected at the IOC Session in 1986 (despite the reservations of some Executive Board members) to approve member visits to bid cities as part of the bid-evaluation process. Bid committees leveraged these opportunities to wine and dine IOC members, "press the flesh," and in some cases offer financial inducements to those individuals inclined toward capitaliz- ing on his/her status as an IOC member. Within a short time (three years) Hodler raised concerns over the behavior and conduct of some IOC members visiting prospective Olympic host cities. Despite all, he could not push Samaranch and the Executive Board to move beyond establishing the so-called "Hodler Rules," dictates that limited the value of gifts that could be provided to IOC members from bid committees to $200, and, as well, setting limits on spending by bid committees.

Gosper conceded that the lack of an oversight or monitoring process with respect to these spending rules was a trigger for the IOC's predicament tied to Salt Lake City. "The real problem was not the lack of rules," offered Gosper, "it was our inclination not to police them." The IOC's structure, he asserted, hampered its functioning in this regard: "We should have been more alert to the risk of cor- ruption and improper practices, but we were a 'club'—an association of members from all walks of life spread around the world—not a corporation where everyone came to work in the same office building each day with their activities monitored by a chief executive and supervisory team."[5] The policy on spending limits had no teeth; in most cases bid committees routinely ignored them. "The Games are an aphrodisiac," SLOC Board of Trustees member Ken Bullock reflected: "If you want something bad enough, you stretch the boundaries."[6]

The system also counted on bid committees blowing the whistle on the behavior of specific IOC members. However, bid committee officials, specifically those on the losing end of competitions, viewed such action as a death knell for any future bid. In 1999, when rumors of questionable conduct surfaced amid the throes of the scandal and certain IOC members were approached for explanation, Dick Pound asserted (in his typically colorful fashion): "You heard enough rumours and it's easy to say where there's that much smoke, there must be some fire. . . . That's a very comforting adage, but when you go to someone and say, 'We're hearing this about you,' they'd say, 'There's absolutely nothing to it. Look at my halo. You can hardly see me for the radiance.' At that point, you don't have any evidence, you've got to put up or shut up. What you hope is that if someone has maybe been a little indiscreet, that will stop them from doing it in the future."[7] Regrettably for the IOC, it did not.

Troubling, too, was the emergence of Olympic "agents" who offered their services to bid committees with promises of delivering blocs of IOC member votes. Samaranch worried about this development's impact on the reputations of the IOC and the Olympic Movement, and, along with the members of the Executive Board, considered transferring power over the selection of host cities to the Executive Board. But, again, Samaranch shied away from taking definitive action. He sensed that IOC members, in general, already believed that too much power and authority devolved to the Executive Board and that their right to inspect and choose the host city should remain in place.[8] He and his closest advisers should have trusted their collective gut. Still, such a decision, if it had been made at the time, would have been too late to avert the disaster waiting in Salt Lake City. These discussions occurred in 1998, mere months before the scandal over activities of some IOC members and Salt Lake City bid officials, dating back to the early to mid-1990s, burst forth. A proactive approach might have lessened the virulence of the attacks in some quarters of the global media if the IOC had been able to trumpet that this soft underbelly of the bid process had been identified and changes were imminent.

While the IOC battled its way through the crisis and sought reform measures to address its policy shortcomings, Pound, in giving weight to Gosper's later assessment, confessed to Eastman Kodak's (a TOP-sponsor company) chairman and CEO, George Fisher, that "it would . . . have been better had all this come about in an evolutionary manner, but I am afraid we had our eye on other matters and did not give this one the attention it deserved."[9]

The Salt Lake City Crisis and the IOC's Response

On a wintry November morning in 1998, Dick Pound pored over a fax message in his Montreal law office. Its contents concerned him. Earlier, he fielded a phone call from a Salt Lake City reporter who told him that he had a lead on a story about payments made by the Salt Lake City bid committee in support of an IOC member's dependent (later identified as Sonia Essomba) to attend college in the United States. The fax message provided further details about the story that aired on Salt Lake City's KTVX Channel 4. With his reading glasses perched on his nose, Pound scanned the fax and concluded that trouble loomed. He alerted Samaranch to the developing story, though neither he nor his IOC colleagues could have foreseen the scale of the crisis in the offing. It was, in the mind of David Miller, *The Times*'s chief sport correspondent, "an initially minor revelation . . . on par with the Watergate break-in. [But] the ramifications were to prove similarly far reaching."[10]

The true flashpoint occurred two weeks later as members of the Executive Board gathered in Lausanne for the last of their four annual meetings in 1998. Salt Lake Organizing Committee (SLOC) officials jetted to Switzerland to provide a scheduled update on preparations for the 2002 Olympic Winter Games, but they also carried with them files that revealed that the activities of the bid committee extended well beyond assistance to Sonia Essomba. François Carrard immediately requested a preliminary forensic audit, one that showed that the financial induce-ments included other tuition-support payments and even cash disbursements to individual IOC members. Samaranch reviewed the files in a meeting with Frank Joklik, SLOC's chairman, Executive Board member Anita DeFrantz, and Hodler. This meeting delayed the first scheduled session with Salt Lake City officials by one full day. Samaranch found the contents of the files disturbing. SLOC officials indicated that $393,817 was spent on "tuition scholarships, book money, living expenses and training fees to 13 unnamed individuals, including six relatives of IOC members."[11] Hodler, too, found the material jarring.

During a break in meetings of the Executive Board in December 1998, from left, Dick Pound, Juan Antonio Samaranch, and IOC director general François Carrard discuss fast-moving events concerning Salt Lake City. (© 1998 / International Olympic Committee (IOC) / Giulio Locatelli. Photo courtesy of the IOC.)

Almost immediately upon learning of the story from Pound, Samaranch had assigned responsibility for the Salt Lake City matter to the Juridical Commission (chaired by Senegal's Kéba Mbaye), as it was the IOC's advisory body on legal issues. Samaranch's action reflected his "finely honed instinct for danger and self-preservation."[12] But following his meeting with Joklik, he realized that additional steps were required. The next morning, he delegated responsibility over the IOC's internal inquiry to an Ad Hoc Commission, chaired by Pound, with a membership composed of Executive Board members Mbaye, Thomas Bach, Jacques Rogge, Pál Schmitt, and Carrard, who served as secretary.

Pound's selection sent an appropriate signal to the media, given his no nonsense reputation and his physical location in North America, such that he could tackle onsite elements of the investigation in Salt Lake City itself. It was, noted Payne, "a very public demonstration of the IOC putting its house in order."[13] The Ad Hoc Commission, known within IOC circles as the Pound Commission, was tasked to wind up its review such that it could report back to the full Executive Board by the end of January (1999). While a shorter timeline might have been desirable in order to bring a swifter resolution to the matter, Bach pressed for the time necessary in order to avoid a rushed effort, one that might well prove vastly more complicated than it might appear. It was sound counsel.

At a midday press briefing, the Executive Board affirmed its support for Salt Lake City, indicated there was no thought of transferring the Games to another host city, and laid out the mandate for, and composition of, the Ad Hoc Commission. While the entire matter was highly discomfiting, it was, for the time being, under control. This sense of restored calm soon changed.

Later, during a break in the afternoon proceedings set aside for the signing of an agreement with SEMA, the company tabbed to replace IBM in TOP, Marc Hodler's simmering anger over the developing incident imploded . . . in a spectacular way. Hodler's impromptu press scrum delayed a ceremony planned for the main lobby of the IOC's headquarters. The deal with SEMA, an agreement negotiated over the previous six months, stood ready to be signed by its chairman, Pierre Bonelli, and senior vice president, Tidu Maini, along with IOC representatives Samaranch, Pound, and Carrard. Costas Bakouris, director general of the Athens Organizing Committee, and Salt Lake City's Frank Joklik also looked on while Hodler held forth, stunning observers by questioning past bids and intimating that some of his IOC colleagues were susceptible to bribes. "Cities have been the victim and not the villain," intoned Hodler, thereby training the focus of his audience squarely on the IOC itself.[14] He raised the issue of agents who pledged to deliver IOC member votes in exchange for payment.

Hodler brushed aside IOC secretary general Françoise Zweifel's effort to move along. He emptied his reservoir of frustrations. He questioned the involvement of

Fiat, owned by the Agnelli family, in Sestriere's bid for the 1997 World Ski Championships, claiming cars had been given away. He had reason to believe Ferraris (built by a Fiat subsidiary) would be distributed in support of Turin's bid for the 2006 Olympic Winter Games. An angered Evelina Christillin, a member of the Agnelli family who was present in Lausanne to present Turin's candidature to the Executive Board, considered withdrawing Turin's bid but was ultimately reassured by Samaranch and Gosper in a private meeting later in the day. Sion, Switzerland, a second contestant for the 2006 Olympic Winter Games, feared a blowback from Hodler's statements, given he was Swiss. An astounded Pound, together with Payne, Carrard, and Samaranch, believed Hodler might have had "a stroke or some other mentally imbalancing episode."[15] Gosper, while genuinely caught off guard by Hodler's interaction with the reporters, later noted that his Swiss colleague "did not seem to be his normal self" in earlier meetings of the Executive Board. He had been far more emotional and talkative than usual.[16] "I thought I might have been in a parallel universe," concluded Executive Board member Anita DeFrantz.[17]

The circus ended abruptly. Hodler retreated, allowing the signing ceremony to proceed. But reporters were little interested in SEMA's commitment to the Olympics, a partnership that staked out one of the largest TOP agreements signed in the program's thirteen-year history.[18] Salt Lake City developments and Hodler's

Marc Hodler shares his thoughts on events evolving in Salt Lake City amid a crush of reporters during the IOC Executive Board's meetings in Lausanne in December 1998. (© 1998 / International Olympic Committee (IOC) / Giulio Locatelli. Photo courtesy of the IOC.)

Juan Antonio Samaranch, flanked by Dick Pound on his right and François Carrard on his left, deal with the fallout from Marc Hodler's comments as they face questions from members of the media at an IOC Executive Board press conference. Michael Payne and Howard Stupp appear in the top right-hand corner of the photograph as they looked on. (© 1998 / International Olympic Committee (IOC) / Giulio Locatelli. Photo courtesy of the IOC.)

comments were now the sole focus of their attention. Samaranch, in response to questions from the assembled journalists, stated that Hodler's thoughts were his own, and henceforth only he (Samaranch) and Carrard would issue public statements.

None of this dissuaded Hodler. Over the remaining days of the Executive Board's meetings and in ensuing weeks he continued to question the integrity of the Olympic bid process. "In an almost Gilbert and Sullivan style performance," observed Gosper, "he continued to walk around the foyer of Olympic House, talking to the press . . . while we continued with our executive board meetings. . . . Here was one of the most respected IOC members and an expert in the winter Olympics talking about bribery and corruption in the Olympic bidding process. It was great news copy. We just couldn't control him."[19] Hodler liked the attention: "The oxygen of publicity can become addictive," mused Payne.[20]

In the waning days of Hodler's IOC membership, the Olympic bid process and its susceptibility to corruption, in his mind, deserved a full and complete review. He was not convinced that the IOC possessed the necessary level of commitment to follow through. "I thought those I trusted most were trying to push things under the carpet and that might put all the blame on Salt Lake City," he stated.[21] In the wake of the extraordinary Vidy event in which he played a starring role, Hodler exclaimed: "No revolution is possible without scandal."[22] Though he later conceded he had very little hard evidence and much of what he related was based on hearsay, the fuse had been lit.

In the aftermath of the Executive Board meeting, Samaranch leaned heavily on three individuals, Pound, Payne, and Carrard, to carry the IOC's crisis management efforts forward, but others, including Kevan Gosper and Jacques Rogge, were drawn into significant roles when suspicion fell on Sydney that its hands were not clean in the context of the bid competition for the 2000 Summer Olympics. Gosper made three return trips to Lausanne from Australia in January 1999 alone and, like the other Executive Board members, dealt with a blizzard of phone calls and fax messages. Rogge, as chairman of the Coordination Commission for the 2000 Sydney Olympics, did his best to calm folks in Australia who saw the crisis as an albatross with respect to their efforts during a critical period of fundraising. Further, he examined files related to the reports that John Coates, president of the Australian Olympic Committee and driving force behind Sydney's bid, routed $70,000 in support payments for African athletes through two IOC members. The record revealed that this beneficence materialized in 1993 through conversations with African IOC members Charles Mukora and Francis Nyangweso on the very eve of the vote on the 2000 Summer Games' site.[23] Unfortunately, this story surfaced just prior to the report of the Ad Hoc Commission to the full Executive Board in late January 1999, a reality that made that phase of the crisis even more intense.

While the optics were far less than ideal, especially given the fact that Beijing lost to Sydney by a mere two votes for the right to host the 2000 Olympics, Samaranch concurred with Gosper that this money flowed to African athletes, not dependents of IOC members, and it ought not to shake the IOC's support for Sydney. It supplemented support already made available to a number of African athletes to train at the country's national sport institute in Canberra. Jacques Rogge met with John Coates in Lausanne in early February. This discussion left Rogge in agreement with Samaranch, but he believed "Coates had broken the spirit of the IOC bidding rules with the special last minute offers to the two IOC members."[24] Gosper breathed easier knowing that the Ad Hoc Commission's mandate would not extend to Sydney; however, this sense of relief was short-lived, as the New South Wales Olympics minister, Michael Knight, soon announced a government inquiry into Sydney's bid.

Pound bore principal responsibility with respect to the internal investigation and marshaling the work of the members of the Ad Hoc Commission, but as chairman of the Marketing Commission he also served as a point person in communications with management teams of TOP partners and Olympic broadcasters. His

1999 day planner shows that in the service of the IOC, with the vast majority of this work tied to crisis management, he logged approximately 149,700 miles in air travel, the equivalent of circumnavigating the globe six times.[25]

Carrard's legal acumen and abilities in strategy formulation were tested, as were his crisis management skills. He struck a committee of IOC departmental directors that met at 8:00 each morning to review overnight developments, chart the way forward that day in terms of how to respond to rumors, and apprise the IOC's stakeholders of its ongoing efforts. Within days, he deemed the job of crisis communications too big for his Lausanne staff, in part, Payne notes, because the IOC was deficient in terms of staffing in the area of communications. Other matters reduced the priority toward staffing this area during Samaranch's presidency. The crisis exposed a glaring weakness. As the trouble deepened, and more than one thousand journalists around the globe tracked and reported on the events, Carrard engaged representatives of Hill & Knowlton, a global public relations company, the sole purpose of which was to guide the IOC's messaging. Hill & Knowlton specialized in crisis communications and distinguished itself in the minds of some IOC officials in its handling of the September 1998 Swissair 111 disaster. The IOC needed the best possible counsel. Members of the IOC Executive Board expressed divergent opinions on Hill & Knowlton's effectiveness over the ensuing months. Pound believed its contribution vital. Mbaye, Schmitt, Bach, Hodler, and Samaranch, who resented the estimated cost of $1.5 million to $1.6 million for its work, dissented. Without Hill & Knowlton, states Payne matter-of-factly, "we'd have been dead with the sponsors."[26]

François Carrard

We interviewed Carrard in March 2016 in Lausanne, where, as a senior partner with Kellerhals Carrard, he oversees a team of 140 lawyers and still supplies outside legal advice to his former employer. He specializes in international arbitration and alternative dispute resolution, sports and media law, and corporate law. While he considered himself "quite the dinosaur" at age seventy-eight,[27] he exuded an energy level of a much younger man and still appreciates a challenge, if judged by his willingness to assist FIFA in 2015 and 2016 with its reform efforts stemming from the financial scandal that enveloped it.

As a youngster during World War II, Carrard gravitated to swimming. Growing up next door to Lausanne's only public swimming pool, his mother demanded that he have the basic skills to manage in the water. While no fan of competition, she did not stand in young François's way when he was recruited to the Lausanne Swim Club, where he developed an interest in improving his skills. In 1955, with a scholarship from the American Field Service, Carrard traveled to California, attending Pasadena's John Muir High School. There, his swimming talents were further honed. Carrard recalled that it was "a fantastic atmosphere," where he mixed with a 30 percent African American population, an opportunity that he could never have enjoyed in Europe at the time. Though his tuition was paid, spending money was in short supply; he supplemented his monthly stipend of $12 with cash earned as a jazz pianist in various clubs. Carrard thinks this money flowed as a result of his being a bit of an "curiosity," as Americans thought a Swiss fellow, if musically inclined, "should be yodeling somewhere in the Alps." The English-language capacity he developed during that year, asserts Carrard, served him well in his professional life.[28]

The California venture "changed his life," and while he could have attended Stanford, he was required to return to Europe before applying for re-entry to the United States. Once home, he realized he missed Europe and the winters filled with hours skiing in the Swiss mountains. His swimming exploits ground to a halt, and he commenced his law studies at the University of Lausanne resulting in his admission to the Swiss bar in 1967. Before his admission to the bar, he spent two years at a law firm in Sweden, a fortuitous circumstance, as once he began his legal work in Switzerland, he possessed a ready cadre of clients from the Swedish film industry, given an exodus of many Swedes to Switzerland at the time. Carrard chuckled when he reflected on his father's opinion of his capacity for legal work. He thought François better suited as a diplomat than a lawyer because he considered him too lazy. As for diplomats, "they eat well, and don't work too hard," stated his father.[29]

Carrard's career trajectory experienced a major shift one morning in the winter months of 1979 when his phone rang in his Lausanne law office. It was Monique Berlioux on the line.

"Madame Berlioux," states Carrard, was a "formidable person"; however, in 1979 when he picked up the phone, Carrard knew little about her or the IOC. In fact, most people in Lausanne knew little about the IOC or its operations at the Château de Vidy. This soon changed for Carrard, and once Samaranch arrived on the scene the following year, it changed for the vast majority of Lausanne's citizens. "I'm told you're a lawyer?" queried Berlioux. "Yes," responded Carrard. Berlioux explained that the IOC needed to file some documents as it faced a legal challenge and sought to claim judicial immunity in the Canton of Vaud. Berlioux's tone, recalled Carrard, suggested she was trolling for a lawyer from Lausanne's "local trash" out of necessity.[30]

Berlioux soon dispatched her aide (and nephew), Alain Coupat, with a letter for Carrard to sign and file with the local court. Carrard reviewed the document and expressed reservations about its content. He indicated he needed to make some inquiries. Coupat left dumbfounded. Carrard rang up a legal colleague in

Bern and asked, "Who is this Monique Berlioux?" "Oh, she's a difficult person," responded his friend. Their subsequent discussion resulted in Carrard learning he'd look foolish and so, too, would the IOC, if the document were filed. The IOC, as an association under Swiss law, had no realistic claim for judicial immunity. He informed Berlioux he would not sign the document. Following an expression of her displeasure, she looked into the matter further, confirming the wisdom of his counsel.[31] The case revolved around IOC member Henry Hsu's efforts to seek an injunction against the IOC for its decision to force Taiwan's NOC to alter its marks and emblems such that the People's Republic of China could be recognized. The following year, Hsu withdrew his legal challenge.

Following Carrard's nine years of outside legal work for the IOC, we fast forward to February 14, 1988, the morning of the men's downhill at the Calgary Olympic Winter Games. High winds postponed the event by a full day. Samaranch telephoned Carrard and said he needed to talk to him. The two met, and Samaranch offered Carrard the job of IOC director general, to succeed Raymond Gafner, who handled the duties for three years in the wake of Berlioux's forced resignation in 1985. Carrard had not applied for the job. Surprised and somewhat abashed, he told Samaranch he was content with his current role as outside legal counsel. "I know, I know," said the IOC president, "you have a firm, you are happy, you are sort of independent." Samaranch argued further: Carrard's services were required by the IOC in a more formal capacity. Samaranch gave him two days to mull things over. Carrard asked for three months. Gruffly, Samaranch consented to the request.[32] Happily for Carrard, Pirmin Zurbriggen and Thomas Müller, two Swiss downhillers, took gold and silver the following day when the event took place.

"It was a Sunday, three months to the day," recounted Carrard, when "Samaranch called me." "You know why I am calling," he said, "what is your answer?" In the interim, Carrard's wife counseled him to take the position, fearing that her husband would be disappointed in hindsight if he did not. "It is not no," replied Carrard. Their discussions on the terms of his hiring soon commenced. Samaranch could fire him when he wanted, and Carrard could leave whenever he chose to move on. Carrard did not have to step back from his law firm. Had Samaranch demanded otherwise, it would have been a deal breaker. But, instead of announcing Carrard's hiring immediately, he sent him to Seoul to view the Olympics as an IOC-accredited guest. Carrard's observations might prove valuable, thought Samaranch.[33]

Through the remaining years of the Samaranch presidency Carrard's reputation grew, earning the respect and admiration of IOC staff members.[34] When Jacques Rogge assumed the presidency in 2001, he well understood Carrard's value to the IOC, a view no doubt informed by his observations of him when the organization faced the gravest crisis of its existence in the context of the Salt Lake City bid scandal. Rogge tried, without success, to convince him to become even more involved with the IOC and to step aside from his law firm. Carrard countered Rogge's offer with a signal; perhaps it was time for renewal in the position. Rogge asked Carrard for another three months until he could find a replacement. The three months turned into two years before the IOC appointed Urs Lacotte.[35]

The IOC's Troubles Continue

Samaranch directed Payne to engage corporate executives in ongoing discussions designed to inform them of the IOC's unfolding plan to "fix the problems."[36] An anxious Payne journeyed to the United States to discuss matters personally with Doug Ivester, chairman and CEO of Coca-Cola, and Paul Allaire, chairman and CEO of Xerox, and then departed for a two-day whirlwind set of meetings in Korea and Japan with the chief executives of Samsung and Matsushita. Weekly missions to the United States soon followed. Before the Ad Hoc Commission filed its report in late January, either Payne personally or representatives of the IOC's U.S.-based marketing agency, Meridian Management, met with the senior executives of all the TOP sponsors.[37] Like Pound, Payne spent a good deal of time over the next few months on an airplane.

Pound wasted little time in reviewing SLOC's files in the wake of the Executive Board meeting in December, flying to Salt Lake City on December 27. There, he met Jim Asperger, formerly a prosecuting attorney with the U.S. Department of Justice, then a lawyer with the IOC's U.S. legal counsel, O'Melveny and Myers (now with Los Angeles–based Quinn Emanuel Urquhart and Sullivan, LLP). Pound was anxious not to commit any breach of U.S. law in conducting the investigation. The files were extensive. Expenses incurred by the bid committee in relation to each IOC member were detailed. Following his preliminary review, they were sent to Lausanne for study by Carrard and Bach, both lawyers. Their arrival in Switzerland relieved Pound, who thought the U.S. Department of Justice, which had launched its own probe, might impound the documents, thereby crippling the Ad Hoc Commission's investigation. Eventually, the Ad Hoc Commission questioned the behavior of thirteen members. Samaranch directed a letter to each, requesting a response to the allegations within two weeks. Further, he extended to them an opportunity to appear before the Ad Hoc Commission before it filed its recommendations. It all pained Samaranch greatly.[38] "We had wonderful years. We had very successful games. And now we are in a storm," he confessed in a media interview one week before the Ad Hoc Commission convened in Lausanne.[39]

The pace and gravity of these events did not deter Pound from delivering a scheduled speech in downtown Kitchener, Ontario, on January 19. In fact, it signaled a willingness to "soldier on" during difficult times. Fighting the effects of a winter cold, Pound appeared "dog-tired," a state that forced him to deliver his comments in a measured pace, while allowing a cough drop to provide some relief. He reaffirmed the IOC's commitment to putting its house in order. Rather than being whisked from the hall when he concluded his remarks, he remained in the room to chat with the affair's attendees.

With the Ad Hoc Commission due to meet on January 22 and 23 in Lausanne before its session with the full Executive Board on January 24, Pound's odyssey continued. Following his Kitchener speech, he flew to New York. Members of the Ad Hoc Commission were already there for a meeting attended by lawyers from O'Melveny and Myers and SLOC's legal counsel, Latham and Watkins.[40] Before leaving New York for Switzerland, Pound delivered an address on January 21 before a gathering of sport officials and corporate sponsors at the International Sport Summit Conference. While Pound spoke, Payne flew to New York to link up with him at the Sport Summit. It was another opportunity to engage Olympic corporate sponsors in face-to-face conversation. Thus far, with one notable exception, senior executives with TOP-sponsor companies and Olympic broadcasters issued few public comments on the scandal dilemma, believing that calling forcefully for definitive action in addressing existing IOC policies in private context, rather than adding to the IOC's public misery in the press, was the preferred path toward protecting their investments.[41]

The Notable Exception: David D'Alessandro and John Hancock

"Boardrooms will shake if this is mishandled," warned David D'Alessandro, president and CEO of John Hancock Mutual Life Insurance, as the days dwindled prior to the release of the Ad Hoc Commission's report.[42] In the early days of the crisis, he criticized the IOC's response as one lacking focus and "a needed sense of urgency."[43] Though D'Alessandro applauded the efforts of Pound as one of the few IOC officials who understood the need for rapid and meaningful reform, others within the IOC hierarchy, including Samaranch, needed prodding.[44] Noting that United States Olympic Committee (USOC) officials sensed a hesitancy within the domestic sponsorship community to partner with the USOC and the Salt Lake City Organizing Committee in light of recent events, D'Alessandro, in public forums, raised the alarm: "The IOC's sponsorships have become radioactive. All corporate Geiger counters are off the chart. [The IOC has] got to find a way to make the sponsorships safe again."[45] As the CEO of a TOP-sponsor company and the individual who orchestrated the company's move from its sponsor relationship with the USOC to the list of global Olympic corporate sponsors for TOP III (1993–1996),[46] despite dissenting opinions within his marketing department, D'Alessandro called for the IOC to "get it right."

Internal corporate issues and his personal advocacy toward striking the TOP sponsorship deal guided D'Alessandro's action concerning the IOC crisis. Alarmed at the exposure of John Hancock's brand to damage in the insurance marketplace, he employed the media as a platform to forcefully press the IOC to embrace meaningful reform. This tack, of course, separated the Boston executive from his fellow TOP CEOs, not in terms of his desire—they all advocated reform—but in terms of his method for advancing its certainty. John Hancock was in the process of transitioning to a publicly traded company: 300 million shares were ready to hit the market; damage to the company's corporate image must not occur. D'Alessandro viewed the TOP sponsorship as a means of growing the company's business profile in Asia before, in his mind, the expected award of the Olympics to China in the near future. With Beijing poised as a strong contender for the 2008 Olympics, John Hancock was prepared to cash in on its investment in the Asian market.

By 1999, John Hancock had invested more than $300 million in its TOP relationship in fees and advertising, and while dropping its TOP sponsorship might be viewed as an "easy PR fix," it was fraught with personal risk for D'Alessandro. "If a company drops a sponsorship, that guy who pushed it is dead; a dead man walking inside the company," he observed. "They don't stay." That "guy" was D'Alessandro. He had to "stick it out."[47] His timeline for IOC reform, as well as its scope, did not match that considered by the IOC's leadership. In the weeks ahead, his sharply worded public criticism of Samaranch and the IOC exasperated Gosper, Payne, and Samaranch, and even National Broadcasting Company (NBC) Sports chairman, Dick Ebersol. D'Alessandro's public comments in mid-January focused even more attention on the Executive Board's deliberations concerning the Ad Hoc Commission's report.

The Ad Hoc Commission Submits Its Report

With the global media having adopted a "pound dog with a bone" mentality following Hodler's comments in mid-December, a steady stream of rumors and allegations surfaced with respect to the Salt Lake City bid, other past bids, and the behavior of IOC members. The revelations kept Carrard's crisis management team occupied. Amsterdam's 1992 bid committee allegedly used prostitutes and gifts of jewelry and video cassette recorders in its attempt to secure votes. Nagano spent an estimated average of over Can$33,000 on courting each of the sixty-two visiting IOC members, lavishing them with gifts, upscale accommodations, and travel expenses in connection with its bid for the 1998 Olympic Winter Games. Jere Longman, the *New York Times*'s Olympic beat writer, following an interview with Tom Welch, Salt Lake City's bid committee chairman and former president of SLOC, wrote that some IOC members "had been given gifts such as shotguns, skis and free lift tickets, helicopter flyovers of Utah's arresting canyons, and tickets to the opera and Utah Jazz basketball games," all in an effort to lure votes.[48] "We didn't do anything different than any other bid committee," Welch stated matter-of-factly.[49]

The son of David Sibandze (IOC member from Swaziland), Sibusiso, was given a year-long internship at Salt Lake City's city hall during the bidding phase. Intermountain Health Care provided medical services to three individuals with "Olympic connections," one of whom was soon identified as Jean-Claude Ganga, an IOC member from the Congo.[50] In the fullness of time, investigations showed Ganga accepted approximately $250,000 in gifts and benefits from Salt Lake City officials.[51] Mahmoud El Farnawani, a Canadian-based, Egyptian-born manufacturer of souvenirs, little known outside of Olympic circles, was identified as one of the agents to whom Hodler referred. He was a paid consultant for the Toronto, Nagano, Sydney, Salt Lake City, and Athens bid committees. Bruce Baird, the New South Wales minister assigned to Sydney's 2000 bid, and Jean Grenier, a member of Quebec City's bid team for the 2002 Olympic Winter Games, observed that they had been approached by Olympic agents. Christer Persson, head of Ostersund's bid, alongside Salt Lake City and Quebec City, called for Salt Lake City to refund its competitors in light of its perceived cheating. Dave Johnson, Tom Welch's right-hand associate in the bidding process, intensively involved in the disbursement of cash and benefits to the identified IOC members, resigned his position as senior vice president with SLOC, followed on the same day by Frank Joklik, who said his decision hopefully offered organizers an opportunity to hit the reset button. When combined with the stunning news from Sydney, the mood in Lausanne in the hours before the Ad Hoc Commission presented its report was grim.

A marathon fifteen-hour session on January 23 brought an end to the Ad Hoc Commission's deliberations, setting the stage for the next phase of the IOC's effort to manage the crisis. Six members—Augustin Arroyo (Ecuador),[52] Zein El Abdin Ahmed Abdel Gadir (Sudan),[53] Jean-Claude Ganga (Congo),[54] Lamine Keita (Mali),[55] Charles Mukora (Kenya),[56] and Sergio Santander Fantini (Chile)[57]—were recommended for expulsion. Anton Geesink (Holland) was recommended for a warning. Earlier, three implicated members, Pirjo Häggman, Bashir Attarabulsi, and David Sibandze, resigned. With respect to Swiss law, this negated any further action on their cases by the commission. Investigations involving Vitaly Smirnov, Un Yong Kim, and Guirandou N'Diaye remained active.

Pound related to his Executive Board colleagues that his labor over the past month in connection with the internal inquiry was "the most discouraging and depressing work he had ever had to do."[58] The individual cases represented but one area of discussion for members of the Executive Board. Mbaye, Carrard, and Gosper were charged with developing the terms of reference for a newly conceived Ethics Commission that would have as its mandate the generation of an IOC member code of conduct and adjudicating future matters pertaining to IOC member conduct. Ad Hoc Commission members were keen to refer continued investigations to the Ethics Commission, but Samaranch balked, stating that such a commission would take time to be formally established. In the meantime, a "vacuum" would persist. Finally, it was also determined that the IOC's investigations would extend back to the 1996 Games bid cycle.

Carrard was under no illusion concerning the way forward; the IOC could expect "a difficult ride" in the days leading up to the World Conference on Doping in Sports, scheduled for Lausanne in early February.[59] At an evening press conference, with some five hundred accredited journalists present in Lausanne, Samaranch said the suspension of IOC member visits to the 2006 Games bid cities, put in place at the outset of the crisis, remained in effect. He also reiterated the IOC's support of Sydney and Salt Lake City. "This is the beginning not the end of our work. I am certain," said Samaranch in a hopeful effort to signal the worst might be over, "the Olympic Movement will emerge stronger than ever."[60]

The World Conference on Doping in Sports

For Dick Pound, doping in sport has been, and is, anathema to sport. A number of months before he and other IOC officials battled for the IOC's survival from the Salt Lake City bid scandal, a scandal of another sort rose in association with the 1998 Tour de France. Race organizers expelled the Festina racing team mere days into the competition as a result of the discovery of a systematic doping program revolving around the use of the red-blood-cell booster EPO (erythropoietin). As the race progressed, a number of other riders, together with six more racing teams, dropped out of the event because of what their representatives claimed were heavy-handed police investigative tactics. Cycling was shamed, but so, too, was the wider international sport community. The IOC determined that what had not been realistic in the past—a unified effort by the International Sport Federations (IFs), the IOC, as the preeminent international sport governing body, and public authorities to combat doping in sport and to share the costs of doing so—was now possible.

The IOC pressed forward with plans for a World Conference on Doping in Sport, to take place in Lausanne in February 1999. This placed the conference on a collision path with the IOC's preoccupation with Salt Lake scandal matters. Nevertheless, the IOC followed through. The conference started as scheduled, the ultimate result being the birth of WADA and, by the end of the year, of Pound himself installed as its inaugural chair. A six-point resolution was accomplished, establishing the framework for WADA. Even so, conference attendees, surrounded by the stench of Salt Lake matters, were hard pressed to separate doping matters from bid irregularities. Government officials who attended the Doping Conference roasted the IOC for its ethical shortcomings and stonewalled Samaranch's call to lead WADA himself; IOC members Johann Olav Koss, Anita DeFrantz, and Pound believed the new body required leadership other than Samaranch's. "Hardly a single speaker missed the chance to comment on the perfidy and corruption of the IOC and its general unworthiness," commented Pound.[61] Journalists grilled IOC officials on the scandal and demonstrated minimal interest in the major thrust of the conference. Samaranch, wrote the *Irish Times*'s Tom Humphries, "chaired the proceedings with the wounded solemnity of a condemned man gnawing his final meal."[62]

The atmosphere at Lausanne's Palace Hotel, where many of the conference attendees stayed, including IOC members, was toxic. Reporters were deluged with "anonymous missives alleging affairs between IOC members, shady business contracts, double-dealing and consorting with prostitutes." A badly fatigued and thoroughly overworked François Carrard, himself subject to some of the scurrilous allegations, sadly reflected: "I'm ready to believe almost anything."[63] More than forty IOC members challenged Samaranch to restore their privilege of determining the host city for the 2006 Olympic Winter Games, even if that meant simply deciding between two finalists. "Stripping us of our right to vote," stated one IOC member, "is creating the impression we cannot be trusted. Some bad apples do not make the whole barrel rotten."[64] Stunned by the media treatment and the unrelenting criticism of his leadership, Samaranch retreated to his office, maintaining a much lower public profile as the 108th Extraordinary IOC Session scheduled in March drew nearer. It would be on that occasion that the wider IOC membership would weigh in on the futures of their implicated colleagues.

The 108th Extraordinary IOC Session

Though Juan Antonio Samaranch scaled back his own interaction with the media, the same cannot be said for John Hancock's David D'Alessandro, who continued to assert his feelings publicly that the IOC was not moving forward with the required pace or seriousness in tackling needed reforms. The catalyst for his renewed public commentary was the release of SLOC's Board of Ethics investigation in early February that revealed more details on the five IOC members who faced expulsion (Charles Mukora resigned in late January). Further, SLOC's report focused attention on the actions of ten more IOC officials, including Australia's Phil Coles. D'Alessandro struggled to understand how the IOC had not deemed John Coates's deal with Charles Mukora and Francis Nyangweso on the eve of the vote for the site of the 2000 Olympics an act of bribery. "The IOC is like a royal family," wrote D'Alessandro in an op-ed piece published on February 14, "one in which the cousins have been marrying each other so long, it's no wonder that their ideas of what means what are a little daft." He believed the IOC's reform efforts were stalled. "The lethargic pace of the IOC in rooting out corruption," he railed, "and its about-faces as to what constitutes corruption are hurting every constituency it serves—the corporate sponsors who write the big checks, the broadcasters who write even bigger checks, and the athletes in places so poor they cannot even afford a team uniform or a pair of shoes."[65]

A frustrated Michael Payne concluded that D'Alessandro's piece was a "Valentine message [for the IOC] with a difference."[66] Payne's anger stemmed from his perception that D'Alessandro did not seem to understand, or perhaps acknowledge, that the structure and membership of the IOC did not parallel that of a corporation, thereby necessitating a different approach for achieving the necessary changes.

Throughout the crisis, in direct, matter-of-fact language, D'Alessandro seldom disappointed journalists eager for quotable material. No one should have been caught off guard by his behavior, asserted the *Boston Globe*'s Joan Vennochi: "Those who cover Boston's business community know there is nothing shy or restrained about D'Alessandro. From his flashy ties to his flashy quotes, he knows how to make irreverent statements and seize the spotlight."[67] While some IOC officials were perplexed and dumbfounded by his approach, there is no doubt that his messages were directed toward spurring the IOC to emerge from the crisis intact. At the time, Pound thought D'Alessandro prevented Samaranch and the IOC from steering a path away from major reform. Jacques Rogge did not relish scanning the daily newspapers for D'Alessandro's latest barbs, but when he met with D'Alessandro in 2002 following his election to the IOC presidency, he told him, "I didn't like it at the time, but you did a great thing for us by keeping us alert."[68]

Pound and Payne convened with TOP sponsors on February 11. They knew beforehand that a difficult reception awaited. A recent action by D'Alessandro further raised their discomfort level—the suspension of negotiations with NBC for Olympic advertising on U.S. broadcasts from Sydney and, as well, the removal of the Olympic rings from John Hancock's letterhead stationery. Pound and Payne encountered a business group whose patience was wearing thin. Definitive action was demanded on a number of fronts. Sponsor representatives expressed a lack of confidence in the IOC's commitment to address its problems in decisive fashion. Time was of the essence. Would Samaranch resign? they asked. The IOC Session must jettison the implicated members, they warned. What would the IOC put in place in terms of new site selection voting procedures? A general undertone focused squarely on an expectation that far greater financial transparency from the organization occur in the future. Pound and Payne listened. It was a charged atmosphere. "They wanted 'Kumba Ya,'" noted a TOP representative, "but instead got 'Fire and Rain.'"[69]

Pound felt that few IOC members fully understood the stakes as they prepared for the opening of the IOC's 108th Extraordinary Session on March 17. He drew some relief from public expressions from IOC members concerning the IOC's task. "We must put on the fire water, not petrol," advised Italy's Mario Pescante. "The situation is delicate. If the situation continues, we risk losing sponsors."[70] Zimba-bwe's Tomas Sithole declared: "The public, sports people and the corporate sector are waiting to see if the IOC is serious about cleaning its house. If they see the IOC is serious, they will support us. If not, there is going to be serious trouble."[71] James Easton (United States) knew the importance of expelling the members identified by the Ad Hoc Commission: "If those who are clearly guilty are not thrown off, I would have real concerns about the credibility of the IOC after that."[72] While Pound found their words comforting, he was uneasy, as it became clear to him that few colleagues had read the in-depth files prepared on the members recom-mended for expulsion. Payne questioned whether those IOC members situated distant from Europe, Australia, and the United States, where the preponderance of media coverage on the scandal existed, realized the seriousness of the situation, despite telephone calls from Samaranch and his personal letter of March 9 sent to all members.

Korea's Un Yong Kim, one of the two highest-profile IOC members, along with Phil Coles, who came under investigation by the Ad Hoc Commission, arrived in Lausanne with a bevy of support staff thought to be a mix of bodyguards and lawyers. Though it had been shown that piano concert dates had been arranged for Kim's daughter in multiple bid cities over time, and that he had enjoined Tom Welch to assist in the acquisition of a green card for the owner of a company that had recorded her music, the investigation into whether Kim was privy to the arrange-ments for his son to work for a Salt Lake City telecommunications firm with money allegedly provided by Salt Lake City bidders, remained under examination. In the end, at the March Session, he received a severe censure. However, Kim's case remained open long enough for Samaranch to transfer its responsibility to the newly formed Ethics Commission. This relieved the Pound Commission from continuing the investigation—not altogether unwelcome, as there existed a definite refusal by Pound to sign on with Samaranch's personal call to "save" Kim.

On the eve of the opening of the Extraordinary Session, at a reception for Mitt Romney, the newly named head of SLOC, Kim, whose ire at allegations rose by the moment, exploded. He confronted Carrard, threatening him by striking a menacing Taekwondo stance. Quickly, Pound intervened. "He jumped at me," recalled Car-rard in animated fashion when we interviewed him, yelling, "Bastard!"[73] Carrard departed the terrace at the Château de Vidy with the words, "I quit!"[74] He retreated to his downtown Lausanne office, leaving a message for Samaranch that he was "out."[75]

For Carrard, Kim's antics and threats were despicable, especially with journal-ists present. "Kim was absolutely out of his mind at that time," he said. With his own law practice to fall back on, Carrard had no qualms about removing himself from further involvement with the IOC. Back in his office, he tried to relax with a few friends, including Pound, who had joined him. The aroma of brandy and the fragrance of fine cigars soothed him. He'd had enough of the "zoo." Samaranch, knowing fully well that the IOC's continued efforts to emerge from the crisis would be crippled without Carrard's daily energy and professionalism, called him in an attempt to convince him to return to the IOC's team. "Listen, listen," said Samaranch, "I've been told that you are leaving." Carrard retorted: "I do not need the IOC," further asserting that the treatment he received from Kim was the last straw. "Listen," replied Samaranch, "I understand, you're right, I would have done the same thing." When Samaranch asked what he needed to return to work, Carrard replied, "I need a written apology from Mr. Kim." "That's all?" an incredulous Samaranch asked. "Yes, Mr. President, I'm an easy man, as you know," Carrard replied, telling Samaranch that the situation on the terrace was "insane," with members of the Executive Board fighting. It had to end.[76]

Within thirty minutes, Samaranch called back. He had Kim's written apology in hand; further, Kim was waiting for him in Samaranch's office to offer a verbal apology. "I still have the letter," said a smiling Carrard, who enjoyed recounting the event for us. In his role of director general, Carrard regards the crisis as the most difficult challenge he faced. He received death threats, and for a period of time he engaged personal protection. There is no doubt that Carrard was well aware that the work being done to safeguard the IOC was extremely important.[77] As for Kim, his survival in 1999 was but a temporary reprieve. He resigned in disgrace from the IOC in 2005 before IOC members voted on his expulsion for embezzling $2.8 million from the World Taekwondo Federation and the General Assembly of International Sport Federations, as well as seeking kickbacks in excess of $675,000 from sport officials. A South Korean Court sentenced Kim to a two-and-a-half-year prison term (subsequently reduced to one year).[78]

Nervous tension filled the hall when Samaranch opened the 108th IOC Extraordinary Session on the morning after the Kim/Carrard confrontation. His central message for all those in attendance was simple: their focus would be IOC membership support of the recommendations forthcoming from the Ad Hoc Commission and the Executive Board with respect to expelling six members; approval of the mandate and framework for the IOC 2000 Commission that would develop needed changes to the *Olympic Charter*; and authorization for the establishment of an Ethics Commission. "There has never been an occasion," stated Samaranch soberly, "on which a President of the IOC has needed to express an opinion, in relation to an issue which so profoundly affects the present and future of the Olympic Movement as much as the current circumstance. . . . It is my conviction that unless we act quickly, decisively and unanimously, at the Extraordinary Session, the damage which may be done to the Olympic Movement and to the IOC as a result of the recent disclosures will be very, very serious."[79] Delivering a thorough assessment of his work on behalf of the IOC over the past nineteen years, he presented an ultimatum: he would lead the IOC through this crisis but would not do so without an expression of support from the members. Samaranch departed the hall while a secret vote unfolded. The result, 86–2 (with one spoiled ballot), endorsed Samaranch with an overwhelming mandate to remain at the helm.

Attention turned to the six members, Augustin Arroyo, Zein El Abdin Ahmed Abdel Gadir, Jean-Claude Ganga, Lamine Keita, Sergio Santander Fantini, and Seiuli Paul Wallwork,[80] each of whom entered the hall to address their colleagues for twenty minutes. Each provided passionate defenses of their actions. Subsequently, through secret balloting, they were expelled.

On the second day of proceedings, IOC members duly approved the plans for the Ethics Commission, the IOC 2000 Commission, and the revised host-city selection procedures for the 2006 Olympic Winter Games. Members would select the host city from two finalists determined by a small electoral college composed of IOC members and sports experts. For Samaranch, the Session achieved his immediate goals. Despite these actions, they did little to temper the tenor of media coverage pertinent to his leadership, in part, due to his steadfast determination to lead the IOC 2000 Commission, one dedicated to recommending needed institutional reforms. U.S. Senator John McCain, who planned to hold hearings on the IOC's tax-exempt status through the Senate Subcommittee on Commerce (which he chaired), commented that Samaranch's decision was "worrisome at best."[81] "Apparently, Mr. Samaranch doesn't understand the gravity of the situation for the future of the Olympic movement," stated McCain.[82] In addition, and with respect specifically to Un Yong Kim and Phil Coles, the IOC faced criticism for a double standard in exacting misconduct punishment: both Kim and Coles escaped expulsion. James Easton, capturing the frustration of IOC members, reluctantly declared: "Other than having a public hanging out in the square, we couldn't have done anything else to satisfy the critics."[83] Anita DeFrantz held the same view: "Everything we do will be criticized until the first athlete begins competing in Sydney."[84]

Phil Coles accepted multiple trips (and hospitality) to the United States from Salt Lake City officials. The total cost was estimated at Au\$60,000. Though Pound conceded that Coles had been unwise and that he should have heard "alarm bells," the Ad Hoc Commission distinguished between those who asked for gifts (Kim) and those who had been unwise in accepting them (Coles).[85] Coles's activities came under renewed investigation within mere days of the Session when his ex-wife, Georgina, revealed that she and Coles accepted jewelry from a representative of the Athens 1996 bid committee. Later, the Australian Broadcasting Corporation revealed that it possessed personal dossiers on IOC members produced by Coles and his partner, Patricia Rosenbrock, which ended up in the possession of Salt Lake City bidders. News also surfaced that Coles had taken *two* instead of the permitted *one* companion on a trip to Atlanta during that city's bid for the 1996 Olympics.

With the Ad Hoc Commission relieved of its duties in the wake of the March Session, Coles's case fell to a three-person committee comprised of Executive Board members, Mbaye, DeFrantz, and Hodler. The committee recommended expulsion, but the case divided the IOC Executive Board. Ultimately, a compromise resulted: Coles's resignation from the Sydney Organizing Committee (a move that SOCOG's leadership had been seeking) in exchange for his continued membership on the IOC (but he was to be banned from serving on any IOC commissions for two years). None of this satisfied John Hancock's David D'Alessandro. "The IOC talks about being held to a higher standard," he intoned, "but it performs at the lowest possible denominator. Phil Coles broke all the rules but he gets a pass because he is one of the boys."[86]

Back from the Abyss

Though Samaranch remained largely silent in the weeks following the World Conference on Doping in Sports, this changed in the waning days before the 108th Extraordinary Session. Unsettled by a sense that a "plot" was active within the IOC to destabilize his leadership, he nevertheless pressed on.[87] To his credit, he admitted a personal failing in ignoring the warning signs and allowing the problems within the bidding environment to fester. Samaranch conceded that he underestimated "everything that was going on around all the bid cities—the money, the interests of all types, the temptations, the weaknesses." The situation demanded his intervention much earlier, he stated. But while he understood the matter was "serious, [even] despicable in certain aspects," he and others were frustrated at the virulence of the media attacks, especially when one considered that the "fraud, nepotism, and corruption" revealed in connection with the European Union scandal of early 1999, one that encompassed $1 billion, received far less media scrutiny. He repeated his commitment to make things right: "We have to clean up everything."[88] He then delivered a forceful and confident performance at the March Session that assisted the organization in moving forward, not merely through the expulsion of the six members but also through gaining the members' support for the IOC Ethics Commission and the IOC 2000 Commission. Michael Payne said that it gave everyone—the IOC's staff in Lausanne and IOC members, most especially members of the Executive Board, whose lives had been consumed by the crisis—a bit of breathing room.[89]

In the early weeks of the scandal, Samaranch's performance had been uninspired and stumbling. Indeed, he had been beaten down by early February, when sport executives and government officials convened at the World Conference on

Doping in Sports. With his presidency and much of his personal legacy on the line, in early March he was able to achieve consensus within his organization on important issues. Though he never did win over the media, he survived.

With the passage of time and upon further reflection, Pound believed that problems associated with the bidding process in the post–Los Angeles years were embedded in Samaranch's otherwise laudable effort to grow the Olympic brand and extend its reach across continents and cultures. "In seeking universality," wrote Pound, "[Samaranch] had to make choices. He got some people in that were not as acquainted with the ethical values that you wish."[90] Olympic scholar John MacAloon minced no words in concluding that Samaranch "made huge mistakes by having members co-opted who had not been properly screened."[91] For instance, Ganga's invitation to join the IOC in 1986, opined Payne, was an element of Samaranch's overall effort to "banish" the boycott agenda "from the Olympic lexicon"[92] and extend the Olympic message in Africa. Ganga, one of the leaders of the African boycott of the 1976 Montreal Olympics, later served a ten-year term as president of the Association of National Olympic Committees of Africa. His gravitas and influence in African sport served a purpose for Samaranch. "Did he personally like dealing with Ganga? I don't think so," said Payne. But for Samaranch, Ganga's presence "inside the tent" had value, and if he "lost an airline ticket now and then, [it] wasn't the end of the world."[93]

Clearly, Samaranch was aware of the undercurrent of corruption involved in the bidding process, but he ignored it; he was, however, staggered by the sums revealed in connection with the Salt Lake City scandal. At the precise moment of Samaranch's passing the IOC leadership baton to Jacques Rogge in 2001 and seeking to place his recruitment of the likes of Ganga to the IOC in context, Pound mused: "Was the price worth it? It got messy, but it was worth it. He got rid of those people and kept the universality."[94]

The Salt Lake City Crisis

In December 1999, Samaranch opened the IOC's 110th Session in Lausanne with a determination to usher through fifty proposed reforms to the *Olympic Charter* recommended by the IOC 2000 Commission. "Barely one year before," stated Samaranch

> the IOC was confronted by one of the most serious crises in its existence. Those present knew all the details: it would thus be pointless to go back over them. The crisis revealed that the institution was faced with serious problems regarding its composition, organization, and role, as well as some of its procedures, in particular the selection of host cities for the Olympic Games. The errors committed by some

members of the IOC and other people, such as the candidate cities, alerted world public opinion to the crisis. The IOC was severely criticized, rightly so, sometimes, and its credibility, and even, in some cases, its integrity was called into question. . . . As in many institutions before the IOC, it had taken a major crisis to bring in major changes.[95]

Former U.S. secretary of state Henry Kissinger echoed Samaranch's call for the approval of the reform measures. The recommendations, said Kissinger, were needed "to anchor the Olympic Movement in the public confidence it deserved, so that it could be given the opportunity to adapt itself to an even greater future. Failure to proceed along these lines," he warned, "would create a crisis of public confidence."[96] One by one, with anxious members of the IOC leadership team looking on, the fifty reform measures were passed.

What had been accomplished in 1999? Had the IOC's leadership been able to employ a crisis as a lever for needed change? Was the result transformational for the IOC?

The need for an Ethics Commission and a member's code of conduct was a high priority. The work fell to Gosper, Mbaye, and Carrard, but Mbaye and Carrard were swamped with the necessary work of the Ad Hoc Commission. Gosper took the lead. He consulted with Simon Longstaff, head of the St. James Ethics Centre in Sydney, and Craig McLatchey, the Australian Olympic Committee's secretary general. At meetings in early February, and in further discussions immediately prior to the March Session, the Executive Board deliberated on the mandate of the Ethics Commission.

At the March Session their proposal met resistance from rank-and-file IOC members who believed the seven-person committee was overly dominated by outside officials. Samaranch informed the membership that a majority of non-IOC members was absolutely required on the Ethics Commission. Seeking compromise, Samaranch proposed that the Committee's final composition could be adjusted such that it encompassed three IOC members, one of whom would be appointed by the president as the committee's chair, one athlete who competed recently in the Olympics, and three other outside members. The IOC members accepted the proposed compromise. The Ethics Commission's mandate involved oversight of the activities of IOC members, candidate cities, and Organizing Committees. Its inaugural meeting was held on May 3. Charter members, Mbaye, Gosper, and Chiharu Igaya (who, interestingly, opposed the establishment of the commission, as he saw it as an investigative body of IOC members in the guise of some sort of police force),[97] along with Howard Baker, Javier Pérez de Cuellar, Robert Badinter, Kurt Fürgler, and Olympian Charmaine Crooks, finalized details with respect to the Code of Ethics. The code received the IOC Session's approval in June. It has been an active committee, willing to recommend reprimands, suspensions, and expulsions of IOC members as a result of behavior thought not reflective of the values of the Olympic Movement.

The IOC 2000 Commission put forward recommendations to bring the IOC in line with best administrative practices in the twenty-first century. In its original form, the IOC 2000 Commission was a small working group of twenty to twenty-four individuals, but Samaranch had second thoughts in the wake of the IOC's Session in March. He assigned more than forty IOC members to the commission, though it welcomed a number of high-profile persons for "heft, credibility and prestige" from outside the Olympic world, including Henry Kissinger and Boutros Boutros Ghali, the former secretary general of the United Nations (and at the time the secretary general of La Francophonie).[98]

Once again, D'Alessandro stepped forward in his inimitable fashion to critique Samaranch's decision making: "You have now loaded your reform committee with people who have Olympic DNA, and clearly the offspring of that union will be as cross-eyed as the other results you have brought so far."[99] It was the type of media coverage that Pound warned Samaranch about when he first learned of the IOC president's thinking relevant to the size of the commission. "A commission [of this size] is simply not credible. What is more the proposal contains the names of some who are clearly inappropriate. . . . Even worse," continued Pound, "the international personalities whose presence we have been emphasizing so much in the media, are completely drowned by the mass of 'the usual suspects' from within the Olympic Movement."[100]

Samaranch was unmoved. He believed that the greater involvement of a greater number of IOC members would achieve the buy-in to pass the reforms later in the year when the IOC Session convened. "The media," offered a resolute Samaranch, "tended to do nothing but criticize anyway . . . [I am] used to the criticism now."[101] Pound defended Samaranch's decision, without sharing his own thoughts. In a lengthy exchange of correspondence with D'Alessandro, who continued to be a vigorous provider of strident critiques to the media, Pound sought to temper the aroused feelings of the Boston-based executive. He even flew to New York to meet with him.

John MacAloon, a member of the Executive Board of the IOC 2000 Commission, offers us a possible glimpse into Samaranch's thinking. Gleaning from a personal conversation with the IOC president, MacAloon wrote: "Although Samaranch's personal genius lay in his backstage ability to make everyone he spoke with feel involved, that was hardly the same as real institutional presence for many members." A few veteran members still believed Samaranch erred in "commercializing and professionalizing" the Olympics. Many more thought the Executive Board had grown too powerful, with a well-placed belief that Samaranch's personal position was that it would be better if the Executive Board decided on the host cities. Others thought little of his broadening of the membership of the IOC through the deliberate recruitment of individuals from the most powerful IFs, the most controversial having been Primo Nebiolo, the kingpin of track and field. "This tinderbox of accumulated resentments," concluded MacAloon, "could be further ignited by the understandable outrage of the great majority of honest members over the vicious public attacks on the IOC as a whole, and many were highly critical of, even furious with the leadership for ever allowing things" to "evolve in this fashion."[102] Members were tarred with the same brush. Most will agree that Samaranch had a strong sense of the "pulse" of the IOC at all times. And, at this critical juncture in his presidency with his legacy teetering, Samaranch could not risk marginalizing the wider IOC membership with the overt perception that the process was being driven in top-down fashion. Its allegiance was required, and Samaranch thought that this would be facilitated by enhancing the profile of IOC members in the process.

Once the meetings commenced, Samaranch asserted a measure of authority. The three discussion groups were chaired by Samaranch allies, Franco Carraro (Composition, Structure, and Organization of the IOC), Thomas Bach (Role of the IOC), and Anita DeFrantz (Designation of Olympic Host Cities).[103] Commission members were puzzled and discomfited by the presence of "public relations" figures roving about in the Session rooms, some of whom presented press releases to the commission members before the discussions concluded. "Such practices," wrote MacAloon, "were familiar to those with top-level corporate and government experience, but for most [commission] members it was an unsettling experience." And yet, reports MacAloon, despite this level of control over the agenda, the discussions were "careful, thoughtful, [and] collaborative."[104]

MacAloon also challenged D'Alessandro's contemporary view that the IOC's approach to the reform process could not possibly yield the needed results. "Although many outside critics at the time were sceptical that an IOC commission to reform itself could be anything but a put-up job," wrote MacAloon, "I and other conferees can assure you that it was, from beginning to end, a cause of the highest uncertainty and anxiety for the IOC leadership. Open debate in large forums had hardly been a hallmark of the Samaranch presidency, and now it was to be conducted in an unprecedented atmosphere of public authority and media attention amidst a real crisis."[105]

In settling on a 115-member organization with fifteen people each from the pools of NOC and IF presidents and the athlete community, and seventy at-large individual members, the IOC 2000 Commission delivered Samaranch a desired result. It had been a goal of Samaranch's for some time to enhance the representation of the IFs and NOCs on the IOC. He reasoned that such a move would buy enhanced loyalty from these factions. But the decision invited potential problems with conflict of interest.

Though this type of cross-fertilization had long existed, with the likes of Sigfrid Edström, Avery Brundage, and the Marquess of Exeter, to name just three individuals who, decades earlier, maintained leadership positions with an IF or NOC (in Exeter's case, both) while serving as an IOC member, this shift institutionalized the practice. How could an IF president (or an NOC president) wear two hats and fairly represent the often competing interests of other federations (and NOCs) not represented on the IOC? As well, proportional representation of the IFs and NOCs was skewed. Fifteen of thirty-five IF presidents were now on the IOC, while only fifteen NOC presidents out of more than two hundred NOCs had a seat at the table. The IOC's history was riddled with bloc voting, along geopolitical lines, and now a new specter emerged.

Pound counseled Samaranch on the dangers of permitting the reform process to spin out of control. "Our responsibility at this time is not to allow the IOC agenda to be taken hostage by the media and 'political circles' nor accept the characterizations of the IOC that may result from lack of knowledge of what the IOC is and what it does. . . . **Transparency** is a catch-phrase that is very difficult to define and it is used in many different ways, often to disguise lazy thinking on the part of the user," wrote Pound. "We should define it the way that is most appropriate for the IOC, which, I suggest, should mean that we will disclose on a timely and informative basis all those actions and decisions of the IOC and its constituent commissions that are not, for some good reason, to be kept confidential. Transparency," concluded Pound, "does not mean that the public-at-large is somehow entitled to participate in the IOC's decision-making process."[106]

By July, with the proposed "new look" of the IOC in view, Pound complimented Carraro on his efforts to chair the committee dealing with the structure of the IOC. At the same, time he warned Samaranch, "I see a tendency within the group to go much farther in matters of structural reform than I believe is necessary to respond to pressures we face at this time. I think we should be cautious before dismantling a system that has served us very well for so long."[107] It was a continuing theme in Pound's advice for Samaranch: "We should avoid over-reacting to the crisis by doing too much within the context of IOC 2000. The problems we encountered were not primarily the result of the IOC structure, but mainly the result of our governance."[108] Yet, this was an area of difference between the two. Samaranch believed the problems rested in the structure of the organization, and he clearly sought to leverage the situation to place more representatives of the IFs and NOCs on the IOC.

One of the more contentious debates within the entire process involved the question of bid visits. The IOC 2000 Commission placed two scenarios before the IOC Session. Members could accept the report of an evaluation commission or, if the member believed he or she needed to visit the bid city, one could apply for such an opportunity from the Executive Board, which could make a determination on the manner in which the trip might be taken and would authorize the IOC staff to arrange for its payment. The second option had originally been one that would have established group-member visits on defined days, at the IOC's expense. Samaranch was not comfortable with the second option—the wording of the proposed second option discouraged members from making such a request. And, while it was a hotly contested matter inside and outside the Session hall, the outright ban achieved consensus in a majority vote; however, the grumbling persisted throughout Jacques Rogge's presidency. The ban remains in place today essentially to govern the optics of the matter and to control costs. It takes little imagination to count the numerous ways in which bribes could be proffered and accepted without a face-to-face interaction.

With Samaranch scheduled to depart shortly after the 110th IOC Session for an appearance before the U.S. House Commerce Subcommittee on Oversight and Investigations, a united front was imperative. When the recommendations were presented to the IOC Session in December 1999, Samaranch and his closest allies encountered an unfamiliar atmosphere. Usually able to have cajoled and convinced members of the desired path on major issues, they were unsure of the collective opinion on the proposed reform measures. "I have never seen Samaranch and his floor generals . . . Dick Pound and François Carrard, so nervous," observed MacAloon.[109] Members of the Executive Board and the outside members of the commission sat on the dais staring out at the membership, signaling both the weighty deliberations that had transpired and the need to accept the recommendations. The Session approved all fifty recommendations. Relief was apparent.

In a command performance in front of Representative Fred Upton's (R-Michigan) congressional committee three days after the close of the 110th IOC Session, stage-managed by IOC officials, Samaranch conveyed the IOC's demonstrated resolve. The IOC, at Anita DeFrantz's suggestion, pressed U.S. officials to have Samaranch provide his testimony in Spanish. The questions were translated into Spanish for him, and his answers were translated into English for Upton and his colleagues. The process allowed him time to gather his thoughts before issuing responses to pointed questioning and blunted the prospect of a heated "back and forth" dialogue for television cameras should this have been Upton's desire.[110] The IOC Executive Board was divided on the wisdom of Samaranch venturing to Washington, but the wily Spaniard did not shy away from the challenge, and in the end, he achieved his goal.[111] U.S. congressional bulldogs, severe critics of the IOC amidst the crisis, retreated. Media criticism diminished.

For many in the outside world, especially those within the IOC's community of critics, the reform path followed was not transformational. For instance, while the IOC released its audited financial records, it guarded the payments received by individual NOCs and IFs and did not disclose the terms of individual TOP agreements. In defense of that exclusion, one can well visualize what internal rancor might have been aroused if transparency had been carried to its extreme. For some, transformation was only possible if Samaranch left the scene. He did not, of course, at least not for another nineteen months. For many folks, including those who invested much time and energy over time in observing the activities of the IOC, the changes were significant and startling in their scope for such a conservative, tradition-laden organization, even if not universally successful in their implementation.

For the IOC, its leaders completed the tightrope walk necessary to satisfy its major partners, the sponsors and broadcasters, while preserving its autonomy. Ultimately, the scandal demonstrated the crisis management ability of those in leadership positions, especially given the volunteer, global nature of the organization and, as well, the strength and resilience of the Olympic brand. Even in the throes of the crisis, the IOC was able to elevate the average value of a TOP IV agreement (2001–2004) from $40 million to $55 million. John Hancock's David D'Alessandro, despite his reservations about Samaranch's leadership in the crisis, re-upped with the IOC on a new TOP agreement for 2001–2004.[112] This development, given D'Alessandro's standing as a fierce critic during the crisis, offered the IOC a powerful opportunity for messaging with the world's media. If D'Alessandro could be won over, the IOC had effectively dealt with the problem.

The IOC survived and thrived; we need look no further than near-term and longer-term results for evidence. The 2000 Sydney Olympics were an overwhelming success with a massive global television audience. So, too, were the Olympic Winter Games in Salt Lake City in 2002. The IOC signed record-breaking television and corporate sponsorship agreements during Jacques Rogge's presidency. If one was part of the Olympic world, those who viewed the IOC's actions as simply window dressing, certainly not the root and branch reform for which they clamored, were people who did not understand the IOC and its history. The development of an Ethics Commission, with its accompanying code of conduct and enhanced input from the athlete community, the establishment of term limits for IOC members and its president, the expansion of the Executive Board from eleven to fifteen members, and the lowering of the IOC member maximum age from eighty to seventy, marked major changes in the character of the IOC. Transformational? It depended on one's vantage point, but in September 2017, those who rejected the IOC's reform efforts viewed early reports of the alleged vote-buying scheme targeting African IOC members—orchestrated by Rio's bid committee chief, Carlos Nuzman, to secure the Brazilian city's right to host the 2016 Olympics—with little surprise and much scorn. Another wave of skepticism washed ashore with reports of financial irregularities tied to Tokyo 2020's successful bid.[113]

Closing Thoughts

For Dick Pound, the Salt Lake City crisis scuttled any chance to succeed Juan Antonio Samaranch as president. Leading the IOC's internal investigation earned him respect within the organization's leadership circles but few friends within the rank-and-file membership. Journalists speculated that Pound's presidential aspirations were endangered. François Carrard confirmed this. Pointing to Pound's role as chief prosecutor of his IOC member colleagues, Carrard bluntly stated: "That cost, in fact, Pound all chances for being elected President. There's no doubt."[114] Carrard may be correct; however, a successful Pound candidacy flew in the face of the IOC's long-standing tradition of European leaders (Avery Brundage, an American, having been the only exception), as well as Samaranch's declared support for Jacques Rogge. It was a tall task for the Canadian with or without his service as the IOC's chief prosecutor. Even so, questions remained: Was Samaranch's support for Jacques Rogge during the succession campaign an indication of Samaranch's desire to prevent Un Yong Kim from gaining control by marshaling support from the European bloc, or did it reflect a lingering resentment that Pound voted against raising the age limit to eighty years of age in 1995 when Samaranch (successfully) sought another five years in office? Did he hope for more sustained influence over Rogge, the younger and less experienced man?

In Moscow at the IOC's 112th Session, amid much pomp and circumstance, Juan Antonio Samaranch stepped down. Some questioned just how much Samaranch actually learned from the struggles of 1999. In demonstrating that his power over the membership remained at least partially secure, Samaranch Sr. orchestrated the appointment of Samaranch Jr. (son, "Juanito") to the IOC. Samaranch Jr. received seventy-one votes, but twenty-seven members opposed and another eleven abstained. Samaranch's move was defended at the time by Carrard, Alex Gilady (Israel), and Pál Schmitt, but Marc Hodler's thoughts represented far from a full-throated endorsement: "I know the boy. He's a good boy. He's very good looking and might be the way to attract more ladies into the IOC."[115]

Samaranch's retirement brought an end to the most transformational two decades in the history of the IOC. It was a transnational body of immense financial resources and revenue-generating capacity, scarcely resembling the organization he inherited from Lord Killanin. In the context of the Salt Lake City scandal, as noted by Michael Payne, it had been "to the brink and back."[116] Pound, having been appointed to the IOC in 1978, was witness to it all. Scarcely in his early forties when Samaranch first anointed him to lead the organization's financial mission,

Pound played a vital role in securing the IOC's fiscal future through his leadership work on television negotiations and in the area of corporate marketing. His efforts were central to the IOC's survival through the depths of its debilitating troubles in 1999. Yet the IOC members turned to the Belgian Jacques Rogge, an Executive Board member, former Olympian, and an orthopedic surgeon to lead them. Though a European, in fact, replaced a European, the leadership style of the new president in carrying forward the Olympic mission was vastly different from that of his predecessor.

CHAPTER 9

The European Television Market

As the global television medium developed in the post–World War II years, the U.S. and European markets evolved in decidedly different ways. This reality had far-reaching ramifications for the IOC, its revenue-generating capacity, and its relations with the United States Olympic Committee (USOC). The "big three" U.S. networks, the American Broadcasting Company (ABC), the National Broadcasting Company (NBC), and the Columbia Broadcasting System (CBS), were fueled by commercial advertising. Galvanized by the advent of satellite technology in the 1960s and the enhanced value of live television broadcasts of events at overseas locations, U.S. television executives pursued Olympic television rights aggressively. The lure of U.S. television rights to the Olympic Games grew noticeably. Roone Arledge likened U.S. television executive teams scrambling for domestic television rights to the 1980 Moscow Olympics to "three scorpions in a bottle."[1] Organizing Committee officials happily capitalized on the competitive U.S. market as the price tag on American television rights for the Summer Olympics ballooned from $394,940 in 1960 (Rome) to $300 million in 1988 (Seoul).[2]

Meanwhile, the European Broadcasting Union (EBU), an alliance of government-operated television networks in Western European countries, relied primarily on government funding and license fees assigned to television owners. The near absence of commercial advertising revenue from its balance sheets led EBU's negotiators to resist the IOC's efforts to elevate Olympic television rights fees in Europe. Nevertheless, from 1960 to 1988 Western European television rights rose from $667,967 in Rome (the only time that EBU paid more than the contracting U.S.

network for the same Games) to $28 million in Seoul. Though ABC purchased the U.S. television rights to the 1988 Calgary Olympic Winter Games for $309 million in a unique auction staged by Dick Pound (chairman of the IOC's Television Rights Commission) and Calgary officials, Juan Antonio Samaranch, who retained control of European negotiations, secured a mere $5.7 million from EBU.[3]

Organizing Committees, and later the IOC, held the better hand in their dealings with U.S. networks in the 1960s, 1970s, and 1980s, but EBU officials enjoyed a preferred set of cards in discussions concerning the sale of European rights. U.S. Olympic television rights became a prized and prestigious commodity that offered an opportunity to burnish the image of a network as well as an effective means of promoting the network's own future drama and sitcom programming to a large and captive audience. Leaders of successive Organizing Committees and IOC officials were alert to the enticing qualities of U.S. rights in the minds of American television executives. A high-spirited bidding environment worked to the Olympic Movement's financial benefit. Conversely, Organizing Committees and the IOC lacked the ability to create a bidding environment in Western Europe because of a veritable absence of private non-EBU networks supported financially by advertising revenue. Given this dearth of competition, EBU refused to bid against itself knowing the degree of reticence of the IOC to any form of blackout or reduced coverage of the Olympics in Europe (should it walk away from signing a deal with EBU).

Even when private networks emerged in the 1980s coincident with the IOC's heightened involvement in direct negotiations with the television networks, Samaranch held fast to the belief that EBU was the only entity capable of providing blanket coverage in the region. Only the nagging efforts of Dick Pound pushed Samaranch to finally employ the prospect of establishing contractual relationships with private networks as a lever in his (and Marc Hodler's) negotiations with EBU in the 1990s. Yet industry experts knew Samaranch lacked serious intent to follow through with a break from tradition. He took less money from EBU than the IOC would have gained from negotiations with private networks. Though EBU contracts did increase in value in the years ahead, Samaranch was devoted to EBU throughout his presidency. His successors, Jacques Rogge and Thomas Bach, felt no such compulsion.

In 2004, when the IOC prepared for European television rights negotiations for 2010 and 2012, Rogge signaled a shift in the organization's approach. The proliferation of private networks in recent years placed the IOC in a more advantageous negotiating position. Rogge announced that the IOC would "consider all options— that is, pan-European, multi-territory or country by country."[4] Advocating this agenda and strategic thinking with his boss behind the scenes was Rogge's chief of staff at the time and future IOC director general (2011), Christophe De Kepper, who also believed the IOC should avoid merely extending NBC's U.S. broadcaster status through the 2010–2012 term without a tender process.

Additional revenue, reasoned De Kepper, assisted Organizing Committees (OCOGs), International Sport Federations (IFs) and National Olympic Committees (NOCs). "If we put [the networks in both the U.S. and European markets] in competition," stated De Kepper, "we might have good surprises coming out of them."[5] It proved to be sound reasoning. NBC stunned IOC officials with a $2.2 billion bid for U.S. rights, which included a $200 million TOP sponsorship tied to its parent company, General Electric. On the Continent, EBU continued to prize its role as Europe's Olympic broadcaster. Having paid $578 million for the 2006 Olympic Winter Games and 2008 Olympic Games, Rogge's posture prompted EBU to step forward with a successful $746 million offer for the 2010 Vancouver Olympic Winter Games and 2012 Summer Olympics.[6] However, private entities Sportfive and Discovery Communications later secured European television rights to the 2014 Sochi Olympic Winter Games and 2016 Rio Olympics (Sportfive), and the four Olympic festivals spanning the 2018–2024 period (Discovery Communications) in 2009 and 2015, respectively, thereby ending EBU's run of longer than fifty years as an Olympic broadcast partner.[7]

The wide discrepancy between television revenue generated in the United States and other markets, and the fact that most TOP-sponsor companies were headquartered in the United States, in combination with the ASA, provided the USOC with needed ammunition in advancing its case for special consideration with regard to revenue sharing in the 1980s and 1990s. However, by the time Jacques Rogge assumed office, not only did Europe contribute more to the Olympic Movement's coffers than in years past, but greater geographical diversity in the ranks of TOP sponsors also existed. By 2004, for the first time, U.S.-based companies did not represent the majority of TOP sponsors.[8] Subsequently, European IOC members increasingly questioned the sums of money channeled to the USOC from U.S. television contracts and TOP. This rancor did little to assist Chicago's bid to host the 2016 Olympics at the IOC's 2009 Copenhagen Session. This tension subsequently discouraged the USOC from entering U.S. bid cities in international bid competitions until the interorganizational differences were resolved.

Peter Ueberroth, the USOC's chairman between 2004 and 2008, took a hard-nosed approach in discussions with IOC officials on possible alterations to the USOC's share of television revenue and TOP dollars. He argued against yielding to IOC pressure. His successor, Larry Probst, and Executive Director Scott Blackmun, who rejoined the USOC's leadership team in 2010, recognized that the changing economics of the European market offered a rationale for listening to the IOC's concerns, as well as cause to negotiate.[9] Such an initiative promised a path to better interorganizational relations and offered an element of strategy toward improving the USOC's standing within the Olympic Movement, where many viewed the USOC as insular and greedy.

European Television and the Postwar Years

EBU, based in Geneva, Switzerland, was founded in 1950 as a successor organization to l'Union Internationale de Radio-diffusion. It brought together twenty-three countries from Europe, North Africa, and the near East. This number grew to twenty-seven by the early 1960s. Its budget was largely derived from license fees paid to federal governments by television set owners in the individual countries. The size of each market and the number of television set owners reported determined the yearly amounts transferred to EBU. Individual EBU networks were responsible for production costs of any programming dealing with sports, news, current affairs, and cultural events they produced. But they undertook such activity knowing that they received access to programming generated by other EBU networks at no cost, through an umbrella mechanism for program sharing known as Eurovision. If a European city hosted an international sport event such as the Olympics, it could not charge EBU a sum for the cost of broadcast installations, cameras, or other equipment required to transmit the signal, but it could solicit a rights fee through negotiations. An individual EBU network could opt in or opt out of such coverage, but if it elected to sign on with the project, it was obliged to contribute to the overall rights fee negotiated by the EBU Programme Committee in accordance with the size of its market in relation to all other contracting EBU partner networks.

The public service broadcasting model that prevailed in Europe and the strict limitations on commercial advertising clearly prioritized "public service over profits."[10] It differed noticeably from the "market economy" model that governed the operations of ABC, NBC, and CBS.[11] "For decennia," report Kees Brants and Els De Bens, "the system [was] self-evident, unchallenged and heralded as a dam against what were considered to be the evils of commercial television: the mediocre and the popular, of which U.S. television was the prime example."[12]

This broadcast environment suppressed the sums available from Europe for the Olympic Movement resulting from negotiations with EBU officials. By the close of the 1960s, U.S. television rights for Mexico City (1968) sold for $4.5 million (ABC), while EBU's territorial rights fetched $1 million. Though Willi Daume's negotiations with ABC for U.S. television rights to the 1972 Munich Olympic Games were memorable for the genesis of the technical services-fee concept, they, too, resulted in a widening gap between the revenue delivered from the United States and Western Europe. ABC paid $7.5 million for the Munich rights and directed an additional $6 million technical services fee to Daume's OCOG. For months, EBU refused to budge from a rights offer of $1.7 million, despite the IOC's valuation of the Western European rights at $3 million for the twenty-seven countries EBU serviced. With no competing bidders, Daume and the IOC accepted EBU's terms, a marginally improved $1,745,000.[13]

IOC member Sir Lance Cross, a New Zealander, confessed his bewilderment that the television rights offer forwarded from the Australia/New Zealand region was turned aside by Munich officials despite the fact that it exceeded EBU's accepted bid on a per-television-set basis for the respective areas. EBU enjoyed live-telecast capacity while such did not exist in Oceania, where the telecasts would be delayed, argued Cross. Australia's Hugh Weir, Cross's IOC colleague, was similarly puzzled. For broadcast executives in Oceania, it reeked of favoritism.[14]

Montreal 1976 and the EBU Monopoly

The first concerted and sustained, albeit failed, effort to break EBU's monopoly on Olympic television coverage in Western Europe occurred in the context of the 1976 Montreal Olympics. The Montreal Organizing Committee (COJO) retained Marvin Josephson as its negotiating agent on television contracts. Founder of Marvin Josephson & Associates (MJA), an agent for Hollywood luminaries such as Burt Lancaster, Marlon Brando, and Ingrid Bergman, as well as global music icons such as Elton John, Josephson inserted himself into Montreal's operations through persistent lobbying of COJO officials in the summer and fall months of 1972. Friends and competitors found it odd that he lacked a suntan even though he claimed to be flying to Bermuda each weekend during this period. On such weekends he did not disembark in St. George or Hamilton; he was in Montreal. His sales pitch was, "If you have a legal problem, get a lawyer. If you have TV rights to sell, get an agent." The Bermuda story was a façade to distract his competitors from his activities.[15] Once the contractual relationship with COJO was settled through discussions with ABC executives, Josephson had moved the value of U.S. television rights (combined with a technical services payment) from Munich's $13.5 million to $25 million.

Like Robert Kane and Barber Conable, Josephson completed his undergraduate studies at Cornell University. He subsequently completed his law degree at New York University Law School in the early 1950s. Following a three-year sojourn with CBS's law department, Josephson branched out on his own to establish Broadcast Management Inc. in 1955, the forerunner company to MJA. Broadcast Management was a one-man show whose first client was Bob Keeshan, known best to American television viewers as children's entertainer Captain Kangaroo. As a talent agency, MJA ranked second in size only to the William Morris Agency by 1973. Josephson employed 250 people in New York, Los Angeles, and London. In his effort to break EBU's privileged negotiating standing, he toured Europe to explore welding together deals with individual networks.

By raising the specter of a blackout if EBU did not meet his asking price, Josephson sought to peel off the British Broadcasting Corporation (BBC) or reach a deal with a German network. Once one network left EBU's umbrella, he thought, others would follow, and EBU's bargaining advantage would dissipate.[16] Josephson's activities drew the ire of his main antagonists, Georges Straschnov (head of EBU's legal division, who surfaced later in the decade as the IOC's legal adviser) and EBU's president, Charles Curran. Both Straschnov and Curran sought to protect EBU's control of the sport broadcast landscape in Western Europe.[17] Straschnov registered his displeasure in a phone call to IOC director Monique Berlioux during which he stated that Josephson's machinations "left a very bad impression."[18] "Mr. Josephson," Curran warned Killanin "is on to a bad bet."[19] COJO's demands, he added, "must lead to the disappointment of millions of people throughout the world whose television services cannot pay the sums now demanded of them."[20]

Curran was not a man who would be bullied easily. A World War II veteran and graduate of Oxford University, Curran rose through the ranks of the BBC commencing in 1947. He was appointed BBC's director general in April 1969, a position he held until September 1977. He was well familiar with the hard jostling that accompanies life in the executive suites of major broadcast companies. In the early 1970s, Britain's Conservative government found the BBC's coverage of the troubles in Northern Ireland too evenhanded and, therefore, too sympathetic to the Irish Republican Army. The BBC documentary *Yesterday's Men*, which aired in 1971, amounted to a takedown of Britain's former prime minister Harold Wilson (1965–1970) and his leadership colleagues in the Labour Party. The documentary damaged the BBC's relations with Wilson and prompted years-long accusations of a Conservative bias resident in the BBC. Curran took much criticism for the £2 million the BBC invested in a widely panned set of television plays, *Churchill's People*, based on the legendary prime minister's multivolume literary work, *History of the English Speaking Peoples*. Conservatives railed at the corporation's production of a set of televised plays on Britain's working class in the post–World War I years, *Days of Hope*, that the *Daily Express*, one of the country's major daily newspapers, labeled as "one long political party broadcast for the Communist Party."[21] Curran, as EBU's president from 1973 to 1978, a period overlapping with his tenure as BBC's director general, would not accede to Josephson's "threats" and abandon the BBC's relationships with fellow EBU networks. Television, he said, was not obliged to fund the Olympic Games for host cities that extended themselves too far. "I see no reason," stated Curran, "why broadcasting audiences should be soaked in order to provide amenities for cities who have overbid their resources in seeking to be hosts to the Games."[22]

For IOC president Lord Killanin, Josephson's role in negotiations offered both promise and the prospect of pitfall. He knew Curran and Straschnov sought to retain EBU's status as Western Europe's holder of Olympic television rights at minimum cost.[23] Josephson's tactics might elicit better terms from EBU and more money for the IOC; however, he also knew that no comparison could be reasonably made between the revenue capacity of the U.S. market and that of Western Europe.[24] If Josephson failed to entice any breakaway networks and pushed EBU too hard, his actions might imperil Olympic coverage in Western Europe.[25] "It will be a slow game of poker," he told members of the IOC's Finance Commission.[26]

The two adversaries, EBU and COJO, stared at each other from their respective corners through 1973 and much of 1974. Curran informed Killanin in December 1973 that EBU had no intention of initiating discussions; rather, the responsibility rested with COJO. Straschnov reiterated Curran's message in January 1974.[27] When the sides did sit down in October 1974 with the IOC's newly named television adviser, Walter Schätz, together with IOC staff member Luc Silance, the gulf between their respective negotiating positions was striking. Josephson's team sought $20 million from EBU for television rights and technical services for Western Europe; Straschnov indicated that EBU would be willing to pay $2 million. EBU officials protested that COJO's demands were not aligned with any reasonable understanding of the broadcast market given EBU paid $1.75 million for rights to the 1974 World Cup soccer competition. Schätz was underwhelmed by Straschnov's offer. Only a week earlier, he pegged the maximum and minimum values of Western European rights at $14.17 and $8.33 million, respectively.[28] EBU and COJO departed the meeting and returned to their respective corners.[29]

For the time being, Killanin was content to see negotiations play out: "I do not wish at this stage to interfere in any way," Killanin informed COJO's president, Roger Rousseau, "but I think Mr. Josephson's budgeted figures and arguments are not real, whilst at the same time of course, the low figure quoted publicly by EBU is far too low."[30]

In late January 1975 the EBU and COJO negotiating teams descended on Lausanne for further discussions. Little progress was made during the day-long talks on January 29. COJO consented to negotiate jointly with EBU and Intervision, Eastern Europe's analogous broadcasting union. Josephson declared that the television rights and technical services payments from Western and Eastern Europe should total $30 million—$20 million from EBU and $10 million from Intervision. Straschnov scoffed at this demand and replied that EBU and Intervision would pay a combined $5.5 million. It was, added Straschnov, a final offer.

A thoroughly discouraged Luc Silance told Killanin that "the parties separated without being able to decide on any point whatsoever."[31] Both Silance and Monique Berlioux questioned COJO's strategy of negotiating with EBU and Intervision in the same room. Further, Berlioux lamented that EBU controlled the media narrative, as Straschnov, alone, issued a press release at the close of the meeting.[32] Castigating COJO's negotiating stance and noting that COJO was asking for ten times the figure that EBU paid for Munich, and twenty times what Intervision paid for the rights to the same festival, Straschnov indicated the EBU/Intervision offer in excess of $5 million reflected Europeans' "immense interest" in the Olympics. He placed the ball in COJO's court: "The answer to the question whether European audiences will be able to see the Olympic Games on their screens is now entirely in the hands of COJO."[33] For his part, Curran stated that the longer the discussions dragged out, the more likely that a blackout would unfold, as the network would lack time to acquire necessary equipment.

As the weeks drifted by, Killanin's alarm at COJO's approach increased, and his concerns about the prospect of a blackout grew. He advised Schätz that the IOC needed "maximum viewing from a propaganda view." "It is for this reason," wrote Killanin, "I feel I must put a word of caution in as neither closed circuit television nor negotiating with one or two countries can be the ultimate answer." COJO would need to alter its demands.[34] Schätz advised COJO that renewed talks with EBU should focus on a figure for EBU and Intervision that did not exceed $15 million. COJO rejected his counsel. Montreal officials dropped their demand to $20 million—payments of $12 million to EBU and $8 million to Intervision.[35] Within days COJO tweaked these numbers. In a press release, COJO called for $14.5 million and $6.4 million from the two European broadcast unions: "The offer made today to EBU and [Intervision] represents a substantial concession by COJO to guarantee television coverage to European viewers, who, as a group, have traditionally shown exceptional interest in the Games." Europeans, noted COJO, represented 59 percent of the competitors. By its calculations, Great Britain, France, West Germany, and Italy would be responsible for $21,000, $23,000, $27,000, and $10,000 per hour of Olympic coverage over the course of the sixteen-day event. In Great Britain, argued COJO, dramatic series and football programming costs were $80,000 and $46,000 per hour. "If the broadcasting unions refuse to pay their share, responsibility for whatever outcome will rest squarely on their shoulders," concluded COJO.[36] This rhetoric did little to calm Killanin's jangled nerves.

Killanin counseled Rousseau that the fundamental difference in the financial foundation of the U.S. and European television markets argued against COJO's strategy that ignored such a reality: "I do not completely share your views that too high a pitch to EBU will not terminate negotiations on the present basis."[37] Killanin charged that Rousseau (Canada's former ambassador to Chad, Gabon, and Cameroon, who was appointed COJO's president in 1972) and Josephson were responsible for the impasse. "I can assure you that I have not been 'indoctrinated by the EBU,'" wrote an increasingly exasperated Killanin, "but look at this on the basis of someone resident in Europe, fully conscious of the economic situation affecting broadcasting overall."[38] Jean de Beaumont, chairman of the IOC's Finance Commission, believed continued delays in settling matters with EBU and Intervision threatened both the quality of European telecasts and the reputation of the Olympic Movement.[39] Agitated NOC and IF executives, already displeased with the IOC's concession to COJO's position that all contracts should contain a 50 percent deduction for technical services, implored Killanin to bring negotiations to a swift conclusion. In late May 1975, Killanin informed Rousseau he wanted them concluded within the next two months.[40]

Over the intervening weeks Curran's role broadened to include negotiating on behalf of EBU, Intervision, Organización de Televisión Iberoamericana (OTI), the world's broadcasting union for Spanish-language nations, the Asian Broadcasting Union (ABU), the Arab States Broadcasting Union (ASBU), and the Union des Radiodiffusions et Televisions Nationales d'Afrique (URTNA). In early August, Curran caucused with COJO officials and indicated that the collective he represented offered $8.6 million in the form of an ultimatum, with the prospect of an additional $600,000 if the terms were accepted by September 1. Further delay, he stated, precluded the possibility of telecasts in Europe, as the time remaining would not permit logistical and technical planning. Curran's offer, Walter Schätz said, "[fell] far short of all expectations."[41] COJO rejected Curran's offer and countered with $18,045,000.[42] EBU concluded that negotiations had "finally broken down"[43] and that the gap between the two sides was "unbridgeable."[44]

Killanin's patience was exhausted. In a press release, the IOC requested that COJO reconsider Curran's offer. If accepted, COJO's share of world television revenue would be $27.5 million compared to Munich's $11.9 million. The IOC's share, prior to allocations to the NOCs and IFs, would increase marginally to $7 million from $5.8 million four years earlier. "The need for money for the COJO, IOC, NOCs, and [IFs] must be balanced off against the publicity for the city, country, and Olympic Movement," intoned the IOC, and its rules "[required] the widest possible dissemination of the events of the Olympic Games."[45] Rousseau wished to continue negotiations, but Killanin's position emboldened Curran. He pounced. "There is no more room for Canadian illusions," Curran stated in an EBU press release. "There is no more money available."[46] He set a September 1 deadline and departed for a holiday,[47] confident he controlled the outcome.

Killanin, firmly committed to a solution, obtained a slightly improved offer from Curran and Straschnov ($9.5 million). Sidelining Rousseau and other COJO officials, Killanin sat down with Montreal's mayor Jean Drapeau in London on September 7. Back from his vacation, Curran met with Killanin the following day. These meetings resulted in a settlement with the broadcast unions for $9.5 million.[48] Rousseau buckled. He signaled that COJO's board of directors acquiesced.

Killanin implored Curran to expedite the drafting of contracts with minimal time spent arguing the "small print."[49] EBU paid $4.5 million (of the $9.5 million) for Western European television rights and technical services. Though COJO's belief that Europe should provide a larger sum was fully justified given the number of competing European athletes and the number of television sets and countries within EBU's and Intervision's broadcast regions, its negotiating figures were impossible goals based on the economic basis of Europe's television market in the 1970s and the IOC's aversion to less-than-blanket coverage on the Continent.

A triumphant Charles Curran could not resist needling Canadian negotiators: "I believe the result of these negotiations will not be so much to get the Olympic games pictures, as to consolidate the association between EBU and the other broadcasting unions," he told the *Times*. "I do not think anybody should take us on in the future."[50] Peter Ueberroth did exactly that six years later in his efforts to maximize television revenue for the 1984 Los Angeles Organizing Committee (LAOOC).

Ueberroth Challenges EBU's Monopoly

Marvin Josephson's effort to secure a significantly elevated sum of money from the European television market failed because private networks were in their nascent stage of development, leaving him bereft of viable private networks with whom to sign deals in individual countries. Even if the options existed, it is highly debatable whether Killanin would have approved the contracts because he favored blanket coverage in Europe, and EBU was the only entity capable of meeting the IOC's need for widespread coverage. Josephson's attempt to rattle EBU executives with financial demands such that some might ponder signing individual domestic contracts did not bear fruit. Curran's EBU colleagues did not abandon their standing as members of a bargaining entity.

In 1981, with a record-setting $225 million deal for U.S. television rights finalized two years earlier, Peter Ueberroth turned his attention to Europe. He stunned EBU officials when he demanded $100 million from Western Europe, a dollar figure he subsequently lowered to $84 million. EBU officials were shocked and considered Ueberroth neither realistic nor serious. The two sides departed their New York meeting with nothing resolved, especially when one considers EBU's stated counter offer was $8.33 million.

Italy's Canale 5 changed the narrative in the months ahead when it offered Ueberroth $10 million for Italian television rights alone. Its founder, Silvio Berlusconi, sought to raise the network's profile and loosen RAI's grip on domestic television rights resulting from its standing as an EBU-affiliated network. Ueberroth pressured Samaranch, without success, to approve the deal which represented nearly $1.7 million more than EBU tendered for thirty-three countries. Samaranch, remaining resolute in his commitment to EBU and its coverage of the Olympics in Europe, refused Ueberroth, who in turn inked a $19.8 million draft contract with EBU (though Ueberroth siphoned off $7.8 million for technical services). Samaranch, who knew his commitment to EBU compromised Ueberroth's ability to maximize revenue in Europe, consented to the inclusion of the technical services fee. While Ueberroth's ultimate plan to undercut EBU's negotiating position collapsed, as had Josephson's, he did succeed in tripling the Western European combined figure for television rights and technical services contracted by the 1980 Moscow Games organizers ($5,652,500).

EBU officials well understood the challenge they faced in maintaining the union's profile in telecasting major sport events within a changing broadcast market highlighted by the appearance of Canale 5 and other private broadcasters. Deregulation within Europe's broadcast industry in the 1980s advanced the fiscal aims of emerging commercial networks and created more meaningful competition within the sphere of sport property acquisitions. Satellite channels, too, altered this landscape. Though EBU considered establishing a satellite "sports" channel as early as 1981, the Sports Working Party, struck by EBU's Administrative Council, did not come forth with a recommendation to proceed until 1986. EBU's vision "was 'pulled' by the EBU's persistent desire for a presence in the growing satellite television market," wrote Richard Collins, "and 'pushed' by its recognition that its bargaining power, with both advertisers and the owners of sports rights, was weakening."[51] In 1986 EBU's secretary general, Regis de Kalbermatten, painted a clear picture for the Administrative Council. Private networks posed a looming threat to EBU in terms of its ability to sustain its profile in the sport television marketplace.[52] Part of the strategy behind the launch of a satellite sport channel involved the revenue possible from advertising, which would "help defray the increasing costs of sports rights."[53]

However, some EBU officials, notably Vittorio Boni, chairman of EBU's Television Programme Commission, believed EBU required a commercial partner that could assume "the major financial risk."[54] EBU resolved to move forward in partnership with Rupert Murdoch's News International, an intriguing choice given its status as a past commercial rival. A consortium of sixteen EBU-member networks and News International put ink to their joint ownership agreement for Eurosport in December 1988. Collins explains the mutual financial interests that brought Rupert Murdoch and the barons of European public television to the table:

> News International was to capitalise the anticipated four or five years of initial losses. EBU members were to acquire programme rights for the channel. The deal was attractive to both parties. The EBU was to charge Eurosport high fees for access to its pool of sports rights and, because of these high fees, Eurosport would make losses which News International would set off against profits made elsewhere. News

International would thus reduce its overall liability to corporation taxes. Profits were to be divided equally between the consortium and News International. Eurosport thus secured public funding, via the tax which otherwise would have accrued to the national exchequers of the countries in which News International's operations were domiciled, for a joint public-private venture.[55]

In short, it was a creative way for EBU to protect its place in the changing sports television property market in Europe by diverting much of its rights payments to taxpayers. This helps to explain the climbing value of EBU's payments for European television rights following the Seoul Olympics.

While creative for EBU and News International, it appeared problematic for the European Commission's Directorate for Competition Policy. In 1991 it ruled the arrangement a breach of existing competition legislation. EBU funneled the sports rights it acquired exclusively to Eurosport, and Eurosport was aligned with a commercial, non-EBU network (BSkyB, following the merger of Murdoch's Sky Channel with British Satellite Broadcasting in 1990) with whom it should have been competing. Murdoch, whose gaze had already shifted to the commercial possibilities of BSkyB, extricated himself from the relationship with EBU, absorbing a £20 million loss. Eurosport was actually off the air for two weeks before a new merger with French channel TF1 permitted its resurrection. Though TF1, too, was a commercial broadcaster, its past life as a public broadcaster and its continuing EBU-member status made this arrangement palatable for the competition watchdogs, though they soon extracted a pledge that EBU would offer sublicensing opportunities to non-EBU-member commercial networks. TF1 Group assumed full ownership of Eurosport in 2001 and retained a flow of sport television properties from EBU.

Samaranch and EBU's Monopoly

"If the IOC switched then," mused Michael Payne, and permitted Peter Ueberroth to reach an agreement with Berlusconi and perhaps other players in the newly emerging community of private networks, "where would the Olympics be today?" Admittedly, this is difficult to know, though such an approach at the time, Payne surmised, would have precluded "free-to-air" telecasts for all Europeans, justifying Samaranch's maintaining ties with EBU. Because of lingering questions about the movement's susceptibility to world geopolitics and a diminished interest in hosting the festivals due to burgeoning costs, Ueberroth's path invited undue risk for the IOC given the Olympics lacked "a locked-in foundation."[56]

Despite irritation very late in his presidency when the Executive Board digested news that a number of EBU-member networks sublicensed elements of their

Sydney Olympic coverage to fund rights payments for World Cup soccer games, Samaranch remained committed to EBU, as did the IOC's lead negotiator in the region, Thomas Bach. Bach was particularly aggrieved because he "believed that the EBU was causing harm to the image of the IOC and the Olympic Games. This was certainly not the sign of a good partnership," commented Bach, registering his disappointment with EBU's activities. "The IOC had always protected the EBU," he said, "and they had enjoyed a very good relationship." He understood also that EBU planned to issue sublicenses to the Kirch Group, a German media conglomerate, for a number of sports for the 2002–2008 Olympics, even though the IOC and EBU did not yet have a contractual relationship for 2004 and beyond. "This situation was like a public bazaar," stated a clearly discomfited Bach, who called for much better communication between the parties. He had no answers for journalists who queried him on these matters. Marc Hodler and Anita DeFrantz, fellow members of Bach's on the IOC Executive Board, too, were displeased. Though EBU had the legal right to issue sublicenses, such tactics required permission from the IOC. Thus, EBU-member networks were not abiding by the terms of the agreement. Samaranch pledged to meet with Arne Wessberg, the newly appointed head of EBU, to discuss the matter. He requested that Jacques Rogge and François Carrard accompany him to the meeting at the upcoming European Youth Games. The IOC "had enjoyed an excellent relationship with the EBU, which they wished to continue," stated Samaranch.[57] Three months later, Bach reported satisfaction with follow-up discussions he pursued with EBU officials.[58]

Where Samaranch might have altered his approach to good effect, offers Payne, would have been to court other European broadcast entities more freely over time to "create competition" as a means of eliciting better monetary offers, even if his intent was to stick with EBU. For instance, in 2004 Jacques Rogge gave Bach, who headed European television rights negotiations, and Payne "a pretty free hand"[59] to generate a competitive bidding environment for the 2010–2012 cycle even if they both still thought EBU best equipped to deliver European broadcasts. In this first European negotiation following EBU's long-term agreement for $1.44 billion negotiated in the 1990s that covered the Sydney, Salt Lake City, Athens, Turin, and Beijing festivals, Bach and Payne closed a $746 million agreement with EBU for the 2010 Vancouver Olympic Winter Games and the 2012 (at the time, yet to be named) London Olympics. The result upped markedly the dollars set aside for the most recent pair of Games, Turin ($135 million) and Beijing ($443 million).[60] Payne said that Rogge's willingness to take this approach permitted Bach and him to "keep EBU honest . . . put them under some real pressure, and get the number up to where it should be."[61]

Bach and Payne, though continuing to prefer EBU and the security embedded in their production capabilities, planted the seed with EBU officials that the IOC had other lucrative options under serious consideration. They hired David Kogan of Reel Enterprises, which Kogan had founded in 1998 and through which Kogan burnished his profile largely around his work with England's Premier League. His past consultancy efforts entailed drafting commercial strategies for "broadcasters, newspaper groups and sports federations."[62] For the public record, Bach and Payne sought Kogan's advice on how to approach the European market in advance of the 2010–2012 negotiations. However, Kogan's presence at the negotiating table was pure artifice, a bid to wrong-foot EBU negotiators, something entirely meant to perplex them. Payne's mandate for Kogan meant less-than-onerous demands on Kogan's time. "I don't want you to do anything," Payne told Kogan, "I just want you there listening because it's going to confuse EBU. And it's going to send messages that we're doing different things."[63] And, as events played out, EBU stepped up with a significant offer, perhaps pushed by Kogan's attendance at bargaining sessions but also likely influenced by the prospect that a European city—London, Paris, Madrid, or Moscow, all finalists with New York—would triumph in the election of the host city for the 2012 Olympics the following year.

Jacques Rogge

In terms of his leadership style and the execution of a vision, Jacques Rogge approached the IOC presidency far differently than Samaranch. His predecessor had been a bank executive and a diplomat, one who valued dialogue and debate. Samaranch understood the need for finesse and how best to steer discussions to arrive at his desired destination. Samaranch would often take a circuitous route to a goal: "Right, that's where we want to go. That's the plan. Okay, all clear?" This was a frequent utterance from Samaranch, according to Michael Payne. "And then he would set off in the other direction, completely the opposite direction. I go: 'Hang on, I thought we were going to go over there?' 'Quiet, watch.' And we always arrived at the point."[64] "He was a man with a vision," states François Carrard, "and his vision was to develop, to grow, to give importance to the IOC everywhere."[65] With only ten years' service on the IOC and three years on the Executive Board, Rogge had limited experience as an IOC member. And, though he led the IOC's Sydney 2000 Coordination Commission with success, served as president of both the European National Olympic Committees (1989–2001) and the Belgian National Olympic Committee (1989–1992), and was committed to restoring the IOC's credibility in the wake of the Salt Lake City scandal, he did not possess an overarching vision.

When he contested Rogge for the IOC presidency, Dick Pound asked him, "'What's your platform?' He said: 'My colleagues will tell me what my platform is.'"[66] Christophe De Kepper believes Rogge focused his energies on the IOC's credibility and governance, with an emphasis on doping policy and recovery from the

Salt Lake City scandal. The stability achieved, along with the notable financial gains, left Thomas Bach in a position to advance the movement's goals further in the years ahead.[67] Labeled by some as a "dull technocrat"[68] and "wooden," Rogge preferred to describe himself as "sober."[69] When he stepped down, Rogge confirmed that part of his focus was on the scourge of doping in sport: "We cannot be naïve. The fight against doping will never be won. But I am convinced it is harder to cheat now than it was when I took over."[70] Within two years of his retirement, the scandal concerning state-sponsored doping in Russia placed emphasis on the continuing nature of the problem for those officials committed to clean sport.

Born in Ghent, Belgium, in 1942, Rogge pursued rugby and yachting in his youth, taking ten caps for the Belgian national rugby team and representing his country three times at the Olympics in yachting. At university he studied medicine,

Thomas Bach, IOC director general Christophe De Kepper, and IOC honorary president Jacques Rogge at the World Track and Field Championships in London, England in August 2017. (© 2017 / International Olympic Committee (IOC) / Greg Martin. Photo courtesy of the IOC.)

leading to a career as an orthopedic surgeon. He became fluent in five languages, something that aided him in communicating with IOC members. Leading such a diverse organization poses many challenges, concluded Richard Carrión: "The politics are very crossed in the Olympic movement. There are National Olympic Committees and the International Sports Federations and very, very different bunches of personalities. Jacques' job is like herding cats. Actually, it is more like herding peacocks, because we are terrible [preeners]," he observed in 2011.[71]

Rogge adopted an assertive decision-making approach, taking straight pathways to goals. Payne attributes this tendency to his training as a surgeon, a characterization echoed by Pound and Carrard. There is a problem, here is the solution.[72] Sometimes this approach worked, as was the case with his resolve in taking large television deals to the market and his determination to establish Olympic Broadcast Services (OBS), a subsidiary of the IOC that, established on a permanent basis, now manages the production of Olympic broadcasts in all host cities.[73] OBS eliminates a measure of risk for the IOC and Organizing Committees in the presentation of the Olympics on television, especially in countries lacking the necessary broadcast infrastructure. But, on occasion, Rogge's firmness in decision making did not serve him as well. If we look for a misstep perhaps triggered by this less-nuanced leadership style, we find the controversy involving Wrestling's temporary removal from the Olympic program of events. For Norway's Gerhard Heiberg, though, "he was absolutely the right person at the right time. We had a lot of turmoil. We had to get out of that. We had to get another image. He [brought] stability to the organization."[74]

EBU's Monopoly Dissipates

Timo Lumme arrived in Lausanne as Payne's successor in August 2004.[75] With respect to developing his own strategy for the European television region, he benefited from the existing long-term agreement that extended through Turin (2006) and Beijing (2008), as well as Bach and Payne's recently completed agreement with EBU officials for 2010 and 2012. These deals afforded him the time necessary to complete an environmental scan of the European television market. Ultimately, Lumme, Bach, and IOC president Jacques Rogge exhibited the nerve necessary to break from past practice with the Sportfive contract for 2014–2016, which, according to media reports, totaled $316 million for forty European countries but still permitted the IOC to reach separate deals with networks in France, Germany, Great Britain, Italy, Turkey, and Spain. It is important to note that IOC officials neither disclosed nor would confirm the $316 million figure to us due to confidentiality agreements, but it rather reflects a sum that circulated in various speculative media reports at the time.[76]

Bach and Rogge's backing for the move, observed Lumme, was "unflinching, unhesitating," and vital. "I have to say it was a . . . somewhat firm conviction from my perspective that if the IOC was ever going to progress in the European market it had to loosen the shackles and find partners apart from EBU. In the past there had always been . . . a little bit of a stand-off, but at the end of the day [EBU] would up their offer a little bit and nobody else effectively got a proper look in." Admittedly, it was "a judgement call" to step away from the safety and security of an EBU bid, notes Lumme, but it was an action whose time had come, and one that exhibited logic when considering "the big picture."[77]

Bach and Lumme initiated the tender process in April 2008, with a closing date for bids set for July 1. They received sixteen bids, some based on pan-European coverage, while others targeted regions or national territories. Bids for Italy and Turkey were viewed favorably, and Sky Italia and Fox Turkey, each pay-TV stations owned by Rupert Murdoch, soon acquired domestic rights. The decision was made to move forward with negotiations on individual deals for Spain, Great Britain, Germany, and France, while three bidders, including Sportfive and EBU, pursued the rights for the remaining forty countries.[78] By the close of the year, Bach and Lumme deemed EBU's bid insufficient, and EBU withdrew from further discussions.[79] "EBU members," stated EBU's president Fritz Pleitgen, "were surprised

Timo Lumme, director, IOC Television and Marketing Services (left), and Thomas Bach share a lighthearted conversation at the meeting of the TOP Leader Group in Lausanne in May 2014. (© 2014 / Comité International Olympique (CIO) / Christophe Moratel. Photo courtesy of the IOC.)

by the high financial expectations of the IOC."[80] "The reality is that there were companies in the market that have given more money than the EBU has done at this stage," countered Rogge. "It appeared the EBU was not the highest bidder."[81] Two months later, Sportfive prevailed in the pursuit of rights within the remaining forty territories.

In our interviews with Timo Lumme and Michael Payne, it is clear that a healthy degree of mutual respect exists between the two men. They both understand the challenge and stress involved in driving the IOC's marketing program; however, they differ on the wisdom of the Sportfive deal in terms of its timing. Lumme believed the IOC "had to step into this new era" by broadening its television partner options in Europe.[82] Payne, on the other hand, felt that the uplift in the revenue from the deal with Sportfive, beyond what was achievable through EBU, did not warrant the "risk." Sportfive, he adds, lost significant money and did not return to the table for the ensuing cycle of negotiations.[83] "The short-term might have been painful," concedes Lumme, "but, I think the outcome was absolutely fine, and actually I don't think there could have been a [Discovery] deal if we hadn't gone through that phase of testing the market and actually starting to educate the European broadcast market that the IOC is open for business beyond the EBU."[84] Both Lumme and Payne sought to make clear the distinction between EBU and EBU-member networks in the current construct of European telecasts of the Olympics. EBU, as a negotiating body, lost out to Sportfive and Discovery, but numerous EBU members reached sublicense agreements with them for broadcast privileges in their respective territories.

Lumme and Payne agree on the sound strategy of the partnership that the IOC established in moving forward with Discovery Communications. As a broadcaster, not merely an agency looking to market the rights to individual networks throughout Europe, as had been Sportfive's role, Discovery is motivated to commit to long-term promotion of the Olympics and will endeavor to push eyeballs to the Olympic Channel, the IOC's new broadcast venture. "We went right to the IOC and said our vision was that the Olympic flame would burn 365 days a year," stated Discovery's CEO David Zaslav after closing the $1.45 billion deal for 2018 through 2024.[85] Two weeks after the purchase of the Olympic television rights package, in a $534 million deal with TF1 Group, Discovery announced its now-complete ownership of Eurosport. Discovery obtained a 20 percent share of Eurosport in 2012 and advanced its ownership position to 51 percent two years later. "I think the Discovery deal is absolutely correct. For coverage, exposure, promotion, and [it is] a much better arrangement than the [Sportfive] one," stated Payne, "but it wasn't available four years previously. It's just that the market had evolved and that's where it now stood."[86] It's a "win-win," he concluded, though some good fortune accompanied

Discovery's motivation to leverage its ownership of Eurosport given Sportfive did not take a seat at the table, and EBU's loss of the rights for 2014/2016 dimmed its energy and enthusiasm to bid aggressively.[87]

Lumme, like Payne, has left a significant imprint on the IOC's television and marketing operations. Beyond piloting the IOC's move away from EBU with Thomas Bach and Jacques Rogge, Lumme and Bach were the chief architects of what is said to be a massive $835 million TOP contract in the mobility category with Toyota running from 2017 through 2024 (signed in 2015 with Toyota's pre-rogative to activate its rights upon signature in Japan). IOC staff members would not confirm this figure to us in interviews due to confidentiality agreements, but it appeared in various speculative media releases in 2015.[88] As a member of the Marketing Commission as early as 2011, Bach raised the idea of linking the TOP program with an automobile company. Clearly, it never left his mind.[89] Launched in 2016 following two years of planning, Lumme was a driving force behind The Olympic Channel, the IOC's in-house media platform for Olympic and international sport events, news, and documentaries.

Lumme manages a team of some fifty-five to sixty employees, a number that reveals the broad scope of the IOC's work in television and marketing within the IOC's wholly-owned IOC Television and Marketing Services, S.A., as well as the extent of the IOC's corporate existence in the early twenty-first century. With respect to the TOP program that "evolved into a very, very powerful marketing platform," Payne believes Bach, Lumme, and their colleagues "breathe[d] major new life into the program" at a time when TOP "was starting to fall behind some of the more aggressive marketing of other big properties."[90] The program was underpriced. The Toyota deal, notes Payne, "is a game-changer." Toyota voluntarily ceded some of its rights to permit South Korean auto giant, Hyundai and Kia Motors, to hold domestic rights and serve as the official automobile company for the Pyeongchang Organizing Committee,[91] but going forward the deal blocks a Chinese car firm from a TOP sponsorship contract in Beijing (2022), and similarly, French and American car companies were unable to link up with Paris or Los Angeles via TOP depending on the IOC's selection of a host city for the 2024 Olympics. We now know this to be Paris. "[Toyota's contract] brings the value of TOP into line [with today's sport sponsorship market] and locks up the major markets wherever the games are and takes out all of the competition," stated Payne.[92] "The TOP program is, I think, making a quantum, quantum leap into a new level now," he concluded.[93]

Trained as a lawyer at London's King's College, Lumme, who speaks five languages, brought a diverse background to Lausanne, including various portfolios at IMG Europe from 1988 through 1996, European Sports marketing director for Nike (1996–1999), managing director, Europe, Quokka Sports Ltd. (1999–2001), and vice president, ESPN, Europe, Middle East, and Africa (2001–2004). As a youngster, Lumme participated in numerous sports while drawing inspiration and motivation from Finnish track and field athletes. Juha Väätäinen's epic showdown with East Germany's Jürgen Hasse in the 10,000 metres at the 1971 European Track and Field Championships, which Lumme witnessed on his grandmother's television, and Lasse Virén's double-gold-medal performance in the 5,000 and 10,000 metres races in the 1976 Montreal Olympics, capped off with a fifth-place finish in the marathon, left indelible impressions on him.[94]

Though long fascinated with sport, Lumme's gravitation to sports marketing was a case of "happenstance." Finnish by birth, his family moved frequently in his youth. He attended school in a number of countries, including Belgium, France, West Germany, and for a ten-year stint from age eight to eighteen in England. Helsinki University did not accept foreign school certificates, forcing Lumme to complete his university studies in England. When he prepared for his return to Helsinki to complete his National Military Service, he picked up a copy of Mark McCormack's book *What They Don't Teach You in Harvard's Business School*. He swiftly devoured its contents, prompting an epiphany of sorts: he knew now how he might fruitfully apply his legal training within the sport industry. Through a number of contacts who helped pave the way, he gained an interview for a junior lawyer's position in IMG Europe's Legal Department. "It was just serendipity," confessed Lumme, "it was just a happy conjuncture of passion and chance."[95]

The European Television Market and IOC/USOC Relations

Samaranch's unwavering commitment to EBU and his hesitancy in crafting even the illusion of a bidding market, imploded on the IOC's relationship with the USOC. The widening disparity in the value of television rights reaped from negotiations in the United States and Europe pushed the USOC to invoke its rights enshrined in the ASA. The result was the BMA. Though Michael Payne is correct in his assertion that Samaranch and the IOC would have been ill-advised to move away prematurely from its long-standing partnership with EBU because of the risk involved, Samaranch demonstrated little inclination in creating a bidding market intended to maximize the IOC's revenue from Europe. Perhaps most unsettling for Pound had been Samaranch's decision to sign an "IOC-EBU Co-operation Agreement" in 1986 that outlined future means of collaboration between the two organizations.[96] This was hardly the way to create a bidding environment, he lamented. Going forward, Samaranch's approach complicated the efforts of Dick Pound to manage the IOC's relations with the USOC concerning revenue matters. Why, railed USOC officials, should the United States continue to fund the development of elite athletes in rival countries?

A breakthrough to this dilemma came in advance of the 1996 Atlanta Olympics when Universum Film AG offered $300 million for European rights, thereby forcing Samaranch and Hodler to seek something close to market value from EBU.[97] Over the ensuing years of the Samaranch presidency, negotiations staged in the 1990s yielded improved financial returns from Europe, in part due to the increasing number of viable private network options on the Continent. U.S. television rights from Sydney, Athens, and Beijing totaled $2.4 billion, while Europe yielded $1.19 billion.[98] And it was this increased revenue from Europe that attracted the attention of European IOC members. It was now time for them to howl. Why should the USOC be receiving so much more money than the other NOCs any longer? Jacques Rogge's willingness to create a competitive bidding environment in Europe for 2010–2012 not only further aided the IOC's revenue goals, but also intensified the spotlight on the money transferred to the USOC.

Closing Thoughts

Under Avery Brundage, Lord Killanin, and Juan Antonio Samaranch, EBU was unrivaled as Western Europe's Olympic broadcaster. Following its merger with Intervision in 1993, it continued its uninterrupted status as an Olympic television partner through the 2012 London Olympics. For years EBU lacked discernible competition, leaving OCOGs and the IOC with no competitive bidding environments to nurture. But even after private networks populated the television landscape in Europe in the 1980s, Samaranch preferred the security of deals with EBU, as well as the quality of EBU's delivery of the Olympic Games to its viewers. Samaranch prized the free-to-air coverage, and he took less money to maintain this relationship than might have been made through parceling television rights to multiple partners in individual European countries.

When Jacques Rogge settled into his new office, he established a different approach. He was comfortable in cultivating a bid environment, even if his European negotiators, Thomas Bach and Michael Payne, saw wisdom in continuing the IOC's contractual ties with EBU. Their decision to deploy David Kogan in 2004 as part of the negotiations with EBU executives for 2010/2012 conveyed an impression of a contested bidding environment in keeping with Jacques Rogge's earlier public pronouncement that the IOC's days of dealing exclusively with EBU were over. Five years later, with Timo Lumme at the helm of the IOC's marketing and television operations, Lumme and Bach, with Rogge's backing, resolved to make a break with EBU through the deal with Sportfive for Sochi and Rio, which they viewed as an acceptable risk to broaden their pool of prospective European television partners in future years. Though Sportfive lost money and did not seek to renew its standing as Europe's Olympic rights holder, CEO David Zaslav and his colleagues at Discovery Communications seized an opportunity in 2015 to carve out a long-term nexus with the Olympic Movement (2018–2024), in part by leveraging and further enhancing its ownership stake in Eurosport.

As revenue from the television and corporate sectors in Europe climbed in the 1990s and early 2000s, so, too, did the scrutiny of European IOC members on the USOC's direct shares of U.S. television money and TOP dollars, first obtained by leveraging the ASA in the 1980s. On behalf of the world's other NOCs, the IOC sought redress. All attempts failed. Anger, resentment, and frustration characterized the message of vocal IOC members such as Hein Verbruggen and Denis Oswald, each of whom championed the cause of NOCs for an enhanced share of commercial revenue.

In 2005, IOC members might well have been disposed toward awarding the 2012 Olympics to a city in Europe, thereby compromising New York's chances, but when one considers the IOC's past tendencies, and without the Olympics having been staged in the United States since 2002, Chicago's solid technical bid should have positioned it well in the ensuing 2016 competition. The time seemed right to exploit the rich American commercial market for the mutual financial benefit of the IOC and its Olympic Tripartite partners, including the USOC. This scenario, as we know, did not play out. Former USOC CEO Scott Blackmun believes that Chicago's bid had been effectively dead on arrival as a result of the lingering dispute over revenue distribution.[99] Rio surged forward to victory with the compelling message that it was South America's moment to welcome the world.

The USOC's interpretation of Chicago's demise was clear. Without resolution, the revenue distribution issue was a severe "impediment" to the aspirations of any U.S. bid city, at least in the short term.[100] The USOC did not advance a U.S. city in the bidding for the 2018, 2020, or 2022 festivals. There remains no debate that the Copenhagen meeting served as a flashpoint. While IOC and USOC officials might not have known it as they winged their way home from Denmark, the 2009 Session was a significant turning point in the narrative of IOC/USOC relations.

CHAPTER 10

The 2009 Copenhagen IOC Session

October 2, 2009

At the International Olympic Committee's (IOC) 121st Session in Copenhagen in October 2009, IOC president Jacques Rogge held the envelope containing the name of the victorious host city for the 2016 Summer Olympics. The Rio and Madrid delegations fell silent. They outlasted Tokyo and Chicago to reach the third, and final, ballot. Somewhat clumsily, Rogge displayed the envelope bearing the Olympic rings inverted for the cameras and paused before opening it. He did not repeat the same mistake with the card he pulled from the envelope. Holding it before the plethora of media cameras for a brief moment with the logo oriented properly, he turned it around to reveal Rio de Janeiro as the winner.

The Brazilian bid delegation, led by Carlos Nuzman and the country's charismatic and controversial president, Luiz Inácio Lula da Silva, launched into a raucous, joyful celebration of its sweeping triumph. "Today is the most emotional day in my life, the most exciting day of my life," gushed a jubilant President Lula. "I've never felt more pride in Brazil. Now, we are going to show the world we can be a great country. We aren't the United States, but we are getting there, and we will get there."[1] An emotional Pelé, the country's legendary football star, hugged fellow bid committee members. While Lula, Nuzman, and Pelé rejoiced, fifty thousand Brazilians on Rio's iconic Copacabana Beach erupted in dance and song. The impending economic burden of the country's effort to host the World Cup and the Olympics within a twenty-four-month period in 2014 and 2016, something that should have triggered second thoughts concerning this ambitious plan, troubled no one. Meanwhile, downcast Madrid, Tokyo, and Chicago officials shuffled out of the hall at Copenhagen's Bella Center.

Deflated Chicago delegates pondered the city's bewildering exit from the voting after the first ballot. Michael Payne, who served as an adviser to Rio's campaign and provided expert commentary for the BBC and BBC World, witnessed the hush that fell over the area populated by U.S. television announcers when Chicago's fate was announced an hour before euphoria gripped Lula, Nuzman, and Pelé. And, recalled Payne, "all hell's broken loose in Japanese and Spanish."[2] "So unexpected, so utterly unfathomable, was Chicago's early departure," wrote the *San Diego Union-Tribune*'s Mark Zeigler, "that [Chicago mayor Richard] Daley wasn't even present to hear it live." En route to the Bella Center, Daley heard the stunning news of Chicago's ouster and then returned to his hotel.[3]

Count ESPN's outspoken talk show anchor, Tony Kornheiser, among those dumbfounded at Chicago's dismissal. Only days earlier he believed the additional money available to the IOC from the sale of U.S. television rights by assigning the Games to an American city, and President Barack Obama's appearance in Copenhagen, would sway IOC members in Chicago's direction: "There's two reasons why the United States is getting this one for Chicago: one is that because Obama is extraordinarily popular around the world right now, and two, and most importantly, . . . the answer to all of your questions is money. We prop up the Olympics. Our TV money bankrolls the Olympics,"[4] wrote Kornheiser. Though his logic was not completely flawed, he had it all wrong in terms of sensing the IOC's willingness to reach out to South America. He had vast amounts of company. U.S. athletes bearing orange "Chicago 2016" T-shirts at the USOC's Olympic Training Center in Chula Vista, California, were still filtering into a television room when Chicago learned its fate. They, too, never contemplated that the city would be the first candidate eliminated. The star power of Barack and Michelle Obama and Oprah Winfrey, all of whom pushed Chicago's candidature in Copenhagen, failed to move votes.

Chicago 2016's Copenhagen Collapse

"Every IOC voter knew that Chicago was the most lucrative place to bring the Games," observed Doug Logan, the (now former) CEO of USA Track & Field. "The calculus became: Is this anti-U.S. sentiment strong enough to trump a financial windfall? And today it was."[5] Logan's analysis highlighted the frustration pervading the European cohort of IOC members riled up for some months by Hein Verbruggen and Denis Oswald over prolonged, failed efforts to reach agreement with American officials on revisions to the USOC's shares of U.S. television money and global TOP dollars. The likes of Verbruggen and Oswald believed that the slate of TOP-sponsor companies, less dominated by U.S.-based corporations than in the 1980s and 1990s when the USOC's cut of TOP revenues had been determined and subsequently elevated, as well as the increasing sums of television money on a percentage basis from Japan and Europe, pointed to the need for redress. In calling out the USOC for its "foot dragging" and the unique nature of its sharing of commercial revenue, Verbruggen charged that the USOC received an "immoral amount of money compared to what other people get."[6]

Reflective of the numerous hats that IOC members wear, Verbruggen and Oswald were equally motivated to secure more money for the International Sport Federations (IFs), including their own, the Union Cycliste Internationale and the Fédération Internationale des Sociétés d'Aviron, respectively. Peter Ueberroth, the USOC's chairman, while willing to listen and negotiate over the previous three years, was not inclined to yield much ground and was well versed on the rights ceded to the USOC through the Amateur Sports Act (ASA). Inter-organization tension was palpable as Jacques Rogge's first eight-year term as IOC president closed.

Scott Blackmun believes, in hindsight, the strained IOC/USOC relations badly undercut Chicago's chances.[7] Hard feelings over failed attempts to solve the revenue issue "certainly didn't help [Chicago]," observed Dick Pound, but the bid commit-tee had "no story" to sell, other than competence and that "we can do it well . . . and that's not persuasive."[8] Michael Payne attributed Chicago's troubles to a "bad campaign." Payne also pointed out that the popular narrative of Chicago's downfall being tied to the difficult relations between the IOC and USOC was problematic, particularly when considering the triumphs of Atlanta (1990) and Salt Lake City (1995) at a time when it could hardly be said the two organizations were seeing eye to eye with respect to revenue sharing.[9] John Krimsky, the USOC's former deputy secretary general and managing director of business affairs, and Harvey Schiller, the two-time USOC executive director, were tough adversaries in negotiations with Pound and Payne in the 1990s. Later, Dick Schultz was as well. Pound viewed Krimsky, nicknamed the "Tank" because of his hard, bulldozer-type approach to representing the USOC's financial interests,[10] as a "bully,"[11] a characterization Payne echoed.[12] They found his dim view of the IOC and his descriptors of its members as "Eurotrash" insulting. "There was constant fighting with him," recalls Pound.[13]

Blackmun, who served the USOC as an outside commercial lawyer for Krimsky in the 1990s, confirms Krimsky's use of the ASA as a tool to leverage money for the USOC: "We don't talk much about it, the Amateur Sports Act, nowadays with the IOC, but back in the nineties when I was the USOC's commercial lawyer, or one of them, that was kind of the beginning, the middle, and the end of every conversation that John Krimsky ever had with [IOC officials]." Krimsky constantly "[reminded] them that they can't even come into the United States without his permission."[14] "The USOC cared nothing about the IOC," states Pound. "We were a complete nuisance to them. They thought we were interfering in their business. Or, at least [they] constructed that model—and simply wanted money. They wanted control of the U.S. television negotiations and revenues."[15]

The USOC hounded Pound for years in pursuit of an enhanced share of U.S. television revenue beyond the 10 percent established in the Broadcast Marketing Agreement (BMA) signed in 1986. In 1997 the two sides agreed on an increase to 12.75 percent, but not without significant rancor. When the Americans tried to move legislation surreptitiously through congressional channels under the cover of the 1996 Atlanta Olympics that would have transferred control of negotiations to the USOC, such that the USOC could have set its own percentage share, Pound, Payne, and other IOC officials "went bananas."[16] Even Samaranch, whose tendency was to try to solve problems and avoid conflict with the USOC, was fuming. He had been holding bilateral talks with USOC executive director Dick Schultz that promised to yield a 15 percent share for the USOC. The deceit playing out on Capitol Hill angered him, yet his focus remained on finding a resolution. The IOC's (former) long-time director of legal affairs, Howard Stupp, once asked Samaranch, "Why aren't we tougher with the USOC?" "If we are tougher," responded Samaranch, "they will lose. But, so will we."[17]

François Carrard found himself in the middle of the conflict pitting Pound and Payne against a "gallery of personalities" in the USOC. In reference to the ASA's terms granting the USOC exclusive rights to the use of the Olympic rings in U.S. territory, repeatedly used as leverage by Krimsky and his USOC colleagues, Carrard recalls telling Samaranch at some point the time had come for a legal challenge. "Look, we've been expropriated. Let's go fight. Let's fight it out and see legally who is right and who is wrong?" "Stop, stop, stop," replied Samaranch. Carrard believes the frequent turnover in the USOC executive offices proved challenging for IOC officials and that he could only move so far in working to improve personal relationships with USOC representatives, as he had to avoid "casting too much shadow over Dick Pound," whose responsibility it was to manage the IOC's commercial interests in North America. Samaranch steered a conciliatory path. Carrard characterized Samaranch's approach: "I don't know Americans well but they are Americans and America is America. Let's not [rock the boat too much]." "And," concluded Carrard, "it was always a bit difficult to find a proper line [with the USOC] you know."[18]

In this particular episode tied to Schultz's lobbying in Washington, a solution was only possible if Samaranch took a hard line. Pound and Payne succeeded in prompting Samaranch to threaten cutting the IOC's ties with the USOC. Pound recalled Samaranch's stern message issued privately to USOC officials: "Listen, you should understand that we can get along very well, thank you very much, without the United States. We'll have less money. We'll all have less money. You'll have less money because you'll have nothing to sell, because you're not going to be part of the Olympics. And, so, make a call, folks. Either we're all in this together and cooperating or you're out."[19] USOC executives took note. It was the "first time that [USOC officials] suddenly said, 'Oh, these guys are serious,'" observed Pound.[20] The settlement that resulted in moving the IOC's share of U.S. television revenue from 10 percent to 12.75 percent soon followed.

Michael Payne is accurate in his view that the IOC awarded the Games to U.S. cities twice in the 1990s when these challenging dynamics in the IOC/USOC relationship existed; however, what perhaps separated Chicago's experience from those of Atlanta and Salt Lake City was that its bid unraveled, in part, because of the public nature of the dispute in 2007–2008. Some IOC members were voicing strong opinions, many of them well reported in the global media, on the USOC's unwillingness to compromise and the need for change in allocation of commercial revenue.

Though not personally sold on Rio's preparedness for the task, Pound says Chicago also committed some errors. He asserts that Tokyo outmaneuvered Chicago on the first ballot. Chicago needed to maintain a firm grasp on those first-ballot votes, Pound observed, because "the crucial round really is the first round. It's not the last round." Tokyo bidders campaigned for support from Chicago backers in the first round voicing a need to avoid an embarrassing result. Tokyo's success in peeling off votes on this tactical pretext spelled doom for Chicago, said Pound, especially when combined with the city's lack of a captivating message. He also believes American officials discounted the allure of Brazil to some IOC members. Brazil, one of the quartet of BRIC countries (Brazil, Russia, India, and China) boasted a newly emerging advanced economy. Pound did not entirely discount the friction between the IOC and USOC as a factor, but it was merely one of a number of issues at play.[21]

The Obama (Non-)Factor

Barack Obama, whose appearance in Copenhagen was eagerly anticipated, did not deliver the votes, and Payne learned later from a friend who served as one of the president's speechwriters that Obama and his team prepared his remarks during the flight to Copenhagen on Air Force One. In contrast, President Lula's speechwriters pored over the task for close to a year.[22] One can imagine that Obama and his team were far more engaged in salvaging their country's ravaged economy, a result of the global recession of 2007 and 2008, laying the groundwork for the upcoming Copenhagen Climate Change Conference (December 2009), and working through the details in formulating the Affordable Care Act, signed into law in March 2010, than they were in stumping for Chicago.

Obama was not inclined to go to Copenhagen but changed his mind when he learned other nations' leaders would be attending the Session. The decision to go, let alone his inability to bring home the prize, drew the rebuke of Republicans such as House Minority Leader John Boehner (soon to be Speaker of the House): "Listen, I think it's a great idea to promote Chicago, but he's the president of the United States, not the mayor of Chicago," declared Boehner, "and the problems we have here at home affect all Americans, and that's where his attention ought to be."[23]

John Hoberman, a keen observer of Olympic affairs and author of *The Olympic Crisis: Sport, Politics, and the Moral Order*, believed Obama should have trusted his gut. While the president prepared to depart for the Danish capital, Hoberman wrote:

> All of this makes Obama's Olympic mission a political gamble both at home and abroad. If he pulls it off and brings the games to Chicago, he will add a gleaming, but low-carat, gem to his crown. For there is nothing that fades more quickly from the American mind than the quadrennial Olympiad. If he fails, the right wing will pillory him as a dilettante who should have kept his eye on weightier affairs of state. Nor would a "loss" to the president of Brazil or the prime minister of Spain do much for Mr. Obama's international stature. All of this suggests that Obama should have left well enough alone and stayed at home.[24]

Years later, as Obama prepared to leave the White House in 2016, Chicago's loss still gnawed at him: "I think we've learned that the IOC's decisions are similar to FIFA's decisions: a little bit cooked," Obama said. "We didn't even make the first cut, despite the fact that, by all the objective metrics, the American bid was the best."[25] Informed people can differ reasonably on how and why Chicago's bid collapsed in Copenhagen, yet for USOC officials, specifically chairman Larry Probst and (then) soon-to-be appointed executive director Scott Blackmun, events dictated a considered and focused response.

The USOC's Response to Chicago's Loss

Years of fruitless discussions between Peter Ueberroth and his team of USOC officials, and the likes of Gerhard Heiberg, the IOC's Marketing Commission chair, Verbruggen, and Oswald preceded events in Copenhagen. Ueberroth grew increasingly annoyed over the drawn-out process, particularly since he believed he shook hands with Heiberg on three occasions, only to have those deals rejected in Lausanne. Ueberroth concluded that the track of negotiations indicated the IOC "would rather have disagreement than agreement."[26] Knowing that U.S. television and corporate sponsorship sources still provided the Olympic Movement with 60 percent of its revenue, discussions angered him because he believed that the IOC was leveraging these negotiations in the context of Chicago's bid. And Ueberroth held firm in granting no further concessions. As he stepped down, he drew his line in the sand: "Who pays the bill for the world Olympic movement? Make no mistake about it. Starting in 1988, U.S. corporations have paid 60 percent of all the money, period."[27] "Be sure you all understand that. The rest of the world pays 40 percent. It's pretty simple math," intoned Ueberroth.[28]

With no solution in sight, the IOC and USOC pushed their chairs back from the table in March 2009, a number of months after Larry Probst succeeded Ueberroth, pledging to renew discussions in 2013. The USOC might have been wise to let things stand there. But instead, before the IOC's concerns were resolved, the USOC pressed forward in announcing its project, two years in the making, for a United States Olympic television network in collaboration with Comcast. With the Copenhagen Session mere months away, the USOC's action flummoxed IOC Finance Commission chairman Richard Carrión, who stated, "They know we have issues. I just find it frankly cavalier on the part of the USOC. It's just vintage USOC."[29] It did nothing to advance Chicago's bid, offered Carrión. Though no longer the USOC's chairman, a miffed Ueberroth shot back: "We started this two years ago. Everybody's known [this] was coming on and so we're not surprising anybody."[30] Probst, sensing trouble, retreated, pledging to Jacques Rogge that the plans would be delayed until a later date. But damage to Chicago's bid was apparent. A source linked to the IOC noted, "While clearly Chicago is not the USOC and vice versa, some members are blind to the fact and only see it as Americans making trouble and that obviously will have an impact on the vote."[31]

In the aftermath of Chicago's defeat, a glum Patrick Ryan, chairman of Chicago 2016's bid committee, rationalized the struggle to counter Rio's campaign. What message could any city offer on its merits when confronted with Rio's intense lobbying based on South America's never having hosted the Olympics in the past? It was hard to "trump" that.[32] And, though he believed the USOC had been a good partner, he hinted at the difficult dynamics in the USOC/IOC relationship—drawing reference, in fact, to persistent squabbling reminiscent of the feuding Hatfields and McCoys of late-nineteenth-century West Virginia and Kentucky. Backlash within America's elite sport community was swift and severe. Though Larry Probst survived, the USOC's acting executive director Stephanie Streeter did not. She removed herself from consideration in the organization's search for a permanent executive director. In early 2010, Scott Blackmun waded into this quagmire in his return to the USOC as Streeter's replacement.

Scott Blackmun: A New Voice

Scott Blackmun's childhood was somewhat nomadic. As the son of a steel salesman, his family lived for various periods in the midwestern cities of Gary, Quad Cities, Indianapolis, Cleveland, Hammond, and Chicago. But one constant in his life was sport. Most of his experiences were with neighborhood friends, in stark contrast to the manner in which many youth engage in sport today: "[I left] the house in the morning [to] go play baseball and football and soccer and other stuff till it was time to come home for lunch and dinner," recalled Blackmun. As an undergraduate at Dartmouth, he played varsity soccer for four years. Blackmun started college as a math major, but transitioned to religion, then, ultimately, to philosophy.[33] He graduated summa cum laude in 1979. From Dartmouth he moved west, studying law at Stanford; he subsequently began his career as a practising lawyer with Denver's Holme Roberts & Owen, LLP following graduation in 1982. The USOC engaged his law firm in its dealings with the IOC and the 1996 Atlanta Organizing Committee, and this experience led the USOC to recruit him in the late 1990s, initially in the role of general counsel and senior managing director of Sport, and subsequently as the acting CEO in October 2000 for a twelve-month stint.[34] "I took a 40 percent pay cut when I took [the USOC] job and I have never been happier," noted Blackmun. This career change offered an opportunity to "make a difference." "I realized the thing that I was enjoying more than anything else was going home and cutting my lawn on Friday afternoon because when I finished, not only could I have a beer, but I could look over my shoulder and see somehow I had made the world look a little better."[35]

Blackmun spent much of his time in his early days on the job assisting USOC chairman William Hybl confront the domestic fallout from the Salt Lake City bid scandal that broke in late 1998. Though not a pleasant experience at the time, given the level of media scrutiny and criticism, Blackmun believes much good came from the various investigations, both for the IOC and the USOC. He credits Hybl with deft management of the USOC's interests through the establishment of the Mitchell Commission headed by former U.S. senator George Mitchell. Mitchell, states Blackmun, "was beyond reproach. It was a brilliant move."[36]

Fast forward a decade when Blackmun returned to the USOC as its executive director and CEO in early 2010 after more than four years as chief operating officer with Los Angeles–based Anschutz Entertainment Group and a four-year return stint with Holme Roberts & Owen, where he became a partner in 2008. Once again, he faced a challenging USOC work environment, this one precipitated by Chicago's demise and the unrest within the American community of national sport governing bodies over the perceived wasted opportunity that defined Chicago 2016's defeat. In 2010, on the positive side, the USOC was far less dysfunctional than it had been during his initial period of employment. Restructuring of the USOC in 2003 and 2004 carved the board of directors from an unwieldy 120-person group to ten. "It was like night and day," Blackmun states. "There literally were no politics domestically when I arrived back in 2010. Zero. I had complete flexibility and freedom to do what was in the best interest of the organization, and it wasn't like that in my first stint." Blackmun does not see himself as a "cheerleading"-type leader who will lift folks from their seats with his oratory but rather as an individual who does his utmost to "walk the talk when it comes to integrity and commitments and preparation."[37]

The Road to Peace: From Vancouver to Quebec City

Scott Blackmun soon realized the challenge ahead in stabilizing and improving the USOC's relationship with the IOC. Blackmun, newly arrived at the USOC, and Probst, with only a year of service but with much of that time dedicated to domestic Olympic affairs, requested a meeting with IOC officials during the 2010 Vancouver Olympic Winter Games to introduce themselves. Blackmun recalls the charged atmosphere in the room:

> We attended a meeting in Vancouver during the Games. It was Larry and I with probably ten IOC members and there was a lot of anger in the room. I mean a lot of anger. They didn't tie their feelings directly to the 2016 outcome but it was obvious

From left, USOC executive director Scott Blackmun, USOC president Larry Probst, and IOC president Jacques Rogge appear at an USOC-sponsored reception during the 2010 Vancouver Olympic Winter Games. These were difficult days in IOC/USOC relations as the IOC grew increasingly frustrated with the inability of the two sides to reach an agreement on revisions to existing revenue-sharing agreements on U.S. Olympic television money and TOP revenue. (© 2010 / International Olympic Committee (IOC) / Richard Juilliart. Photo courtesy of the IOC.)

there was no love lost for the USOC. In that group that included [Christophe] De Kepper, [Jacques] Rogge, Denis Oswald, René Fasel, people I would call leaders of the IOC . . . and we walked into a buzz saw in that meeting and it became crystal clear that the USOC was an impediment to the U.S. ever hosting the Games again because they had a hard time being in the same room with us.[38]

While not referring directly to this meeting, Christophe De Kepper confirmed that Blackmun and Probst soon processed that "there could not be the right interaction and the right place for the U.S. Olympic family within the Olympic Movement if [the revenue issue] did not get solved." Olympic stakeholders, confirmed De Kepper, believed the revenue-sharing deal, last modified in 1996 and 1997, required review and amendment. "There was a very genuine feeling within the movement that you cannot have an open-ended contract. Very positive for the USOC with revenues from the U.S. that were declining," stated De Kepper.[39]

Blackmun's initial environmental assessment revealed a need for action on a number of fronts. The state of IOC/USOC relations troubled him and represented his biggest challenge. However, the situation was more complicated than the existence of the dispute over commercial revenue. Blackmun conceded that the USOC was not an "engaged participant" in the Olympic Movement. For instance, the USOC did not send high-level representation to the meetings of the Pan-American Sports Organization (PASO), the umbrella-like body for the some forty NOCs from the Americas. "That's just not right. It was something very flawed about our role in the global movement and we needed to change that," stated Blackmun.[40] Americans were (and remain) underrepresented in the presidential offices of the IFs. For years, as the president of the International Softball Federation (1987–2013), American Don Porter labored as the only U.S. citizen to hold such presidential authority within the IF community. This same mantle soon fell on David Haggerty, elected president of the International Tennis Federation in 2015. In general, this is an "unfortunate" circumstance, notes Blackmun. He viewed such realities as contributing to the USOC's "isolation."[41] He also sought better working relations with America's national sport governing bodies. "I think for a long, long time," he reflected, "we viewed ourselves as only supervising our national governing bodies—disciplining them, writing the rules, as opposed to empowering the national federations to be more successful." He believed the path forward was best laid if the USOC enhanced its efforts to serve the federations in more effectively executing their collective mandate to produce the nation's elite athletes and Olympic medals. The national federations and their athletes should be viewed as the USOC's "customers." And, last, from a revenue standpoint, there was much room to grow the organization's charitable donations by targeting modifications to its philanthropy program.[42]

The launching pad for discussions on television and global sponsorship revenue matters involved bringing resolution to a second confounding financial issue separating the two organizations. The USOC had not previously contributed to the cost of staging the Games (Games Cost fund), as had other NOCs, by subsidizing the onsite work of the World Anti-Doping Agency, the Court of Arbitration of Sport, and other IOC commissions.

Christophe De Kepper arrived at the IOC in 2001 as President Jacques Rogge's chief of staff, but in 2011 he was appointed the successor to Urs Lacotte as the IOC's director general. A graduate of Leuven University's law school, De Kepper pursued further studies in European law at Brussels University, then served in a number of capacities before assuming duties in Lausanne, including assistant to the Belgian Olympic Committee's legal director, as an adviser on the European Commission's development of sport policy in the European Union (EU), and as director of the liaison office between the European Olympic Committees (EOC) and the EU. As a youngster he was drawn to the Olympics as they were displayed on television in the early 1970s, and he had various sporting interests, including soccer, tennis, and field hockey. In adulthood he continues to enjoy mountaineering, ski mountaineering, and cycling. He admits deriving much personal fulfillment from sport and, like many working within the Olympic world, is committed to the promotion of sport's benefits to "the widest circle of people."[43]

Philip Hersh, the *Chicago Tribune*'s well-informed former Olympic beat writer, commented that De Kepper, as Rogge's chief of staff, labored to "calm the waters" between the parties, as did Gerhard Heiberg. Still, Verbruggen and Ueberroth struggled mightily to find common ground.[44] De Kepper witnessed both the failed talks leading up to the Copenhagen Session and the IOC's pent up frustration with the USOC's unwillingness to work toward resolution of the Games Cost issue. An even greater issue concerned the distribution of television and corporate sponsorship monies. The IOC well understood the unique nature and size of the USOC's share of television and global corporate sponsorship dollars. "Why, then, are you not participating in the costs?" De Kepper asked rhetorically. The other NOCs, whose share of such revenue was much, much less, assisted in meeting the IOC's operational costs in Olympic cities. He put forward the IOC's exasperation: "How do you, USOC, explain that you receive a big part of the cake . . . you participate in the party, but you do not pay for your drinks? Whereas everyone [else paid for their drinks], you take the biggest part of the cake?"[45]

During Jacques Rogge's first term the IOC could never get USOC officials to answer this question. It was repeatedly brushed aside with the thought that the USOC might in time review the matter. De Kepper concedes that numerous changes in the holders of USOC executive offices at the time impeded discussions, as the two sides never built a relationship that provided a platform for meaningful negotiations. But, he affirms, "that changed with Probst and Blackmun." They brought "stability" to the negotiations and expressed a clear willingness to address the IOC's concerns.[46] The USOC and IOC engaged in discussions over a number of months, culminating with a breakthrough at the Youth Olympic Games in Singapore in August 2010. Within a month the USOC announced its intent to transfer $18 million to the IOC as its share of the NOCs' payments for Vancouver and London. As a result of its share of the proceeds from the newly signed ten-year TOP sponsorship between the IOC and Dow Chemical, the USOC moved forward in this direction. "This was something that we needed to focus on sooner rather than later if we wanted to have a constructive relationship," offered Blackmun.[47] Admittedly, bridging the bitter, public divide over commercial revenue between the IOC and the USOC, and the likes of differences between Ueberroth and Verbruggen, posed a more severe challenge. With the Games Cost issue behind them, both parties turned their attention to the bigger issue—the USOC's part of the cake.

Within six months Probst and Blackmun were appointed to the IOC's International Relations Commission and its Marketing Commission, respectively, offering opportunities to further engage with Lausanne officials. The IOC pressed its case over a series of ten to fifteen meetings with USOC officials between 2010 and the announcement of a deal in May 2012.[48] Threading the needle, and finding a suitable deal, tested the USOC. Blackmun needed to satisfy the IOC, an end that furthered his and Probst's mission to improve IOC/USOC relations, yet, at the same time, not abdicate his duty to the USOC and the U.S. athletes who depended on their NOC for financial support.[49] The IOC's deal makers De Kepper, Heiberg, and Carrión stated that the commercial environment was different than when the USOC's share of U.S. television revenue and TOP dollars had been originally set. "There's a fundamental principle," states Blackmun, "that the IOC articulated that gave me the comfort that it wasn't a breach of my duty to the USOC to entertain an idea of changing, [that being] that when these percentages, both for broadcast and sponsorship, were established, the U.S. represented the majority of the revenue."[50] Clearly, the global marketplace for Olympic properties experienced a transformation with greater sums of commercial revenue forthcoming from Europe and Japan, as well as other markets.

It took a year and a half for the two sides to find a "structure" workable to the parties after having batted around five to ten different approaches.[51] Discussions staged at the 2012 Youth Olympic Winter Games in Innsbruck provided a breakthrough. Fine-tuning of the agreement occupied both teams for the next few months,[52] with Blackmun and De Kepper completing the work in Washington a week before the international sport community convened at the 2012 Sport Accord Convention in Quebec City. The status quo prevailed until 2018, but from 2020 through 2040, the USOC's historical percentages, 12.75 percent of U.S. television revenue and 20 percent of TOP revenue, would be applied to the sums equal to those accrued during the 2009–2012 quadrennium. But once those minimums, adjusted for inflation year over year, were reached, the USOC's share on any overage dropped to 7 percent for U.S. television money and 10 percent for global sponsorship dollars.

IOC and USOC leaders found little difficulty in selling the deal to their respective constituencies. The IOC needed the USOC to contribute to the Games Cost fund going forward, as well as accept amendments to the USOC's shares of U.S. television and TOP money. Any deal signed by Blackmun and Probst had to protect USOC revenues, not decrease them. The IOC, in reaching a deal that had eluded its representatives for years, enhanced the Olympic Movement's share of commercial revenue somewhat, but the USOC's privileged sharing position concerning these monies by virtue of the ASA remained intact. "A good deal is always a deal where there are two winning parties and no losing parties," concluded De Kepper.[53]

Larry Probst understood the agreement did not the end the USOC's mission to reposition the organization within the Olympic Movement. "I think we have to continue our international outreach," Probst said, and "continue to show up at the meetings, events, competitions, seminars, whatever it happens to be, and build those relationships with those individual IOC members. That responsibility falls on me, on Scott [Blackmun], on our IOC members. I would say that's Job One now that we've solved the revenue-sharing issue."[54] Still, Jon Tibbs, chairman of Jon Tibbs Associates, a consultancy firm with broad experience in advising various international sport organizations, neatly summarized the Probst-Blackmun tandem's contribution: "It seems as if the USOC has found the right balance between listening and communicating. They are treated more as equals than as an exception, and they're behaving like equals rather than an exception. That means people are viewing them more as partners, and there's a greater sense of partnership with the USOC now."[55]

Keen observers of relations between the two organizations, Dick Pound and Michael Payne, confirmed the improved interorganizational dynamics and credited Probst and Blackmun for their efforts. "I think you got, in Larry Probst and Scott Blackmun," stated Pound, "a team that understands the bigger picture and the need for the USOC to be part of it."[56] "A key part of their strategic agenda" in the aftermath of the Copenhagen Session, echoed Payne, was to reach out to Lausanne officials and other partners within the Olympic Movement to "build a better rapport and relationships."[57] In their minds, as a result of the consensus reached in 2012, the USOC preserved its fundamental interests, and the IOC was able to trumpet success, even though, in real dollars, little changed. "I think it's like Vietnam. Everyone declared victory and pulled out," said Pound. Both sides "punted" the issue to "thirty years down the road."[58]

All smiles! From left, Scott Blackmun, Larry Probst, Jacques Rogge, and IOC Finance Commission chairman Richard Carrión are shown after signing the terms of the new IOC/USOC revenue-sharing agreement in Quebec City in May 2012. (© 2012 / Comité International Olympique (CIO) / Renaud Philippe. Photo courtesy of the IOC.)

In reference to the IOC/USOC accord, concludes Michael Payne, "there's no question that the [IOC/USOC] relationship is significantly improved," but "as it relates to the business terms of the agreement, there's no difference to what it's always been. It's got an awful lot of nice ribbon around it and wrapping paper and everything around it, but there's no real difference."[59] Perhaps in this case, after years of quarreling and tumult, it mattered less what was committed to paper than the simple fact that the paper existed. After all, symbolism plays a key role in driving the Olympic Movement.

"Hey, Partner. Congratulations."

Especially with respect to the role played by USOC officials, one lens with which to view repaired IOC/USOC relations is through an examination of the processes involved in negotiating the 2010–2012 and 2014–2020 U.S. television rights agreements under Jacques Rogge and the manner in which Thomas Bach handled talks that resulted in the $7.75 billion contract with NBCUniversal spanning six Olympic festivals during the 2022–2032 period. Largely bystanders for the former two sets of negotiations, in 2003 and 2011 respectively, Bach brought USOC executives to the table as the private discussions between the IOC and NBCUniversal reached their advanced stages for the latter deal in 2014.

Much as had been Rogge's mission with European television rights negotiations, he wished to put the U.S. rights for 2010 and 2012 out to the marketplace. It was necessary to do so, in part, to assist in repairing relations within the U.S. broadcast community, specifically with NBC's rival networks who were shut out of the IOC's move to long-term rights agreements in the territory dating back to the mid-1990s.

Rogge entrusted responsibility in the negotiations to Richard Carrión and Michael Payne, after having rebuffed Dick Ebersol's efforts to secure a simple renewal of the agreement. On the decision to take the U.S. rights to the market, Payne states, "Rogge, in my view, made absolutely the right call," adding that it was the most effective method to secure a spike in the value of the television rights in a territory. As a result, Carrión and Payne turned their focus toward creating competition. "The more brides you get to the altar, the better the result," Payne observed matter-of-factly. CBS lacked interest, but it appeared ABC and FOX were ready to challenge NBC. All parties were informed that the IOC's target figure was $2 billion. However, two weeks before the scheduled negotiations, Dick Glover, ABC's Olympic point person, called Payne to tell him they could only proceed with a deal based, in part, on revenue sharing. A frustrated Rogge was ready to call off the negotiations, but Carrión convinced him to let events play out; Payne invited Glover to Lausanne irrespective of the network's bid concept.[60]

Richard Carrión, then chairman and CEO of Banco Popular de Puerto Rico (now executive chairman of Popular Inc.), headed the IOC Finance Commission under Rogge at a time that coincided with the growth of the IOC's financial reserves from $100 million to $900 million. He served on the IOC Executive Board from 2004 through 2012, holds a B.A. from the University of Pennsylvania's Wharton School of Finance and Commerce and an M.S. in management information systems from the Massachusetts Institute of Technology. Rogge entrusted Carrión with the responsibility to negotiate many of the television agreements signed during his IOC presidency, as Samaranch had similarly entrusted Pound. Carrión ran for the IOC presidency in 2013, basing his campaign on his business experience and proven ability to manage large companies during challenging economic times. He finished second to Bach. Interestingly, Carrión advocated placing IOC permanent staff in host cities to assist in preparations for the staging of Olympic festivals, basing his advocacy for such a move on his service with the IOC's Coordination Commission for the 2016 Rio Olympics. While financial security for the IOC and his role in safeguarding it underpinned his candidacy, he asserted that money, while important, was not his only focus: "This is an organization based on values," he said. "I am a person that is very much attuned to financial trends, but I recognize very deeply [that] the moment we forget our values, it doesn't matter how many TV contracts you have, it doesn't matter how much money is in the bank."[61] Other challenges facing the Olympic Movement that he highlighted in his campaign included "the financial downturn, doping, match-fixing, youth obesity and [the] threat of natural disasters."[62]

If Carrión failed to stiffen Rogge's resolve less than two weeks before the bidding, ABC's bid would disappear and the target figure would dissolve. Carrión was resolute in his counsel for Rogge in terms of the IOC's monetary goals in the U.S. market and what might be forthcoming from U.S. executives: "If it's less than $2 billion, we are walking. If there is any hint that we will accept less than $2 billion, the thing will unravel."[63] ABC, FOX, and NBC delegations convened in Lausanne. Rumors circulated that Rupert Murdoch, who hosted Rogge for a "get to know you" meeting some six months earlier, would be making FOX's pitch personally; though not true, it was a rumor David Hill, the network's president of Sports, did little to quell. In the end, though, FOX's presentation was professional and captivating, and Hill's offer was not competitive—which Hill knew, but he energetically engaged in the process as a means of driving up the price for NBC to deprive his competitor of money for battles for other sports properties. ABC's revenue-sharing concept was not workable for the IOC. Dick Ebersol and his NBC colleagues were convinced FOX was willing to at least come close to the $2 billion floated by the IOC. NBC's contemplative process brought it to the point that it could come up with $2.2 billion if its parent company, General Electric (GE), joined the TOP-sponsor community.[64]

As the NBC presentation involving various executives unfolded (marked by the presence of Jeffrey Immelt, GE's chairman and CEO), Payne sized up the direction in which things were moving. He recalled a conversation over drinks with NBC's senior vice president Gary Zenkel a year earlier when Zenkel dismissed Payne's call for him to convince GE officials to join TOP. Yet, on this day, that is exactly how NBC and GE planned to sideline Rupert Murdoch. Payne leaned over to Rogge, who was listening intently, and whispered, "They're going to throw GE into TOP." "What are you talking about?" Rogge asked. "Watch," said Payne.[65] NBC officials duly rolled out the concept of linking a GE TOP sponsorship with NBC's bid as a means of supplementing the size of the overall financial package. Soon after, IOC officials learned that Mark Lewis, who headed marketing operations for the 2002 Salt Lake City Organizing Committee, had been spirited into Lausanne by NBC's team to work with IOC officials on a TOP deal on GE's behalf, if the IOC welcomed the approach. But how could GE, with its many products and business portfolios, work within the TOP structure?[66] It was all unbelievably good fortune for Rogge and the IOC, and after a number of hours of deliberations, the IOC, NBC, and GE arrived at a deal.

However, there was a sticking point—the USOC. Acting USOC executive director Jim Scherr brought his own delegation to Lausanne—in Payne's words, "to try to muscle in on negotiations."[67] Clearly, the USOC, too, was caught off guard by NBC/GE collaborative approach. USOC legal counsel, Jeff Benz, announced that he and his colleagues would have to give further consideration to GE's proposal after returning to Colorado Springs. Nothing could be consummated that evening. IOC officials were adamant that the deal proceed. Payne, now an actor in a drama, invited Scherr and other members of the USOC's delegation to come to a press conference to offer their opinion on the collapse of discussions with the networks. "Pale faced and nervous," Rogge watched as Payne staged a number of "theatrical tantrums"[68] that ultimately had the desired effect of bringing the USOC in line. On June 7, 2003, around 2:30 A.M., the IOC and NBC teams proceeded to Lausanne's majestic Beau Rivage Hotel to unwind over a festive and celebratory meal.

In 2011, when Rogge and Comcast's (NBC's parent company) CEO Brian Roberts fielded press questions pertinent to their signed $4.38 billion deal for U.S. rights to the 2014–2020 Olympics, Larry Probst viewed the proceedings from the same vantage point as reporters. Once again, despite the departure of Dick Ebersol only three weeks before the bidding when contract negotiations with Comcast executives on a four-year deal with Ebersol broke down, NBC walked away with the prize. Ebersol's exit unsettled Carrión and his IOC team of negotiators, but Mark Lazerus slid seamlessly into the role of chairman of NBC Sports Group. The network's enthusiasm for the U.S. rights remained strong.

Following Ebersol's departure, NBC and Comcast staff held a "town hall" meeting aimed at bolstering morale and making clear that Comcast was all in for the upcoming negotiations. Bob Costas, NBC's veteran Olympics anchor, and some twenty other officials made the trip to Lausanne. NBC delivered a presentation "that knocked your socks off," recalled Timo Lumme, the IOC's director of IOC Television and Marketing Services. In the moment, Rogge leaned to his right and told Lumme, "There are no questions possible after a presentation like that."[69] Not only did the IOC find the value of Comcast's bid a remarkable expression of its commitment to the Olympics,[70] so, too, did they find Ebersol's return to NBC Sports as a senior adviser before the end of the summer an excellent omen for NBC's coverage of the upcoming 2012 London Olympics.

Three years later, when Roberts and President Bach fielded similar questions in the happy afterglow of having signed a $7.75 billion contract for U.S. rights running from 2022 through 2032, Probst sat next to them on the podium. Though Bach and NBC officials held preliminary talks about the future television landscape in the United States during the 2012 London Olympics, the notion of an extension was not proposed by the IOC until November 2013. When the private talks entered the final stages of negotiations in March 2014, Bach brought USOC officials to the table. Lumme, a key individual driving the IOC's interests with Bach throughout the process, valued the USOC's contributions: "The cooperation from the USOC was absolutely excellent," he said. "They were totally supportive, and if they hadn't been, we wouldn't have been able to get from the end of March to the beginning of May [in the negotiations]. That's evidence of the great collaboration and strong relationship between the IOC and USOC."[71]

Whether the IOC left money on the table by not taking the contract years to the market is an open question, says Michael Payne, but there's financial security for the IOC when one considers that Bach has his own agenda to work through and the IOC was interested in advancing its Olympic Channel initiative.[72] With respect to the USOC, it all gave weight to Bach's impromptu comment when he saw Probst in the hall after the deal on revenue sharing through 2040 brokered by Rogge and USOC officials had been reached in Quebec City in 2012. Bach (an IOC vice president at the time) walked up to him, smiling, and uttered words not often shared by USOC and IOC officials in the past: "Hey, partner. Congratulations."[73]

Closing Thoughts

The city of Chicago's connection with the Olympics runs deep despite having not hosted the games. In 1901, backed by what John MacAloon refers to as the first Olympic bid committee, a group populated heavily with luminaries from the University of Chicago, such as founding president William Rainey Harper and football coach Amos Alonzo Stagg, Chicago won the right to host the 1904 Olympics. Reports indicated as many as six thousand students celebrated the announcement on the school's Marshall Field. A real estate investor and lawyer with the city's Steere & Furber law firm, Henry J. Furber Jr., headed the bid committee and Chicago's efforts. He asserted that the cost would be $200,000, revised upward later to $250,000, but revenues would reach $375,000. The design vision presented by Holabird & Roche, an architectural firm inextricably linked with Chicago's late-nineteenth- and early-twentieth-century burgeoning streetscape, was highlighted by a main stadium with "70,000 seats, a movable roof, an extraordinary neoclassical construction, the kind of wonder of the time," observed MacAloon.[74]

Alas, regrettably for the city's contemporary sporting community, the stadium never rose from the ground on what is today Grant Park, where Barack Obama gave his historic presidential acceptance speech on the night of November 4, 2008. In early 1903, Coubertin moved the Games to St. Louis to coincide with that city's staging of the Louisiana Purchase Exposition in 1904 when it became clear that St. Louis organizers planned to marginalize Chicago's festival with an athletics program that drew many of the country's best athletes. Chicago subsequently failed to prevail in Summer Olympic bid competitions for the 1952 and 1956 games, as well as the contest for the right to host the 2016 Summer Olympics. Chicago stands second only to New York in the United States in terms of Olympians born in the city, numbering in excess of 270.

In 2009 an IOC poll revealed that two-thirds of the city either "strongly supported" or "supported" Chicago's bid for 2016. However, local polling completed by the *Chicago Tribune* mere weeks before the Copenhagen Session revealed a more divided population.[75] Still, on the morning of October 2, 2009, fifteen satellite trucks from various news outlets, parked on Clark Street, which borders Daley Plaza, complemented thousands of Chicagoans who congregated, thinking a celebration awaited. All were astonished and confounded when they learned Chicago's fate. "Given Chicago's status as the favorite," wrote the *Chicago Tribune*'s David Haugh, "this was the equivalent of a No. 1 seed being ousted by a No. 16 on the first day of March Madness. A shocker."[76]

For the supporters of Chicago's bid, 2009 was littered with the makings of a perfect storm. There lingered the dispute between the IOC and the USOC over commercial revenue, the fires of which had been stoked in recent months. There remained, too, the shortcomings in Chicago's messaging as alleged by the likes of Pound and Payne. Finally, the hard charging, enthusiastic backers of Rio's bid made a strong case that if the IOC truly supported ambulatory games and sought to promote the Olympic ideal in all regions of the world, much as had been the case with Beijing's campaign for the 2008 Olympics, there really was no choice other than to reach out to South America for 2016.

In Olympic history, the Copenhagen Session looms large for many because of the IOC's decision to venture to South America, but in the commercial history of the IOC itself, it is a milestone event, one that provided a decisive change in the narrative of IOC/USOC relations. The USOC's chairman, Larry Probst, and executive director, Scott Blackmun, following a period of introspection and soul searching in the wake of Chicago's defeat, understood that America's image within the Olympic Movement was at low ebb and the country's aspirations in terms of hosting future Olympic Games would be unrealized without a change. They needed to invest time and energy in building relationships, and they did so. Though not a winning motto for Hillary Clinton's 2016 U.S. presidential campaign, there is little doubt the IOC and USOC are "Stronger Together." They cannot possibly agree on all issues, but the ability to sit down, discuss matters, and respectfully debate them as a means of seeking consensus is a welcome development for the Olympic Movement.

As we neared the completion of our manuscript and then, again, in the later stages of the production of this book, the USOC's leadership picture changed. In September 2018, Larry Probst revealed his decision to step down in December. He was replaced by Susanne Lyons, a USOC Executive Board member since 2010. In late February 2018, Scott Blackmun announced his retirement, urged by a prostate cancer diagnosis and the need for ongoing treatment following surgery. Sarah Hirshland, formerly the United States Golf Association's chief commercial officer, stepped into Blackmun's former role in late August. He also faced external pressure to resign as a result of perceived failings of the USOC in handling the Larry Nassar case (USA Gymnastics), together with additional revelations concerning past sexual abuse of athletes within USA Swimming. The graphic, heart-wrenching testimony of Nassar's victims during his sentencing hearing in January 2018 did little to quell those voices. Ultimately, Blackmun, Probst, and the USOC board of directors concurred that the organization's ability to engage in effecting additional positive change in this sphere of its operations, something that would likely require changes to the ASA to obtain further oversight responsibilities over the country's national sport federations, necessitated the leadership of a CEO unimpeded by the health challenge Blackmun faced.[77]

Epilogue

We could have written much more. Paring down the history of the International Olympic Committee's (IOC) evolving nexus with commercial revenue to ten milestone occurrences provided an immense challenge and prompted more than a few debates between us. Readers, too, might question our decision making, but one of the roles of the historian is to prompt discussion and dialogue. It is one way of stimulating further historical research as a means of advancing knowledge.

One such event that might have deserved in-depth treatment was Juan Antonio Samaranch's successful campaign to open up the Olympics to professional athletes in the 1980s. Unanimity for such a direction did not exist within the IOC, and he encountered substantial resistance, especially from Soviet-bloc IOC members who knew the status quo worked in their favor in terms of their countries' production of medals, though opposition was not limited to this region. It represented a key element of Samaranch's strategy to enhance the financial standing of the IOC, as well as its financial security, as the Olympic Movement emerged from the 1970s. He understood the enhanced value of the Olympic property in the minds of television executives and corporate sponsors if the world's best athletes competed, a development that would also spur ever-increasing numbers of television viewers globally.

Lord Killanin made inroads with the eligibility issue in the 1970s by removing the word "amateur" from the *Olympic Charter* and establishing the trust-fund system for Olympic competitors, but the issue of athlete compensation still plagued the Games in the early 1980s.

Enough with the hypocrisy, said Samaranch. He deftly managed the process over a number of years by leading from behind. He well understood this was not an initiative that he could impose on the membership, and he saw to it that the International Sport Federations (IFs) were empowered to set eligibility regulations in their respective sports. They shared a desire that the best athletes compete as a means of driving the promotion of their sports under the glare of the Olympic spotlight. Willi Daume's Eligibility Commission did much of the heavy lifting in terms of steering the IOC's collective thinking, and then Samaranch pounced at the 1987 IOC Session in Istanbul.

The trigger for an open Olympics was the admission of tennis and its touring professionals to the 1988 Seoul Olympics, and Samaranch, in steely-eyed fashion, much as Coubertin had done at the Sorbonne in 1894 when he convinced members of Europe's elite to back his enterprise, used his control of the Session agenda to good effect. He scheduled the discussion of the issue just before lunch at the end of a morning session without a scheduled coffee break. More than thirty IOC members weighed in on the debate and talked themselves out. They needed lunch. The tennis professionals were admitted without a formal vote, as Samaranch simply concluded: "So, we are agreed that tennis is accepted!" Lunch was duly served. Samaranch's push for professional athletes attracted significant criticism from those who lamented the perceived loss of the Olympics' innocence, even though money found its way into athletes' pockets for years before Samaranch arrived in Lausanne. For his biographer, David Miller, "[this] was the day the Olympic Movement finally acknowledged the truth which it had sought to camouflage for thirty years or more; that the Games had to be opened up."[1]

However, we focused on *money matters* in this book—specifically, negotiations concerning commercial revenue as the primary means of driving the narrative, as well as the people who represented the engaged parties: negotiations between the IOC and its Olympic Tripartite partners, the IFs and National Olympic Committees (NOCs), negotiations between the IOC and those entrusted to lead Organizing Committees (OCOGs), negotiations between the IOC and the United States Olympic Committee (USOC), and, once the IOC's corporate basis took shape, direct negotiations between the IOC and executives from the private sector. If one tries to visualize the history, the words and stories within this book chart a learning curve for an organization and its leadership concerning commercial revenue and the means possible through the embrace of television and corporate sponsorship to generate it and protect it.

The steepest trajectory in this curve represents two successive phases of learning: the 1970s, when Lord Killanin set in motion a plan to elevate the IOC's knowledge about the television industry and the negotiations process; and the 1980s and 1990s, when Dick Pound and Michael Payne served as the chief architects of Samaranch's vision to wed the Olympics to the corporate world in an era of globalization. The knowledge gained was further leveraged to good effect by Presidents Rogge and Bach, and those working on the IOC's behalf such as Payne, Richard Carrión, Gerhard Heiberg, Timo Lumme, and Christophe De Kepper.

With respect to this second phase of the learning curve, Dick Pound believes a shift in the IOC's outlook in terms of its relationship with broadcasters and sponsors was crucial. Part of his contribution, he says, "was getting us to understand that even though we aren't a business, we're dealing with businesses. We have to at least understand their needs, as well as our needs, and to deliver on the promises." As a member of the Executive Board in the 1980s and 1990s, he endeavored to build relationships within the Olympic business community and worked "to defend their interests in front of the IOC." It was a necessary role and service, reflected Pound, "to get from where we were to where we needed to go."[2]

One battle that Pound and Payne fought steadily in the early years of Samaranch's term was to maintain the "clean venue" policy—in other words, no corporate advertising within competition venues. Samaranch saw money there, and building the IOC's reserves was a central element of his presidential mission, but they eventually convinced him to abandon the thought of change. Payne adds that the 1996 Atlanta Olympics transformed the IOC's thinking with respect to the Olympics representing a "brand," something that needed to be nurtured and protected. In Payne's early days of employment in Lausanne, if he'd uttered the phrase, "Olympic brand," he would have been fired. But when much of the Atlanta Olympics, at least its projected image, was hijacked by overcommercialization Samaranch was resolute in his response, telling Payne, "You take control and you don't ever let that happen again." What followed, asserts Payne, was a transformation in "the concept of the IOC as franchisor and the Organizing Committees as franchisees." Once fully aware of the "magic" and the "intangibles" and their role in making Olympics special, and the need to burnish and protect its asset value, there "was a transformational leap in the value of the Olympics."[3]

In Olympic historiography, Samaranch has received a significant amount of attention given the sea change that occurred during his presidency. His policy of seeking maximum value for television contracts (with the European market standing as a notable exception) and the genesis of the TOP program drove the IOC's reserves from some $200,000 in 1980 to approximately $100 million when he stepped aside in 2001.[4] In historical depictions and Olympic "lore," Samaranch's impact on the IOC's financial foundation has cast a long shadow over Jacques Rogge, with our own past work contributing to this situation. Indeed, one of the central motivations in writing this book was to extend our own analysis of IOC leadership related to the generation of commercial revenue through the Brundage, Killanin, Samaranch, *and* Rogge presidencies. Rogge empowered his chief television negotiators, Richard Carrión and Thomas Bach, to use the marketplace and the tendering process to boost the IOC's revenue-generating capacity. "Rogge got the jump," confirms Payne, "got the increase over inflation" on major deals, and orchestrated change in the IOC's connection with the European television market.[5] Payne and, later, Timo Lumme pushed the value of TOP sponsorships. The returns were impressive.

Mere months into his own presidency, Thomas Bach could look at a favorable circumstance with IOC's reserves exceeding $1 billion.[6] The momentum achieved from the resolution of the USOC/IOC dispute under Rogge, one of his most important achievements, paid handsome dividends in the early years of the Bach presidency with the 2022–2032 NBC agreement, other television deals, and TOP renewals totaling close to $10 billion. NBC likely factored the possibility of U.S. host cities in this time frame, as a result of the settlement reached between the USOC and IOC in 2012, when working through the numbers on its $7.75 billion renewal signed in 2014. This sum, generated "in a minimum period of time," asserts Christophe De Kepper, "has no parallel in Olympic history."[7] Though McDonald's withdrawal from the TOP program in 2017 three years before the expiration of its deal sent a mild tremor through the Olympic world given its forty-year-plus relationship with the Olympics, recently signed agreements with Bridgestone (2014), Toyota (2015), Alibaba Group (2017), and Intel (2017) leave the TOP program in a healthy circumstance with thirteen sponsors.

The soundness of the IOC's financial foundation permitted Bach the opportunity to sidestep the lingering uncertainty of the Olympic-bid-city environment. With an increasing number of bid cities withdrawing from the process in recent years due to financial concerns, despite the passage of his Olympic Agenda 2020 reforms aimed at encouraging expressions of interest and bolstering cities' ability to execute their hosting mandate, the IOC was left with only two bid cities for the 2024 Olympics, Paris and Los Angeles. Rather than dismissing Paris for the third time within a short period (2008, 2012) in its pursuit of a third Olympic festival (1904, 1924) or losing a quality bid from Los Angeles, especially when one considers the Olympics' absence from U.S. soil since 2002, Bach orchestrated a process in 2017 leading to the IOC's approval of both cities hosting successive festivals in 2024 and 2028. And, while Bach was not initially inclined to bring such a plan to fruition with the use of financial resources, in exchange for Los Angeles accepting the 2028 Olympics, the Los Angeles bid committee pressed successfully for concessions. It received a guaranteed minimum of $1.8 billion from the IOC's television and corporate sponsor deals with a possible additional $200 million, $180 million to fund the operations of the Organizing Committee for an additional four years, and a supplemental transfer of $160 million for youth sport programs in the region. The IOC also waived its 20 percent take of any surplus revenue generated.

As the close of his initial eight-year term approaches, Thomas Bach has been extremely active in pushing forward his agenda, headlined by Olympic Agenda 2020, but has also had to divert his attention to deal with issues as they arise, such as the messy fallout from the Russian doping scandal. All eyes are trained on him while he steers the IOC through a scandal in Rio de Janeiro tied to the alleged efforts of Rio's bid committee chairman and president of Brazil's National Olympic Committee, Carlos Nuzman, and associates, Arthur César de Menezes Soares Filho and Sergio Cabral, to buy votes for Rio from African IOC members before the host-city vote at the IOC's 2009 Copenhagen Session, and as he navigates the troubling developments tied to Tokyo 2020's bid. Dick Pound notes that while Olympic Agenda 2020 is perhaps overly ambitious in some areas, such as the international educational component, the flexibility granted to bid cities in pursuing their path to hosting makes good sense. "You can't have these cookie cutter, made-in-Lausanne games all over the world anymore," but he also warns too much decentralization of the mission must be guarded against.[8] The IOC advanced this cost-savings platform prior to the 2018 Pyeongchang Olympic Winter Games when the Executive Steering Committee for Olympic Games Delivery, under the leadership of Australia's John Coates, presented a set of 118 recommendations, labeled the "New Norm," to the IOC Session. The document outlines means of realizing maximum savings of $959 million and $527 million for future organizers of the Summer Olympic Games and Winter Olympic Games, respectively. These savings possibilities remain just possibilities, but the study underpinning the recommendations makes clear the IOC's focus on generating a more robust host-city bid environment. So, too, was the IOC Executive Board's decision (March 2019) to constitute a five-person working group, composed of IOC members Danka Bartekova, Lingwei Li, Gerardo Werthein, Lydia Nsekera, and John Coates (chairman), to examine thoroughly the bid-city-candidature process with a mandate to forward recommendations to the IOC Session to enhance the attractiveness of bidding ahead of the 2030 and 2032 cycles.[9]

Born in Würzburg, West Germany, in 1953, Bach was a member of West Germany's gold-medal-winning men's foil fencing team in the 1976 Montreal Olympics. He completed his law degree at the University of Würzburg in 1983 and launched his own law firm soon after. For two years Bach headed promotions operations for Adidas under Horst Dassler (until Dassler's passing in April 1987). Payne believes this experience served Bach well: "Dassler was the original executive who understood the brokerage between business and sport politics and how to bring it together." With Dassler, "you were exposed to a level of real, political training and global management," observes Payne, "which is at the core of what is required of leadership when you're running the IOC."[10] At the time, he was still a founding member of the IOC Athletes Commission, and he was co-opted by Samaranch and the IOC in 1991, the same year as his predecessor, Jacques Rogge. Professionally, he applied his legal training to the world of business with Michael Weinig AG, Siemens Schweiz AG, and seven years of service as the president of the Ghorfa Arab-German Chamber of Commerce and Industry. Within the IOC he was an Executive Board member and a vice president, and he served stints on numerous commissions including, Marketing, Juridical, and Sport and Law, while also completing a seven-year term as the president of the Deutscher Olympischer Sportbund.[11] Bach is "very focused and very astute," says the IOC's long-time (former) director of legal affairs Howard Stupp, and he attributes this to his array of sport administration experience, legal training, and attention to detail. "And, I think he has the courage to do what he thinks needs to be done," adds Stupp.[12] Pound believes Bach is determined and fully aware of the direction he wishes to take the IOC but suggests he would be wise to channel Samaranch a little more in terms of a willingness to encourage discussion and exhibit some flexibility in how best to achieve his aims based on advice.[13]

The financial gains for the IOC and the Olympic Movement under Bach have been noteworthy, perhaps best reflected in the long-term television rights agreement with NBC in the United States from 2022 through 2032 and the massive TOP sponsorship agreement signed with Toyota in the mobility category in 2015. The latter posed a unique challenge given the need to seek agreement from the multitude of NOCs already in possession of a domestic automobile sponsorship deal. The push given to the Olympic Channel concept and its launch in 2016 offer powerful opportunities in Olympic messaging on a 365-days-a-year basis. Michael Payne credits Bach and Lumme with revitalizing the TOP program. It "was seriously underpriced," stated Payne. "The TOP program evolved into being a very, very powerful marketing platform. I think for a few years, until recently, it stagnated,"[14] he added, but the opportunities offered by the Olympic Channel are exciting. Executives with Bridgestone, Toyota, and Alibaba Group must concur, as their companies jumped in as founding partners for the channel. But, cautions Pound, the IOC will only truly leverage the Olympic Channel if it "doesn't become a PR ploy. . . . It can't be a house organ. You've got to have some journalism. If there are some things that need to be improved, somebody's got to be able to say something about it. And you can't have the Lausanne attitude that everything has to be perfect. Always perfect."[15] In 2017 the USOC launched its own Olympic Channel in collaboration with NBCUniversal, an initiative long stifled by strained IOC/USOC relations but whose existence further illuminates the improved state of affairs between officials in Lausanne and Colorado Springs.

Closing Thoughts

When we interviewed Michael Payne, we walked him through the milestone events we had isolated and explained our approach in writing the book. We asked him, while conceding that people might challenge our selection of event signposts and that reasonable individuals could differ on and debate our choices, if we were missing something that should be staring us in the face. "A good bottle of wine," mused Payne, might spark an interesting discussion on the subject, but he did offer that "everybody's always very focused on the tangible, specific results, moments, contracts, deals. But in my view, it was often the intangible that really made the magic—and the understanding of what it was that really made the Olympics special and different" was essential. This translated into a commitment to creating the right environment for the athletes, spectators, and television viewers, but also, from the perspective of brand management, "how to make the Olympic symbol the hero."[16]

He recalled events in the waning months before the 2000 Sydney Olympics. For months he pressed Michael Knight, Australia's minister for the Olympics and the chairman of the Sydney Organizing Committee's (SOCOG), to put the Olympic Rings on Harbour Bridge. Rogge, then chairman of the Sydney Coordination Commission, could not grasp Payne's fascination for the project, believing there were more important priorities. Knight said the resources were not available. Payne doggedly pressed forward. He saw an opening at the IOC Executive Board's last meeting before the Games, one attended by Knight, who was required to provide a detailed briefing on the status of preparations. He scribbled a message on a piece of paper and slid it to Samaranch. "Sir," he whispered to Samaranch, "at the end of the meeting, read this out. Please trust me." Samaranch duly complied as he brought the meeting to a close: "Mr. Knight, thank you for your presentation, and, oh, just one other matter. I understand you were thinking about whether to put the Olympic Rings on the Harbour Bridge and weren't sure whether you needed IOC approval. I think it is an excellent idea. Idea approved. Meeting closed." Knight knew Payne "ambushed" him, and he expressed his displeasure upon exiting the boardroom, but in the wake of the Games, he appreciated that Payne's commitment to the plan was not misplaced. It remains one of the lasting iconic images of Sydney's Olympics.[17]

Coubertin could not possibly have imagined the future earning power and resilience of the five-ring logo he fashioned more than one hundred years ago. There is no denying the warts and imperfections of the Olympic Games revealed during the course of their history—the intrusion of world geopolitics, the decades-long propensity of some athletes to cheat through the use of banned performance-enhancing drugs, infighting among those individuals and agencies entrusted to deliver the Games, the exorbitant cost of staging them that has produced financial debt in some cities (and countries), underutilized facilities sometimes left behind, bid scandals, and, for others, the Games' overcommercialization. Payne's reflections reminded us that while our tendency in examining the IOC's commercial history has been to focus "on the tangible, specific results, moments, contracts [and] deals," the underlying story of transformation and change in the IOC's financial foundation, and the commercially-generated revenue underpinning the Olympic Games, depended on the Olympic symbol's stability in representing the best that the Olympics can be and the message it carried for representatives of the corporate world who envisioned it, and continue to view it, as a premier promotional vehicle for their products and services in the global consumer marketplace.

Notes

Abbreviations

ABC	Avery Brundage Collection
GRFPL	Gerald R. Ford Presidential Library, University of Michigan, Ann Arbor, USA
ICOSA	International Centre for Olympic Studies Archives, Western University, London, Canada
IOC	International Olympic Committee
IOCA	International Olympic Committee Archives, Lausanne, Switzerland
PCFRP	Personal Computer Files of Richard Pound
PFRP	Personal Files of Richard Pound
PPRJK	Personal Papers of Robert J. Kane
PPRKB	Personal Papers of Robert K. Barney, London, Canada
PPSW	Personal Papers of Stephen Wenn, Waterloo, Canada
USOC	United States Olympic Committee
USOCA	United States Olympic Committee Archives, Colorado Springs, USA
WLUA	Wilfrid Laurier University Archives, Waterloo, Canada

Preface

1. Barney, Wenn, and Martyn, *Selling the Five Rings*. Dr. Scott Martyn, a faculty member in human kinetics at the University of Windsor, is also a co-author of this book.

2. Simson and Jennings, *Lords of the Rings*.

3. Email correspondence from Stephen Wenn to William Regier, September 11, 2014; Regier to Wenn, September 11, 2014.

4. Despite the tenor of that statement, *Selling the Five Rings* sold approximately three thousand copies over two editions, a fairly notable achievement for a university press

production. Then, too, *Selling the Five Rings* won the 2003 North American Society award for Sport History Book of the Year, one of the organization's most prestigious annual distinctions.

5. Email correspondence from Stephen Wenn to Richard Pound, September 18, 2014.

6. Email correspondence from Richard Pound to Christophe De Kepper, September 22, 2014.

7. Email correspondence from Christophe De Kepper to Richard Pound, September 24, 2014.

8. Email correspondence from Stephen Wenn to Maria Bogner, September 24, 2014; September 29, 2014; November 21, 2014; email correspondence from Bogner to Stephen Wenn and Bob Barney, November 21, 2014. A follow-up conference call in December 2014 involving Bogner, Barney, and Wenn addressed our future hope to travel to Lausanne to view additional files. We received the Session minutes in April 2015, and the Executive Board and Marketing Commission minutes in June 2015. Email correspondence from Bogner to Wenn and Barney, April 15, 2015; email correspondence from Bogner to Wenn and Barney, June 9, 2015. Our research mission to Lausanne occurred March 5–12, 2016.

Introduction

1. For a recent thorough treatment of the history of the IOC's articulation with the amateur ideal, see Llewellyn and Gleaves, *Rise and Fall of Olympic Amateurism*.

2. Miller, "Evolution of the Olympic Movement," 9.

3. Longman, "Juan Antonio Samaranch Dies."

4. Miller, *Olympic Revolution*.

5. *Minutes of the Meeting of the Executive Board*, Dubrovnik, October 23–27, 1969, 8, IOCA. The contemporary U.S. dollar figures were calculated using historic exchange rates at http://fxtop.com/en/historical-exchange-rates.php.

6. Monique Berlioux to Lord Luke, January 21, 1970, "Lord Luke 1970" Folder, IOCA. Yet another breakdown of the IOC's current photocopier during President Killanin's recent working visit triggered Berlioux's contact with Lord Luke.

7. Payne, *Olympic Turnaround*, 9. Dick Pound pegged the reserves at $250,000 sitting in the Banque Rivaud, which was owned by the IOC Finance Commission chairman (1972–1988), Count Jean de Beaumont. See, Pound, *Inside the Olympics*, 250.

8. Email correspondence from Estel Hegglin, research coordinator, Olympic Studies Centre, to Stephen Wenn, August 6, 2018. Similarly, the television networks sought protection through "force majeure" clauses in television contracts that permitted them to cancel a contract or renegotiate its value, depending on the circumstance. Email correspondence from Richard Pound to Stephen Wenn, August 14, 2018.

9. *Minutes of the IOC Executive Board Meeting*, Lausanne, December 11–12, 2001, 6, IOCA.

10. *Minutes of the Meeting of the IOC Executive Board*, Lausanne, December 10, 2013, and Montreux, December 14, 2013, 21, IOCA. U.S. dollar figure calculated using the OANDA currency converter (http://www.oanda.com/currency/converter). All figures cited are U.S. dollars unless otherwise stated. Still, the cancellation of the Games for any reason,

and the loss of revenue from television and corporate sponsorship sources, would be a trying circumstance for the IOC and the Olympic Movement despite the impressive sum set aside for this possibility.

11. Monique Berlioux took the lead role in developing a licensing program designed to market summer and winter pictograms first employed by the 1972 Munich and 1976 Innsbruck Organizing Committees. The IOC, with Killanin's blessing, entered into an agreement with Intelicense Corporation S.A., the company that would operate the program, but the plan foundered when the USOC resisted Intelicense's encroachment on its territory, and eventually the IOC, Intelicense, and the USOC found themselves in protracted legal proceedings. See, Martyn and Wenn, "A Prelude to Samaranch: Lord Killanin's Path to Olympic Commercialism," 43–45.

12. Pound, *Inside the Olympics*, 141. For Dassler's efforts in pushing forward his sport-marketing agenda, see, Tomlinson, "The Making—and Unmaking?—of the Olympic Corporate Class," 233–47. Dassler's self-interest was readily apparent as his company, ISL, teamed with the IOC to construct the TOP program.

13. Timo Lumme and Evan Hunt, "Marketing Commission: Marketing Development Update," Lausanne, July 2, 2013, IOCA (this is a PowerPoint presentation); see also *Olympic Marketing Fact File, 2019 Edition*, 8.

14. Avery Brundage to Armand Massard, David Lord Burghley, S.A.R. The Prince Axel of Denmark, S.E. Mohammad Taher, Miguel A. Moenck, and Count Paolo Thaon de Revel, August 3, 1955, ABC, box 114, WLUA.

15. The Amateur Sports Act was the legislative result of the President's Commission on Olympic Sports (PCOS) struck by U.S. president Gerald Ford in 1975. Significant concern pervaded Washington with respect to the United States' declining success in international sport competition, especially the Olympics. Athletes from behind the Iron Curtain were setting world records and outperforming their American rivals. The U.S. Olympic team's performance at the 1972 Munich Olympics was below expectations, and internecine administrative squabbles with the National Collegiate Athletic Association and the Amateur Athletic Union plagued the USOC. Signed into law by U.S. president Jimmy Carter in 1978, the act streamlined the administration of Olympic affairs and left the USOC squarely in charge of effecting a change to the Olympic medals (by country) table. Michael T. Harrigan served as PCOS's executive director. Less understood at the time was the future effect of the act on the USOC's fiscal bottom line. When the USOC was incorporated in 1950, the USOA (then the United States Olympic Association) was granted exclusive rights to the use of the Olympic rings in U.S. territory. This clause did not serve as a lever for meaningful revenue generation in the ensuing years. The act reconfirmed these rights and established the (now) USOC's ability to pursue companies that made unauthorized use of the rings for financial compensation. Several years passed before the USOC recognized the financial windfall possible if it invoked the terms of the act in its dealings with the IOC. It did so in two ways: in 1983 the USOC withheld support for Samaranch's TOP global sponsorship initiative for two years until it received 15 percent of the revenue generated in exchange for permitting the contracted multinational firms to use the Olympic rings in their marketing efforts in U.S. territory; and, in 1985,

the USOC informed the IOC that it required compensation should companies purchasing advertising time on U.S. Olympic television broadcasts wish to continue their use of Olympic marks and emblems, including the five-ring logo, in their commercials. Without this privilege granted to the advertisers, the IOC understood the diminished ability of bidding U.S. networks to offer market value for the U.S. television rights because of the deleterious impact on advertising revenue. In 1986 the USOC and IOC signed the Broadcast Marketing Agreement that channeled 10 percent of the value of the U.S. Olympic television contracts to the USOC in perpetuity. A decade later, follow-up negotiations between the parties pushed this percentage to 12.75.

16. *Minutes of the IOC Marketing Commission Meeting*, Lausanne, June 21, 2012, 4; *Minutes of the Meeting of the 124th IOC Session*, London, July 24–26, August 12, 2012, 5, IOCA.

Chapter 1. Paul Helms versus Avery Brundage

1. Galbraith, *Affluent Society*. Galbraith, a liberal economist and holder of a professorship at Harvard for fifty years, instructs us that most goods produced are not of urgent importance for carrying out our lives. But if "production is to increase, wants must be effectively contrived" (132). An "elaborate myth" (114) surrounds demand for goods, much of it perpetrated by advertising. But Galbraith's "elaborate myth" has proved to be reality. Indeed, the well-known slogan "It pays to advertise" is testimony to that which a multi-trillion-dollar industry worldwide can attest.

2. *Rapport official de jeux de la VII Olympiade, Anvers 1920*, 52. Brackets in original.

3. Barney, Wenn, and Martyn, *Selling the Five Rings*, 28.

4. As cited by Pendergrast in *For God, Country and Coca-Cola*, 173.

5. Barney, "Resistance, Persistence, Providence," 156. Knowing that California's "athletic carnival" would cost in excess of $2 million, Hoover was sensitive about being associated with the project. He reportedly told friends: "It's a crazy thing. And it takes some gall to expect me to be a part of it." Cited in Stump, "Games That Almost Weren't," 67. Stump offers no documentation for Hoover's statement. An in-depth research mission across the United States, including sources at the Herbert Hoover Presidential Library in Indianola, Iowa, has failed to ratify Stump's undocumented assertion.

6. "Dummy" Hoy's major-league career was auspicious. Over a twelve-year career, he accumulated 2,044 hits, stole 607 bases, and established a lifetime batting average of .288. For more on Hoy see, Garron, *Deaf Heritage*, 291–95.

7. For biographical notes on Helms, see ABC, box 225, ICOSA. The term "Bakeries," as expressed in signage decorating Helms's fleet of delivery trucks, as well as that mounted above the entrance to Helms's plant operation in Culver City, refers to a variety of bakery products, rather than a conglomerate of individual bakery shops. There was but one Helms shop, the vast plant at Venice and Washington Streets in Culver City.

8. In every state of the union (with the exception of Washington, denied mainly because of prior registrations associated with the state's popular beer, Olympia) and in the U.S. territories of Hawaii and the Philippines, Helms was successful in registering the Olympic five-ring symbol; the latinized Olympic motto, *Citius, Altius, Fortius*; the so-called Olympic shield; and the relative uses of the word *Olympic*.

9. Further clarification is warranted here. No prior registration of Olympic marks had ever been attempted. No precedent existed for preventing such action. In each Olympic Village supplier's agreement with the Los Angeles Olympic Organizing Committee, except Helms's, there appeared an injunction clause against publicly advertising contracted products with Olympic emblems included. Suppliers of toilet articles, laundry supplies, beverages, food products, and the like adhered. In a final review of his agreement document, Helms removed the injunction clause. Organizing Committee officials duly signed the amended agreement. See John T. McGovern to Avery Brundage, October 18, 1949, ABC, box 225, ICOSA. It is fact that the idea of duly registering the Olympic marks in the United States had occurred to the USOC well before the opening of the 1932 Games. In an exchange of correspondence between Frederick W. Rubien, secretary of the USOC, and Colonel A. G. Berdez, secretary of the IOC, Rubien sought clarification on how the five rings of different colors should be sequenced. Berdez responded with the proper counsel. In the final communication on the subject, Rubien thanked Berdez and added: "We have taken up the matter of having the IOC emblem registered with a patent firm here in New York City but I doubt very much if it is possible to arrange this. I will forward to you the official opinion as soon as it is announced." See Frederick Rubien to A. G. Berdez, May 16, 1932, IOCA. Well over a month earlier, Avery Brundage himself registered concern relative to the symbol-copyright issue. In a letter to Colonel Wait C. Johnson, a U.S. Olympic Team fundraiser in Fort Hayes, Kansas, Brundage stated: "The problem of preventing the misuse of the word 'Olympic' as well as the appropriation of the emblems and insignia attached to the Olympic Games by various promoters for personal profit, is a most difficult one. The fact that the Games are to be held in the United States this year has made this problem much more acute than usual. All sorts of rackets have been started, particularly in Southern California. Various articles have been sold to people who thought they were assisting the American Olympic Committee. We finally enlisted the help of newspapers and the Chamber of Commerce in Los Angeles, and while most of the attempts to commercialize the Games have been stamped out there are still a number operating. . . . Unfortunately, neither the name or the emblem of the Games have been copyrighted so we must rely on public opinion." See Avery Brundage to Colonel Wait C. Johnson, March 28, 1932, ABC, box 225, ICOSA.

10. Although Helms applied for the registration of the Olympic marks and words in 1932, his official application (#360,431) was not granted final and permanent license by the United States Trade Mark Registration Office until September 20, 1938. See "Draft of proposed agreement between Paul H. Helms and Counsellors for the United States Olympic Committee," appended to letter from Arthur M. Smith (counselor) to Avery Brundage, December 30, 1949, ABC, box 225, ICOSA.

11. See *Los Angeles Times*, July 30–August 30, 1932.

12. Johnson, "Defender of the Faith."

13. Brundage's letter to Schroeder has not survived, but Brundage (fortunately) sent a copy to fellow IOC member William May Garland, a Los Angeles resident. Garland acknowledged having received it. See William May Garland to Avery Brundage, October 14, 1938, ABC, box 225, ICOSA.

14. Ibid. The "shield of the IOC" referred to by Garland was a misidentification; the "shield" was, in fact, the well-known logo of the American Olympic Association.

15. Avery Brundage to William May Garland, October 19, 1938, ABC, box 225, ICOSA. Brackets ours.

16. This scenario was related to Brundage by USOA attorney John T. McGovern. John T. McGovern to Avery Brundage, October 18, 1949, IOCA. By the time Helms completed the three-stage Helms Foundation building project, located at 8760 Venice Boulevard in Los Angeles, his investment totaled just short of $500,000. See "Helms Athletic Foundation."

17. For the intricacies of these machinations, see Guttmann, *Games Must Go On*, 99–100.

18. This bit of information is contained in the document, "Outline of Circumstances Leading to Present Activities of the United States Olympic Association's Legislation Sub-Committee in Negotiations with Paul Helms," ABC, box 225, ICOSA.

19. Ibid.

20. In a letter written to Avery Brundage on October 1, 1949, McGovern recalled what Paul Helms had told him at their personal meeting in New York that the 1948 Olympic Games bread contract had been "let to the highest bidder with no suggestions even that advertising be forbidden, although it had been known at that time that Helms had been using advertising matter and a package covered with the emblem, and the bread was accepted in packages containing all the advertising matter." McGovern to Brundage, October 1, 1949, ABC, box 225, ICOSA.

21. Van Camp, "Report of the Treasurer," 362–64, 369.

22. Avery Brundage to John Jewett Garland, December 18, 1948, ABC, box 225, ICOSA. Despite Brundage's assertion that he had "received many protests from the general public," there is not a single bit of extant evidence for this in the huge Avery Brundage Collecton of archival materials. Young Garland replaced his father, William May Garland, as an IOC member from the United States on June 28, 1948. See "Minutes, 43rd IOC Session, London, 1948," in Lyberg, ed., *IOC Sessions*, 3:250.

23. The USOA's headquarters at the time were located in the Biltmore Hotel at 43rd Street and Madison Avenue. One of Terry McGovern's last acts before his death in 1960 was to finalize the legal work for the USOA's eventual 1959 purchase of billionaire Jay Piermont Morgan's New York townhouse, a luxurious six-story mansion located at 57 Park Avenue. See Terry McGovern to the USOA "Board of Directors," February 10, 1959, ABC, box 225, ICOSA. For more, see Posey, "Homeless No More," 106.

24. Farrell, "Birthday Party."

25. *New York Herald Tribune*, May 27, 1960.

26. Philip Noel-Baker to Cornell University, July 4, 1960, Cornell University Archives. Brackets added. We are grateful to the late Professor John A. Lucas of Pennsylvania State University for this informative source.

27. John T. McGovern to Avery Brundage, June 13, 1949, ABC, box 225, ICOSA.

28. J. Lyman Bingham to Avery Brundage, July 6, 1949, ABC, box 225, ICOSA.

29. Ibid.

30. John T. McGovern to Avery Brundage, July 7, 1949, ABC, box 225, ICOSA. Brackets added.

31. Avery Brundage to W. R. Schroeder, July 20, 1949, ABC, box 225, ICOSA.

32. Avery Brundage to Daniel J. Ferris, September 27, 1949, ABC, box 225, ICOSA.

33. Paul H. Helms to Avery Brundage, September 30, 1949, ABC, box 225, ICOSA. Brundage made several handwritten comments on the margins of Helms's September 30 letter, among them challenges to the bakery owner's statements and listing possible actions, such as a boycott of Los Angeles track and field meets by American athletes. Brundage's impression of Helms is graphically captured in his final jotting notations: "has money, wants respect and esteem."

34. This is detailed in McGovern's letter/report to Brundage, October 18, 1949, ABC, box 225, ICOSA.

35. Ibid.

36. Arthur M. Smith to Avery Brundage, December 30, 1949, ABC, box 225, ICOSA. Smith's letter conveyed his thanks to Brundage for hosting him and Cross as houseguests for two days at his Santa Barbara, California, "second home." At Brundage's majestic home overlooking the Pacific Ocean, prior to proceeding to Los Angeles, the trio discussed the strategies to be employed in meeting with Helms. Finally, Smith's letter outlined to Brundage the essence of the agreement reached in Los Angeles. The importance of Arthur Smith's presence in the proceedings should not be underestimated. Smith, a member of Cross's Detroit law firm, was an expert in patent law; in fact, at the time he was president of the Michigan Patent Law Association.

37. Avery Brundage to Paul Helms, December 28, 1949, ABC, box 225, ICOSA.

38. The shield, displaying vertical red and white stripes, set off at the top by a blue horizontal band referred to by trademark officials as an escutcheon, was used by more than one American organization and business, the most prominent of which was the Union Pacific Railroad Company.

39. John T. McGovern to Avery Brundage, March 21, 1950, ABC, box 225, ICOSA.

40. John T. McGovern to Avery Brundage, June 15, 1950, ABC, box 225, ICOSA.

41. John T. McGovern to Avery Brundage, June 27, 1950, ABC, box 225, ICOSA.

42. Ibid.

43. John T. McGovern to Avery Brundage, October 2, 1950, ABC, box 225, ICOSA.

44. Arthur Smith to Terry McGovern, February 24, 1950, ABC, box 225, ICOSA.

45. "81st Congress, 2nd Session, Chapter 975, September 21, 1950, Public Law 805: An Act to Incorporate the United States Olympic Association," 901.

46. Ibid.

47. Ibid., 902.

48. Avery Brundage to Fred C. Matthei, October 4, 1950, ABC, box 225, ICOSA.

49. International Olympic Committee, "About Protection," 20.

50. J. Sigfrid Edström to John J. Garland, September 9, 1949, ABC, box 225, ICOSA.

51. John J. Garland to J. Sigfrid Edström, October 14, 1949, ABC, box 225, ICOSA.

52. International Olympic Committee, "About Protection," 20.

53. John T. McGovern to Avery Brundage, Gustavus Kirby, USOA Officers, Members of the Executive Board, Associate Counsel Jeremiah Mahoney, Richard Cross, Arthur Smith, and Esquire Pincus Sober and Fred Steers, July 5, 1950. ABC, box 225, ICOSA. The

"U.S.O.C." mentioned in McGovern's letter was a subcommittee of the USOA; its chief responsibility was to organize and administer the means for getting American athletes to the Olympic Games.

54. Avery Brundage to John T. McGovern, July 6, 1950, ABC, box 225, ICOSA.

55. John T. McGovern to Avery Brundage, July 7, 1950, ABC, box 225, ICOSA.

56. John T. McGovern to Avery Brundage, October 31, 1950, ABC, box 225, ICOSA.

57. John T. McGovern to Avery Brundage, February 19, 1951, ABC, box 225, ICOSA.

58. Cited in John T. McGovern to USOA, July 5, 1950, ABC, box 225, ICOSA.

59. Avery Brundage to Fred. C. Matthei, October 4, 1950, ABC, box 225, ICOSA.

Chapter 2. Melbourne, 1956

1. Though a written source from Killanin directly to Brundage on this issue is not extant, Brundage referred to Killanin's entreaty in a letter to members of the Executive Board in early August 1955. See Avery Brundage to Members of the Executive Board, August 3, 1955, ABC, box 114, ICOSA. Readers should note that portions of text in this chapter appear in Barney and Wenn, "Nothing in Hand."

2. IOC chancellor Otto Mayer reminded Brundage of Ahearne's statements regarding television uttered at the Executive Board meeting in June. See Otto Mayer to Avery Brundage, July 31, 1955, ABC, box 114, ICOSA. Ahearne's statements were offered with the thought that future television revenue be shared by the IOC, OCOGs, and IFs.

3. Avery Brundage to Members of the Executive Board, August 3, 1955.

4. Ibid.

5. David, Lord Burghley to Avery Brundage, September 23, 1955, ABC, box 58, ICOSA. Brackets added.

6. Lord Killanin to Avery Brundage, August 24, 1955, ABC, box 58, ICOSA.

7. Lyberg, *IOC Sessions*, 3:261.

8. A measure of explanation is required. Though the BBC beamed its signal to about eighty thousand television sets in and around London, and the events were seen as far away as the Channel Islands (about 150 miles distant), the 1,000 guineas (approximately $3,000) pledged to Lord Burghley and the London Organizing Committee purportedly did not change hands. The BBC pleaded difficult financial circumstances, and London officials purportedly did not cash the check. See IOC Marketing Department, "History of Olympic Marketing," 20. Cortina's approach contrasted sharply with that espoused by Kent Hughes. The Cortina Organizing Committee and Radiotelevisione Italiana (RAI) entered into agreement concerning telecast arrangements for eight Western European nations. RAI was obliged to fund the operation, but in seeking maximum publicity for their own enterprise, Cortina officials contributed to the financial demands placed on RAI, with differing sources pegging this contribution at $16,000 and $64,000 respectively. See *The Official Report of the Games: VIIth Olympic Winter Games*, 421; *Procès-verbal de la Réunion de la Commission Executive*, Cortina d'Ampezzo, January 23, 1956, 1, IOCA.

9. For an extended biographical treatment of Wilfrid Kent Hughes, see Howard, *Kent Hughes*.

10. For more on Kent Hughes's incarceration, see Hancock, "Kent Hughes."

11. Kent Hughes performed both his cabinet duties and his Organization Committee presidential work until January 1956.

12. See W. S. Kent Hughes, "Report on Television and Films—Olympic Games 1956," March 25, 1957, ABC, box 114, ICOSA.

13. Roger Tatarian to Avery Brundage, January 23, 1956, ABC, box 114, ICOSA.

14. Film rights translated into filming Olympic events in Melbourne, having the film flown directly to North America and Europe for showing on a delayed basis as special "short subject" presentations in movie theaters and as abbreviated programs on television. As for the threat to the economic viability of the official Olympic film, the production's director, Peter Whitchurch, echoed Kent Hughes's thoughts. Peter Whitchurch to Avery Brundage, September 15, 1959, ABC, box 114, ICOSA.

15. See George Moir to Wilfrid Kent Hughes, January 3, 1956, Moir Collection, Australian Gallery of Sport and Olympic Museum, Melbourne, Australia, as cited in Cahill, "Very Hard Crowd," 17; see also p. 5.

16. Cited by Howard, *Kent Hughes*, 187.

17. The chief areas of the world with television capability by 1956 were North America and Europe. Thus, the British Broadcasting Corporation (BBC), the European Broadcasting Union (EBU) on the Continent, the Canadian Broadcasting Corporation (CBC), and all major outlets in the United States were party to the boycott. The Melbourne Organizing Committee, however, eventually established its own film unit, providing one thousand feet of film daily during the Games. This film was subsequently employed by independently owned movie theaters in Australia and a few minor television stations in America. The international/theater newsreel boycott, though extensive, was not complete.

18. See *Melbourne Herald and Weekly Times*, May 10, 1957. Italics added.

19. See Cahill, "Very Hard Crowd," 9.

20. Williams's utterance to Kent Hughes is cited by Howard, *Kent Hughes*, 188, as well as by Cahill, "Very Hard Crowd," 4.

21. See Cahill, "Very Hard Crowd," 12; Gould, "Nobody Was First"; Lucas, "Descriptive History," 11.

22. Lewis Luxton to Avery Brundage, May 13, 1957, ABC, box 114, ICOSA.

23. Gould, "Nobody Was First."

24. Paul Talbot to Wilfrid Kent Hughes, July 20, 1960, cited by Howard, *Kent Hughes*, 247n43.

25. See Hancock, *Kent Hughes*. Brackets added.

26. We have posited this argument previously. See Barney and Wenn, "Nothing in Hand."

27. See Howard, *Kent Hughes*, 188; Cahill, "Very Hard Crowd," 4. Kent Hughes's outburst was communicated directly to Brundage by John T. McGovern, an old Kent Hughes friend from his Oxford days. It will be remembered from the previous chapter that McGovern, the esteemed New York lawyer, USOC Executive Board member, and "savior" in the Helms Bakeries–Olympic Insignia Protection case, was well acquainted with having to repair circumstances generated by Brundage's acerbic nature.

28. Brundage summarized his thoughts in: Avery Brundage to Members of the IOC Executive Board, August 3, 1955.

29. *Minutes of the 51st Session of the International Olympic Committee*, Cortina d'Ampezzo, January 24–25, 1956, 20, IOCA.

30. Ibid.

31. For elaboration, see Alan E. Bartholemy (general secretary, VIIIth Winter Olympic Games Organizing Committee) to Otto Mayer, July 10, 1957, ABC, box 165, ICOSA; Guilio Onesti (president, Rome Organizing Committee) to Avery Brundage, May 6, 1960, box 165, ICOSA.

32. "Athletics in the Modern World and the Olympic Games" (analysis and extracts from a lecture by Coubertin to the Parnassus Club, Athens, 1894), 83.

33. The "nine minutes" free-coverage standard, appearing in the 1958 version of the *Olympic Charter*, represented a concession on Brundage's part. Brundage's original stance favored a total of six minutes of free coverage per day. The news-film industry, however, lobbied Brundage aggressively for a nine-minute limit, the same position steadfastly pursued and just as earnestly rejected by Kent Hughes and his MOCOG colleagues.

34. See, for instance, Alan E. Bartholemy to Otto Mayer, July 10, 1957; Giulio Onesti to Avery Brundage, May 6, 1960.

35. Brundage's reference to "picnic ground" is in Avery Brundage to Cortlandt T. Hill, November 12, 1955, ABC, box 165, ICOSA. For Cushing's "superb" bid campaign, see Avery Brundage to Kenneth "Tug" Wilson (president, United States Olympic Association), August 20, 1955, ABC, box 165, ICOSA.

36. Alan E. Bartholemy to Otto Mayer, July 10, 1957.

37. Ibid.

38. John M. Pierce (director of finance, State of California) to Avery Brundage, May 7, 1956, ABC, box 165, ICOSA.

39. Avery Brundage to Otto Mayer, August 4, 1959, ABC, box 168, ICOSA. Brackets added.

40. Guilio Onesti to Avery Brundage, May 6, 1960.

41. *Minutes of the Meeting of the 56th Session of the International Olympic Committee*, San Francisco, February 15–16, 1960, 7–8, IOCA. See also, Otto Mayer to Guilio Onesti, September 18, 1961; Onesti to Avery Brundage, October 19, 1961, box 61, ICOSA.

42. See Guttmann, *Olympics*, 105. Guttmann attributes the quote to German journalist, Heinz Maegerlein.

43. International Olympic Committee Marketing Department, *1999 Olympic Marketing Fact File*, 35.

44. Wenn, "History of the IOC and Television," 88, 93. CBS televised twenty hours of the events in Rome (five of them in prime time, utilizing tape delays), while the British sent home approximately forty hours of live telecasts. See Senn, *Power, Politics, and the Olympic Games*, 121.

45. "Droits de télévision versés par les organismes de télévision pour les Jeux d'Olympiade (en dollars U.S.)" 1986, IOCA.

46. Otto Mayer to Guilio Onesti, September 18, 1961, and Guilio Onesti to Avery Brundage, October 19, 1961. In his October 19 letter to Brundage, Onesti stated that the final

transfer of funds, which brought the total channeled to the IOC to $53,521, provided closure for the IOC/OCOG arrangement.

Chapter 3. The Rome Formula

1. Pound, *Inside the Olympics*, 235. Brackets added.

2. Avery Brundage to Ivar Vind, IOC member, Denmark, September 13, 1965, ABC, box 64, WLUA.

3. *Minutes of the Meeting of the Executive Board of the IOC*, Tehran, May 2–8, 1967, 4–5, IOCA.

4. Ivar Vind to Avery Brundage, April 30, 1964, ABC, box 64; Vind to Brundage, January 24, 1966, ABC, box 64; Marquess of Exeter to Brundage, May 7, 1966, ABC, box 55; Exeter to Brundage, August 12, 1968, ABC, box 55, WLUA.

5. Georg von Opel to Lord Luke, Chairman, IOC Finance Commission, December 17, 1970, ABC, box 61, WLUA.

6. The IOC Finance Commission first met in September 1967 under the chairmanship of Lord Luke. *Minutes of the IOC Finance Commission*, Lausanne, September 24–25, 1967, IOCA. For Brundage's concerns about the IOC's dependence on television money and loose spending practices, see Avery Brundage to Reginald S. Alexander, IOC member, Kenya, October 24, 1967, ABC, box 98; Brundage to Lord Luke, IOC member, Great Britain, October 4, 1967, ABC, box 98; Brundage to Alexander, November 4, 1967, ABC, box 98; Jean de Beaumont, IOC member, France, to Avery Brundage, March 1, 1968, ABC, box 51; Brundage to Beaumont, April 9, 1968, ABC, box 51, WLUA.

7. Guttmann, "Games Must Go On," 219. Brackets added.

8. *Minutes of the Meeting of the IOC Executive Board*, Lausanne, May 27–30, 1972, 7, IOCA.

9. Ibid., 7–8.

10. Llewellyn and Gleaves, *Rise and Fall of Olympic Amateurism*, 139.

11. *Minutes of the Meeting of the IOC Executive Board*, Lausanne, May 27–30, 1972, 7–8.

12. Reginald S. Alexander to Avery Brundage, March 12, 1969, ABC, box 98, WLUA. Brackets added.

13. Marquess of Exeter to Dr. Bear (editor, *World Sports*), July 20, 1957, ABC, box 54, WLUA. "Bunny" Ahearne encouraged the IFs to claim one-third of Olympic television revenue as early as 1955. See *Seduta Delle Federazoni Internazionali Sportive*, April 22, 1966, 2/22, ABC, box 81, WLUA.

14. *Seduta Delle Federazoni Internazionali Sportive*, 2/9. See also Marquess of Exeter to Avery Brundage, June 10, 1965, ABC, box 55; Avery Brundage to Guru Dutt Sondhi, IOC member, India, July 3, 1965, ABC, box 63, WLUA.

15. *Seduta Delle Federazoni Internazionali Sportive*, 2/13–14.

16. Roger Coulon to Avery Brundage, March 10, 1967, ABC, box 207, WLUA.

17. *Seduta Delle Federazoni Internazionali Sportive*, 2/13–14.

18. Otto Mayer, IOC Chancellor, to Friedl Wolfgang, General Secretary, Innsbruck Organizing Committee, March 23, 1961, ABC, box 169; Avery Brundage to Armand Massard, April 1, 1963, ABC, box 60, WLUA.

19. Guttmann, *Sports*, 271.

20. Oliver, *Commonwealth Games*, 125.

21. Hennessy, as quoted in, Owen, "Tale of Marius." Brackets added.

22. Pound, *Inside the Olympics*, 253.

23. Owen, "Tale of Marius." Brackets added. GAIF was reconstituted as the General Assembly of International Sport Federations in the late 1970s.

24. Berlioux, "Fédération Internationale des Luttes Amateurs," 104–5. In January 1971, Coulon's sudden passing after an evening out in Lausanne with a number of colleagues, including Berlioux, shook many in the Olympic world.

25. Coulon received frequent mention in Exeter's letters to Avery Brundage and the IOC's secretary general, Johann Westerhoff, concerning the ongoing efforts of the IFs to collaborate on the establishment of such a body. See, for instance, Marquess of Exeter to Avery Brundage, January 16, 1967; Exeter to Brundage, January 18, 1967; Exeter to Brundage, January 23, 1967; Exeter to Brundage, October 7, 1967; Exeter to Johann Westerhoff, October 14, 1967; Exeter to Brundage, November 20, 1967; Exeter to Brundage, September 2, 1968. All letters found in, ABC, box 55, WLUA.

26. "Burghley: Bermuda's Olympic Champion."

27. Mason, "Yesterday's Anti-heroes." The use of this dramatic license, along with the inaccurate depiction of the Trinity Court run where the moviemakers depicted Burghley being defeated by Harold Abrahams, when his feat was achieved as a result of a solo run, explains why Exeter did not permit the filmmakers to use his name.

28. Barker, "Lord Burghley." Brackets added.

29. Guttmann, *Games Must Go On*, 175.

30. Avery Brundage to Marquess of Exeter, March 31, 1961, ABC, box 51, WLUA.

31. Marquess of Exeter to Avery Brundage, April 7, 1961, ABC, box 54, WLUA.

32. Marquess of Exeter to Avery Brundage, May 31, 1961, ABC, box 54, WLUA.

33. Exeter recounted this story in a letter to Rudyard H. Russell, president of the Association Internationale de Boxe Amateur (AIBA), some six years later. See Marquess of Exeter to Col. Russell, March 8, 1967, ABC, box 101, WLUA. Russell was elected AIBA's president in 1962, and Exeter viewed him as a more reasonable individual who might be employed as a counterweight to the more aggressive individuals such as Coulon. Russell served as AIBA president until 1974. Exeter's feelings on this matter are implied in Marquess of Exeter to Rudyard Russell, January 11, 1967, ABC, box, 55. Exeter received an inquiry from Roger Coulon's secretary. He was asked if a meeting between the IFs and the IOC Executive Board was advisable in the short term. Exeter queried Russell as to why such a request had not come from him, given he served as an unofficial liaison with the IOC in past years. If such a meeting were organized with the IOC Executive Board, offered Exeter, the arrangements should flow through Russell's office.

34. "Circular Letter to the International Federations," July 1961, #182, ABC, box 70. The need for the Olympics to be designated as the individual IF's World Championships that year had been in discussion for some time. See Marquess of Exeter to Avery Brundage, January 24, 1960, ABC, box 54, WLUA.

35. In 1966, when the IFs were greatly agitated about the way that television money was distributed, Rudyard Russell conceded that the IFs were generally satisfied with the

process employed with regard to the Tokyo/Innsbruck money and the decisions made by Exeter and Brundage in 1961 and 1962. However, the advent of satellite technology changed the terrain and prompted the IFs to aggressively pursue one-third of the television revenue, something that Ahearne advocated for a number of years. *Seduta Delle Federazoni Internazionali Sportive*, 2/9.

36. Pelton, "Start of Commercial Satellite Communications," 25. Whether industry scientists grasped the seminal nature of this work at the time is open to question. As Pelton points out, it was not even the cover article in the issue. For Clarke's article, see Clarke, "Extra-Terrestrial Relays," 305–8.

37. Clarke, "Extra-Terrestrial Relays," 305.

38. Pelton, "Start of Commercial Satellite Communications," 25.

39. "Olympic Games Television Rights Summary: Summer Games," February 2, 1999, "IOC TV Data" File, PCFRP.

40. "Summary of Olympic Television Rights: Olympic Winter Games," July 27, 1998, "IOC TV Data" file, PCFRP.

41. *Minutes of the 58th Session of the International Olympic Committee*, Athens, June 19–21, 1961, 2–3, IOCA. Interestingly, verbal interaction between Brundage and Massard was often facilitated by colleague Giorgio de Stefani when he served on the Executive Board between 1964 and 1968 as Brundage spoke no French, and Massard, no English. See "Obituary," 662; Martucci, "Giorgio de Stefani," 452.

42. Armand Massard to Avery Brundage, September 23, 1960, ABC, box 60, WLUA. The original letter is in French.

43. Avery Brundage to Armand Massard, October 14, 1960, ABC, box 60, WLUA.

44. *Minutes of the 58th Session of the International Olympic Committee*, Athens, June 19–21, 1961, 2–3.

45. Guru Dutt Sondhi to Avery Brundage, June 17, 1965, ABC, box 63, WLUA. Brackets added.

46. Ibid.

47. Ibid.

48. Posey, *Olympic Century*, vol. 16, 107.

49. Guttmann, *Games Must Go On*, 175.

50. *Minutes of the IOC Executive Board with the Delegates of the National Olympic Committees*, Madrid, October 4, 1965, Annex 5, IOCA; *Minutes of the 63rd Session of the International Olympic Committee*, Madrid, October 6–8, 1965, IOCA; Giulio Onesti to Ivar Vind, September 8, 1965, ABC, box 61, WLUA.

51. Giulio Onesti to Avery Brundage, June 24, 1965, ABC, box 61, WLUA. Onesti called for 50 percent transferable to the IOC, 25 percent to the OCOGs, who would cover the costs of the judges and officials of the IFs, and 25 percent to the NOCs.

52. Avery Brundage to Ivar Vind, September 13, 1965.

53. *Minutes of the IOC Executive Board with the Delegates of the National Olympic Committees*, Madrid, October 4, 1965, 5–6.

54. *Minutes of the 63rd Session of the International Olympic Committee*, Madrid, October 6–8, 1965, 5.

55. Giulio Onesti to Avery Brundage, October 2, 1965, ABC, box 81, WLUA. Proposals emanating from the NOCs' meeting in Madrid dealing with the independence of NOCs, television money, amateurism, regional games, and needed increases to the number of officials assigned to Olympic teams can be found in *Minutes*, Madrid, October 4, 1965. Onesti also pressed the NOCs' case with Ivar Vind. See Giulio Onesti to Ivar Vind, July 31, 1965, ABC, box 61, WLUA; Onesti to Vind, September 8, 1965. Onesti presented his thoughts on the need for an association of NOCs in a detailed five-page letter to Swiss IOC member Albert Mayer, in the process reassuring Mayer that the NOCs recognized the IOC as the world's leader in Olympic sport. See Onesti to Mayer, December 14, 1965, ABC, box 81, WLUA.

56. "Study and Co-ordinating Committee of NOCs, Rome, April 20, 1966," 2, ABC, box 81, WLUA.

57. Ibid., 3. The minutes read: "An agreement should therefore be reached between the IOC and the International Federations regarding the definition of the rules of amateur status, so that the athlete should have a precise and clear status in the world of sport, always the same whatever the event in which he participates, from regional championships to the Olympic Games." Onesti believed a set of commonly accepted principles between the IOC and IFs could then be interpreted by the individual IFs, lending autonomy in this decision making to the IFs. Llewellyn and Gleaves, *Rise and Fall of Olympic Amateurism*, 140.

58. Ibid., 4.

59. Ibid.

60. *Seduta Delle Federazoni Internazionali*, 2/10.

61. Marquess of Exeter to Avery Brundage, May 6, 1964, ABC, box 55, WLUA.

62. Guttmann, *Olympics: A History of the Modern Games*, 115.

63. *Seduta Delle Federazoni Internazionali*, 2/10.

64. Marquess of Exeter to Avery Brundage, June 10, 1965.

65. *Seduta Delle Federazoni Internazionali*, 2/10. The Winter IFs were slated to share $30,000. See Johann Westerhoff to Marquess of Exeter, November 30, 1966, ABC, box 55, WLUA.

66. "Amendments to the Minutes of the Executive Board Meeting in Paris on 9th and 10th July, 1965," ABC, box 55, WLUA.

67. Avery Brundage to Giulio Onesti, January 25, 1966, ABC, box 101, WLUA.

68. Marquess of Exeter to Avery Brundage, February 8, 1966, ABC, box 55, WLUA.

69. Marquess of Exeter to Avery Brundage, February 23, 1966, ABC, box 55, WLUA.

70. Ibid.

71. Marquess of Exeter to Giulio Onesti, March 31, 1966, ABC, box 55, WLUA; Exeter to Avery Brundage, June 10, 1965.

72. Giulio Onesti to Marquess of Exeter, April 7, 1966, ABC, box 61, WLUA.

73. "Preliminary Report to the IOC Executive Board on IOC Television Policy," ABC, box 101, WLUA.

74. Ibid.

75. *Seduta Delle Federazoni Internazionali*, 2/15–19.

76. Ibid., 2/11–12.

77. Ibid., 2/14.

78. Ibid., 2/14–15.

79. Ibid., 2/14.

80. Ibid.

81. Ibid., 2/15.

82. Ibid., 2/16–18.

83. Ibid., 2/19.

84. Ibid., 2/19–20.

85. Ibid., 2/20–21.

86. Ibid., 2/22.

87. Ibid., 2/24–28. Bonet-Maury queried forcefully: "But if we have no rights, I don't really see what we are doing here?"

88. Ibid., 2/23.

89. *Meeting of the Executive Board of the IOC*, Rome, April 21–24, 1966, 7–9, IOCA.

90. *Minutes of the Meeting of the 64th Session of the International Olympic Committee*, Rome, April 25–29, 1966, 4–5, IOCA.

91. Avery Brundage to Albert Mayer, May 19, 1966, ABC box 60, WLUA. In his letter to Exeter in mid-January 1967, Brundage recalled: "You will remember how obnoxious some of the Federation representatives were in Rome and I can assure you that in their private meetings with me they were even worse. You would have been horrified, as I was." See Brundage to Exeter, January 18, 1967.

92. Avery Brundage to Marquess of Exeter, January 18, 1967.

93. Avery Brundage to Marquess of Exeter, May 19, 1966. Brackets added.

94. Llewellyn and Gleaves, *Rise and Fall of Olympic Amateurism*, 140–41. In his correspondence with Exeter, Brundage wrote, "As for the Winter Games, it would have been better if they had never been organized." See Brundage to Exeter, November 16, 1966, ABC, box 55, WLUA.

95. Marquess of Exeter to Avery Brundage, May 31, 1966, ABC, box 55, WLUA.

96. Avery Brundage to Marquess of Exeter, July 1, 1966, ABC, box 55, WLUA.

97. Avery Brundage to Albert Mayer, IOC member, Switzerland, May 19, 1966.

98. Marquess of Exeter to Rudyard Russell, January 11, 1967.

99. Marquess of Exeter to Avery Brundage, January 16, 1967. In early March, Rudyard Russell reported that Track and Field, Football, and Yachting would not attend Coulon's meeting, while a number of others were undecided. Russell to Exeter, March 6, 1967, ABC, Box 55, WLUA.

100. Avery Brundage to Marquess of Exeter, January 24, 1967, ABC, box 55, WLUA.

101. Marquess of Exeter to Avery Brundage, January 23, 1967.

102. Ibid.

103. Roger Coulon to Avery Brundage, March 10, 1967. Brackets added.

104. "Report of the Commission No. 3—Finances," GAIF, Lausanne, April 22, 1967, 3, ABC, box 207, WLUA.

105. Marquess of Exeter to Avery Brundage, July 12, 1966, ABC, box 55.

106. Marquess of Exeter to Avery Brundage, June 12, 1967, ABC, box 55.

107. *Minutes of the 65th Session of the International Olympic Committee*, Tehran, May 6–9, 1967, 13, IOCA; J. W. Westerhoff to Pedro Ramirez Vasquez, president, Mexico City Organizing Committee, July 6, 1967, ABC, box 179, WLUA.

108. Marquess of Exeter to Avery Brundage, June 12, 1967.

109. Johann Westerhoff to Marquess of Exeter, March 7, 1967, ABC, box 55, WLUA.

110. "Compte-rendu de l'entreuve du 22 juillet 1967, á Winnipeg, Hôtel Fort Garry entre Avery Brundage, Roger Coulon, et Charles Palmer (Pres Judo—Assistant—Interprète)," 2, ABC, box 207, WLUA. Whether Exeter knew of this meeting before its occurrence is open to question, but he fretted about any contact between Brundage and Coulon. "I think I should tell you that I hear rumours that you have been meeting with Coulon in his capacity as Secretary of GAIF. I feel sure that this must be incorrect as the whole IOC has said categorically that we do not recognise them and deal with all the IFs whose sports are included in the Games, so if you get a chance of denying this I hope you will do so." Marquess of Exeter to Avery Brundage, September 2, 1968. Brundage seemed weary of the whole matter. "My meetings with Coulon," responded Brundage, "have been in his capacity as President of FILA. On the other hand we cannot ignore the GAIF, it exists and they claim now, I understand, all the International Federations except yours." Avery Brundage to Marquess of Exeter, September 9, 1968, ABC, box 55, WLUA. Coulon was not FILA's president but its secretary general.

111. Johann Westerhoff to Marquess of Exeter, August 8, 1967, ABC, box 55, WLUA.

112. Marquess of Exeter to Avery Brundage, August 27, 1967, ABC, box 55, WLUA.

113. Avery Brundage to Roger Coulon, September 11, 1967, ABC, box 207, WLUA. Brundage neglected to highlight Berge Phillips's FINA contribution as it demonstrated the second highest return from gate receipts over the previous three festivals. And Phillips played a high-profile role within GAIF, serving as its first president. Exeter's plan is found in *Minutes of the 65th Session of the International Olympic Committee*, Tehran, 6–9 May 1967, Annex XIIIa.

114. *Minutes of the 65th Session of the International Olympic Committee*, Tehran, May 6–9, 1967, Annex XIIIa. FILA, Coulon's federation, due $2,340 on the basis of gate receipts alone, received $5,900.

115. *Minutes of the IOC Executive Board with the International Sport Federations*," Lausanne, January 27–28, 1968, 5, ABC, box 93, WLUA.

116. "Summarised Minutes of the Meeting of the Finance Commission of the IOC and Representatives of the International Federations' Commission and Representatives of the International Federations of Judo, Shooting, and Athletics," Mexico City, October 6, 1968, 1–2, *Commission des Finances—Finance Commission*, October 6, 1968, IOCA.

117. Ibid., 3.

118. The discussion and data can be found in, "Meetings of the GAIF—IFs—IOC and IFs," Lausanne, May 31, June 1–2, 1969, ABC, box 207, WLUA. It should be noted that a portion of the drop in the IAAF's receipts under the GAIF formula were due to the inclusion of FIFA in the distribution because the decision to stage an IF's world championships in an Olympic year no longer resulted in its removal from the allocation formula. Interestingly, while the IAAF's formula had it in receipt of $420,000, there was a sizable

drop off until Football and Swimming, both of whom could expect $210,000. Under GAIF's proposal, FIFA was due $280,727. One wonders if this situation was linked in any way to Exeter's belief, shared with Brundage eight years earlier, "that the football people are full of money." Exeter to Brundage, March 26, 1961, ABC, box 54, WLUA. Whether this type of consideration influenced its decision is open to speculation, but FIFA joined GAIF in early 1970, serving as a further challenge to Exeter in his efforts to squelch its growth and search for official recognition. Brundage to Exeter, April 20, 1970, ABC, box 55, WLUA; Exeter to Brundage, June 5, 1970, ABC, box 55, WLUA; Brundage to Exeter, June 16, 1970, ABC, box 55, WLUA.

119. For this discussion, see "Meeting of the Three Vice-Presidents and the Representatives of the International Federations," Munich, September 1, 1972, in *Minutes of the Meeting of the Finance Commission*, Munich, August 17, 28 and September 1, 1972, 7–8, IOCA.

120. In 1962 the IOC warned South Africa that its application of federal government edicts concerning apartheid to sport could no longer be tolerated in the Olympic Games. Ultimately, the South African National Olympic Committee (SANOC) was given until December 31st, 1963, to rectify the situation. SANOC did not comply, and the IOC withdrew its invitation to the 1964 Tokyo Olympics. Searching for a way to re-admit South Africa for 1968, Brundage sent Killanin, Reginald Alexander, and Nigeria's Sir Ade Ademola, the IOC's first black African member, to South Africa in September, 1967. South African officials pledged a mixed-race team, which was good enough for Brundage and enough IOC members such that the IOC duly reinstated South Africa in early 1968. But it was not close to enough for those who sought the elimination of apartheid. The thirty-two-nation-strong Organization of African Unity called for a boycott of the 1968 Mexico City Olympics. Individual nations, as Guttmann notes, in the Caribbean, the Islamic region, and the Communist bloc, threatened boycott. Under this pressure the Executive Board recommended withdrawing the invitation, after polling the rank-and-file IOC members. It was a massive blow for Brundage in his lifelong quest to separate sport from politics. Senn, *Power, Politics, and the Olympic Games*, 134–36; Guttmann, *Games Must Go On*, 234–40. Because the Israelis did not participate in the First Mediterranean Games in 1951 (its NOC had not been approved by the IOC), Arab interests used this fact as a means of pressuring successive organizers to exclude Israel throughout the 1950s and 1960s. As for the IVth Asian Games, this was the work of Indonesian president Sukarno as was the GANEFO as a response to Indonesia's suspension from the IOC for its actions tied to the IVth Asian Games. Sukarno boldly stated in advance of the GANEFO that he understood sport's place in the world: "Let us declare frankly that sport and politics are inseparable. And Indonesia now proposes to mix sport with politics." Guttmann, *Games Must Go On*, 224–30. For Brundage, the 1960s denoted a time when state amateurism was "the elephant in the room." East German and Soviet athletes certainly did not abide by amateur regulations, but his efforts to persuade Communist sport officials to embrace amateur regulations failed dismally. And, knowing it a battle he could not win, he abandoned it. He skirmished with a number of IFs that persisted with the award of cash prizes. He fended off an effort in the early 1960s to permit broken-time payments,

training, clothing, and living expenses for amateur athletes, in part, by declaring that a two-thirds vote would be required, but he yielded in permitting broken-time payments for those who could make a case for "financial hardship." Under Australia's Hugh Weir, a subcommittee revisited amateur policy and did so again later in the decade under the leadership of Romania's Alexandru Siperco, but Brundage's fervently held beliefs on the amateur ideal were in their death throes. The Shoe Wars in Mexico City involving Puma and Adidas, the machinations of ski manufacturers, and athletes such as France's ski champion Jean-Claude Killy in Grenoble left him apoplectic. "Throughout the remainder of the decade, Brundage's threats continued to ring hollow. The IOC's authority was increasingly mocked, athletes were corrupted by the lure of financial riches, money flowed, governments encroached, hypocrisy flourished, and the Olympic Games gradually transformed itself into a branch of commercial entertainment," concluded Llewellyn and Gleaves. *Rise and Fall of Olympic Amateurism*, 129–31, 139–41, 147–53.

121. Giorgio de Stefani to Avery Brundage, March 24, 1966, ABC, box 81, WLUA.

122. Avery Brundage to Giorgio Stefani, March 28, 1966, ABC, box 81, WLUA.

123. Guttmann, *Games Must Go On*, 182.

124. Ibid., 181–83. Beaumont's verbatim comment is on 181.

125. Avery Brundage to Giulio Onesti, August 31, 1971, ABC, box 61, WLUA.

126. Avery Brundage to Marquess of Exeter, January 18, 1967.

127. Killanin, *My Olympic Years*, 21–22.

Chapter 4. Willi Daume and Munich, 1972's Television Legacy

1. Finalists for the right to host the 1972 Olympic Winter Games were Banff, Canada; Lahti, Finland; and Salt Lake City, USA. Munich's competitors for the 1972 Summer Olympics were Detroit, USA; Madrid, Spain; and Montreal, Canada. See "Minutes of the 64th Session of the I.O.C. (excerpts)," 80–81.

2. Of course, this framework experienced adjustment in the context of the award of the 2024 and 2028 Olympics to Paris and Los Angeles at its 2017 Session in Lima, Peru.

3. Rode, "Introduction," 99.

4. Large, *Munich 1972*, 26, 29–30.

5. Ibid., 34–36. Following his passing in 1996, Daume's own Nazi past became the subject of investigation. Daume became a member of the National Socialist Party in 1937. He assumed control of his family's foundry business in Dortmund when his father died the following year. He served briefly in the Wehrmacht during the Poland campaign but was released from military duty in 1940. Daume operated a foundry in Antwerp during the war, while the family's Dortmund operation used forty to sixty slave laborers. In 1943 he provided service to the Sicherheitsdienst des Reichsführers (SD), the intelligence wing of the SS. Daume claimed he did this with no enthusiasm, only to avoid service on the Eastern Front, and that he provided the SD with nothing of substance. Biographer Jan Rode speculates that his decision may also have been prompted by accusations that he "remained too loyal to the Catholic Church." At the war's end, though British authorities labeled him a "follower" and issued him a DM 1000 fine, the classification was removed on appeal (before a German court) in 1949. Rode, who explored this element of Daume's

life, concluded that he was not a full-throated supporter of the Nazis, even though "he supported and benefitted from the regime." "According to my research he was no more than a follower" reported Rode, leaving the initial classification of "Mitläufer" an accurate one. Ibid., 26–28; "Willi Daume (1913–1996), Sportfunktionär"; "Historiker stellt klar: Daume nur ein Mitläufer"; email correspondence from Jan C. Rode to Stephen Wenn, September 27, 2016.

6. Herbert Kunze to Avery Brundage, April 11, 1969, ABC, box 98; Brundage to Kunze, April 24, 1969, ABC, box 98, WLUA.

7. *Minutes of the Meeting of the IOC Finance Commission*, Warsaw, June 4 and 6–8, 1969, 1–2, 5, IOCA.

8. Ibid., 2–3.

9. Ibid., 8–10.

10. Tomoo Sato to Lord Luke, October 2, 1969, "Droits de TV Sapporo 1972," Binder (hereafter Sapporo Binder), IOCA.

11. Tomoo Sato to Lord Luke, October 6, 1969, Sapporo Binder, IOCA.

12. *Minutes of the Meeting of the IOC Executive Board*, Dubrovnik, October 23–27, 1969, 10, IOCA. For Lord Luke's commitment to ensuring the IOC's interpretation of the Rome Formula in its dealings with Sapporo and Munich, see Lord Luke to Members of the Finance Commission, and Monique Berlioux, December 2, 1969, ABC, box 98.

13. Marquess of Exeter to Avery Brundage, November 17, 1969, ABC, box 55, WLUA. Brackets added.

14. Marquess of Exeter to Avery Brundage, January 15, 1970, ABC, box 55, WLUA.

15. Avery Brundage to Marquess of Exeter, January 30, 1970, ABC, box 55, WLUA.

16. *Minutes of the Meeting of the IOC Executive Board*, Lausanne, February 21–23, 1970, 13, IOCA.

17. "Pertaining to the distribution of the proceeds from television between the International Olympic Committee and the Organizing Committee for the Games of the XXth Olympiad Munich 1972," *Minutes of the Meeting of the Finance Commission*, Lausanne, February 20, 1970, Annex 1, IOCA.

18. *Minutes of the Meeting of the Finance Commission*, Lausanne, February 20, 1970, Annex 3, 29.

19. Avery Brundage to Lord Luke, January 7, 1970, ABC, box 98, WLUA.

20. Lord Luke to Herbert Kunze, November 3, 1969, ABC, box 98; Lord Luke to Shohei Sasaka, Sapporo Organizing Committee, March 3, 1970, Sapporo Binder, IOCA.

21. *Minutes of the 69th Session of the International Olympic Committee*, Amsterdam, May 12–16, 1970, 47, IOCA.

22. Lord Luke to Willi Daume, July 28, 1970, *Minutes of the Meeting of the IOC Finance Commission*, Lausanne, October 1, 1970, Annex 2, IOCA. Brackets added.

23. Willi Daume to Lord Luke, September 11, 1970, *Minutes of the Meeting of the Finance Commission*, Lausanne, October 1, 1970, Annex 3, 9. Lord Luke tried to defuse tensions. "I am sorry if I have misjudged the situation in any way, but I have most chiefly been concerned at the lack of progress we seem to have been making over the settlement of the main principle of the amounts due to the IOC from your Committee and that has yet

to be resolved." Luke to Daume, September 11, 1970, *Minutes of the Meeting of the Finance Commission*, Lausanne, October 1, 1970, Annex 4.

24. Tomoo Sato to Lord Luke, March 25, 1970, Sapporo Binder, IOCA.

25. Tomoo Sato to Lord Luke, September 4, 1970, Sapporo Binder, IOCA.

26. Lord Luke to Willi Daume, October 15, 1970, "Lord Luke Personal" File, IOCA.

27. Willi Daume to Lord Luke, November 20, 1970, ABC, box 98, WLUA.

28. Ibid.

29. Jean de Beaumont to Lord Luke, September 29, 1967; Luke to Avery Brundage, October 10, 1967; Brundage to R. S. Alexander, October 24, 1967; Alexander to Brundage, October 31, 1967. All letters found in ABC, box 98, WLUA.

30. Monique Berlioux to Lord Luke, September 25, 1969, ABC, box 98, WLUA.

31. Lord Luke to Monique Berlioux, October 9, 1969, ABC, box 98, WLUA.

32. Avery Brundage to Jean de Beaumont, May 23, 1969, ABC, box 51, WLUA. Beaumont concurred. See Beaumont to Brundage, March 12, 1969, ABC, box 98, WLUA.

33. Avery Brundage to Jean de Beaumont, December 12, 1969, ABC, box 51, WLUA.

34. Avery Brundage to Jean de Beaumont, November 19, 1969; Brundage to Beaumont, December 12, 1969, ABC, box 51, WLUA.

35. Avery Brundage to Members of the IOC Finance Commission, Lord Luke, R. S. Alexander, February 28, 1969, ABC, box 98, WLUA.

36. Monique Berlioux to Avery Brundage, November 24, 1969, ABC, box 98, WLUA.

37. Monique Berlioux to R. S. Alexander, November 25, 1969, ABC, box 98, WLUA.

38. R. S. Alexander to Monique Berlioux, December 22, 1969, ABC, box 98, WLUA.

39. Monique Berlioux to R. S. Alexander, January 15, 1970, ABC, box 98, WLUA.

40. Jean de Beaumont to Avery Brundage, December 2, 1969, ABC, box 51, WLUA.

41. Avery Brundage to Lord Luke, R. S. Alexander, Count Jean de Beaumont, Jose de J. Clark, July 27, 1970, ABC, box 98, WLUA.

42. Lord Luke to Avery Brundage, September 3, 1970, ABC, box 98, WLUA.

43. Avery Brundage to Lord Luke, September 17, 1970, ABC, box 98, WLUA.

44. *Minutes of the Finance Commission Meeting*, Munich, January 28, 1971, 4–5, IOCA.

45. *Minutes of the Meeting of the IOC Executive Board*, Lausanne, March 13–14, 1971, 20, IOCA.

46. Jean de Beaumont to Avery Brundage, February 24, 1971, ABC, box 51, WLUA.

47. Jean de Beaumont to Avery Brundage, February 8, 1971, ABC, box 51, WLUA.

48. Jean de Beaumont to Avery Brundage, February 24, 1971.

49. Lord Luke to Avery Brundage, February 10, 1971, ABC, box 98, WLUA.

50. Avery Brundage to Lord Luke, February 19, 1971, ABC, box 98; and, Brundage to Jean de Beaumont, February 20, 1971, ABC, box 51, WLUA.

51. *Minutes of the 69th Session of the International Olympic Committee*, Amsterdam, May 12–16, 1970, Annex 14a, 47.

52. Berlioux, "Managing a 'Gentlemen's Club,'" 8.

53. "Killanin, Lord; Morris, Michael; 3rd Baron Killanin, cr. 1900, of Galway; 3rd Baronet Morris, cr. 1885, of Galway, *British Army Officers, 1939–1945*." Killanin was recommended for the MBE by Brigidier N. W. Duncan, Commanding Officer, 30th Armoured Brigade,

and it was subsequently approved by Major General Percy C. S. Hobart, Commanding Officer, 79th Armoured Division. The recommendation made clear that Killanin had been a key player in the logistics and planning for the service of the "flail" tanks:

This officer has been Brigade Major of this Brigade for the past eighteen months. In December 1943 it converted from its normal Armoured Brigade role and was equipped throughout with flail tanks. The resultant change in establishment involved an immense amount of additional work which largely fell on the Brigade Major. The training consequent on the new role with exercises further added to the duties which fell to him. The special role of the Brigade which involves cooperation with many other formations meant additional work on a different level from that which falls on the Brigade Major in an ordinary Armoured Brigade. Lord Killanin has spared no pains to ensure that his duties are efficiently carried out. His cheerful willingness has ensured the efficient working of the Brigade staff while his high moral sense and devotion to duty have always been an admirable example to all who come into contact with him. Operations have presented many new problems with other formations but they have always been met by a display of efficiency and courtesy which have done much to smooth the path for all concerned and ensure the success of the Brigade and of the units working with it.

54. "The man who almost sent Monty to his doom." Killanin's wife, Mary Sheila Cathcart Dunlop, with whom he had four children following their marriage in 1945, served as part of the code-breaking team at Bletchley Park during the war. Her record of service (1940–1945) can be found at "Miss Mary Sheila Cathcart Dunlop (Killanin)," *Bletchley Park Roll of Honour.*

55. Goldstein, "Lord Killanin, Olympic Leader, Dies at 84."

56. Hersh, "Killanin's IOC Presidency."

57. Goldstein, "Lord Killanin, Olympic Leader, Dies at 84."

58. Espy, *Politics of the Olympic Games,* 40.

59. Hersh, "Killanin's IOC Presidency."

60. Gonzalez, "Lord Killanin."

61. Guttmann, *Games Must Go On,* 247. Brackets added.

62. Rodda, "Lord Killanin."

63. Todd, "1976 Montreal Olympics."

64. Kaufman, "Jean Drapeau." Brackets added.

65. Todd, "40-Year Hangover." Brackets added.

66. Ibid.

67. Todd, "40-Year Hangover."

68. Riga, "Montreal Olympics."

69. Ibid.

70. Lord Luke to the Mayors of Denver and Montreal, May 15, 1970, *Minutes of the Meeting of the Finance Commission,* Lausanne, February 1 and 3, 1973, Annex 5, 33, IOCA.

71. "Extract—President's Visit to Montreal, 3rd/7th November 1972," "N.1 Droits de TV Montreal Du 4.12.69 Au 30.6.73" File (hereafter Montreal File #1), IOCA.

72. "Minutes of the IOC Finance Commission with the Representatives of the Organising Committee of the Games of the XXIst Olympiad, London, November 28, 1972," 4, Montreal File #1, IOCA.

73. "Extract—President's Visit to Montreal, 3rd/7th November 1972."

74. "Minutes of the IOC Finance Commission with the Representatives of the Organising Committee of the Games of the XXIst Olympiad," London, November 28, 1972," 5.

75. Ibid., 6–7.

76. Lord Killanin to Monique Berlioux, December 5, 1972, Montreal File #1, IOCA.

77. Lord Killanin to Roger Rousseau, December 8, 1972, Montreal File #1, IOCA.

78. "ABC Will Spend $25 Million."

79. Deford, "Roone Arledge 1931–2002."

80. *Minutes of the Meeting of the IOC Executive Board*, Lausanne, February 9–11, 1974, Annex 4, 12–13, IOCA.

81. Ibid; and Lord Killanin to Count de Beaumont, Lord Luke, Marc Hodler, Willi Daume, Herman van Karnebeek, Monique Berlioux, March 6, 1974, "N.2 Droits TV Dossier General Innsbruck ABC UER 1972–1976" File (hereafter Innsbruck File #2), IOCA.

82. Arledge's comment appears in Lucas, "Descriptive History," 46.

83. *Minutes of the Meeting of the IOC Finance Commission*, Lausanne, February 1 and 3, 1973, 7–8, IOCA.

84. *Minutes of the Meeting of the IOC Executive Board*, Lausanne, February 2–5, 1973, 6–7, IOCA.

85. Ibid., 9.

86. *Minutes of the Meeting of the IOC Finance Commission*, Lausanne, February 1 and 3, 1973, 2.

87. In an exchange of correspondence between Killanin and Rousseau, little was resolved. Killanin informed Rousseau that all future contracts needed to be sent to Lausanne prior to being signed or their terms being released to the media. Rousseau wanted to sign the contracts, forward them to the IOC, with their becoming valid only after the IOC issued its approval. He maintained that Montreal wanted to maintain a technical services component in all future contracts. Killanin responded that the Rome Formula already favored the OCOGs. Rousseau was unmoved on the Rome Formula and called for a different tone in future discussions concerning television agreements. All contracts, said Rousseau, must "be discussed in a spirit of partnership in the interest of the Olympic movement rather than the highly pecuniary motives which animated past discussions." Lord Killanin to Roger Rousseau, February 5, 1973; Rousseau to Killanin, February 15, 1973; and Killanin to Rousseau, February 27, 1973. All letters found in Montreal File #1, IOCA.

88. *Minutes of the Meeting of the IOC Finance Commission*, Paris, June 12, 1973, 2, and Annex 3, 19–25, IOCA. IOC records issued later indicate two new clauses were added to the ABC contract that was approved on this same date by the IOC lawyer's signature. *Minutes of the Meeting of the IOC Executive Board*, Lausanne, February 9–11, 1974, 4. The occurrence is also detailed in Lord Killanin to Count Jean de Beaumont, Lord Luke, Marc Hodler, Herman van Karnebeek, and Willi Daume, April 18, 1974, Innsbruck File #2.

89. *Minutes of the Meeting of the IOC Finance Commission*, Varna, October 4 and 7, 1973, 2–4, IOCA. The $40 million figure is found in "Minutes of the IOC Finance Commission with the Representatives of the Organising Committee of the Games of the XXIst Olympiad, London, November 28, 1972," 5.

90. *Minutes of the Meeting of the IOC Finance Commission*, Paris, January 28, 1974, 4, IOCA.

91. *Minutes of the Meeting of the IOC Executive Board*, Lausanne, February 9–11, 1974, 4, 11–12.

92. Lord Killanin to Marc Hodler, March 5, 1973, "N.1 Droits de TV Innsbruck Du 1.2.73" File (hereafter Innsbruck File #1), IOCA.

93. *Minutes of the Meeting of the IOC Finance Commission*, Paris, June 12, 1973, 4. Klee's estimate was accurate: Innsbruck succeeded in reaching $11.63 million in global television revenue. See "Summary of Olympic Television Rights Olympic Winter Games," PCFRP.

94. *Minutes of the Meeting of the IOC Finance Commission*, Varna, October 4 and 7, 1973, 5–6. There was a misunderstanding between the two parties in terms of the schedule of payments, but Klee, Killanin, and Beaumont settled this matter. See Lord Killanin to Karl Heinz Klee, October 7, 1973; Klee to Killanin, October 10, 1973; Killanin to Klee, October 15, 1973; Killanin to Jean de Beaumont, November 3, 1973. All letters in Innsbruck File #1, IOCA. See also "Meeting of Monday 5th November 1973," Innsbruck File #1, IOCA; Killanin to Marc Hodler, November 17, 1973, Innsbruck File #1, IOCA.

95. Lord Luke to Monique Berlioux, February 20, 1974, Montreal File #1, IOCA.

96. *Minutes of the Meeting of the IOC Finance Commission*, Lausanne, October 8, 1974, 4, IOCA.

97. *Minutes of the Meeting of the IOC Finance Commission*, Vienna, October 18, 1974, 4, IOCA.

98. *Minutes of the Meeting of the IOC Executive Board*, Vienna, October 18–24, 1974, 2, 3, 6–9, 15, IOCA; "Report of Dr. Schätz on Television Broadcasting Rights for the Games of the XXIst Olympiad—Montreal 1976," *Minutes of the IOC Finance Commission,* Lausanne, October 8, 1974, Annex 2, 12–19.

99. Monique Berlioux to Lord Killanin, March 15, 1973; Killanin to Berlioux, March 21, 1973; Killanin to Berlioux, May 14, 1973, Montreal File #1, IOCA.

100. Lord Killanin to Jim Worrall, September 9, 1975, "N.5 Droits de T.V. Montreal Du 1.9.75 Au 30.4.76" File (hereafter Montreal File #2), IOCA.

101. Roger Rousseau to IOC, Lausanne, September 11, 1975, Montreal File #2, IOCA. A fuller analysis of the EBU/COJO negotiations for Montreal television rights appears in chapter 9.

102. Lord Killanin to Monique Berlioux, March 21, 1973, Montreal File #1.

103. *Minutes of the Meeting of the 74th Session of the International Olympic Committee*, Varna, October 5–7, 1973, 27–28, IOCA.

104. *Minutes of the Meeting of the IOC Executive Board*, Lausanne, February 9–11, 1974, Annex 4, 12–13; and, Lord Killanin to Count de Beaumont, Lord Luke, Marc Hodler, Willi Daume, Herman van Karnebeek, Monique Berlioux, March 6, 1974.

105. Monique Berlioux to Roone Arledge, March 8, 1974, Innsbruck File #2, IOCA.

106. The membership included, Berlioux, Georges Straschnov (EBU), Georges Croses (ABC), Helmut Käser (general secretary, FIFA), Walter Schätz, and IOC legal advisers Luc Silance and Daniel Mortureux. See *Minutes of the Meeting of the Television Sub-Committee*, Lausanne, October 4, 1974, Annex 2, IOCA.

107. Ibid.; "Notes on the Work of the Television Sub-Committee," June 23, 1974, "TV/Divers 1974–1985" Binder (hereafter TV Subject Binder), "1974–1979" Folder, IOCA; "Memorandum on the Television Rights," 1–4, TV Subject Binder, "1974–1979" Folder, IOCA; "Role and Function of the Expert," 1–3, TV Subject Binder, "1974–1979" Folder, IOCA.

108. *Minutes of the 79th Session of the International Olympic Committee*, Prague, June 15–18, 1977, 35, 99–103, IOCA.

Chapter 5. Los Angeles, 1984

Some text and the table in this chapter appeared previously in Stephen R. Wenn, "Peter Ueberroth's Legacy: How the 1984 Los Angeles Olympics Changed the Trajectory of the Olympic Movement," *International Journal of the History of Sport* 32, no. 1 (2015): 157–71. This material appears with permission of the Taylor & Francis Group.

1. Avery Brundage, "Stop, Look, and Listen," 1948, ABC, box 245, WLUA.

2. Boykoff, *Power Games*, 133.

3. Guttmann, as cited in La Rocco, "Rings of Power," 10.

4. Peter Ueberroth (with Richard Levin and Amy Quinn), *Made in America*, 28.

5. Dyreson and Llewellyn, "Los Angeles is *the* Olympic City," 1991.

6. Athens hosted the Olympic Games in 1896 and 2004. However, in the early years of the modern Olympics, their future success teetered as Coubertin and his colleagues struggled to embed the Games within the world's sporting consciousness. Greek officials, seizing on their success in hosting the 1896 Olympics, offered to host what became known as the Intercalated Games in 1906. Though not officially recognized as Olympic Games, their staging lent stability to the nascent Olympic Movement in the aftermath of less-than-memorable editions hosted by Paris and St. Louis. Though conceived as Games that could be staged in Athens on a staggered quadrennial basis with the Olympic Games, Athens hosted them on only this occasion.

7. Bernstein, "Parting a Sea."

8. Much of this biographical text on Ueberroth appears verbatim in Wenn, "Peter Ueberroth's Legacy," 159.

9. Kennedy, "Miser with the Midas Touch."

10. *Minutes of the Meeting of the IOC Executive Board*, Athens, May 13–14, 16, and 18, 1978, 17, IOCA.

11. *Minutes of the Meeting of the IOC Executive Board*, Puerto Rico, June 26–29, 1979, 8, IOCA.

12. Paul Ziffren, Chairman, LAOOC Board of Directors, and Rodney W. Rood, Secretary, LAOOC Board of Directors, to ABC Sports Inc., c/o Charles Stanford, Director, Legal and Business Affairs, April 9, 1979, "Los Angeles TV General 1984, 1978–1979–1980" File (hereafter LA File #1), IOCA; Ueberroth, *Made in America*, 52.

13. Monique Berlioux to Peter Ueberroth, April 30, 1979, LA File #1, IOCA.

14. Lord Killanin to Paul Ziffren, May 4, 1979, LA File #1, IOCA.

15. Paul Ziffren to Lord Killanin, May 5, 1979, LA File #1, IOCA.

16. Lord Killanin to Paul Ziffren, May 11, 1979, LA File #1, IOCA. Brackets added.

17. Peter Ueberroth to Monique Berlioux, May 10, 1979, LA File #1, IOCA; Berlioux to Ueberroth, May 11, 1979, "Los Angeles TV General 1984, LA File #1, IOCA; *Minutes of the Meeting of the IOC Executive Board*, Puerto Rico, June 26–29, 1979, 7–8.

18. "Report on the Meeting between Mr. Wolper, Chairman of the Los Angeles Television Committee and the Director and Financial Adviser of the IOC 11th June 1979," LA File #1, IOCA.

19. Reich and Margulies, "Talks on Olympic TV Pact Begin." An undated clipping of this article appears in, LA File #1, IOCA. Online research revealed the precise date and page information. The following day, another article in the *Los Angeles Times* projected a possible $175 million sale price for the U.S. deal. See "$175 Million Olympics TV Deal Predicted," *Los Angeles Times*, September 12, part II, 4, LA File #1, IOCA.

20. Ueberroth, *Made in America*, 68.

21. *Minutes of the Meeting of the IOC Executive Board*, Nagoya, October 23–25, 1979, 7–8, IOCA.

22. "Untitled Document," 2, "Los Angeles TV General 1984, 1981" File (hereafter LA File #2), IOCA.

23. "Olympic Games Television Rights Summary: Summer Games," PCFRP.

24. "Untitled Document," 2.

25. Ibid.

26. Ibid., 2–3.

27. Ibid., 2–4.

28. Ibid., 2.

29. Regis de Kalbermatten to Peter Ueberroth, June 10, 1981, LA File #2, IOCA.

30. Peter Ueberroth to Regis de Kalbermatten, June 17, 1981, LA File #2, IOCA.

31. *Minutes of the Meeting of the 84th IOC Session*, Baden Baden, September 29–30, October 1–2, 1981, 4, IOCA.

32. Ibid., 5.

33. Peter Ueberroth to Juan Antonio Samaranch, November 11, 1981, LA File #2, IOCA.

34. *Minutes of the Meeting of the IOC Executive Board*, Sarajevo, December 2 and 4, 1981, 6, IOCA.

35. Ibid.

36. Peter Ueberroth to Juan Antonio Samaranch, November 27, 1981, LA File #2, IOCA.

37. Ibid.

38. Peter Ueberroth to Juan Antonio Samaranch, December 2, 1981, LA File #2, IOCA; Samaranch to Ueberroth, December 3, 1981, LA File #2, IOCA; *Minutes of the Meeting of the IOC Executive Board*, Sarajevo, December 2 and 4, 1981, 6–7.

39. Tomokazu Sakamoto, President, Nippon Hoso Kyokai (NHK) and, Yoshizumi Asano, President, National Association of Commercial Broadcasters in Japan, to Monique Berlioux, May 21, 1980, LA File #1, IOCA; Berlioux to Sakamoto and Asano, May 30, 1980, LA File #1, IOCA.

40. *Minutes of the Meeting of the IOC Executive Board*, Rome, May 25–26, and 28, 1982, 27, IOCA.

41. Michael O'Hara to Takeshi Tanaka, Managing Director, NHK and, Taiji Kawate, Director, National Association of Commercial Broadcasters in Japan, June 15, 1982, "Los Angeles TV General 1984, Avril-Dec 1982" File (hereafter LA File #3), IOCA.

42. Katsuji Shibata to Juan Antonio Samaranch, June 12, 1982, LA File #3, IOCA.

43. Juan Antonio Samaranch to Katsuji Shibata, June 23, 1982, LA File #3, IOCA; Monique Berlioux to Masaji Kiyokawa, Member, IOC Executive Board, August 12, 1982, LA File #3, IOCA.

44. Daniel Russell to Monique Berlioux, November 24, 1982, LA File #3, IOCA. Earlier in the month, Ueberroth had set LAOOC's opening position at $20 million. See Berlioux to Masaji Kiyokawa, November 10, 1982, LA File #3, IOCA.

45. Monique Berlioux (sent by Danny Russell) to Juan Antonio Samaranch, January 26, 1983, "Los Angeles TV General 1984, Janv/Mars 1983" File (hereafter LA File #4), IOCA.

46. Michael O'Hara to Monique Berlioux, January 26, 1983, LA File #4, IOCA.

47. Monique Berlioux to Peter Ueberroth, February 1, 1983, LA File #4, IOCA.

48. Peter Ueberroth to Monique Berlioux, February 2, 1983, LA File #4, IOCA.

49. Lieser, "Los Angeles and the 1984 Olympic Games," 130.

50. Ueberroth, *Made in America*, 61.

51. Wilson, "Sports Infrastructure," 146.

52. Ueberroth, *Made in America*, 70.

53. Kennedy, "Miser with the Midas Touch."

54. Hula, "Updated."

55. Ibid.

56. Interview, Howard Stupp, March 7, 2016, Lausanne, Switzerland.

57. Miller, *Olympic Revolution*, 33.

58. Berlioux, "Managing a 'Gentlemen's Club,'" 11–12. Jonas and Westerhoff carried the title of secretary general. It was a title that would be changed to director at the time that Berlioux took over the role. Jonas, stated Berlioux, rolled into Lausanne "with all the subtlety of a decent Swiss peasant." He drove around town in his car, which was newly adorned with an Olympic pennant, earning a scolding from Brundage. Jonas "rubbed some members the wrong way, and exasperated others," reported Berlioux. In less than a year, the Executive Board sent him packing; however, this action embroiled the IOC in a legal tussle when Jonas claimed four years' salary in Swiss Court. Westerhoff moved to enlarge the staff, and then initiated discussions to transfer the IOC's headquarters to Zurich without consulting Brundage, "who looked unfavourably on the growing administration developing outside his orbit." Westerhoff drew an element of his motivation toward the IOC's departure from Mon Repos, its original headquarters in Lausanne, given his residence was only 30 kilometers distant from Zurich. Westerhoff's activities did spur the City of Lausanne to offer the Château de Vidy rent free, with utilities also covered. A grand "world tour" to various NOCs that Westerhoff launched in the wake of the 1968 Grenoble Olympic Winter Games greatly angered Brundage, who considered Westerhoff's styling himself as an Olympic "Head of State" as an "attack on his authority" as president. By the time of the 1968 Summer Olympics in Mexico City, the two were

no longer on speaking terms. Brundage's re-election in 1968 afforded him the security to obtain Westerhoff's resignation, and he did so in January 1969.

59. Davenport, "Monique Berlioux," 15.

60. Pound, *Inside the Olympics*, 170–72. Howard Stupp confirmed that Berlioux bugged Samaranch's office. Personal interview, Howard Stupp.

61. Pound, *Inside the Olympics*, 172–73.

62. Email correspondence from Michael Payne to Stephen Wenn, February 1, 2018.

63. Miller, *Olympic Revolution*, 34–35.

64. Email correspondence from Michael Payne to Stephen Wenn, February 1, 2018.

65. Pound, *Inside the Olympics*, 240.

66. Ibid., 238–40. Pound was co-opted in 1978. He elected not to attend the Athens Session in that year, thinking it rather awkward to presume his appointment. The following year at the IOC's Session in Montevideo, Pound was wearing the standard IOC Session badge, along with a white ribbon denoting his IOC member status, issued to him by Berlioux's office. Berlioux spied Pound wearing the badge and tasked a junior staff member to retrieve it as according to protocol, or at least, in Berlioux's mind, Pound was not yet able to wear it because he had not yet been officially sworn in as a member. Pound avoided a scene by simply exchanging it for a Session badge minus the white ribbon denoting IOC member status. He duly located a piece of white paper, fashioned that paper into the shape of a ribbon, and wore it for twelve hours, replete with the phrase "I Love Monique" written on it, much to the amusement of his colleagues.

67. Ibid., 237–38; Davenport, "Monique Berlioux," 13. For preparations for Berlioux's departure as discussed by the IOC Executive Board, and the terms of Raymond Gafner's appointment to take up her former duties as "administrator ad interim," see *Minutes of the Meeting of the IOC Executive Board*, East Berlin, May 31, June 1–3, and 6, 1985, 69, 71, IOCA.

68. Miller, *Olympic Revolution*, 35. Brackets added.

69. Ibid., 39–40.

70. Handwritten Notes, Robert J. Kane, undated, "Kane Box 55 874–894 Los Angeles Olympic Organizing Committee (LAOOC) Correspondence (19) 1979–1984" (hereafter USOC box #1), USOCA.

71. *Minutes of the Meeting of the Board of Directors of the Los Angeles Olympic Organizing Committee*, December 19, 1984, 3, "Kane Box 56 895–914 Los Angeles Olympic Organizing Committee (LAOOC) Minutes, reports, legal (20) 1978–1984" (hereafter USOC box #2), USOCA.

72. Ibid., 4.

73. Zimbalist, *Circus Maximus*, 1.

74. Booth, "Olympic City Bidding," 371.

75. Ibid., 372.

76. "IOC 'Agenda 2020.'"

Chapter 6. "Total Olympic Programme"

1. "Remarks by Donald R. Keough—News Conference, The Olympic Programme, November 25, 1985, Pierre Hotel, New York," "J-TOP/0A2, SD4 Coca-Cola Correspondance, 1985" File (hereafter TOP/Coca-Cola File #1).

2. "Signature of the Agreement Coca-Cola-ISL Marketing, New York, 25th November 1985—Speech of the IOC President," TOP/Coca-Cola File #1.

3. "Donald R. Keough, President, The Coca-Cola Company," TOP/Coca-Cola File #1, IOCA.

4. Email correspondence from Michael Payne to Stephen Wenn, February 1, 2018.

5. For instance, see "Meeting with Juan Antonio Samaranch, Johnny De Vicuna and Gary P. Hite," May 3, 1983, "J-TOP/0A2 SD2 Coca-Cola Correspondance, 1983" File (hereafter TOP/Coca-Cola File #2), IOCA; "Report of the Meeting with the Coca-Cola Company—Atlanta, 8th November 1983," TOP/Coca-Cola File #2, IOCA; Gary P. Hite (Manager, International Sports and Consumer Promotions, Coca-Cola Company) to Juan Antonio Samaranch, February 1, 1984, "J-TOP/0A2 SD3 Coca-Cola Correspondance, 1984" File (hereafter TOP/Coca-Cola File #3), IOCA; Gary P. Hite to Juan Antonio Samaranch, March 6, 1985, TOP/Coca-Cola File #1, IOCA.

6. "Signature of the Agreement Coca-Cola-ISL Marketing, New York, 25th November 1985—Speech of the IOC President."

7. Schmitt, "Revamping the Olympic Franchise."

8. Interview with Dick Pound, December 19, 2016, Montreal, Canada.

9. "Signature of the Agreement Coca-Cola-ISL."

10. Email correspondence from Michael Payne to Stephen Wenn, February 1, 2018; Payne, *Olympic Turnaround*, 80–81; Jürgen Lenz to F. Don Miller, August 5, 1984, "ISL/TOP I General" File (hereafter ISL/TOP File #1), IOCA.

11. Email correspondence from Michael Payne to Stephen Wenn, February 1, 2018.

12. "Remarks by Donald R. Keough."

13. Email correspondence from Michael Payne to Stephen Wenn, March 7, 2018.

14. Email correspondence from Michael Payne to Stephen Wenn, February 1, 2018.

15. Earl Ramer to Gerald Ford, December 4, 1972, Vice-Presidential Papers, box 154, "Olympics" Folder (hereafter Gerald R. Ford File #1), GRFPL. Attached to this letter was a report composed by the NCAA's International Relations Committee titled "United States Olympic Crisis: The Problem That Won't Go Away."

16. For the best survey treatment of the rise of intercollegiate athletics in America, see Smith, *Sports and Freedom*.

17. Cecil N. Coleman to Gerald Ford, November 9, 1972, Gerald R. Ford File #1, GRFPL.

18. As recounted in a memorandum, Mike Harrigan to Bill Casselman, April 22 1974, Vice-Presidential Papers, box 74, "Amateur Sports Legislation" Folder (hereafter Gerald R. Ford File #2), GRFPL.

19. Presidential Commissions are federally created task forces formed to investigate or research specific issues. Such commissions can be empowered as a quasi-judicial body, conferred with powers of arbitration and dispute resolution, or they can be formed to provide information and extend recommendations. Presidential commissions are relatively rare—roughly thirty had been formed by the mid-1970s, the first of which, the Schurman Commission, was formed in 1899. In essence, the rarity of a presidential commission generally speaks to the importance of an issue as evaluated by the president and his inner administration. Other notable commissions include the Roberts Commission

(to investigate the attack on Pearl Harbor), Committee on Civil Rights, Committee on the Status of Women, the Warren Commission (to investigate John. F. Kennedy's assassination), and the 9/11 Commission.

20. Memorandum from Tod Hullin to Ken Cole and Jim Cavanaugh, January 4, 1975, White House Central Files Subject File, boxes 5–6, "RE 14: Olympics" Folder (hereafter Gerald R. Ford File #3), GRFPL. Executive Order 11868 was not formally announced until June 19, 1975. The text of the executive order is available via the University of California–Santa Barbara online entry, "The American Presidency Project: Executive Order 11868—President's Commission on Olympic Sports," *American Presidency Project*, http://www.presidency.ucsb.edu/ws/?pid=23939.

21. For an abbreviated overview of the PCOS and its implementation, see Harrigan, "Class Act." See also, *The Final Report of the President's Commission on Olympic Sports 1975–1977—Executive Summary*, U.S. Government President's Commission on Olympic Sports 1975–1977, box 1, "RG15.01 President's Commission on Olympic Sports—Executive Summary" File (hereafter USOC File #1), USOCA.

22. Interview with Dick Pound. Brackets added.

23. Kéba Mbaye, "Notes on the 'Intelicense Case,'" 7, "F-A01-AF/071: SD4: Rapport de Keba M'Baye, 1985" File (hereafter Intelicense File #1), IOCA.

24. Samaranch asked Mbaye to review the files on the Intelicense case and offer his opinion. For Mbaye's findings, see Kéba Mbaye to Juan Antonio Samaranch, September 2, 1985, "F-A01-AF/062: Affaires juridiques: pictogrammes: Intelicense: correspondance 1985–1986" File (hereafter Intelicense File #2), IOCA.

25. "Report on the Informal Meeting Held in London—19th March 1986," "F-A01-AF/072: Affaires juridiques: pictogrammes: Intelicense: reunions, 1981–1986" File (hereafter Intelicense File #3), IOCA. This document is a summary of a meeting between Samaranch, IOC outside legal counsel, François Carrard, and Killanin. Its content confirms that Killanin delegated almost complete authority in the matter to Berlioux and the IOC's legal adviser, Georges Straschnov.

26. Richard Pound to Monique Berlioux, August 2, 1979, "F-A01-AF/056 SD2: Correspondance, 1979" File (hereafter Intelicense File #4), IOCA. COJO assigned the rights to the Summer pictograms to the Canadian Olympic Association, but eventually they were transferred to the Olympic Installations Corporation. The cost of acquiring the pictograms from the Munich Organizing Committee was $60,000. See "Telephone Conversation Intelicense 3rd October 1983," 4, "F-A01-AF/072 SD1: Reunions concernant Intelicense, 1981–1986" File (hereafter Intelicense File #5), IOCA. This is a verbatim transcript of a conversation between Georges Straschnov, John Huhs, a U.S.-based lawyer for the IOC, and three lawyers, Richard Kline, Robert Rachlin, and Edward Colbert, who acted on behalf of the USOC in its legal dispute with Intelicense.

27. Georges Straschnov to Walter Tröger (West German Olympic Committee), July 17, 1979, Intelicense File #4, IOCA.

28. Stan R. Shefler to Lord Killanin, September 13, 1978; Monique Berlioux to Shefler, September 27, 1978, "F-A01-AF/056 SD1: Correspondance 1978" File (hereafter Intelicense File #6), IOCA. Shefler disputed Berlioux's position, citing a contract with COJO

permitting it to market the pictograms through 1982. See Shefler to Berlioux, October 2, 1978, Intelicense File #6, IOCA. Berlioux's tone became more strident in telling Shefler to cease and desist with any activities concerning the Montreal pictograms. See Berlioux to Shefler, October 23, 1978, Intelicense File #6, IOCA. "I underline once again," wrote Berlioux, "that you are not entitled to commercialize the pictograms of the Montreal Games, the Olympic Rules being very specific on this point." Time drifted by, but Berlioux's irritation did not subside. See Berlioux to Shefler, July 10, 1979, Intelicense File #4, IOCA. Berlioux warned Shefler of the murky copyright situation with the Munich/Montreal pictograms and sought assurance that the IOC would not be held liable for any legal suits prompted by Intelicense's activities.

29. "Telephone Conversation Intelicense 3rd October 1983," 4–5.

30. Ibid., 5.

31. Ibid., 4.

32. Karl Heinz Klee (President, 1976 Innsbruck Organizing Committee) to Monique Berlioux, May 31, 1979; Klee to Berlioux, July 4, 1979; Berlioux to Klee, July 11, 1979, Intelicense File #4, IOCA.

33. Mbaye, "Notes on the 'Intelicense Case,'" 2–3.

34. Ibid., 4.

35. "Report in re Intelicense Corporation, 14.3.83," 9, "F-A01-AF/071 Affaires juridiques: pictogrammes; Intelicense: rapports 1982–1987" File (hereafter Intelicense File #7), IOCA.

36. F. Don Miller to Stanley Shefler, May 26, 1981, "F-A01-AF/057 SD1: Correspondance, janvier-juillet 1981" File (hereafter Intelicense File #8), IOCA.

37. "Report on the Informal Meeting Held in London—19th March 1986," 1–2.

38. 737 F.2d 263, 222 U.S.P.Q. 766, United States Olympic Committee, Plaintiff—Appellee, v. Intelicense Corporation, S.A., International Sports Marketing, Inc., Defendants—Appellants. International Sports Marketing Inc., Intelicense, S.A., Plaintiffs—Appellants v. United States Olympic Committee, Defendant—Appellee. Nos. 1324, 1331, Dockets 83-9025, 83-9063. United States Court of Appeals, Second Circuit, Argued May 30, 1984, Decided June 18, 1984, Certiorari Denied Nov. 5, 1984. See 105 S.Ct. 387, Sec. I, para. 5, https://law.resource.org/pub/us/case/reporter/F2/737/737.F2d.263.83-9063.83-9025.1324.1331.html.

39. Juan Antonio Samaranch to Mr. S. R. Shefler, June 5, 1981, "F-A01-AF/057 Affaires juridiques: pictogrammes: Intelicense: correspondence 1981–1982" File (hereafter Intelicense File #9), IOCA.

40. "Report in re Intelicense Corporation, 14.3.83," 13–15. See also John I. Huhs, Pisar & Huhs (Attorney and Counselors) to Monique Berlioux, September 15, 1983; Huhs to Berlioux, September 15, 1983; telex, Samuel Pisar (Pisar & Huhs, Attorneys and Counselors) to Berlioux, November 23, 1983, "F-A01-AF/060 Affaires juridiques: pictogrammes: Intelicense: correspondance, 1983–1984" File (hereafter Intelicense File #10), IOCA.

41. "Telephone Conversation Intelicense 3rd October 1983," 11, 13–14.

42. Telex, F. Don Miller to Monique Berlioux, November 23, 1983, Intelicense File #10, IOCA. Samuel Pisar, a U.S.-based legal counsel, commented on the victory, but his comments are contained in a telex whose first page is not extant. Therefore, it is unclear to

whom he sent it, or its precise date; however, it is clear that the comments were provided shortly after Judge Oakes's decision was announced. The last two pages of the telex are found in Intelicense File #10, IOCA. John Huhs, Pisar's senior law partner, provided a more detailed assessment following some reflection over the ensuing three weeks. John I. Huhs to Monique Berlioux, December 13, 1983, Intelicense File #10, IOCA. Huhs reported that "the USOC is, of course, preparing as large a damage claim as it can reasonably justify." Beyond its "substantial" legal costs, reported Huhs, the USOC "will ask for an accounting of all license revenues earned by Intelicense in the United States, with the objective of having these revenues awarded to the USOC under an 'unjust enrichment' theory of damages."

43. 737 F.2d 263, 222 U.S.P.Q. 766, Sec. II, para. 16.

44. "Report in re Intelicense Corporation S.A., July 5, 1984," 1–2, Intelicense File #7, IOCA. With respect to Judge Oakes's original decision that the USOC had control of the use of the five-ring logo alone, or in combinations with other marks, the three judges on the appeal panel noted: "There is absolutely nothing in the legislative history of Sec. 380, or elsewhere, to support the argument that the Olympic symbol loses its identity when combined with other elements. Moreover, such a strained reading of (a)(1) vitiates the very interests sought to be safeguarded by the enactment of Sec. 380. This statute does not merely prohibit marketing the Olympic symbol itself, but more significantly, it forbids any commercial use without the consent of the USOC." Sec. 380 refers to the pertinent section of the Amateur Sports Act. 737 F.2d 263, 222 U.S.P.Q. 766, Sec. II, para. 17. Intelicense also unsuccessfully argued that the USOC's denial of access represented a "taking of property" in light of its standing as the official agent of the IOC with respect to the marketing of the pictograms on a worldwide basis. The claim clearly puzzled the judges who noted you could not take something from Intelicense if Intelicense did not have it in the first place. 737 F.2d 263, 222 U.S.P.Q. 766, Sec. II, para. 20. The judges determined that the Amateur Sports Act (ASA), passed in Washington in 1978, trumped the *Olympic Charter*. The Intelicense/IOC agreements were signed one year after the ASA became law. A concise summary of the legal case as it unfolded in the United States can be found in Hay, "Guarding the Olympic Gold," 484–86. See also "Report in re Intelicense Corporation S.A.," May 24, 1985, 1, Intelicense File #7, IOCA. The breakdown on the $212,000 award was as follows: damages against International Sports Marketing—$50,000; damages against Intelicense—$80,000; jointly shared attorneys' fees by International Sports Marketing and Intelicense—$74,000; and attorneys' fees charged to Intelicense alone—$8,000.

45. "Report on the Intelicense Corporation S.A. Affair," November 17, 1983, 4, Intelicense File #7, IOCA.

46. "Report in re Intelicense Corporation, 14.3.83," 15–16.

47. Ibid., 16–17.

48. "Report in re Intelicense Corporation S.A.," May 25, 1984, 5–6.

49. François Carrard to Richard W. Pound, November 9, 1986, "F-A01-AF/063 SD:2 Correspondance, 1987–1988" File (hereafter Intelicense File #11), IOCA. Strub was thought by Carrard to be an effective judge, one who would consider the case carefully.

50. "Report in re Intelicense Corporation S.A.," May 25, 1984, 6.

51. "Report in re Intelicense Corporation S.A.," July 5, 1984, 4–5. Shefler stated that Intelicense lost SF 3 million through 1983, another SF 2 million in "uncollected minimums," and the rest represented "missed profits."

52. "Report on the Intelicense Corporation S.A. Affair Presented by Mr. Francois Carrard, Lawyer of the IOC," undated, 1–2, Intelicense File #7, IOCA. This document is an appendix in the *Minutes of the Meeting of the IOC Executive Board*, Mexico City, November 7–8, 1984, IOCA.

53. Telex, Stan Shefler to Juan Antonio Samaranch, September 10, 1985; telex, Samaranch to Shefler, September 11, 1985, Intelicense File #2, IOCA. Shefler provided a detailed summary of what he thought had been determined in their meetings with a possible path forward to reboot the 1979 agreements. Samaranch's reply was brief and blunt: "With reference to your telex of September 10th 1985, this is to advise you that I do not agree with its contents."

54. "Report in re Intelicense Corporation S.A.," April 18, 1986, 2–3, Intelicense File #7, IOCA; "Report in re: Intelicense Corporation S.A.," September 12, 1986, 3–4, Intelicense File #7, IOCA.

55. François Carrard to Richard W. Pound, November 9, 1986. Carrard appended an obituary notice from Lausanne's *Le Matin* to his letter.

56. This information was gleaned from her website: http://sarashefler.ch/sara-shefler-2.shtml. In the 1990s she established a line of skincare products in collaboration with the Givaudan laboratory that was marketed in the United States and Europe.

57. *Minutes of the Meeting of the IOC Executive Board*, Lausanne, December 6–8, 1989, 17, IOCA.

58. In February 1988 Carrard reported that the IOC had an agreement with the Shefler brothers, who were actively "taking legal steps to block Intelicense's activities," but their efforts were being challenged by Sara Shefler. See *Minutes of the Meeting of the IOC Executive Board*, Calgary, February 6–7, 1988, 9, IOCA. For news of the final settlement, see *Minutes of the Meeting of the IOC Executive Board*, Tokyo, September 13–16, 1990, 5–6, IOCA. Interestingly, the lawyer for the Shefler brothers owned Intelicense at the time of its dissolution. By this date, the IOC had paid half of the settlement, with the other half withheld until all creditors identified themselves. In December, Carrard reported that Intelicense's liquidation "was proceeding smoothly." *Minutes of the Meeting of the IOC Executive Board*, Lillehammer, December 9–10, 1990, 9–10, IOCA.

59. *Minutes of the Meeting of the IOC Executive Board*, Seoul, April 22–24, 1986, 47, IOCA.

60. "Report in re Intelicense Corporation S.A.," April 18, 1986, 6.

61. Interview with Dick Pound.

62. "Report in re Intelicense Corporation, 14.3.83," 1. In this report, written by Carrard, he provides the date when he was first consulted on matters pertaining to Intelicense.

63. Interview with François Carrard, March 8, 2016, Lausanne, Switzerland.

64. For the following synopsis, see Hay, "Guarding the Olympic Gold," 472–503; San Francisco Arts & Athletics, Inc. and Thomas F. Waddell, Petitioners v. United States Olympic Committee and International Olympic Committee, 483 U.S. 522 (107 S.Ct. 2971,

97 L.Ed.2d 427), Legal Information Institute (Cornell University Law School), http://www/law.cornell.edu/supremecourt/text/483/522. The Intelicense case did not mark the USOC's entry to the legal arena in defense of its rights granted by the Amateur Sports Act. However, it did have a place within a flurry of cases in the early 1980s. The USOC was more often the appellant, bringing legal proceedings against a perceived transgressor of its rights; however, in the first case decided in the context of the ASA, the USOC was the defendant. A nonprofit advocacy group, Stop the Olympic Prison (STOP) asserted its right to employ the Olympic rings for a noncommercial purpose. STOP opposed the plan to construct housing for Lake Placid's Olympic athletes that would be converted to a prison following the 1980 Olympic Winter Games. It produced a poster that depicted the Olympic rings and torch with the tagline, "Stop the Olympic Prison." The USOC duly requested that the organization cease and desist in the distribution of the poster and the use of Olympic insignia. STOP's response was to seek a legal judgment in support of its right to use the rings for a noncommercial purpose. A New York District Court concurred with STOP's claim that the ASA did not prevent its use of the rings in this instance. Similarly, the USOC could not claim that the poster confused the public into believing that the USOC supported STOP's cause.

With respect to San Francisco Arts & Athletics' (SFAA) efforts to promote the "Gay Olympic Games," the IOC and USOC collaborated in bringing suit against the organization as a means of halting its branding initiative. SFAA began to promote the Gay Olympic Games, scheduled for 1982, the previous year "on its letterheads and mailings, in local newspapers, and on various merchandise sold to cover the costs of the planned Games." The USOC held that the promotional campaign falsely advertised a connection between the USOC and the Gay Olympic Games. SFAA claimed that the USOC's actions discriminated against the homosexual community. The IOC's and USOC's claims were supported by a Northern California District Court. SFAA was prevented from continuing its promotional campaign in conjunction with the use of the term "Olympic," a decision later upheld by the Court of Appeals, and the U.S. Supreme Court in 1987.

In 1982 the USOC sought to prevent the International Federation of Bodybuilders (IFBB) from using the label, "Mr. Olympia" for its yearly, professional, and increasingly high-profile bodybuilding contest. The court turned aside the USOC's legal claims that the contest implied a connection between the USOC and the IFBB and that the trademark should be stripped from the IFBB (the Trademark Trial and Appeal Board consented to its use by the IFBB against the USOC's wishes in 1974). It was a professional event, held since 1965, that bore no resemblance, in the eyes of the court, to the quadrennial amateur Olympic Games; however, a number of co-defendants—Weider Health & Fitness, I. Brute Enterprises, and two Washington, D.C., health-food stores—were found in violation of the Amateur Sports Act for marketing and/or selling products emblazoned with the Olympic five-ring logo. This element of the case revolved around the concept of the "dilution of the value of the Olympic designations."

Executives with Union Sport Apparel were advised as early as 1979 that the company's practice of attaching an interlocking three-ring logo with the letters "U.S.A." to its clothing products might invite a legal suit from the USOC, but they forged ahead with the tradition. Again, the company's lawyers voiced concern, to no avail in 1980. A Virginia District Court found Union Sport Apparel in violation of the ASA in 1983, granting the USOC "treble damages, its costs and attorney's fees, and defendant's wrongful profits," the latter totaling more than $762,000.

65. Klaus Hempel to Juan Antonio Samaranch, ca. December 1982, "J-ISL 004 SD1: Correspondance, 1982—avril 1985" File (hereafter ISL File #2), IOCA.

66. For a semi-scholarly biographical treatment of Adolf and Rudolf Dassler, see Smit, *Sneaker Wars*.

67. Ibid., 123.

68. Email correspondence from Michael Payne to Stephen Wenn, February 1, 2018.

69. At an IOC-orchestrated memorial service held in Lausanne following Dassler's death from cancer in 1987, Samaranch exclaimed: "We are gathered here this morning in order to pay tribute to a great man and to pray for him. . . . We are proud to count ourselves as his friends and I am sure that each one of us holds very special memories of an extraordinary man [to] whom sport owes so much." Cited in Simson and Jennings, *Lords of the Rings*, 21–22.

70. Cited by Simson and Jennings, *Lords of the Rings*, 23.

71. "Preliminary Agreement between The International Olympic Committee, (IOC) and ISL Licensing, (ISL)," June 2, 1983, "J-ISL 002 SD1: Contrat préliminaire entre le CIO et ISL (TOP I), 2 juin 1983" File (hereafter ISL File #1), IOCA.

72. Interview with Michael Payne, March 10, 2016, Lausanne Switzerland; email correspondence from Michael Payne to Stephen Wenn, February 1, 2018.

73. Interview with Dick Pound. Pound clarified this process in subsequent communication with the authors on April 19, 2018.

74. Interview with Michael Payne, 2016.

75. Email correspondence from Michael Payne to Stephen Wenn, March 7, 2018.

76. Ingle, "Chinese Company Alibaba."

77. Email correspondence from Michael Payne to Stephen Wenn, March 7, 2018.

78. Ibid.

79. Downes's article was accessed via Michael Payne's personal website, and the article, originally published in the June 30, 2004, edition of the *Times*, can be found at http://www .michaelrpayne.com/articles.

80. Ibid.

81. Howard M. Stupp to Raymond Gafner, November 6, 1985, "J-ISL 004 SD4: Correspondance, mai—décembre 1985" File (hereafter ISL File #3), IOCA.

82. Juan Antonio Samaranch to Charlie L. Brown (CEO, AT&T) November 13, 1985; Samaranch to William A. Schreyer (CEO, Merrill Lynch), November 13, 1985; Samaranch to Robert W. Galvin (CEO, Motorola), November 13, 1985; Samaranch to R. Gordon McGovern (Campbell Soup Company), November 13, 1985, ISL File #3, IOCA.

83. Robert R. Prazmark to Anne Wickham (Manager, Special Projects, American Express), September 27, 1985; Anne Wickham to Robert Prazmark, September 12, 1985, "E-REO8 001 SD 2: Correspondance, 1985–1987" File (hereafter American Express File #1), IOCA.

84. Mickle, "25 Years Ago."

85. Espinosa, "Olympic Rainmaker."

86. Email correspondence from Michael Payne to Stephen Wenn, February 1, 2018.

87. Mickle, "25 Years Ago."

88. Espinosa, "Olympic Rainmaker."

89. Payne, *Olympic Turnaround*, 85.

90. Charles T. Russell (President, Visa International) to William P. Breen (President, ISL Marketing, U.S.A.), April 25, 1986, "J-TOP 049 SD 1 Correspondance 1986" File (hereafter TOP File #1), IOCA.

91. Thomas Klooz (Legal Manager, ISL) to John H. Bennett, undated, TOP File #1, IOCA.

92. Payne, *Olympic Turnaround*, 89. Brackets added. For Samaranch's letter to Robinson as the IOC and ISL prepared to launch TOP, see Juan Antonio Samaranch to James D. Robinson III, November 13, 1985, American Express File #1, IOCA.

93. Email correspondence from Michael Payne to Stephen Wenn, March 7, 2018.

94. Interview with Dick Pound.

95. *Olympic Marketing Fact File, 2017 Edition*, 11.

96. Email correspondence from Michael Payne to Stephen Wenn, February 1, 2018.

97. Philips and Whannel, *Trojan Horse*, 59. Brackets added.

98. Hersh, "Dassler's Death."

99. Ibid.

100. Interview with Michael Payne, 2016.

101. Ibid.

102. Email correspondence from Michael Payne to Stephen Wenn, February 1, 2018. Pound provided his characterization of the process in communication with the authors on April 19, 2018.

103. Ibid.; and interview with Michael Payne, 2016.

Chapter 7. The Broadcast Marketing Agreement

Readers should note that this chapter blends original research with portions of text appearing in three previously published works: Wenn, "Riding into the Sunset"; Wenn, "IOC/USOC Relations"; and Wenn, "Long and Winding Road."

1. In 1991 or 1992, based on the content of the handwritten summary, Robert Kane outlined the process he followed in securing assistance from Conable, and Conable's efforts in Washington on the USOC's behalf. See Robert Kane, "TV Rights Sharing," undated, PPRJK, box 4c, USOC Archives, Colorado Springs, Colorado.

2. Pertinent Kane/Conable correspondence on the matter includes: Kane to Conable, July 11, 1985; Conable to Kane, August 6, 1985; Conable to Kane, December 6, 1985, box 4c, PPRJK.

3. Phone conversation, Dick Pound, July 20, 2015.

4. Interview with François Carrard.

5. Kane, "TV Rights Sharing."

6. Ibid.

7. Ibid.; Kane, "Alumni Who Aid Athletics." While Kane did not mention Stratton's name directly, an examination of the historical list of congressmen whose district encompassed Ithaca left this as the unalterable conclusion.

8. Robert J. Kane to Barber Conable, June 23, 1981; Conable to Kane, July 20, 1981; Kane to Conable, August 4, 1981, Kane Box 55 874–894 Los Angeles Olympic Organizing Committee (LAOOC) Correspondence (19) 1979–1984 (hereafter USOC box #1), USOCA.

9. Fleming, *Window on Congress*, 22.

10. Ibid., 7. For details on the manner in which the Watergate scandal and Nixon's conduct disappointed Conable, see 156–78. Following Nixon's resignation, the two never spoke, despite Nixon's efforts in 1980 and 1986 to reach out to Conable.

11. Ibid., 1–2.

12. Kane, "TV Rights Sharing."

13. For Kane's buoyed feelings, see Robert J. Kane to Barber B. Conable Jr., July 11, 1985. For Vander Jagt's efforts, see Kane, "TV Rights Sharing"; Kane, "Alumni Who Aid Athletics."

14. A copy of the draft bill can be found in the PPRJK, box 4c.

15. Miller sought Kane's permission to approach the IOC directly given the slow pace of developments in Washington. See Kane, "TV Rights Sharing."

16. Miller's strategy was revealed by Dick Pound, IOC Executive Board member and chairman of the IOC's Television Rights Negotiations Commission, in two missives to Juan Antonio Samaranch. See Pound to Samaranch, September 26, 1985; Pound to Samaranch, September 30, 1985, "Seoul 1988 TV-General II" File (hereafter Seoul File #1), IOCA.

17. The installation took place on February 9, 1985, at the Broadmoor Hotel in Colorado Springs. See Personal Correspondence, Teri Hedgpeth, Archivist and Historical Steward, USOC, to Stephen Wenn, March 3, 2015.

18. Holbreich, "After 2½ Years."

19. Janofsky, "Miller Quits as U.S.O.C. Chief." Mere days before he submitted his resignation at the close of the Xth Pan American Games in Indianapolis, Miller and Helmick clashed on the possible fallout from a U.S. State Department decision concerning the denial of a visa request from a Chilean athlete who had been "involved in killings as a member of the Chilean Intelligence Service." Helmick thought the decision, shortsighted as it was, might have negative repercussions for U.S. bid cities seeking hosting privileges for major sport events, while Miller did not envision it serving as a "hindrance" to cities such as Anchorage that was well underway with its campaign for the 1994 Olympic Winter Games. In explaining his understanding of Miller's motivation to resign, Helmick stated, "George said it was for personal reasons, and I respect his desire to leave it at that." Miller, for his part, remained tight-lipped about his departure. Holbreich, "After 2½ Years."

20. For instance, see Howard M. Stupp to Juan Antonio Samaranch, October 3, 1985, Seoul File #1, IOCA. The problem for the IOC was that the Amateur Sports Act and the *Olympic Charter*, in terms of the rights assigned to the USOC, stood in conflict. The IOC calculated that its chances of prevailing in a court challenge in the United States were slim.

21. Ibid.

22. Interview with Howard Stupp.

23. Interview with Michael Payne, 2016.

24. Samaranch did understand that the USOC would need to be accommodated at some point and delegated the job to Pound. Juan Antonio Samaranch to Richard Pound, October 1, 1985, Seoul File #1, IOCA.

25. Barber B. Conable Jr. to Robert J. Kane, December 6, 1985.

26. Phone conversation with Dick Pound, July 20, 2015.

27. *Minutes of the Meeting of the Board of Directors of the Los Angeles Olympic Organizing Committee*, December 19, 1984, 5–8, Kane Box 56 895–914 Los Angeles Olympic Organizing Committee (LAOOC) Minutes, reports, legal (20) 1978–1984 (hereafter USOC box #2), USOCA.

28. Ibid., 6–8. The LAOOC board of directors approved the plan by majority vote (20–5) subject to receipt of legal permission to do so from the attorney general of California. USOC representatives present at the meeting abstained.

29. Reich, "'Friendship' Plan."

30. *Minutes of the Meeting of the IOC Executive Board*, Calgary, February 25–28, 1985, 54–56, IOCA.

31. Juan Antonio Samaranch to Richard Pound, October 1, 1985, Seoul File #1, IOCA. Brackets added.

32. "Report to the Finance Commission Paris 6th June 1986," 6, "Seoul 1988 TV General Août-Décembre 1986" File (hereafter Seoul File #2), IOCA.

33. "TV Rights Sharing"; *Minutes of the Meeting of the IOC Executive Board*, Lausanne, February 11–12, 1986, 5, 7; *Minutes of the Meeting of the IOC Executive Board*, Seoul, April 22–24, 1986, 4, IOCA.

34. Kane opposed the decision to withdraw the excise tax. "TV Rights Sharing." See also, George D. Miller to Barber Conable, March 6, 1986, box 4c, PPRJK. George Miller met with Guy Vander Jagt in Washington in late February to explain recent developments concerning negotiations with IOC officials. Vander Jagt expressed his pleasure that HR 3770 and the Tax Reform Act had assisted the USOC in achieving its goal. In his letter to Conable, Miller confirmed that the Tax Reform Act served as "insurance" in the event that the IOC considered "reneging" on the deal and that nothing would be done to "perturb" the Tax Reform Act until the IOC signed the Broadcast Marketing Agreement.

35. "TV Rights Sharing."

36. Kane, "Alumni Who Aid Athletics." See also George D. Miller to Barber Conable, March 6, 1986; Miller to Robert J. Kane, April 7, 1986, RJKPP, box 4c. Brackets added.

37. See Kane, "TV Rights Sharing." Brackets are Miller's.

38. Phone conversation with Dick Pound, July 20, 2015.

39. The USOC gladly accepted $15 million, plus 10 percent of future U.S. Olympic television revenue in 1992 and beyond, from the IOC in exchange for removing the excise tax language from the Tax Reform Act. Kane opposed backing away from legislative action, but George Miller believed it the prudent thing to do in terms of the USOC's relations with the IOC. See Kane, "TV Rights Sharing"; George D. Miller to Barber Conable, March 6, 1986; Miller to Kane, April 7, 1986.

40. "Richard W. Pound C.C., O.Q., Q.C., Ad. E., FCA, Montreal."

41. Revue Politique—Tête à Tête—Dick Pound, 2008. This is a televised interview conducted by Pierre Donais. CPAC is the Cable Public Affairs Channel in Canada, and it is analogous to C-SPAN in the United States in terms of its focus on government affairs.

42. Interview with Dick Pound.

43. Chigbo, "The Go-to Guy." Books written by Pound include, *Five Rings over Korea: The Secret Negotiations Behind the 1988 Olympic Games in Seoul*; *Chief Justice W.R. Jackett: By the Law of the Land*; *Stikeman Elliott: The First Fifty Years*; the aforementioned, *Inside the Olympics*; *Inside Dope: How Drugs Are the Biggest Threat to Sports, Why You Should Care, and What Can Be Done about Them*; *Unlucky to the End: The Story of Janise Marie Gamble*; and, *Rocke Robertson: Surgeon and Shepherd of Change*.

44. Ibid.

45. Ibid. Cleghorn and Pound wrote the Uniform Evaluation (UFE), the standardized exam for those aspiring to be chartered accountants in Canada, in the mid-1960s. His early observations of Pound were based on watching his preparation for the UFE.

46. Miller, *Olympic Revolution*," 52. Brackets added.

47. Longman, "Juan Antonio Samaranch."

48. The USOC did not net this same percentage (20 percent) given certain fees it was required to pay into the program.

49. Personal communication from Dick Pound to the authors, February 9, 2015.

50. Lawrence, "Fools' Gold," 5–10.

51. Ibid., 6.

52. *Minutes of the Meeting of the IOC Executive Board*, Lausanne, July 24–26, 1988, 26, IOCA. The minutes read: "Mr. Pound thought the amounts EBU paid to cover the Games derisory in comparison to large amount made available for events comparatively less important."

53. American networks paid $401 million (NBC) and $300 million (CBS) for the rights to the 1992 Barcelona and 1994 Lillehammer Olympic Winter Games, while EBU acquired European rights for the same festivals for $75 million and $24 million, respectively.

54. "Notes on the Meeting with Congressman Tom McMillen, Washington, D.C.," January 17, 1991, "IOC-USOC" File, PCFRP; Richard Pound to Edward J. Markey (Chairman, Committee on Energy and Subcommittee on Telecommunications and Finance), September 30, 1991 (draft), "IOC-USOC" File, PCFRP.

55. "Notes on the Meeting with Congressman Tom McMillen, Washington, D.C."

56. Ibid. Brackets added.

57. Ibid. It is assumed "not/not" appears as a means of emphasis provided by Pound.

58. A former president of the Fédération Internationale de Natation Amateur (FINA), the international sport federation for aquatic sports, Helmick succeeded William Simon as USOC president in 1985. In September 1991 he resigned his office in light of revelations that he had accepted more than $300,000 in consultancy fees for services that placed him in a conflict of interest. Former deputy U.S. attorney general Arthur Burns conducted an investigation for the USOC, and Samaranch tasked Kèba MBaye, Marc Hodler, and IOC

director general, François Carrard, to conduct a parallel IOC exploration of Helmick's activities. Helmick fought to retain his place on the IOC Executive Board, but he was forced to resign his IOC membership in December. Miller, *Olympic Revolution*, 220–21. Journalist Michael Janofsky was scathing in his analysis of Helmick's violation of USOC bylaws and the manner in which he had sullied the IOC. His resignation from the IOC triggered his immediate loss of positions with the executive boards of the Atlanta Organizing Committee and the USOC, leaving Helmick to "do little more to help future Olympic efforts than cheer from the sidelines." Janofsky, "Olympics: As Helmick Resigns, His Familiar Rationale Misses the Ethical Point."

59. *Minutes of the Meeting of the IOC Executive Board*, Barcelona, April 14–16, 1991, 56, IOCA.

60. *Minutes of the Meeting of the IOC Executive Board*, Birmingham, June 10–11, 1991, 43, IOCA. While not privy to Pound's suggestion concerning the possible wisdom in securing the services of a lobbyist in his memo to Samaranch, dated January 17, 1991, he knew of the suggestion through Pound's statement in, "Marketing Report to the Executive Board Birmingham June 1991," in Annex 12, 108–12 of the aforementioned minutes.

61. "Marketing Report to the IOC Executive Board, 14–16 April 1991, Barcelona," *Minutes of the Meeting of the IOC Executive Board*, April 14–16, 1991, Barcelona, Annex 15, 127.

62. Richard Pound to Harvey, Schiller (draft), November 11, 1992, "IOC-USOC" File, PCFRP.

63. Richard Pound to Harvey Schiller, (draft), November 11, 1992, (revised) December 3, 1992, "IOC-USOC" File, PCFRP.

64. Interview with Michael Payne, 2016.

65. Richard Pound to Harvey Schiller (draft), April 12, 1993, "IOC-USOC" File, PCFRP.

66. Ibid.

67. *Minutes of the Meeting of the IOC Executive Board*, Berlin, September 17–19, 1991, 42, IOCA.

68. *Minutes of the Meeting of the IOC Executive Board*, Lausanne, December 4–6, 1991, 43–44, IOCA. The minutes read that EBU's offer was $235 million with add-ons that took the value of the proposed deal to $250 million. The $247 million figure appears in Dick Pound's files, a result of his crafting a complete summary of rights fees paid in all markets through 1996. "Olympic Games Television Rights Summary: Summer Games," February 2, 1999, "IOC TV Data" File, PCFRP.

69. "Olympic Games Television Rights Summary: Summer Games," February 2, 1999, "IOC TV Data" File, PCFRP. Pound alerted us to the challenge in dealing with this broadcast union given the direct channel to Samaranch in an email to Stephen Wenn, dated August 12, 2018.

70. Interview with Michael Payne, 2016. Brackets added.

71. Ibid.

72. Sandomir, "TV Sports: All Are to Blame for Baseball Network's Demise." Baseball's troubles in the early 1990s left it looking for alternative means of placing its games on U.S. television as CBS exited what had been an unsuccessful contract (four years, $1.06 billion) in terms of its financial returns for the network. In 1993, Major League Baseball

(MLB) reached a six-year agreement with ABC and NBC to establish The Baseball Network on a revenue-share basis. ABC and NBC did not have rights fees to put forward, but each contributed $10 million in start-up money for the network. They did have advertising revenue targets, but MLB, at the last minute before signing the deal, withdrew the networks' protection if it failed to meet the 1995 target ($330 million) irrespective of whether a labor disruption occurred (as it eventually did in 1994). Ultimately, it provided MLB with an escape hatch, as the strike precluded the ability of ABC and NBC to reach the advertising revenue target. MLB wanted to maintain an ability to move in a different direction if there were any noticeable changes in the industry that might have made MLB a more enticing sport property. There is little doubt the networks would have insisted upon such protection if they invested sizeable rights fees through a standard contract for the acquisition of a major sports property. Ebersol and Denis Swanson, head of ABC Sports, could have walked away, but they continued with the project despite the removal of the protection. MLB cited issues with The Baseball Network's broadcast format that deprived fans across the country from seeing all games in the respective League Championship Series, problems with start times, and the absence of Saturday afternoon games. In the interim, Commissioner Bud Selig saw FOX as a rising player in the sport television industry, and CBS might have renewed interest.

73. Stewart, "Fox Gets Baseball."

74. Interview with Michael Payne, 2016.

75. "Dick Ebersol '69 Speaks of Passion for Sports at 2008 Kiphuth Fellowship Public Lecture."

76. Ibid.

77. The London Olympics, much to NBC's surprise, actually broke even, with the losses incurred in conjunction with its coverage of the 2010 Vancouver Olympic Winter Games. NBC acquired the two festivals in a package deal negotiated in 2003. Szalai, "Comcast"; see also "NBC Posts $223 Million First-Quarter Loss on Winter Olympics," April 16, 2010, http://bc.ctvnews.ca/nbc-posts-223-million-first-quarter-loss-on-winter-olympics-1.502918.

78. Pound clarified this matter in terms of the length of the second NBC contract in communication with the authors dated April 19, 2018.

79. Six months of secret discussions yielded NBC a six-festival (2022, 2024, 2026, 2028, 2030, and 2032) contract through 2032 for $7.75 billion in May 2014. This deal followed up on a four-festival agreement (2014, 2016, 2018, and 2020) acquired through a competitive bid process for $4.38 billion in June, 2011. NBC can boast an uninterrupted series of seventeen Olympic festivals, having been already broadcast or scheduled for ensuing years. See Wilson, "NBC Extends Olympic Deal." CBS was the U.S. Olympic broadcaster for the 1994 Lillehammer and 1998 Nagano Olympic Winter festivals.

80. Grossman, "Dick Ebersol." Ebersol credits Randy Falco with a valuable contribution to NBC's efforts.

81. Richard Pound to Harvey Schiller, draft, revised, December 3, 1992, "IOC-USOC" File, PCFRP.

82. Ibid.

83. *Minutes of the Meeting of the IOC Executive Board*, Lausanne, October 8–10, 1996, 16, IOCA. Dick Pound provided clarification on the thinking behind the new distribution policy in a communication with the authors (dated April 19, 2018).

84. "Briefing Memorandum: IOC-USOC Meeting October 8 1996," "IOC-USOC" File, PCFRP.

85. Interview with Michael Payne, 2016.

86. Email correspondence from Michael Payne to Stephen Wenn, March 7, 2018.

87. Interview with Michael Payne, 2016.

88. Ibid.

Chapter 8. The Salt Lake City Bid Scandal

1. Gosper, *Olympic Life*, 350.

2. *Minutes of the Meeting of the 109th IOC Session*, Seoul, June 17–20, 1999, Annex 20, "Report to the 109th IOC Session by the Director of Communications," 220, IOCA.

3. Interview with Michael Payne, June 18, 2007, Lausanne, Switzerland.

4. Interview with François Carrard.

5. Gosper, *Olympic Life*, 312.

6. Payne, *Olympic Turnaround*, 230.

7. Starkman, "IOC Bigwigs' Heads Buried Deep in the Sand."

8. Gosper, *Olympic Life*, 311.

9. Richard W. Pound to George Fisher, May 13, 1999, PFRP.

10. Payne, *Olympic Turnaround*, 226.

11. Gorrell, "IOC Official."

12. Pound, *Inside the Olympics*, 198.

13. Payne, *Olympic Turnaround*, 232.

14. Clarey, "Olympics; Samaranch Vows Cleanup If Needed"; Payne, *Olympic Turnaround*, 228.

15. Gorrell, "IOC Official."

16. Gosper, *Olympic Life*, 313.

17. Wilson, "Corruption Scandal."

18. SEMA's TOP status in the information technology category has been continuous through successive takeovers.

19. Gosper, *Olympic Life*, 315.

20. Payne, *Olympic Turnaround*, 230.

21. Clarey, "Olympics: Bribery Charged."

22. Wilson, "Corruption Scandal."

23. *Minutes of the Ad Hoc Executive Board Meeting*, Lausanne, January 24, 1999, 15, PFRP.

24. Gosper, *Olympic Life*, 330.

25. Richard W. Pound, "Day Planner—1999," PFRP.

26. Payne, *Olympic Turnaround*, 233–34; *Minutes of the Meeting of the IOC Executive Board*, Seoul, June 13–15, 1999, 9–10, PFRP; email correspondence from Michael Payne to Stephen Wenn, March 7, 2018.

27. Interview with François Carrard.

28. Ibid.

29. Ibid.

30. Ibid.

31. Ibid.

32. Ibid.

33. Ibid.

34. We have had the pleasure to know a good number of retired IOC staff members, as well as staff who still work for the IOC today, people who helped us to further our research endeavors over the years. All who served under Carrard when he was director general are universal in their high opinion of him.

35. Interview with François Carrard.

36. Payne, *Olympic Turnaround*, 232.

37. *IOC Marketing Commission—Report to the IOC Executive Board*, Lausanne, March 16, 1999, 2, PFRP; email correspondence from Michael Payne to Stephen Wenn, March 7, 2018.

38. *Minutes of the Ad Hoc Executive Board Meeting*, Lausanne, January 24, 1999, 2–3, IOCA.

39. "13 IOC Members."

40. *Report of the IOC Ad Hoc Commission to Investigate the Conduct of Certain IOC Members and to Consider Possible Changes in the Procedures for the Allocation of the Games of the Olympiad and Olympic Winter Games*, January 24, 1999, 2, PFRP.

41. *IOC Marketing Commission—Report to the 109th Session*, Seoul, June 17–20, 1999, 2, PFRP.

42. Longman, "Olympics: Corporate Backer."

43. Wenn, Barney, and Martyn, *Tarnished Rings*, 28.

44. Email correspondence from David D'Alessandro to Stephen Wenn, July 14, 2009 and July 17, 2009.

45. Longman, "Potential Olympic Sponsors."

46. Email correspondence from David D'Alessandro to Stephen Wenn, July 14, 2009.

47. Madkour, "Unplugged David D'Alessandro."

48. Longman, "Olympics: More Reports."

49. Carter, "Joklik."

50. Longman, "Olympics: More Reports."

51. *Minutes of the 108th Extraordinary IOC Session*, Lausanne, March 17–18, 1999, Annex 5, 48, PFRP.

52. Arroyo, the former president of Ecuador's National Olympic Committee, admitted to seeking employment assistance for his stepdaughter, vacationed with his family in Park City, Utah (at the expense of the bid committee), and accepted a dog from Tom Welch. *Minutes of the 108th Extraordinary IOC Session*, Annex 3, 42–43; Abrahamson, "Ousted Olympics Official."

53. Gadir's son, Zuhair, received educational assistance, and Gadir himself accepted cash transfers ($7,000) to an account in his daughter's name, a daughter that did not exist. In total, Gadir's family received approximately $25,000. Dave Johnson, Tom Welch's right hand in the bidding phase, sent the money to the bank account but was unaware that the daughter did not exist. See "IOC Member's Fictitious Daughter."

54. Ganga, dubbed the "human vacuum cleaner" by Salt Lake City officials, accepted gifts and benefits totaling approximately $250,000. Calvert, "How to Buy the Olympics"; Thomas, Johnson, and Longman, "Rise and Fall."

55. Keita's son received educational assistance of not less than $97,000 to attend Washington's Howard University. See "Expelled IOC Member."

56. Mukora received in excess of $34,000 in cash payments. Penner, "Kenya's Mukora Quits."

57. Fantini denied receiving money in support of failed mayoralty run in Talca in December 1993. *Minutes of the 108th Extraordinary IOC Session*, Annex 7, 53–56.

58. *Minutes of the Ad Hoc Executive Board Meeting*, Lausanne, January 24, 1999, 3.

59. Ibid., 4–6.

60. "IOC Cleans House."

61. Pound, *Inside the Olympics*, 72.

62. Humphries, "IOC."

63. Copetas and Thurow, "IOC Moping"; interview with François Carrard.

64. "Olympic Games—Palace Revolt."

65. D'Alessandro, "With Sponsorship Money."

66. Payne, *Olympic Turnaround*, 235. Brackets added.

67. Vennochi, "Olympic-Sized Ethical Dilemma."

68. Madkour, "Unplugged David D'Alessandro."

69. Siddons, "Sponsors to IOC."

70. Longman, "Olympics: I.O.C. Expulsion Vote."

71. Longman, "Olympics: Reform Process."

72. Longman, "Olympics: I.O.C. Expulsion."

73. Interview with François Carrard.

74. See "Korean IOC Member."

75. Interview with François Carrard.

76. Ibid.

77. Ibid.

78. "International Olympic Committee Ethics Commission."

79. *Minutes of the 108th Extraordinary IOC Session*, Annex 1, 25.

80. Wallwork's wife received a $30,000 loan from Tom Welch. Wallwork denied knowledge of the loan. "Expelled IOC Member."

81. "(Olympics) Sponsors and U.S. Senator."

82. Sandomir, "Olympics: Samaranch Declines."

83. Roche, "IOC Event Fails."

84. Dodd, "Samaranch to Lead Reforms."

85. See "With Severe Warnings."

86. Hersh, "Major Sponsor Blasts I.O.C. Reform."

87. See "With Vote Approaching."

88. See "Samaranch Says He Erred."

89. Interview with Michael Payne, 2016.

90. Garber, "Samaranch's Legacy."

91. MacAloon, "Scandal and Governance," 296.

92. Payne, *Olympic Turnaround*, 14.

93. Interview with Michael Payne, 2007.

94. Garber, "Samaranch's Legacy."

95. *Minutes of the Meeting of the 110th IOC Session*, Lausanne, December 11–12, 1999, 3, PFRP.

96. Ibid., 6.

97. *Minutes of the Meeting of the IOC Executive Board*, Lausanne, February 1, 1999, 13–14, PFRP.

98. MacAloon, "Scandal and Governance," 294.

99. Wilson, "NBC Sports Chief." D'Alessandro sent this AP report to Pound along with a fax message. Fax from David D'Alessandro to Richard Pound, June 1, 1999, PFRP.

100. Richard Pound to Juan Antonio Samaranch, April 19, 1999, PCFRP. Brackets added.

101. *Minutes of the Meeting of the IOC Executive Board*, Lausanne, May 4, 1999, 2, 4, PFRP. Brackets added.

102. MacAloon, "Scandal and Governance," 294.

103. Ibid., 295.

104. Ibid. Brackets added.

105. Ibid., 294.

106. Richard Pound to Juan Antonio Samaranch, April 19, 1999. Emphasis Pound's.

107. Richard Pound to Juan Antonio Samaranch, July 6, 1999, PCFRP.

108. Richard Pound to Juan Antonio Samaranch, September 24, 1999, PCFRP.

109. MacAloon, "Scandal and Governance," 295.

110. Email correspondence from Michael Payne to Stephen Wenn, March 7, 2018.

111. *Minutes of the Meeting of the IOC Executive Board*, Athens, October 1–4, 1999, 8–11, 20, PFRP.

112. *Minutes of the Meeting of the IOC Executive Board*, Seoul, June 13–15, 1999, 30–31; *Minutes of the Meeting of the IOC Executive Board*, Athens, October 1–4, 1999, Annex 16, "Marketing Report to the IOC Executive Board, Athens, October 2nd, 1999," 159, PFRP.

113. In early 2019, stories resurfaced about possible violation of host-city bidding procedures linked with Tokyo's successful bid for the 2020 Summer Olympics tied to $2 million having been funneled to a consulting company, Black Tidings, run by ex-IOC member Lamine Diack's son. Tsunekazu Takeda, president of the Japanese Olympic Committee and chairman of the IOC Marketing Commission (who headed Tokyo's bid committee), faced pressure to resign his leadership of Japan's NOC. Wade, "Takeda Corruption Probe"; Nuga, "Tokyo Governor Won't Speculate." He did so in March 2019, while at the same time tendering his resignation from the IOC. See "Tokyo 2020."

114. Interview with François Carrard.

115. Longman, "Olympics: Rogge."

116. This is the title of the chapter Payne devoted to the Salt Lake City scandal in his book, *Olympic Turnaround*. It appears on pp. 225–54.

Chapter 9. The European Television Market

1. Osnos, "'Mysterious' Impresario."

2. "Olympic Games Television Rights Summary: Summer Games," "IOC TV Data," File, PCFRP.

3. Ibid.

4. "IOC Opens Tender Process."

5. Interview with Christophe De Kepper, March 10, 2016, Lausanne, Switzerland.

6. This deal did not include Italy.

7. Six countries, the United Kingdom, Italy, Spain, France, Germany, and Turkey were not part of the Sportfive/IOC agreement.

8. *Marketing Commission Meeting Minutes*, Lausanne, June 24–25, 2004, 3, IOCA.

9. Interview with Scott Blackmun, February 21, 2017, Colorado Springs.

10. Dahlgren, "Key Trends," 2.

11. Brants and De Bens, "Status of TV Broadcasting in Europe," 8.

12. Ibid.

13. *Minutes of the Meeting of the IOC Finance Commission*, Munich, January 28, 1971, 5–6, and Annex 3, 9–10, IOCA; Lord Luke to Avery Brundage, February 10, 1971, ABC box 98; Brundage to Luke, February 19, 1971, ABC, box 98, WLUA; *Minutes of the Meeting of the IOC Finance Commission*, Luxembourg, September 13 and 16, 1971, 9, IOCA.

14. *Minutes of the Meeting of the IOC Finance Commission*, Sapporo, January 29–30, 1972, 5, 8, IOCA; Hugh Weir to Luke, February 10, 1971, ABC, box 98, WLUA.

15. This information was retrieved from a 1973 trade magazine article, "Profile: A muscle man behind the television scenes: Marvin Josephson," posted on *VintageAdsandBooks.com*. http://vintageadsandbooks.com/profile-1973-marvin-josephson-associates-television-vintage-article-ze296.html.

16. Josephson's possible strategy was reported by Curran in a letter to Killanin, February 26, 1974, "N.2 Droits T.V. Dossier General Innsbruck ABC UER 1972/1976," File (hereafter Innsbruck File #2), IOCA.

17. Monique Berlioux to Lord Killanin, March 15, 1973, "N.1 Droits de T.V. Montreal Du 4.12.69 Au 30.6.73," File (hereafter Montreal File #1), IOCA; Charles Curran to Lord Killanin, February 26, 1974.

18. Monique Berlioux to Lord Killanin, March 15, 1973.

19. Charles Curran to Lord Killanin, February 26, 1974, Innsbruck File #2, IOCA.

20. Charles Curran to Lord Killanin, ca. December 1973, Innsbruck File #2, IOCA.

21. Aylett, "Charles Curran Revisited."

22. Lord Killanin to Count Jean de Beaumont, Lord Luke, Marc Hodler, Herman van Karnebeek, and Willi Daume, April 18, 1974, Innsbruck File #2, IOCA. Killanin was reporting on a speech delivered by Curran in November 1973.

23. Lord Killanin to Monique Berlioux, March 21, 1973, Montreal File #1, IOCA.

24. Lord Killanin to Count Jean de Beaumont, Lord Luke, Marc Hodler, Herman van Karnebeek, and Willi Daume, April 18, 1974.

25. Lord Killanin to Monique Berlioux, May 14, 1973, Montreal File, #1, IOCA.

26. Lord Killanin to Count Jean de Beaumont, Lord Luke, Marc Hodler, Herman van Karnebeek, and Willi Daume, April 18, 1974.

27. Charles Curran to Lord Killanin, December 12, 1973, Innsbruck File #2, IOCA; "Meeting with Straschnov," January 11, 1974, "N.1 Droits de T.V. Innsbruck Du 1.2.73," File (hereafter Innsbruck File #1, IOCA).

28. "Report of Dr. Schätz on the Television Broadcasting Rights for the Games of the XXIst Olympiad—Montreal 1976," *Minutes of the IOC Finance Commission*, Lausanne, October 8, 1974, Annex 2, 15, IOCA.

29. "Meeting of the 14th October 1974—Montreal Television," 2, 7, 9, "N.3 Droits de T.V. Montreal Du 1.9.74/31.12.74" File (hereafter Montreal File #2), IOCA.

30. Lord Killanin to Roger Rousseau, December 13, 1974, Montreal File #2, IOCA.

31. "Confidential Report on the Meeting of 29th January 1975 at Lausanne: Montreal COJO/EBU Negotiations Concerning Television Rights," February 6, 1975, "N.4 Droits de T.V. Montreal Du 1.1.75 Au 31.8.75," File (hereafter Montreal File #3), IOCA.

32. Ibid. See also "Director's Report on Television," February 1975, Montreal File #3, IOCA.

33. "Joint EBU/OIRT Communiqué," Montreal File #3, IOCA.

34. Lord Killanin to Dr. Walter Schätz, March 3, 1975, Montreal File #3, IOCA.

35. Roger Rousseau to Lord Killanin, March 11, 1975; Monique Berlioux to Dr. Schätz, March 12, 1975; Dr. Walter Schätz to Monique Berlioux, March 13, 1975, Montreal File #3, IOCA.

36. "Press Release—COJO Television Rights Statement," March 25, 1975, Montreal File #3, IOCA.

37. Lord Killanin to Roger Rousseau, March 26, 1975, Montreal File #3, IOCA.

38. Ibid.

39. Jean de Beaumont to Lord Killanin, May 6, 1975, Montreal File #3, IOCA; *Minutes of the Meeting of the IOC Finance Commission*, Lausanne, May 19 and 22, 1975, 2, IOCA.

40. Lord Killanin to Roger Rousseau, May 29, 1975, Montreal File #3, IOCA.

41. "Transcript of Letter from Dr. Walter Schätz, dated Montreal 12th August 1975," Montreal File #2, IOCA.

42. E. Howard Radford (Secretary Treasurer, COJO) to Lord Killanin, August 12, 1975, Montreal File #3, IOCA; "Olympians Reject $9.3 Million TV Bid."

43. "Negotiations on Olympic TV Collapse."

44. "Olympic Committee Fights."

45. "Correspondence by Telex," Lord Killanin to Roger Rousseau, August 14, 1975, Montreal File #2, IOCA. Brackets added.

46. Charles Curran to Lord Killanin, August 20, 1975, Montreal File #3, IOCA; "No More Money for TV Rights."

47. Antony Dean (EBU) to IOC, Lausanne, August 25, 1975, Montreal File #3, IOCA.

48. Lord Killanin, "Aide Memoire—Montreal—TV," September 5, 1975, "N.5 Droits de T.V. Montreal Du 1.9.75 Au 30.4.76," File (hereafter Montreal File #4), IOCA; "Killanin, Drapeau Discuss TV Snag"; "Olympics TV Deal Nearer"; Lord Killanin to Jim Worrall, September 9, 1975, Montreal File #4, IOCA.

49. Roger Rousseau to IOC, Lausanne, September 11, 1975, Montreal File #4, IOCA; Lord Killanin to Charles Curran, September 15, 1975, Montreal File #4, IOCA.

50. "BBC Will Pay £500,000."

51. Collins, *From Satellite to Single Market*, 119–120.

52. Ibid., 120.

53. Ibid., 121.

54. Ibid.

55. Ibid., 122.

56. Interview with Michael Payne, 2016.

57. *Minutes of the IOC Executive Board Meeting*, Dakar, February 5–7, 2001, 6–8, IOCA. See also, "Marketing Report to the IOC Executive Board," *Minutes of the IOC Executive Board Meeting*, Dakar, February 5–7, 2001, Annex 11, 1, IOCA. Kirch Group filed for bankruptcy in 2002. Werdigier, "Leo Kirch."

58. *Minutes of the IOC Executive Board Meeting*, Lausanne, May 15–17, 2001, 21, IOCA.

59. Interview with Michael Payne, 2016.

60. "Marketing Report to the IOC Executive Board, Lausanne, 4–6 March 1996," in *Minutes of the Meeting of the IOC Executive Board*, Lausanne, March 4–6, 1996, Annex 6, 93, IOCA; "IOC Confirms European TV Rights Contract." Italy was not included in the EBU contract for 2010/2102.

61. Interview with Michael Payne, 2016.

62. "David Kogan, Trustee."

63. Interview with Michael Payne, 2016.

64. Ibid.

65. Interview with François Carrard.

66. Interview with Dick Pound.

67. Interview with Christophe De Kepper.

68. Bond, "Jacques Rogge."

69. "Jacques Rogge in Final Days."

70. Bond, "Jacques Rogge."

71. Magnay, "Interview." Brackets in original.

72. Interview with François Carrard; interview with Michael Payne, 2016; interview with Dick Pound.

73. Interview with Dick Pound. Pound indicates Rogge saw the need for such action and credits Manolo Romero and Yiannis Exarchos with carrying forward its mandate with distinction.

74. "Jacques Rogge in Final Days."

75. To be precise, Payne was named the IOC's director of global broadcast and media rights in 2003, while Chris Welton, formerly of Meridian Management, which had handled the sale of TOP sponsorships since 1996, directed IOC's marketing operations for a brief period of time before Lumme's arrival. *Minutes of the Meeting of the IOC Executive Board*, Lausanne, December 4–5, 2003, 33, IOCA; Mickle, "Chris Welton, Terrence Burns."

76. "IOC Awards European Broadcast Rights." Tripp Mickle pegged the figure at $312.5 million. Mickle, "IOC Inks Deal."

77. Interview with Timo Lumme.

78. "Report by the Chairman of the TV Rights and New Media Commission to the IOC Executive Board," Lausanne, November 10–12, 2008, 2, IOCA; "IOC Rejects Bid."

79. *Minutes of the Meeting of the IOC Executive Board*, Lausanne, December 10–11, 2008, 24, IOCA; Holmwood, "BBC's Olympic Coverage."

80. Pfanner, "Is Europe Ready?"

81. "Rogge: IOC."

82. Interview with Timo Lumme.

83. Interview with Michael Payne, 2016.

84. Interview with Timo Lumme.

85. Stelter, "Discovery Nabs European TV Rights."

86. Interview with Michael Payne, 2016.

87. Email correspondence from Michael Payne to Stephen Wenn, May 3, 2017.

88. Connolly, "Toyota Joins IOC TOP Tier"; Greimel, "Toyota Signs On"; Wharton, "Olympics"; "Toyota Olympic Sponsorship 'Game Changing.'"

89. *Minutes of the IOC Marketing Commission Meeting*, Lausanne, May 20, 2011, 5, IOCA.

90. Interview with Michael Payne, 2016. Brackets added.

91. Premack, "Why South Korea's Biggest Auto Brand."

92. Wilson, "Toyota Drives onto Olympic Stage." Brackets added.

93. Interview with Michael Payne, 2016. Brackets added.

94. Interview with Timo Lumme.

95. Ibid.

96. "Draft Co-Operation Agreement (IOC-EBU)," March 12, 1986, "Calgary 1988 TV-General 1986" File (hereafter Calgary File #1), IOCA; Richard Pound to Howard Stupp, June 19, 1986, "RWP-IOC 7398-026 Seoul TV" File, PFRP; *Minutes of the Meeting of the IOC Executive Board*, February 11–13, 1987, 20, IOCA.

97. Eventually, the IOC and EBU finalized an agreement for $247 million for Europe, a noticeable increase in the $94.5 million for all of Europe for Barcelona (EBU, $75 million; Intervision, $4.5 million; Spain [TVE], $15 million).

98. "Olympic Games Television Rights Summary"; "Summary of Olympic Television Rights: Olympic Winter Games," PCFRP.

99. Interview with Scott Blackmun.

100. Ibid.

Chapter 10. The 2009 Copenhagen IOC Session

1. Macur, "Rio Wins 2016 Olympics." President Obama once dubbed Lula "the most popular politician on earth," but Lula suffered a massive personal setback in 2017 when he was found guilty of corruption and money laundering. He received a prison sentence of 9½ years, though he remained free on appeal with the promise of protracted legal proceedings ahead. He began a jail sentence in April 2018 that had been extended to twelve years. Phillips, "Brazil's Ex-president Lula."

2. Interview with Michael Payne, 2016.

3. Zeigler, "Brazil's Passion." Brackets added.

4. "Race for '16 Olympics."

5. Zeigler, "Why Can't the U.S. Get an Olympics?"

6. Hersh, "IOC Official."

7. Interview with Scott Blackmun.

8. Interview with Dick Pound.

9. Interview with Michael Payne, 2016.

10. Longman, "Olympics; Interim Deputy."

11. Interview with Dick Pound.

12. Interview with Michael Payne, 2016.

13. Interview with Dick Pound.

14. Interview with Scott Blackmun. Brackets added.

15. Interview with Dick Pound. Brackets added.

16. Personal communication from Dick Pound to the authors, May 12, 1999. Brackets added.

17. Interview with Howard Stupp.

18. Interview with François Carrard. Brackets added. When searching for a means of completing his thought, Stephen Wenn floated the words "rock the boat too much," and Carrard expressed agreement.

19. Interview with Dick Pound.

20. Ibid. Brackets added.

21. Ibid.

22. Interview with Michael Payne, 2016.

23. Keck, "Obama."

24. Hoberman, "Why Is Obama Going to Copenhagen?"

25. Rubinroit, "President Obama."

26. Hersh, "IOC-USOC Deal."

27. Macur, "International and U.S. Olympic Leaders."

28. Pells, "USOC Paid Its Way."

29. "IOC Official Expresses Frustration." Brackets added.

30. Ibid. Brackets added.

31. Ibid.

32. "Chicago Bid Boss."

33. Interview with Scott Blackmun.

34. Ibid.; "Executive Profile: Scott Blackmun."

35. Interview with Scott Blackmun. Brackets added.

36. Ibid.

37. Ibid.

38. Ibid.

39. Interview with Christophe De Kepper. Brackets added.

40. Interview with Scott Blackmun.

41. Ibid.

42. Ibid.

43. Interview with Christophe De Kepper.

44. Hersh, "Hoist a Cold One."

45. Interview with Christophe De Kepper.

46. Ibid.

47. Gomez, "USOC Gives $18 Million."

48. Interview with Christophe De Kepper.

49. Interview with Scott Blackmun.

50. Ibid.

51. Interview with Christophe De Kepper.

52. Ibid.

53. Ibid.

54. Zeigler, "Why Can't the U.S. Get an Olympics?" Brackets added.

55. Mickle, "Improved USOC-IOC Relationship."

56. Interview with Dick Pound.

57. Interview with Michael Payne, 2016.

58. Interview with Dick Pound. When the agreement expired, offered Pound, he and his two interviewers would all be retired when the "rubber hits the road" in 2040. When Bob, approaching his eighty-fifth birthday, chuckled and countered that we'd all likely be well beyond retirement, the seventy-year-old Pound deadpanned, "I certainly won't be interested." Reflecting in the moment on this jocular exchange following a swift mental calculation, Stephen, then age fifty-two, held out some hope to witness the wind-up to the agreement, but he kept that thought to himself.

59. Interview with Michael Payne, 2016.

60. Ibid.

61. Wilson, "Richard Carrión Declares IOC Presidential Bid."

62. Ibid. Brackets added.

63. Interview with Michael Payne, 2016.

64. Ibid.

65. Ibid.

66. Ibid.; Payne, *Olympic Turnaround*, 61–65.

67. Payne, *Olympic Turnaround*, 65.

68. Ibid., 66.

69. Interview with Timo Lumme.

70. Ibid.

71. Mickle, "Improved USOC-IOC Relationship on Display."

72. Interview with Michael Payne, 2016.

73. "IOC, USOC Finalize Revenue Deal."

74. Kelly, "Hyde Park's Olympic History."

75. Bryant, "Support for Olympics Waning."

76. Haugh, "In Retrospect."

77. Our work focused on the USOC's interaction with the IOC on matters pertaining to Olympic finance. In this regard, Scott Blackmun's performance (as well as that of Larry Probst) was solid. Blackmun was central to putting IOC/USOC relations on a better footing. This ultimately is to the long-term benefit of the U.S. Olympic community. The

Nassar case complicates his overall legacy at the USOC in the wake of the publication of the Ropes and Gray report detailing the USOC's and Blackmun's response to information concerning Nassar's activities. McPhee and Dowden, "Report of the Independent Investigation." The Nassar case and its fallout provide a stark message to the USOC that it must confront this issue aggressively, and those efforts must buttress the work of the U.S. Center for SafeSport that commenced formal operations in 2017, an entity whose organizational impetus had been provided by Blackmun and USOC staff members.

Epilogue

1. Miller, *Olympic Revolution*, 76.

2. Interview with Dick Pound.

3. Interview with Michael Payne, 2016.

4. *Minutes of the IOC Executive Board Meeting*, Lausanne, December 11–12, 2001, 6, IOCA.

5. Interview with Michael Payne, 2016.

6. *Minutes of the Meeting of the IOC Executive Board*, Lausanne, December 10, 2013, and Montreux, December 14, 2013, 21, IOCA.

7. Interview with Christophe De Kepper.

8. Interview with Dick Pound.

9. "Olympic Agenda 2020—Olympic Games: The New Norm," 48; "IOC Shakes Up Olympic Bidding."

10. Interview with Michael Payne, 2016.

11. Bach, "Curriculum Vitae."

12. Interview with Howard Stupp.

13. Interview with Dick Pound.

14. Interview with Michael Payne, 2016.

15. Interview with Dick Pound.

16. Interview with Michael Payne, 2016.

17. Ibid.

Bibliography

"ABC Gets TV Rights to Summer Games." *New York Times*, April 15, 1966.

"ABC Warns NBC on '76 Olympics." *New York Times*, December 21, 1972.

"ABC Will Spend $25 Million for the Summer Olympic Rights." *New York Times*, January 4, 1973.

Abrahamson, Alan. "IOC Move Could Spark Nepotism Questions." *Los Angeles Times*, May 18, 2001. http://articles.latimes.com/2001/may/18/sports/sp-65015.

———. "Ousted Olympics Official Tells His Side of Scandal." *Los Angeles Times*, June 13, 1999.

"America's Cup Appoints Dr. Harvey Schiller as Commercial Commissioner." *America's Cup*, August 28, 2014. http://www.americascup.com/en/news/111_Americas-Cup -appoints-Dr-Harvey-Schiller-as-Commercial-Commissioner.html.

". . . And the Heat Is Turned Up concerning Salt Lake City's Bid." *Toronto Star*, January 20, 1999.

"An Interesting and Varied Career." *History Ireland* 20 (July/August 2012). http://history ireland. com/20th-century-contemporary-history/an-interesting-and-varied-career.

"Apology Ends Fraser Case." *The Age* (Melbourne), February 29, 1968.

"Arledge Brought Modern Innovation to TV Sports." December 9, 2002. http://www.espn .com/classic/obit/NEWarledgeobit.html.

"Armand Emile Massard." 2016. https://www.olympic.org/armand-emile-massard.

"Armand Massard." *Olympic Review* 43 (April 1971): 194–95.

Axon, Rachel. "Bill Would Make U.S. Center for SafeSport Eligible for Federal Funding." June 23, 2017. https://www.usatoday.com/story/sports/olympics/2017/06/23/ senate-bill-would-give-u-s-center-safesport-financial-independence/424100001.

———. "USOC names new CEO at critical time for Olympic movement." *USA Today*, July 12, 2018. https://www.usatoday.com/story/sports/olympics/2018/07/12/usoc -names-sarah-hirshland-new-ceo-critial-time-olympic-sports/778461002.

Aylett, Glenn. "Charles Curran Revisited." *Transdiffusion.org*, July 1, 2007. https://www .transdiffusion.org/2007/07/01/charles_curran.

"Bach Appoints Pound as Head of Olympic Broadcast Services." *TSN*, April 4, 2014. http:// www2.tsn.ca/Olympics/story/?id=448282.

Bach, Thomas. "Curriculum vitae." Undated. http://www.dosb.de/fileadmin/Bilder_ allgemein/ Praesidium/lebenslauf_bach_thomas_englisch.pdf.

Barber, Russell B. "The European Broadcasting Union." *Journal of Broadcasting* 6, no. 2 (1962): 111–24.

Barker, Philip. "Lord Burghley—Britain's Most Powerful Ever Sports Adminis-trator." *Insidethegames.biz*, October 15, 2009. http://www.insidethegames.biz/ articles/107535/philip-barker-lord-burghley-britains-most-powerful-ever-sports -administrator.

Barney, Robert K. "Born from Dilemma: America Awakens to the Modern Olympic Games, 1901–1903." *Olympika: The International Journal of Olympic Studies* 1 (1992): 92–135.

———. "This Great Symbol." *Olympic Review* 301 (November 1992): 627–31, 641.

———. "An Olympian Dilemma: Protection of Olympic Symbols." *Journal of Olympic History* 10, no. 3 (2002): 7–29.

———. "Resistance, Persistence, Providence: The 1932 Los Angeles Olympic Games in Perspective." *Research Quarterly for Exercise and Sport* 67 (June 1996): 148–60.

———. "Righteous Regent: Avery Brundage and the Modern Olympic Movement." In *Historical Dictionary of the Modern Olympic Movement*, edited by John E. Findling and Kim-berley D. Pelle, 366–79. Westport, Conn.: Greenwood, 1996.

Barney, Robert K., and Stephen R. Wenn. "Nothing in Hand but Billions in Precedent: Wilfrid Kent Hughes and the 1956 Melbourne Olympic Games Television Stalemate." *Journal of Olympic History* 12 (January 2004): 29–35.

Barney, Robert K., Stephen R. Wenn, and Scott G. Martyn. "Family Feud: Olympic Rev-enue and IOC/USOC Relations." *Olympika: The International Journal of Olympic Studies* 9 (2000): 49–90.

———. *Selling the Five Rings: The International Olympic Committee and the Rise of Olympic Com-mercialism*. Rev. ed. Salt Lake City: University of Utah Press, 2004.

"BBC Will Pay £500,000 for Olympics Television." *Times*, September 16, 1975. "Lord Luke Personal File, 1969–1978," 1975–1978 folder, IOCA.

"Belgian Is New IOC President." *The Guardian*, July 16, 2001. http://www.theguardian .com/ sport/2001/jul/16/olympicgames.theguardian.

Berlioux, Monique. "Fédération Internationale des Luttes Amateurs." *Olympic Review* 40–41 (January–February 1971): 104–5.

———. "Managing a 'Gentlemen's Club.'" *Journal of Olympic History* 23, no. 1 (2015): 8–14.

Bernaudeau, Eric. "FIFA Still Weighing Independent Oversight—Carrard." *YAHOO! Sports*, March 5, 2016. http://sports.yahoo.com/news/fifa-still-weighing-independent -oversight-carrard-073410543--sow.html.

Bernstein, Fred. "Parting a Sea of Olympic Red Ink, Organizer Peter Ueberroth Says the '84 Games May Even Make Money." *People*, August 1, 1983. http://people.com/archive/parting-a-sea-of-olympic-red-ink-organizer-peter-ueberroth-says-the-84-games-may-even-make-money-vol-20-no-5.

Berry, Alex. "The In-house Transfer Window: Legal Moves at Pret a Manger, LinkedIn and the International Olympic Committee." *Law.com*, February 26, 2018. https://www.law.com/2018/02/23/the-in-house-transfer-window-legal-moves-at-pret-a-manger-linkedin-and-the-international-olympic-committee.

"Biography." *Dow.com*, 2010. http://www.dow.com/news/multimedia/media_kits/2010_07_16a/pdfs/Timo_Lumme_Bio.pdf.

Bishop, Greg. "In Need of Rescue, International Baseball Turns to Harvey Schiller." *New York Times*, April 20, 2009. http://www.nytimes.com/2009/04/20/sports/baseball/20schiller.html?_r=0.

Blood, Michael R. "USOC Endorses Los Angeles for 2024 Olympics Bid." *YAHOO! News*, September 1, 2015. https://www.yahoo.com/news/los-angeles-poised-vote-2024-olympic-plan-060332846-spt.html?ref=gs.

Bond, David. "Jacques Rogge: Departing IOC Chief Transformed Olympic Body." *BBC.com*, September 9, 2013. http://www.bbc.com/sport/olympics/24017134.

Booth, Douglas. "Gifts of Corruption? Ambiguities of Obligation in the Olympic Movement." *Olympika: The International Journal of Olympic Studies* 8 (2000): 43–68.

———. "Lobbying Orgies: Olympic City Bids in the Post-Los Angeles Era." In *Global Olympics: Historical and Sociological Studies of the Modern Games, Research in the Sociology of Sport*, edited by Kevin Young and Kevin B. Wamsley, 3:201–25. Amsterdam: Elsevier, 2005.

———. "Olympic City Bidding: An Exegesis of Power." *International Review for the Sociology of Sport* 46, no. 4 (2011): 367–86.

Bose, Mihir. "Today in Sport: Samaranch Bows Out as Rogge Takes Reins." *The Telegraph*, July 16, 2001. http://www.telegraph.co.uk/sport/olympics/3009031/Today-in-Sport-Samaranch-bows-out-as-Rogge-takes-the-reins.html.

Boswell, Thomas. "Something's Rotten at the Top." *Washington Post*, March 19, 1999.

Boykoff, Jules. *Power Games: A Political History of the Olympics*. Foreword by Dave Zirin. Verso: London, 2016.

Brants, Kees, and Els De Bens. "The Status of TV Broadcasting in Europe." In *Television across Europe: A Comparative Introduction*, edited by Jan Wieten, Graham Murdock, and Peter Dahlgren, 7–22. London: Sage, 2000. http://dx.doi.org/10.4135/9781446220344.n2.

Brennan, Christine. "Olympic World Not Better Off after USOC's Scott Blackmun Resigning." *USA Today*, February 28, 2018. https://www.usatoday.com/story/sports/olympics/2018/02/28/olympic-world-not-better-off-after-usocs-scott-blackmun-resigning/383668002.

Brichford, Maynard. "Avery Brundage on Amateurism: Preaching and Practice." In *Rethinking Matters Olympic: Investigations into the Socio-Cultural Study of the Modern Olympic Movement; Proceedings of the 10th International Symposium for Olympic Research*, edited by Robert

K. Barney, Janice Forsyth, Michael K. Heine, 90–93. London, Ontario: Centre for Olympic Studies, University of Western Ontario, 2010.

Briel, Robert. "The Olympic Channel Has Launched." *Broadbandtvnews.com*, August 22, 2016. http://www.broadbandtvnews.com/2016/08/22/the-olympic-channel-has-launched.

"Brigadier General Harvey W. Schiller, USAF Ret., Ph.D." *The Citadel Directors' Institute*, 2015. http://www.citadeldirectorsinstitute.com/panelists/harvey-w-schiller.

Brown, Bobbi. "Susan Saint James at 68: The Emmy-Winning TV Star Looks Back." *YAHOO! Beauty*, June 4, 2015. https://www.yahoo.com/beauty/susan-saint-james-at-68-the-emmy-winning-tv-star-120687998633.html.

Bryant, Steve. "Support for Olympics Waning: Poll." *NBCChicago.com*, September 2, 2009. http://www.nbcchicago.com/news/politics/Support-for-Olympics-Dwindling-Poll-56804857.html.

Bulman, Erica. "Australian IOC Vice President Resigns from Ethics Commission." *SlamSports*, March 6, 2000. http://www.canoe.ca/SlamOlympicScandal/mar6_aus.html.

Burbank, Matthew J., Gregory D. Andranovich, and Charles H. Heying. *Olympic Dreams: The Impact of Mega-Events on Local Politics*. Boulder: Rienner, 2001.

"Burghley: Bermuda's Olympic Champion." *Bernews.com*, March 31, 2012. http://bernews.com/2012/03/burghley-bermudas-olympian-governor.

Cahill, Shane. "The Friendly Games? The Melbourne Olympic Games in Australian Culture, 1946–1956." MA thesis: University of Melbourne, 1990.

———. "A Very Hard Crowd to Have Dealings With: International and Australian Television Networks' Resistance to the Demands of the 1956 Melbourne Olympic Organizing Committee for a Fee For Television Coverage, 1955–1956." In *On-line Proceedings: Forty Years of Television Conference*. Melbourne: Monash University, 1996.

Calmes, Jackie. "Peter Ueberroth Drops Out of California Governor Race." *Wall Street Journal*, September 10, 2003. http://www.wsj.com/articles/SB106312851096443500.

Calvert, Jonathan. "How to Buy the Olympics." *Observer* (London), January 6, 2002.

"Candidature Process 2024." *Olympic.org*, 2017. https://www.olympic.org/current-candidature-process-2024.

Carbaugh, Robert J. *International Economics*. 16th ed. Boston: Cenage Learning, 2017.

Carlson, Michael. "Roone Arledge: Innovative U.S. Television Producer Who Made His Mark on Sport and News." *The Guardian*, December 11, 2002. https://www.theguardian.com/news/ 2002/dec/11/guardianobituaries.television.

Carter, Bill. "Roone Arledge, 71, a Force in TV Sports and News, Dies." *New York Times*, December 6, 2002. http://www.nytimes.com/2002/12/06/business/roone-arledge-71-a-force-in-tv-sports-and-news-dies.html.

Carter, Bill, and Richard Sandomir. "Ebersol to Rejoin NBC Sports as a Senior Adviser." *New York Times*, August 30, 2011. http://mediadecoder.blogs.nytimes.com/2011/08/30/ebersol-to-rejoin-nbc-sports-as-a-senior-adviser/?_r=0.

Carter, Mike. "Joklik Says Charges That Fund Was Used for Bribery Are Defamatory." *Associated Press Newswires*, December 2, 1998.

Catlin, D. H., K. D. Fitch, and A. Ljungqvist. "Medicine and Science in the Fight against Doping in Sport." *Journal of Internal Medicine* 264 (2008): 99–114. doi:10.1111/j.1365-2796.2008.01993.x.

Chalaby, Jean K. *Transnational Television in Europe: Reconfiguring Global Communications Networks*. London: Tauris, 2009.

Chappelet, Jean-Loup. *Autonomy of Sport in Europe*. Strasbourg: Council of Europe, 2010.

———. "Towards Better Olympic Accountability." *Sport in Society* 14 (April 2011): 319–31.

Chappelet, Jean-Loup, and Brenda Kübler-Mabbott. *The International Olympic Committee and the Olympic System: The Governance of World Sport*. New York: Routledge, 2008.

"Charles R. Ebersol; Executive, 85." *New York Times*, November 5, 2001. http://www.nytimes.com/2001/11/05/nyregion/charles-r-ebersol-executive-85.html.

"Chicago Bid Boss Says Regional Voting, IOC-USOC Friction Costly." October 6, 2009. http://blogs.reuters.com/sport/2009/10/06/chicago-bid-boss-says-regional-voting-ioc-usoc-friction-costly.

Chigbo, Okey. "The Go-To Guy, Richard Pound." *CA Magazine*, August 2000. http://www.camagazine.com/archives/print-edition/2000/aug/features/camagazine26378.aspx.

Christie, James. "Koss Delivers Blow to Samaranch: Athletes Leader Doesn't Want IOC Boss to Become First Head of Antidoping Body." *Globe and Mail*, February 3, 1999.

———. "Reconcile with U.S. TV Networks, IOC Is Warned." *Deseret News*, February 27, 2001. http://www.deseretnews.com/article/828136/Reconcile-with-US-TV-networks-IOC-is-warned.html?pg=all.

Christopherson, Walter. "Your New Home—Real Estate Business Moves into Jet Age." *Montreal Gazette*, June 23, 1962.

Clarey, Christopher. "Olympics: Bribery Charge Studied by Special I.O.C. Board." *New York Times*, December 15, 1998.

———. "Olympics: Samaranch Vows Cleanup If Needed." *New York Times*, December 14, 1998.

Clarke, Arthur C. "Extra-Terrestrial Relays: Can Rocket Stations Give World-wide Radio Coverage?" *Wireless World* 51 (October 1945): 305–8. http://www.americanradiohistory.com/Archive-Wireless-World/40s/Wireless-World-1945-10.pdf.

Cohan, Peter. "How Success Killed Eastman Kodak." *Forbes*, October 1, 2011. http://www.forbes.com/sites/petercohan/2011/10/01/how-success-killed-eastman-kodak/#751ddac24d86.

Collins, Richard. *From Satellite to Single Market: New Communication Technology and European Public Service Television*. London: Routledge, 2005.

"Communiques and News in Brief." *Olympic Review* 91 (August 1965): 52.

Connelly, Eoin. "Toyota Joins IOC TOP Tier." March 13, 2015. http://www.sportspromedia.com/news/toyota_joins_ioc_top_tier.

Copetas, A. Craig, and Roger Thurow. "IOC Moping at Meeting on Doping; S. L. Bribery Scandal Splits Membership into Self-Serving Factions." *Wall Street Journal*, February 5, 1999.

———. "IOC President Samaranch Gets an Olympian Send-Off." *Wall Street Journal*, July 12, 2001. http://online.wsj.com/article/SB994886836875316393.html.

"Cost Threat to Olympics on TV." *London Times*, January 31, 1975.

Coultan, Mark. "The Phil Factor." *Sydney Morning Herald*, March 13, 1999.

"Count Jacques Rogge." Undated. https://www.olympic.org/count-jacques-rogge.

Cruise, David, and Alison Griffiths. *Net Worth: Exploding the Myths of Pro Hockey*. Toronto: Viking, 1991.

Curthoys, Ann. "The Getting of Television: Dilemmas in Ownership, Control, and Culture." In *Better Dead than Red: Australia's First Cold War, 1949–1956*, edited by Ann Curthoys and John Merritt, vol. 2. Sydney: Allen and Unwin, 1986.

Dahlgren, Peter. "Key Trends in European Television." In *Television across Europe: A Comparative Introduction*, edited by Jan Wieten, Graham Murdock, and Peter Dahlgren, 23–34. London: Sage, 2000. http://dx.doi.org/10.4135/9781446220344.n3.

D'Alessandro, David. "With Sponsorship Money on the Line, the IOC Must Take Radical Steps." *New York Times*, February 14, 1999.

Davenport, Joanna. "Monique Berlioux: Her Association with Three IOC Presidents." *Citius, Altius, Fortius* 4 (Autumn 1996): 10–18.

"David George Burghley." https://www.olympic.org/david-george-burghley. 2017.

"David Kogan, Trustee." *BBC Media Action: Transforming Lives through Media around the World*. Undated. Originally available at http://www.bbc.co.uk/mediaaction/about/management-and-trustees/david-kogan; see archived page at https://web.archive.org/web/20161216134347/http://www.bbc.co.uk/mediaaction/about/management-and-trustees/david-kogan.

"Dawn Fraser Claims Letters Defamed Her." *Sydney Morning Herald*, February 27, 1968.

Dawson, Thomson. "Brand Management: The Last Kodak Moment?" *Branding Strategy Insider* 6 (December 2011). http://www.brandingstrategyinsider.com/2011/12/brand-management-the-last-kodak-moment.html#.WBdjdUozWUk.

de Coubertin, Pierre. "Athletics in the Modern World and the Olympic Games." Analysis and extracts from a lecture by Coubertin to the Parnassus Club, Athens, 1894. In *Pierre de Coubertin: The Olympic Idea—Discourses and Essays*. Schorndorf: Hoffman, 1967.

Deford, Frank. "Roone Arledge 1931–2002: In Presenting the Olympics, Wide World, Howard Cosell and Much More, This Visionary Revolutionized Sports Television." December 16, 2002. http://www.si.com/vault/2002/12/16/334171/roone-arledge-1931-2002-in-presenting-the-olympics-wide-world-howard-cosell-and-much-more-this-visionary-revolutionized-sports-television.

Dewan, Shaila. "When the Germans, and Rockets, Came to Town." *New York Times*, December 31, 2007. http://www.nytimes.com/2007/12/31/us/31huntsville.html?_r=0.

"Dick Ebersol '69 Speaks of Passion for Sports at 2008 Kiphuth Fellowship Public Lecture." *Yale University Athletics*, December 5, 2008. http://www.yalebulldogs.com/genrel/120508aaa.html.

"Discovery Communications Agrees to Take Full Control of Eurosport." *Discovery Communications*, July 22, 2015. https://corporate.discovery.com/discovery-newsroom/discovery-communications-agrees-to-take-full-control-of-eurosport.

"Dispute over Olympic Revenue Sharing May Impact Chicago Bid." *USA Today*, June 3, 2008. http://usatoday30.usatoday.com/sports/olympics/2008-06-03-chicago-share_N.htm.

Dodd, Mike. "Samaranch to Lead Reforms." *USA Today*, March 19, 1999.

Downes, Steven. "Kim Will Dish Dirt on IOC to Save His Skin—Olympics." *Sunday Times*, March 21, 1999.

"Drapeau Accuses Malouf Inquiry of Choosing Him as a Scapegoat." *Montreal Gazette*, June 16, 1980. https://news.google.com/newspapers?nid=1946&dat=19800616&id=OYkxAAAAIBAJ&sjid=dKQFAAAAIBAJ&pg=1217,2610362&hl=en.

Dwyre, Bill. "Peter Ueberroth's L.A. Olympics: Bigger, Better, Richer." *Los Angeles Times*, July 18, 2009. http://articles.latimes.com/2009/jul/18/sports/sp-dwyre-ueberroth18/2.

Dyreson, Mark, and Matthew Llewellyn. "Los Angeles Is *the* Olympic City: Legacies of the 1932 and 1984 Olympic Games." *International Journal of the History of Sport* 25, no. 14 (December 2008): 1991–2018.

Edelman, Robert Simon. "The Russians Are *Not* Coming! The Soviet Withdrawal from the Games of the XXIII Olympiad." *International Journal of the History of Sport* 32 (January 2015): 9–36.

"Elections of the Presidents of the International Olympic Committee: Reference Document; Candidates and Voting Results." September 23, 2013, 7. https://stillmed.olympic.org/media/Document%20Library/OlympicOrg/factsheets-Reference-Documents/Olympic-Movement/IOC-Presidents/Reference-document-Elections-of-the-IOC-Presidents.pdf.

Espinosa, Patricia. "The Olympic Rainmaker." *Wag*, June 29, 2012. http://www.wagmag.com/the-olympic-rainmaker.

Espy, Richard. *The Politics of the Olympic Games: With an Epilogue, 1976–1980*. Berkeley: University of California Press, 1981.

"Ex-Brazil President Lula Leaves Prison to Attend Grandson's Funeral." *The Guardian*, March 2, 2019. https://www.theguardian.com/world/2019/mar/02/ex-brazil-president-lula-leaves-prison-to-attend-grandsons-funeral.

"Executive Profile: Scott Blackmun." Undated. https://www.bloomberg.com/research/stocks/private/person.asp?personId=32853755&privcapId=4278213.

"Expelled IOC Member Says He's Innocent." *SlamSports*, March 14, 1999. http://www.canoe.ca/SlamOlympicScandalArchive/mar14_ex.html.

"Expelled IOC Member Vows to Defend Himself." *SlamSports*, January 27, 1999. http://www.canoe.ca/SlamOlympicScandalArchive/jan27_exp.html.

"Explorer and Early Satellites." 2015. https://www.nasa.gov/mission_pages/explorer/explorer-overview.html.

"F1 Gets Two Marketing Bosses." November 6, 2012. http://www.pitpass.com/46546/F1-gets-two-marketing-bosses.

Farrell, Frank. "Birthday Party." *World Telegram*, December 10, 1959.

FIFA. "François Carrard to Lead FIFA Reform Process." Media release. August 11, 2015. http://www.fifa.com/about-fifa/news/y=2015/m=8/news=francois-carrard-to-lead-fifa-reform-process-2670347.html.

Findling, John E. "Chicago Loses the 1904 Olympics." *Journal of Olympic History* 12 (October 2004): 24–29.

Fleming, James S. *Window on Congress: A Congressional Biography of Barber B. Conable Jr.* Foreword by Richard F. Fenno Jr. Rochester, N.Y.: University of Rochester Press, 2004.

"Former USTA President David Haggerty Elected as President of ITF." September 25, 2015. http://www.tennis.com/pro-game/2015/09/american-david-haggerty -elected-to-head-world-tennis-body/56436.

"France and Olympism." *Olympic Review* 72–73 (November–December 1973): 501–40.

Friedman, Thomas L. *The World Is Flat: A History of the Twenty-First Century*. Updated and expanded. New York: Farrar, Straus and Giroux, 2007.

Friedman, Wayne. 2011. "Veteran NBC Sports Chief Dick Ebersol Resigns." *Media-DailyNews*, May 19, 2011. http://www.mediapost.com/publications/article/150863/ veteran-nbc-sports-chief-dick-ebersol-resigns.html.

Futterman, Matthew. "USOC Moves to Nominate Los Angeles for 2024 Games." *Wall Street Journal*, August 12, 2015. http://www.wsj.com/articles/usoc-moves -to-nominate-los-angeles-for-2024-games-1439420605.

Galbraith, John Kenneth. *The Affluent Society*. 4th ed. Boston: Houghton Mifflin, 1984.

Galbraith, Kate. "Introduction." In *The Economist: Globalisation*, edited by Kate Galbraith. London: Economist/Profile, 2001.

The Games of the Xth Olympiad Los Angeles 1932: Official Report. Los Angeles: Xth Olympiade Committee of the Games of Los Angeles, U.S.A. 1932, 1933.

Garber, Greg. "Samaranch's Legacy: Controversy, Corruption." July 12, 2001. http://static .espn.go.com/oly/columns/garber_greg/1225329.html.

Gardner, David. "Slap in the Face for Obama as His Personal Plea to Back Chicago Backfires for the U.S. and the 2016 Olympics Goes to Rio." *MailOnline*, October 3, 2009. http://www.dailymail.co.uk/news/article-1217595/Rio-Janeiro-awarded-2016 -Olympics.html.

Garron, Jack. *Deaf Heritage: A Narrative History of Deaf America*. Silver Springs, Md.: National Association of the Deaf, 1981.

"George D. Miller Scholarship." *National Fire Protection Association*, updated 2015. Originally available at http://www.nfpa.org/news-and-research/archived/for-students/george-d-miller-scholarship; see archived page at https://web.archive .org/web/20160611162707/http://www.nfpa.org/news-and-research/archived/ for-students/george-d-miller-scholarship.

Giannoulakis, Chrysostomos, and David Stotlar. "Evolution of Olympic Sponsorship and Its Impact on the Olympic Movement." In *The Business of Sports*, edited by Scott R. Rosner and Kenneth L. Shropshire, 470–76. Sudbury, Mass.: Jones and Bartlett Learning, 2011.

Gibson, Owen. "Russia Accused of State-Sponsored Doped as Wada Calls for Athletics Ban." *The Guardian*, November 9, 2015. http://www.theguardian.com/sport/2015/ nov/09/wada-iaaf-russia-dick-pound-banned.

Gold, John R., and Margaret M. Gold. "From A to B: The Summer Olympics, 1896–2008." In *Olympic Cities: City Agendas, Planning, and the World's Games, 1896–2016*, edited by John R. Gold and Margaret M. Gold, 17–55. Rev. ed. Abingdon: Routledge, 2011.

Goldpaper, Sam. "John B. Kelly Jr. Dead at 57; Olympic Committee Leader." *New York Times*, March 4, 1985. http://www.nytimes.com/1985/03/04/sports/john-b-kelly-jr -dead-at-57-olympic-committee-leader.html.

Goldstein, Richard. "Lord Killanin, Olympic Leader, Dies at 84." *New York Times*, April 26, 1999. http://www.nytimes.com/1999/04/26/sports/lord-killanin-olympic-leader -dies-at-84.html.

Gomez, Brian. "USOC Gives $18 Million to IOC, Resolves Games-Cost Dispute." *Colorado Springs Gazette*, September 9, 2010. http://gazette.com/article/104360.

Gonzalez, Arturo. "Lord Killanin: The Kissinger of the Sweatsuit Set." *People* 2 (August 12, 1974). http://www.people.com/people/archive/article/0,20064356,00.html.

Gorrell, Mike. "IOC Official: Games Are for Sale." *Salt Lake City Tribune*, December 13, 1998.

———. "Joklik Hopes His Sacrifice Will Push Games Forward; Joklik Hopes His Sacrifice Will Save Games." *Salt Lake Tribune*, January 9, 1999.

Gosper, Kevan. With Glenda Korporaal. *An Olympic Life: Melbourne 1956 to Sydney 2000*. St. Leonards: Allen and Unwin, 2000.

Gould, Jack. "Nobody Was First." *New York Times*, December 9, 1956.

———. "When TV Lost the Olympics." *New York Times*, October 18, 1964. http://www .nytimes.com/1964/10/18/when-tv-lost-the- olympics.html?_r=0.

Green, Catherine. "L.A. Riots: Rebuild L.A.'s Ambitious Attempts to Revive the City." *Neon Tommy: Annenberg Digital News*, April 24, 2012. http://www.neontommy.com/ news/2012/04/la-riots-rebuild-las-ambitious-attempts-revive-neighborhood.

Greimel, Hans. "Toyota Signs on as Global Olympics Sponsor: Deal Reportedly Valued at $835 Million." *Automotive News*, March 13, 2015. http://www.autonews .com/article/20150313/ RETAIL03/150319934/toyota-signs-on-as-global-olympics -sponsor.

Grossman, Ben. "Dick Ebersol." *Broadcasting and Cable*, October 21, 2005. http://www .broadcastingcable.com/news/news-articles/dick-ebersol/108441.

Guide des Jeux Olympiques: VIIIe Olympiade—Paris 1924. Paris: Games of the VIIIth Olympiad Organizing Committee, 1924.

Guttmann, Allen. *The Games Must Go On: Avery Brundage and the Olympic Movement*. New York: Columbia University Press, 1984.

———. *The Olympics: A History of the Modern Games*. Urbana: University of Illinois Press, 1992.

———. *The Olympics: A History of the Modern Games*. 2nd edition. Urbana: University of Illinois Press, 2002.

———. *Sports: The First Five Millennia*. Amherst: University of Massachusetts Press, 2004.

Hampton, Janie. *The Austerity Olympics: When the Games Came to London in 1948*. Foreword by Sebastian Coe. London: Aurum, 2008.

Hancock, I. R. "Kent Hughes, Sir Wilfrid Selwyn (Billy), 1895–1970." In *Australian Diction- ary of Biography*, 15th edition. Melbourne: Melbourne University Press, 2000.

Harmon, Joanie. "A Look Back: Velodrome Built for 1984 Olympics Brought CSU Domin- guez Hills Recognition as Sports and Entertainment Venue." *Dateline Dominguez*, August 13, 2009. http://www.csudhnews.com/2009/08/velodrome.

Harrigan, Michael T. "A Class Act." *The Olympian* (January 1989): 8–15.

Harvey, Randy. "Olympic Official Schiller Joins Turner Broadcasting: USOC Had Expected Its Executive Director to Stay through the Year 2000." *Los Angeles Times*, July 26, 1994.

http://articles.latimes.com/1994-07-26/sports/sp-19913_1_assistant-executive
-director.

———. "Search Committee Recommends Schiller: Olympics: Southeastern Conference Commissioner Is Expected to Be Named, for the Second Time, as Executive Director of United States Olympic Committee." *Los Angeles Times*, October 12, 1989. http://articles .latimes.com/1989-10-12/sports/sp-343_1_executive-director-s-position.

Haugh, David. "In Retrospect, Losing 2016 Olympics to Rio a Big Victory for Chicago." *Chicago Tribune*, August 2, 2016. http://www.chicagotribune.com/sports/columnists/ ct-haugh-olympics-spt-0803-20160802-column.html.

Hay, Steven B. "Guarding the Olympic Gold: Protecting the Marketability of Olympic Trademarks through Section 110 of the Amateur Sports Act of 1978." *Southwestern University Law Review* 16, no. 2 (1986): 461–503.

Hazlehurst, Cameron. "The Advent of Commercial TV." *Australian Cultural History* 2 (1982– 1983): 104–19.

"Helms Athletic Foundation." *Olympic Review* 1951: 26–28.

Hersh, Phil. "Dassler's Death Could Have Olympic Repercussions." *Chicago Tribune*, April 13, 1987. http://articles.chicagotribune.com/1987-04-13/sports/8701280232 _1_horst-dassler-adidas-international-sports.

———. "Hoist a Cold One: $18 Mill Taking Chill out of USOC–IOC relationship." *Los Angeles Times*, September 9, 2010. http://latimesblogs.latimes.com/olympics_blog/ 2010/09/hoist-a-cold-one-18-mill-taking-chill-out-of-usoc-ioc-relationship.html.

———. "IOC Official Rips USOC's Share of Olympic Funding." *Chicago Tribune*, June 4, 2008. http://articles.chicagotribune.com/2008-06-04/sports/0806030739 _1_usoc-chairman-peter-ueberroth-chicago-bid-denis-oswald.

———. "IOC-USOC Deal: Some Ado about Nothing." *Chicago Tribune*, April 1, 2009. http://newsblogs.chicago-tribune.com/sports_globetrotting/2009/04lets-make-a -few-things-clear-about-the-net-result-so-far-of-the-volatile-revenue-sharing -negotiations-between-the-us-o.html.

———. "Killanin's IOC Presidency Filled with Crises." *Chicago Tribune*, April 29, 1999. http://articles.chicagotribune.com/1999-04-29/sports/9904290083_1_ioc-lord -killanin-monique berlioux.

———. "Major Sponsor Blasts Latest IOC Moves." *Chicago Tribune*, May 5, 1999. https:// www.chicagotribune.com/news/ct-xpm-1999-05-05-9905050010-story.html.

———. "New USOC Chief Schiller Quits." *Chicago Tribune*, January 21, 1988. http://articles .chicagotribune.com/1988-01-21/sports/8803240225_1_usoc-president-helmick -fractious-organization-robert-helmick.

———. "Peter Ueberroth Leaves a Reformed USOC." *Chicago Tribune*, October 12, 2008. http://articles.chicagotribune.com/2008-10-12/sports/0810110213_1_ usoc-state-of-mass-confusion-chicago-guarantee.

Hill, Christopher R. *Olympic Politics: Athens to Atlanta, 1896–1996.* 2nd edition. Manchester: Manchester University Press, 1996.

Hitchen, Adrian. "An Interview with Timo Lumme, Managing Director of Quokka Sports Ltd." *International Journal of Sports Marketing and Sponsorship* 2, no. 1 (2000): 2–13.

Hoberman, John. "Why Is Obama Going to Copenhagen?" *Foreign Policy*, September 29, 2009. https://foreignpolicy.com/2009/09/29/why-is-obama-going-to-copenhagen.

Hobson, Will. "Scott Blackmun Steps Down as U.S. Olympic Committee Chief Executive." *Washington Post*, February 28, 2018. https://www.washingtonpost .com/sports/olympics/scott-blackmun-steps-down-as-us-olympic-committee -chief-executive/2018/02/28/742775b2-1cc2-11e8-9de1-147dd2df3829_story .html?utm_term=.5fd34a5691d6.

Holbreich, Curt. "After 2½ Years, Miller Quits as USOC Director." *Los Angeles Times*, August 25, 1987. http://articles.latimes.com/1987-08-25/sports/sp-3998 _1_executive-director.

Holmwood, Leigh. "BBC's Olympic Coverage under Threat after TV Bid Is Rejected." *The Guardian*, December 3, 2008. https://www.theguardian.com/sport/2008/dec/03/ olympics-2012-bbc-itv-sky.

"Homage to the Marquess of Exeter." *Olympic Review* 109–110 (November–December 1976): 586–87.

Howard, Frederick. *Kent Hughes: A Biography*. South Melbourne: Macmillan, 1972.

Huebner, Stefan. *Pan-Asian Sports and the Emergence of Modern Asia, 1913–1974*. Singapore: National University of Singapore Press, 2016.

Hula, Ed. "Updated—IOC Members Remember Monique Berlioux, Former IOC Director General." *Around the Rings*, September 9, 2015. http://aroundtherings .com/site/A__52930/Title__ Updated——IOC-Members-Remember-Monique -Berlioux-Former-IOC-Director-General/292/Articles.

Humphries, Tom. "IOC Will Not Direct New Testing Body." *Irish Times*, February 3, 1999.

Hunt, Thomas M. "Countering the Soviet Threat in the Olympic Medals Race: The Amateur Sports Act of 1978 and American Athletics Policy Reform." *International Journal of the History of Sport* 24 (June 2007): 796–818.

"India and Olympism." *Olympic Review* 149 (March 1980): 123–29.

Ingle, Sean. "Chinese Company Alibaba Signs Deal to Be Major Sponsor of Olympic Games." *The Guardian*, January 19, 2017. https://www.theguardian.com/sport/2017/ jan/19/chinese-e-commerce-company-alibaba-major-olympic-games-sponsor.

"Interior Design for Businesses." *Town of Mount Royal Weekly Post*, October 29, 1959, 12.

International Olympic Committee. "About Protection of Olympic Words, Emblems, and Rings." *IOC Bulletin* 18 (November 1949): 20.

"International Olympic Committee Ethics Commission: Decision Containing Recommendations N° D/01/05—CASE N° 1/04, Un Yong Kim." February 4, 2005. http://www .olympic.org/ Assets/ImportedNews/Documents/en_report_913.pdf.

IOC. *Marketing Matters: The Olympic Marketing Newsletter* 18 (May 2000). http://www .olympic.org/Documents/Reports/EN/en_report_274.pdf.

———. *Marketing Matters: The Olympic Marketing Newsletter* 21 (June 2002). http://www .olympic.org/Documents/Reports/EN/en_report_456.pdf.

"IOC 'Agenda 2020' Allows Olympics in Different Host Countries." December 8, 2014. http://www.dw.com/en/ioc-agenda-2020-allows-olympics-in-different-host -countries/a-18116022.

"IOC Awards European Broadcast Rights to Sportfive." *New York Times*, November 8, 2009. http://www.nytimes.com/2009/02/18/sports/18iht-olytv18.20285494.html.

"IOC Cleans House: 6 Kicked Out in Influence-Peddling Scandal." *Kitchener-Waterloo Record*, January 25, 1999.

"IOC Confirms European TV Rights Contract." July 6, 2004. https://www. olympic.org/news/ioc-confirms-european-tv-rights-contract.

"IOC Ethics Commission Statement on the R. Kevan Gosper Case." May 15, 2000. http://www.olympic.org/content/news/media-resources/manual-news/1999-2009/2000/05/15/ioc-ethics-commission-statement-on-the-r-kevan-gosper-case.

"IOC Executive Board Sets Dates for 2024 Olympic Games Bid Process." December 5, 2014. https://www.olympic.org/ news/ioc-executive-board-sets-dates-for-2024-olympic-games-bid-process.

"IOC Facing Up to Key Expulsion Votes." *SlamSports*, March 15, 1999. http://www.canoe.ca/ SlamOlympicScandalArchive/mar15_ioc.html.

IOC Marketing Department. "The History of Olympic Marketing." *Olympic Marketing 1999 Fact File*. Lausanne: IOC, 1999.

"IOC Member's Fictitious Daughter Sent $7,000." January 22, 2001. http://www.cbc. ca/sports/ioc-member-s-fictitious-daughter-sent-7-000-1.283836.

"IOC Official Expresses Frustration with New USOC TV Network." *Street and Smith's Sports Business Daily*, July 9, 2009. www.sportsbusinessdaily.com/article/131587.

"IOC Opens Tender Process for Sale of European Olympic Broadcast Rights." January 29, 2004. https://www.olympic.org/news/ioc-opens-tender-process-for-sale-of-european-olympic-broadcast-rights-1.

"IOC Shakes Up Olympic Bidding—Again: Top Story Replay." *Around the Rings*, March 30, 2019. http://aroundtherings.com/site/A__76172/Title__IOC-Shakes-Up-Olympic-Bidding—-Again——Top-Story-Replay/292/Articles.

"IOC, USOC Finalize Revenue Deal." May 24, 2012. http://espn.go.com/olympics/story/_/id/7967000/ioc-usoc-resolve-differences-revenues.

"IOC, USOC to Revisit Olympic Revenue Sharing." *CBS Sports*, June 4, 2008. http://sportsline.com/worldsports/story/10852373.

"Ireland and the Olympic Games." *History Ireland* 6 (Spring 1998). http://www.historyireland.com/20th-century-contemporary-history/ireland-the-olympic-games.

"Jacques Rogge in Final Days as IOC President." September 3, 2013. http://www. cbc.ca/sports/olympics-sochi-old/jacques-rogge-in-final-days-as-ioc-president-1.1364696.

Janofsky, Michael. "Miller Quits as U.S.O.C. Chief." *New York Times*, August 25, 1987. http://www.nytimes.com/1987/08/25/sports/miller-quits-as-usoc-chief.html.

——. "Olympics: As Helmick Resigns, His Familiar Rationale Misses the Ethical Point." *New York Times*, December 5, 1991. http://www.nytimes.com/1991/12/05/sports/olympics/as/helmick/resigns/his/familiar/rationale/misses/the/ethical/point.html.

——. "Olympics: Under Fire for Business Ties, Helmick Resigns." *New York Times*, September 19, 1991. http://www.nytimes.com/1991/09/19/sports/olympics-under-fire-for-business-ties-helmick-resigns.html.

———. "U.S.O.C. Cutting Foreign Aid Program." *New York Times*, May 1, 1988. http://www
.nytimes.com/1988/05/01/sports/usoc-cutting-foreign-aid-program.html.

"Japan Irked by 3-hr. Delay." *New York Times*, October 11, 1964.

Jenkins, Sally. "Peacock Power—Talk about Smoking the Competition: With the 1996
Atlanta Games Already in Hand, Dick Ebersol of NBC Sports Has Grabbed Five More
Olympics—In the Years 2000–2008." *Sports Illustrated*, December 25, 1995. http://
www. si.com/vault/1995/12/25/209185/peacock-power-talk-about-smoking-the
-competition-with-the-1996-atlanta-games-already-in-hand-dick-ebersol-of-nbc
-sports-has-grabbed-five-more-olympics---in-the-years-2000-to-2008.

———. "The USOC Needs a Leader Who Cares about Athletes More than Expense
Accounts." *Washington Post*, July 5, 2018. https://www.washingtonpost.com/sports/
olympics/the-usoc-needs-a-leader-who-cares-about-athletes-more-than-expense-
accounts/2018/07/03/9554ded87ae5-11e8-80be d32e182a3bc_story.html?utm_term
=.9d16d78448d1.

Johnson, William. "Defender of the Faith." *Sports Illustrated*, July 24, 1972. http://www.si
. com/vault/1972/07/24/612579/defender-of-the-faith.

Kane, Robert J. "Alumni Who Aid Athletics." *Cornell Alumni News*, June 1986, 65–66. https://
ecommons.cornell.edu/bitstream/1813/28022/1/088_10.pdf.

Kaufman, Michael T. "Jean Drapeau, 83, Mayor Who Reshaped Montreal." *New York
Times*, August 14, 1999. http://www.nytimes.com/1999/08/14/world/jean-drapeau
-83-mayor-who-reshaped-montreal.html?_r=0.

Keck, Kristi. "Obama, Chicago Come Up Short in Olympics Bid." *CNN*, October 2, 2009.
http://www.cnn.com/2009/POLITICS/10/02/denmark.olympics.obama.

Keh, Andrew. "I.O.C. Paves Way for Paris and Los Angeles to Host Summer Games." *New
York Times*, June 9, 2017. https://www.nytimes.com/2017/06/09/sports/olympics/paris
-2024-los-angeles-2028-summer-games.html.

Kelly, Jason. "Hyde Park's Olympic History." *University of Chicago Magazine*, May–June
2009. http://magazine.uchicago.edu/0906/chicago_journal/olympic_history.shtml.

Kelner, Martha. "Rio Games Vote-Winner Questioned by Police over 'Rigged Bidding Process,'" *The Guardian*, September 5, 2017. https://www.theguardian.com/
sport/2017/sep/05/head-rio-2016-organising-committee-questioned-vote-buying
-investigation.

Kennedy, Ray. "Miser with the Midas Touch." *Sports Illustrated*, November 22, 1982. http://
sportsillustrated.cnn.com/vault/article/magazine/MAG1126135/index.htm.

Kidd, Bruce. "Montreal 1976." In *Encyclopedia of the Modern Olympic Movement*, edited by
John D. Findling and Kimberly D. Pelle, 191–98. Westport, Conn.: Greenwood, 2004.

"Killanin, Drapeau Discuss TV Snag." *New York Times*, September 8, 1975.

Killanin, Lord. *My Olympic Years*. London: Secker and Warburg, 1983.

"Killanin, Lord; Morris, Michael; 3rd Baron Killanin, cr. 1900, of Galway; 3rd Baronet
Morris, cr. 1885, of Galway." *British Army Officers, 1939–1945*. http://www.unithistories
.com/officers/Army_officers_K01.html#Killanin_Lord.

"Korean IOC Member Takes Threatening Stance." *Kitchener Waterloo Record*, March 17,
1999.

Landry, Fernand, and Magdeleine Yerlés. "The Presidencies of Lord Killanin (1972–1980) and of Juan Antonio Samaranch (1980–)." In *The International Olympic Committee—One Hundred Years: The Idea—The Presidents—The Achievements*, vol. 3. Lausanne: IOC, 1996.

Large, David Clay. *Munich 1972: Tragedy, Terror, and Triumph at the Olympic Games*. Lanham, Md.: Rowman and Littlefield, 2012.

La Rocco, Claudia. "Rings of Power: Peter Ueberroth and the 1984 Los Angeles Olympic Games." *Financial History* 81 (Spring 2004): 10–12, 36.

Latouche, Daniel. "Montreal 1976." In *Olympic Cities: City Agendas, Planning, and the World's Games, 1896–2016*, edited by John R. Gold and Margaret M. Gold, 197–217. Rev. ed. London: Routledge, 2011.

Lawrence, Robert Z. With Jeffrey D. Pellegrom. "Fools' Gold: How America Pays to Lose in the Olympics." *Television Quarterly* (Fall 1989): 5–10.

LeBlanc, Gilles. "Dale McMann Elected President of the International Softball Federation." *Softball Canada*, October 25, 2013. http://www.softball.ca/english/news/dale-mcmann-elected-president-of-the-international-softball-federation.htm

Lechner, Frank J., and John Boli. "General Introduction." In *The Globalization Reader*, edited by Frank J. Lechner and John Boli. 3rd edition. Oxford: Blackwell 2008.

Lenskyj, Helen. *Inside the Olympic Industry: Power, Politics, and Activism*. Albany: State University of New York, 2000.

Lieser, Josh R. "Los Angeles and the 1984 Olympic Games: Cultural Commodification, Corporate Sponsorship, and the Cold War." PhD diss., University of California, Riverside, 2014. http://search.proquest.com/docview/1656486865.

Llewellyn, Matthew P., and John Gleaves. "1984 Olympic Games, Los Angeles." In *American Sports: A History of Icons, Idols, and Ideas*, edited by Murry Nelson, 3:945–51. Santa Barbara: ABC-CLIO, 2013.

———. *The Rise and Fall of Olympic Amateurism*. Urbana: University of Illinois Press, 2016.

Longman, Jere. "Juan Antonio Samaranch Transformed the Olympics." *Globe and Mail*, August 23, 2010. http://www.theglobeandmail.com/news/world/juan-antonio-samaranch-transformed-the-olympics/article4315993/?page=all.

———. "Juan Antonio Samaranch, Who Transformed the Olympics, Dies at 89; Led I.O.C." *New York Times*, April 21, 2010. http://www.nytimes.com/2010/04/22/sports/22samaranch.html?ref= sports&pagewanted=print.

———. "Olympics: An Interim Deputy with the Skills of a Sheriff." *New York Times*, November 13, 1994.

———. "Olympics: Corporate Backer Tells I.O.C. to Come Clean." *New York Times*, January 13, 1999. http://www.nytimes.com/1999/01/13/sports/olympics-corporate-backer-tells-ioc-to-come-clean.html. http://www.nytimes.com/1994/11/13/sports/olympics-an-interim-deputy-with-the-skills-of-a-sheriff.html.

———. "Olympics: I.O.C. Expulsion Vote Is Key for Samaranch." *New York Times*, March 17. 1999.

———. "Olympics: More Reports of I.O.C. Favors Emerge in Utah." *New York Times*, December 18, 1998.

———. "Olympics: Reform Process Could Change Entire I.O.C. Structure." *New York Times*, February 20, 1999. http://www.nytimes.com/1,99/02/20/sports/olympics-reform -process-could-change-entire-ioc-structure.html.

———. "Olympics: Rogge Takes Olympic Reins from Samaranch." *New York Times*, July 17, 2001. http://www.nytimes.com/2001/07/17/sports/olympics-rogge-takes-olympic -reins-from-samaranch.html?pagewanted=all.

———. "On the Olympics: Lack of I.O.C. Ethics Is Business as Usual." *New York Times*, May 17, 2000. http://www.nytimes.com/2000/05/17/sports/on-the-olympics-lack-of-ioc -ethics-is-business-as-usual.html.

———. "Potential Olympic Sponsors Said to be Uneasy." *New York Times*, January 21, 1999.

"Lord Killanin Suffers 'Mild' Heart Attack." *Spartanburg Herald*, April 13, 1977.

Lucas, Robert Joseph. "A Descriptive History of the Interdependence of Television and Sports in the Summer Olympic Games, 1956–1984." MA thesis, San Diego State University, 1984.

Lyberg, Wolf, ed. *The IOC Sessions, 1894–1955*. Vol. 3. Lausanne: IOC, 1992.

MacAloon, John. "Scandal and Governance: Inside and Outside the IOC 2000 Commission." *Sport in Society* 14, no. 3 (2001): 292–308.

Macur, Juliet. "International and U.S. Olympic Leaders Agree on Revenue-Sharing Plan." *New York Times*, May 23, 2012. http://www.nytimes.com/2012/05/24/sports/olympics/ international-and-us-olympic-leaders-agree-on-revenue-sharing-plan.html.

———. "Rio Wins 2016 Olympics in a First for South America." *New York Times*, October 2, 2009. http://www.nytimes.com/2009/10/03/sports/03olympics.html.

Madkour, Abraham D. "The Unplugged David D'Alessandro." *Sport Business Daily*, February 3, 2014. http://www.sportsbusinessdaily.com/Journal/Issues/2014/02/03/ Opinion/From-the-Executive-Editor.aspx.

Maese, Rick. "U.S. Olympic Committee Names Sarah Hirshland New CEO." *Washington Post*, July 12, 2018. https://www.washingtonpost.com/news/sports/wp/2018/07/12/ u-s-olympic-committee-names-sarah-hirshland-new ceo/?noredirect=on&utm _term=.6f72b3ae326a.

Magnay, Jacquelin. "Interview: Jacques Rogge, IOC President." *The Telegraph*, July 15, 2011. http://www.telegraph.co.uk/sport/olympics/8636963/Interview-Jacques-Rogge -IOC-president.html.

———. "Pound of Flesh." *Sydney Morning Herald*. March 20, 1999.

Mallon, Bill. "The Olympic Bribery Scandal." *Journal of Olympic History* 8 (May 2000): 11–27.

"The Man Who Almost Sent Monty to His Doom." *Galway Advertiser*, August 9, 2012. http://advertiser.ie/galway/article/54208/the-man-who-almost-sent-monty-to-his -doom.

"Marriages: Shefler-Feldman." *Jewish Historical Review*, January 29, 1954, 4.

Martucci, Donato. "Giorgio de Stefani, the Guardian." *Olympic Review* 275–276 (September–October 1990): 450–52.

Martyn, Scott G., and Stephen R. Wenn. "A Prelude to Samaranch: Lord Killanin's Path to Olympic Commercialism." *Journal of Olympic History* 16 (July 2008): 40–48.

Mason, Nick. "Yesterday's Anti-heroes." *The Guardian*, September 28, 2000. https://www
.theguardian.com/sydney/story/0,374383,00.html.

McCullough, Erskine. "(Olympics) Samaranch 18-Year Rule Savaged by White House,
Euro Ministers." *Agence France-Presse*, February 2, 1999.

"McDonald's Olympic Swim Stadium." *Los Angeles Sports Council*. Undated. http://www
.lasports.org/lafacilities/display.php?s=Specialized&id=67.

McKay, Jim, Brett Hutchins, and Janine Mikosza. "'Shame and Scandal in the Family':
Australian Media Narratives of the IOC/SOCOG Scandal Spiral." *Olympika: The International Journal of Olympic Studies* 9 (2000): 25–48.

McMullen, Andrew. "Fraud, Mismanagement, and Nepotism: The Committee of Independent Experts and the Fall of the European Commission 1999." *Crime, Law and Social Change* 32 (1999): 93–108.

McPhee, Joan, and James P. Dowden. "Report of the Independent Investigation:
The Constellation of Factors Underlying Larry Nassar's Abuse of Athletes." December
10, 2018. https://www.ropesgray.com/-/media/Files/USOC/ropes-gray-full-report
.pdf.

Meda, Sergio. "The Honest (and Curious) Story of Giulio Onesti." June 23, 2013. http://
www.panorama.it/sport/storie-di-sport/giulio-onesti-coni-anniversario.

Meltz, Mark. "Hand It Over: Eurovision, Exclusive EU Sports Broadcasting Rights, and
the Article 85(3) Exemption." *Boston College International and Comparative Law Review* 23,
no. 1 (1999): 105–20.

"Members." *TAS/CAS Tribunal Arbitral du Sport/Court of Arbitration for Sport*. Undated. http://
www.tas-cas.org/en/icas/members.html.

Merriman, Chris. "NBC Sports Chief Talks Yale, Olympics." *Yale Daily News*, December 5, 2008.
http://yaledailynews.com/blog/2008/12/05/nbc-sports-chief-talks-yale-olympics.

Mertin, Evelyn. "The Soviet Union and the Olympic Games of 1980 and 1984: Explaining
the Boycotts to Their Own People." In *East Plays West: Sport and the Cold War*, edited by
Stephen Wagg and David L. Andrews, 235–52. New York: Routledge, 2007.

Meyer, John. "Embattled USOC Chief Streeter Leaving Post." *Denver Post*, October 7,
2009. http://www.denverpost.com/2009/10/07/embattled-usoc-chief-streeter
-leaving-post.

Mickle, Tripp. "An American Original." *Street and Smith's Sports Business Journal*, March 11,
2013. http://www.sportsbusinessdaily.com/Journal/Issues/2013/03/11/Champions/
Harvey-Schiller.aspx.

———. "Chris Welton, Terrence Burns Leave Helios to Join Advisory Firm Teneo." *Street
and Smith's Sport Business Daily*, February 6, 2013. http://www.sportsbusiness daily.com/
Daily/Closing-Bell/2013/02/06/Helios.aspx.

———. "Improved USOC-IOC Relationship on Display." *Street and Smith's Sport Business
Journal*, May 12, 2014. http://www.sportsbusinessdaily.com/Journal/Issues/2014/05/12/
Olympics/USOC-NBC-side.aspx.

———. "IOC Inks Deal with Sportfive for Euro Olympic Broadcast Rights." *Street and
Smith's Sport Business Daily*, February 18, 2009. https://www.sportsbusiness daily.com/
Daily/Issues/2009/02/18/Sports-Media/IOC-Inks-Deal-With-Sportfive-For-Euro
-Olympic-Broadcast-Rights.aspx.

———. "25 Years Ago, IOC's TOP Teetered, Then Thrived." *Street and Smith's Sports Business Journal*, June 21, 2010. http://www.sportsbusinessdaily.com/Journal/ Issues/2010/06/20100621/This-Weeks-News/25-Years-Ago-Iocs-TOP-Teetered-Then -Thrived.aspx?hl=Xerox&sc=0.

Miller, David. "Evolution of the Olympic Movement." In *From Moscow to Lausanne*, 9–21. Lausanne: International Olympic Committee, 1990.

———. *The Official History of the Olympic Games and the IOC - Athens to London—Part II: The Modern Era 1984–2012*. Edinburgh: Mainstream, 2012.

———. *Olympic Revolution: The Biography of Juan Antonio Samaranch*. London: Pavilion, 1992.

"Minutes, 43rd IOC Session, London, 1948." In *The IOC Sessions, 1894–1955*, edited by Wolf Lyberg, 3:256–61. Lausanne: IOC, 1992.

"Minutes of the 64th Session of the I.O.C. (excerpts)." *Olympic Review* 95 (August 1966): 80–81.

"Miss Mary Sheila Cathcart Dunlop (Killanin)." *Bletchley Park Roll of Honour*. Undated. http://rollofhonour.bletchleypark.org.uk/search/record-detail/2700.

Monroe, Scott. "Landmark Stowe Restaurant Closes Swisspot's Gone; New Tenant Sought." April 30, 2008. http://www.stowetoday.com/stowereporter/archives/landmark- stowe-restaurant-closes/article_ced8f928-c4f4-51e4-b720-20d75ea528c9.html.

"Morgan News: 2010 |IOC| Small UK Firm to Sell 2010 TV Rights in Europe." *Morgan:News:2010:Bronze Edition*, October 15, 2010. http://morgan-news-2010bronze .blogspot.com/2003/10.

"Mr. Richard W. Pound, Q.C., AD.E." Undated. http://www.olympic.org/mr-richard -w-pound-q-c-ad-e.

Murdoch, Alan. "Obituary: Lord Killanin." *The Independent*, April 28, 1999. http://www .independent.co.uk/arts-entertainment/obituary-lord-killanin-1090066.html.

"Nagano Games Tainted by Scandal." *Toronto Star*, January 18, 1999.

Nagourney, Adam, and Jere Longman. "Los Angeles Makes Deal to Host 2028 Olympics." *New York Times*, July 31, 2017. https://www.nytimes.com/2017/07/31/sports/olympics/ los-angeles-2028-summer-olympics.html.

"NBC Posts $223 Million First-Quarter Loss on Winter Olympics." *BC CTV News*, April 16, 2010. http://bc.ctvnews.ca/nbc-posts-223-million-first-quarter-loss -on-winter-olympics-1.502918.

"NBC Protests ABC's Olympic Pact." *New York Times*, December 20, 1972.

Neff, Craig. "I Enjoy Stress." *Sports Illustrated*, November 21, 1989. http://www.si.com/ vault/1989/11/13/121000/i-enjoy-stress.

Neubauer, Deane. "Modern Sport and Olympic Games." *Olympika: The International Journal of Olympic Studies* 17 (2008): 1–40.

Neufeld, Michael J. "Wernher von Braun's Legacy." *NOVA* (newsletter), June 11, 2007. http://www.pbs.org/wgbh/nova/space/von-braun.html.

"'No More Money' for TV Rights of Olympics." *The Times*, August 21, 1975.

Nuga, Haruka. "Tokyo Governor Won't Speculate on Olympic Bribery Scandal." *San Francisco Chronicle*, February 17, 2019. https://www.sfchronicle.com/news/crime/article/ Tokyo-governor-won-t-speculate-on-Olympic-bribery-13624400.php.

"Obituary [Giorgio de Stefani]." *Olympic Review* 302 (December 1992): 662.

O'Coughlin, Seamus. *Squaw Valley Gold: American Hockey's Olympic Odyssey*. New York: iUniverse, 2009.

The Official Report of the Games: VIIth Olympic Winter Games. Cortina d'Ampezzo: Comitato Olimpico Nazionale Italiano, 1956.

Official Report: The Games of the Tenth Olympiad—Los Angeles 1932. Los Angeles: Tenth Olympiad Committee, 1933.

Official Report of the Games of the XXIIIrd Olympiad Los Angeles, 1984: Volume 1—Organization and Planning. Los Angeles: LAOOC, 1985.

Oliver, Brian. *The Commonwealth Games: Extraordinary Stories behind the Medals*. London: Bloomsbury, 2014.

"Olympic Agenda 2020—Olympic Games: The New Norm." Report by the Executive Steering Committee for Olympic Games Delivery. February 2018. https://stillmed .olympic.org/media/Document%20Library/OlympicOrg/News/2018/02/2018-02 -06-Olympic-Games-the-New-Norm-Report.pdf.

"Olympic Channel Launches Global Digital Platform in Six Additional Languages." February 15, 2017. https://www.olympic.org/news/olympic-channel-launches -global-digital-platform-in-six-additional-languages.

"Olympic Games—Palace Revolt Rocks Samaranch." *The Guardian*, February 4, 1999.

Olympic Games, London, 1908—Marathon Race. London: Vail, 1908.

"Olympics Just Part of $10 mln. Business for Marv Josephson." *Montreal Gazette*, ca. April, 1973. "N.1 Droits de T.V. Montreal Du 4.12.69 Au 30.6.73," File, IOCA.

Olympic Marketing Fact File, 2017 Edition. IOC: Lausanne, 2017. https://stillmed.olympic .org/media/Document%20Library/OlympicOrg/Documents/IOC-Marketing-and -Broadcasting-General-Files/Olympic-Marketing-Fact-File-2016.pdf.

Olympic Marketing Fact File, 2019 Edition. IOC: Lausanne, 2019. https://stillmed.olympic .org/media/Document%20Library/OlympicOrg/Documents/IOC-Marketing -and-Broadcasting-General-Files/Olympic-Marketing-Fact-File-2019.pdf#_ga=2 .45340643.677913899.1551280257-1852196685.1501771186.

"(Olympics) Sponsors and U.S. Senator Rip Samaranch for Non-reforms." *Agence France-Presse*, March 19, 1999.

"(Olympics) Sponsors Worried about IOC Double Standards." *Agence France-Presse*, March 13, 1999.

"Olympics TV Deal Nearer." *The Times*, September 9, 1975.

"$175 Million Olympics TV Deal Predicted." *Los Angeles Times*, September 12, 1979.

Osnos, Peter. "'Mysterious' Impresario of NBC's Olympics." *Washington Post*, March 4, 1977. https://www.washingtonpost.com/archive/lifestyle/1977/03/04/mysterious -impresario-of-nbcs-olympics/16109222-95c6-4df2-956f-e70be397a2d1/?utm _term=.3751547f0ef0.

Ourand, John. "The Great Communicator: Icon in Sports and Entertainment Television Built His Career on Relationships, Vision." *Street and Smith's Sport Business Journal*, May 18, 2015. http://www.sportsbusinessdaily.com/Journal/Issues/2015/05/18/Sports -Business-Awards/Ebersol-main.aspx.

Owen, David. "A Tale of Marius, Juan Antonio and Two Thomas-es, or Did History Repeat Itself on the Shores of the Black Sea?" *Inside the Games*, May 17, 2015. http://

www.insidethegames.biz/articles/1027376/a-tale-of-marius-juan-antonio-and-two
-thomas-es-or-did-history-repeat-itself-on-the-shores-of-the-black-sea.

"Parliamentarians at the Olympic and Paralympic Games: Full List." 2016. http://
www.parliament.uk/about/living-heritage/building/cultural- collections/archives/
parliamentary-olympians/the-olympians.

"Paul Helms Dead; Noted Sportsman; Millionaire Baker Who Set Up Coast Athletic Foundation Aided Many U.S. Stars; Backed Olympic Games; Host to President." *New York
Times*, January 6, 1957.

Payne, Michael. *Olympic Turnaround*. Twyford, Berks: London Business, 2005.

Peart, Harry. "Samaranch: Stylish Exit." *BBC Sport*, July 16, 2001. http://news.bbc.co.uk/
sport2/hi/in_depth/2001/olympic_votes/1442271.stm.

Pells, Eddie. "McDonald's Ends Olympic Sponsorship Three Years Early." *Toronto Star*,
June 16, 2017. https://www.thestar.com/sports/amateur/2017/06/16/mcdonalds-ends
-olympic-sponsorship-deal-three-years-early.html.

———. "USOC Paid Its Way Back Into Bidding Game; LA Could Benefit." *US News and World
Report*, May 16, 2017. https://www.usnews.com/news/sports/articles/2017-05-16/
usoc-expenses-included-10m-to-smooth-friction-for-la-bid.

———. "USOC Still Looking for Answers in Wake of Chicago's Embarrassment in
Vote for 2016 Olympics." *Gaea Times—Sports*, October 3, 2009. http://blog.taragana
.com/sports/2009/10/03/usoc-still-looking-for-answers-in-wake-of-chicagos
-embarrassment-in-vote-for-2016-olympics-34010.

Pelton, Joseph N. "The Start of Commercial Satellite Communications." *IEEE Communications Magazine* 48 (March 2010): 24–31.

Pendergrast, Mark. *For God, Country and Coca-Cola*. New York: Scribner's, 1993.

Penner, Mike. "Kenya's Mukora Quits the IOC." *Los Angeles Times*, January 28, 1999.

Perez, A. J. "U.S. Olympic Committee Chair Larry Probst to Step Down at Year's
End." *USA Today*, September 10, 2018. https://www.usatoday.com/story/sports/
olympics/2018/09/10/usoc-chairman-larry-probst-step-down-end-year/1256774002.

Pfanner, Eric. "Is Europe Ready for U.S.-Style Olympics Coverage." *New York Times*, December 3, 2008. http://www.nytimes.com/2008/12/03/business/worldbusiness/03iht
-rights.4.18373705.html.

Philips, Deborah, and Garry Whannel. *The Trojan Horse: The Growth of Commercial Sponsorship*. New York: Bloomsbury, 2013.

Phillips, Dom. "Brazil's Ex-president Lula Sentenced to Nearly Ten Years in Prison for
Corruption." *The Guardian*, July 12, 2017. https://www.theguardian.com/world/2017/
jul/12/brazil-president-lula-convicted-corruption.

Posey, Carl. *The Olympic Century: Tokyo 1964 Grenoble 1968*. Vol. 16. Los Angeles: World
Sport Research, 1996.

Pound, Dick. *Inside Dope: How Drugs Are the Biggest Threat to Sports, Why You Should Care, and
What Can Be Done about Them*. Toronto: Wiley, 2006.

———. *Inside the Olympics: A Behind-the-Scenes Look at the Politics, the Scandals, and the Glory
of the Games*. Toronto: Wiley, 2004.

Pound, Richard W. *Chief Justice W. R. Jackett: By the Law of the Land*. Montreal: McGill-Queen's
University Press, 1999.

——. *Five Rings over Korea: The Secret Negotiations Behind the 1988 Olympic Games in Seoul.* Toronto: Little, Brown, 1994.

——. *Rocke Robertson: Surgeon and Shepherd of Change.* Montreal: McGill-Queen's University Press, 2008.

——. *Stikeman Elliott: The First Fifty Years.* Montreal: McGill-Queen's University Press, 2003.

——. *Unlucky to the End: The Story of Janise Marie Gamble.* Montreal: McGill-Queen's University Press, 2007.

Powers, John. "Boston Could Benefit from Better Relationship between IOC, USOC." *Boston Globe*, January 18, 2015. http://www.bostonglobe.com/sports/2015/01/18/boston-could-benefit-from-better-relationship-between-ioc-and-usoc/m1RTtCjkVBXTSqgmo1I2dM/story.html.

Premack, Rachel. "Why South Korea's Biggest Auto Brand Isn't Advertising Cars at Its Own Winter Olympics." February 21, 2018. https://www.forbes.com/sites/rachelpremack/2018/02/21/hyundai-south-koreas-biggest-auto-brand-isnt-advertising-its-cars-at-the-winter-olympics-but-will-it-matter/#432e60a24242.

Price, Christopher, and Patrick Harverson. "Sema Seals Olympic Games Contract." *Financial Times*, December 8, 1998.

Purdy, Mark. "Purdy: Peter Ueberroth Thinks L.A.'s Bid for 2024 Olympic Games Is Looking Good." *San Jose Mercury News*, March 22, 2016. Updated August 11, 2016. http://www.mercury news.com/2016/03/22/purdy-peter-ueberroth-thinks-l-a-s-bid-for-2024-olympic-games-is-looking-good.

"Race for '16 Olympics Remains Tight Heading into Final Hours." *Street and Smith's Sport Business Daily*, October 1, 2009. http://m.sportsbusinessdaily.com/Daily/Issues/2009/10/Issue-14/Olympics/Race-For-16-Olympics-Remains-Tight-Heading-Into-Final-Hours.aspx.

Rader, Benjamin G. *In Its Own Image: How Television Has Transformed Sports.* New York: Free Press, 1984.

Rand, Abby. "Big Alp vs. Little Alp." *Ski*, September 1977: 74–77, 144.

Rapport official de jeux de la VII Olympiade, Anvers 1920. Leuven, Belgium: Sportsmusuem Flanders, 1921.

Reich, Kenneth. "'Friendship' Plan Will Be Studied by Olympic Leaders." *New York Times*, February 12, 1985. http://articles.latimes.com/1985-02-12/news/mn-3846_1_u-s-olympic-committee.

——. *Making It Happen: Peter Ueberroth and the 1984 Olympics.* Santa Barbara, Calif.: Capra, 1986.

Reich, Kenneth, and Lee Margulies. "Talks on Olympic TV Pact Begin." *Los Angeles Times*, September 11, 1979.

"Report: Boosters Paid for Scholarships for IOC Children." *Associated Press Newswires*, November 25, 1998.

"Report on Schiller Due Soon." *Orlando Sentinel*, December 19, 1991. http://articles.orlandosentinel.com/1991-12-19/sports/9112190614_1_schiller-ski-usoc.

Revue Politique. "Tête à Tête—Dick Pound." 2008. http://www.cpac.ca/en/programs/tete-a-tete/episodes/14417441.

"Richard L. Carrión." *Federal Reserve Bank of New York*, January 2008. Originally available at http://www.newyorkfed.org/aboutthefed/orgchart/board/Carrión.html; see archived page at https://web.archive.org/web/20080704135654/http://www.newyorkfed.org/aboutthefed/orgchart/board/carrion.html.

"Richard Carrión Quits IOC Finance." *ESPN* [via Associated Press], October 16, 2013. http://www.espn.com/olympics/story/_/id/9832678/puerto-rico-richard-carrion-quits-head-ioc-finance-commission.

"Richard W. Pound C.C., O.Q., Q.C., Ad. E., FCA, Montreal." Undated. http://www.stikeman.com/cps/rde/xchg/se-en/hs.xsl/Profile.htm?ProfileID=32065.

Riga, Andy. "Montreal Olympics: Cost Overruns Tarnished Jean Drapeau's Legacy." *Montreal Gazette*, July 17, 2016. http://montrealgazette.com/sports/montreal-olympics-cost-overruns-tarnished-jean-drapeaus-legacy.

Rishe, Patrick. "Los Angeles Makes Financially Savvy Move in Accepting 2028 Summer Olympics." August 1, 2017. https://www.forbes.com/sites/prishe/2017/08/01/los-angeles-makes-financially-savvy-move-in-accepting-2028-summer-olympic-games/3/#33fe6a0723f1.

"Robert J. Kane Succeeds Lynah as AA Director." *Cornell Daily Sun*, March 3, 1942, 1. http://cdsun.library.cornell.edu.

Roche, Lisa Riley. "IOC Event Fails to Live Up to Hype." *Deseret News*, March 21, 1999. http://www.deseretnews.com/article/686908/IOC-event-fails-to-live-up-to-hype.html?pg=all.

Rodda, John. "Lord Killanin." *The Guardian*, April 27, 1999. http://wwwtheguardian.com/news/1999/apr27/guardianobituaries.johnrodda.

——. "Lord Killanin, 1915–1999, Seventh President of the International Olympic Committee." *Journal of Olympic History* 7 (September 1999): 12–16.

Rode, Jan C. "Introduction to the Research Project 'Willi Daume.'" *Journal of Olympic History* 14 (December 2006): 99–101.

"Rogge: IOC Will Weather Financial Storm." Undated. http://www.eurosport.com/olympic-games/ioc-will-weather-storm_sto1781365/story.shtml.

Rosen, Daniel M. *Dope: A History of Performance Enhancement in Sports from the Nineteenth Century to Today*. Westport, Conn.: Praeger, 2008.

Rubinroit, Seth. "President Obama: IOC's Decisions Are 'A Little Cooked.'" *NBC Sports*. October 6, 2016. http://olympics.nbcsports.com/2016/10/06/president-obama-iocs-decisions-are-a-little-cooked.

Ruiz, Rebecca R., and Matthew Futterman. "Scott Blackmun Steps Down as Head of U.S.O.C. under Pressure from Nassar Case." *New York Times*, February 28, 2018. https://www.nytimes.com/2018/02/28/sports/scott-blackmun-usoc-nassar.html.

Samaranch, Juan Antonio. "A Tribute to Lord Exeter." *Olympic Review* 169 (November 1981): 651–52.

"Samaranch Says He Erred by Not Acting Earlier against Bidding Abuses." *Associated Press Newswires*, March 12, 1999.

Sandomir, Richard. "NBC Extends Olympic Deal into Unknown." *New York Times*, May 7, 2014. http://www.nytimes.com/2014/05/08/sports/olympics/nbc-extends-olympic-tv-deal-through-2032.html.

———. "Olympics; Samaranch Declines to Speak Before Senate." *New York Times*, March 31, 1999. http://www.nytimes.com/1999/03/31/sports/olympics-samaranch-declines -to-speak-before-senate.html.

———. "TV Sports; All Are to Blame for Baseball Network's Demise." *New York Times*, June 27, 1995. http://www.nytimes.com/1995/06/27/sports/tv-sports-all-are-to-blame -for-baseball-network-s-demise.html.

Sandomir, Richard, and Bill Carter. "Dick Ebersol Resigns from NBC Sports." *New York Times*, May 19, 2011. http://www.nytimes.com/2011/05/20/sports/dick-ebersol -resigns-from-nbc-sports.html?_r=0.

Sarantakes, Nicholas Evan. *Dropping the Torch: Jimmy Carter, the Olympic Boycott, and the Cold War*. New York: Cambridge University Press, 2011.

Saxon, Wolfgang. "Barber B. Conable, 81, Congressman and Bank Chief, Dies." *New York Times*, December 2, 2003. http://www.nytimes.com/2003/12/02/nyregion/02/CONA .html.

Sbetti, Nicola. "Italy and the Olympic Movement after the Second World War from Exclusion to Glory." *Final Report: IOC Olympic Studies Centre 2014 PhD Students Research Grant Programme*, 2015. https://doc.rero.ch/record/255153/files/Final_report_-_Italy_and_ the_OM_after_the_Second_World_War_-_N. Sbetti.docx.pdf.

Scheiner, Brett. "Popular Announces Appointment of Richard Carrión as Executive Chairman and Ignacio Alvarez as Chief Executive Officer." *Popular Newsroom*, April 25, 2017. http://newsroom.popular.com/press-release/english/popular-announces -appointment-richard-Carrión-executive-chairman-and-ignacio-a.

Schiller, Kay, and Christopher Young. *The 1972 Munich Olympics and the Making of Modern Germany*. Berkeley: University of California Press, 2010.

Schmitt, Eric. "Revamping the Olympic Franchise." *New York Times*, February 16, 1986. http://www.nytimes.com/1986/02/16/business/revamping-the-olympic-franchise .html?pagewanted=all.

Schöbel, Heinz. *The Four Dimensions of Avery Brundage*. Translated from the original German to English by Joan Becker. Leipzig: Edition Leipzig, 1968.

Schwoch, James. *Global TV: New Media and the Cold War, 1946–1969*. Urbana: University of Illinois Press, 2009.

Seelye, Katharine Q. "Boston's Bid for Summer Olympics Is Terminated." *New York Times*, July 27, 2015. http://www.nytimes.com/2015/07/28/sports/olympics/boston-2024 -summer-olympics-bid-terminated.html?_r=0.

Senn, Alfred Erich. *Power, Politics, and the Olympic Games: A History of the Power Brokers, Events, and Controversies That Shaped the Games*. Champaign, Ill.: Human Kinetics, 1999.

Shambora, Jessica. "King of Pebble Beach." *Fortune*, March 17, 2010. http://archive.fortune .com/2010/03/17/news/pebble_beach_us_open.fortune/index.htm.

Shipley, Amy. "USOC, IOC Reach Deal That Will Pave the Way for Future Olympics in United States." *Washington Post*, May 23, 2012. https://www.washingtonpost .com/ sports/olympics/usoc-ioc-reach-deal-that-will-pave-the-way-for-future -olympics-in-united-states/2012/05/23/gJQAddXelU_story.html?utm_term= .615b8c7e6b4a.

Siddons, Larry. "Sponsors to IOC: Clean Up this Scandal Fast." *Associated Press Newswires*, February 12, 1999.

Simon, William E. With John M. Caher. *A Time for Reflection: An Autobiography*. Washington, D.C.: Regnery, 2004.

Simson, Vyv, and Andrew Jennings. *The Lords of the Rings: Power, Money and Drugs in the Modern Olympics*. Toronto: Stoddart, 1992.

"Sir Ninian Stephen Appointed to IOC Ethics Commission." May 18, 2000. http://www.olympic.org/content/news/media-resources/manual-news/1999-2009/2000/04/18/sir-ninian-stephen-appointed-to-ioc-ethics-commission.

Smit, Barbara. *Sneaker Wars: The Enemy Brothers Who Founded Adidas and Puma and the Family Feud That Forever Changed the Business of Sport*. New York: HarperCollins, 2008.

Smith, Ronald A. *Sports and Freedom: The Rise of Big-Time College Athletics*. New York: Oxford University Press, 1988.

"Sport and Society." In *Encyclopedia of Contemporary Italian Culture*, edited by Gino Moliterno, 787–88. New York: Routledge, 2000.

Stanaway, Glenn. "Olympics Chiefs Split over Coles Allegations." *Courier Mail*, March 22, 1999.

Stanaway, Glenn, and Malcolm Farr. "Coles' Ex-wife Tells IOC of Gifts." *Daily Telegraph*, March 20, 1999.

Starkman, Randy. "IOC Bigwigs' Heads Buried Deep in the Sand." *Toronto Star*, January 23, 1999.

———. "A Pound of Prevention." *Toronto Star*, January 23, 1999.

Starkman, Randy, and Ashante Infantry. "Games Bribery Scandal Grows." *Toronto Star*, December 19, 1998.

Steen, Alex. "From FILA to UWW: How a Once Innovative Organization Almost Killed Wrestling." *Open Mat*, September 2, 2016. http://news.theopenmat.com/international-wrestling/from-fila-to-uww/58368.

Steinberg, Brian. "NBCUniversal's Olympic Channel to Launch July 15." *Variety*, June 15, 2017. http://variety.com/2017/tv/news/nbcuniversal-olympic-channel-launch-1202467959.

Stelter, Brian. "Discovery Nabs European TV Rights to 2018–2024 Olympics." June 29, 2015. http://money.cnn.com/2015/06/29/media/discovery-communications-olympics-europe.

Stewart, Larry. "Fox Gets Baseball; NBC Is Part of Deal." *Los Angeles Times*, November 6, 1995. http://articles.latimes.com/1995-11-06/sports/sp-65431_1_baseball-network.

Stoddart, Brian. *Saturday Afternoon Fever: Sport in Australian Culture*. North Ryde, NSW: Angus and Robertson, 1986.

Stump, A. J. "The Games That Almost Weren't." *American Heritage* 33, no. 5 (1982): 64–71.

———. "1932, The 'Hopeless' Dream of William May Garland." *Olympic Review* 274 (August 1990): 381–87.

Stynes, Tess. "Two Coca-Cola Directors to Retire amid Board Renovation." *Wall Street Journal*, February 19, 2015. http://www.wsj.com/articles/two-coca-cola-directors -to-retire-amid-board-renovation-1424381549.

Sullivan, Rohan. "IOC Accused of Betraying Athletes, Sponsors." *SlamSports*, April 28, 1999. http://www.canoe.ca/SlamOlympicScandalArchive/apr28_ioc.html.

Szalai, George. "Comcast: NBCUniversal Broke Even on London Olympics, Expects Profits from Future Games." *Hollywood Reporter*, October 26, 2012. http://www .hollywoodreporter.com/news/comcast-nbcuniversal-london-summer-olympics -breakeven-383380.

"Television Revenue Not Important Insists Rogge." *More Than the Games*, October 5, 2009. http://www.morethanthegames.co.uk/121st-ioc-session/056536-television -revenue-not-important-insists-rogge.

Tétrault-Farber, Gabrielle. "Doping Scandals Prompt Soul Searching in Russian Athletics Community." *Moscow Times*, February 1, 2015. http://www.themoscowtimes .com/news/article/doping-scandals-prompt-soul-searching-in-russian-athletics -community/515199.html.

"13 IOC Members Caught in Scandal's Web." *Seattle Post-Intelligencer*, January 15, 1999.

Thomas, Jo, Kirk Johnson, and Jere Longman. "The Rise and Fall of Olympic Ambitions Tactics May Have Been Pointless." *New Orleans Times-Picayune*, March 14, 1999.

"Thomas Keller—FISA's Patriarch." *World Rowing* 9 (July 2009). http://www.worldrowing .com/mm//Document/features/Featuressection/11/84/21/FISA_e mag09_July2009_ Neutral.pdf.

Todd, Jack. "The 40-Year Hangover: How the 1976 Olympics Nearly Broke Montreal." *The Guardian*, July 6, 2016. https://www.theguardian.com/cities/2016/jul/06/40-year -hangover-1976-olympic-games-broke-montreal-canada.

———. "1976 Montreal Olympics: Drapeau's Baby from Bid to Billion-Dollar Bill." *Montreal Gazette*, July 26, 2016. http://montrealgazette.com/sports/1976-montreal -olympics-drapeaus-baby-from-bid-to-billion-dollar-bill.

"Tokyo 2020: Chairman of the Japanese Olympic Committee Set to Quit." March 19, 2019. https://www.cnn.com/2019/03/19/sport/tsunekazu-takeda-japanese-olympic -committee-spt-intl/index.html.

Tomlinson, Alan. "The Commercialisation of the Olympics: Cities, Corporations, and the Olympic Community." In *Global Olympics: Historical and Sociological Studies of the Modern Games*, edited by Kevin Young and Kevin B. Wamsley, 3:179–200. Amsterdam: Elsevier, 2005.

———. "The Making—and Unmaking?—of the Olympic Corporate Class." In *The Palgrave Handbook of Olympic Studies*, edited by Helen Lenskyj and Stephen Wagg, 233–47. New York: Palgrave MacMillan, 2012.

"Toyota Olympic Sponsorship 'Game Changing.'" March 13, 2015. http://aroundtherings .com/site/A__50528/Title__Toyota-Olympic-Sponsorship-Game-Changing/292/ Articles.

Tumblety, Joan. *Remaking the Body: Masculinity and the Uses of Physical Culture in Interwar and Vichy France*. Oxford: Oxford University Press, 2012.

Ueberroth, Peter. With Richard Levin and Amy Quinn. *Made in America: His Own Story*. New York: Morrow, 1985.

United States Statutes at Large, 1950–1951. Vol. 64, part 1: *Public Laws and Reorganization Plans*. Washington, D.C.: GPO, 1952.

"USOC Delays Olympic Television Network—Boost for Chicago 2016." August 16, 2016. https://gamesbids.com/eng/summer-olympic-bids/chicago-2016/usoc-delays-olympic-television-network-boost-for-chicago-2016.

Van Camp, Owen V. "Report of the Treasurer." In *Report of the United States Olympic Committee - 1948 Games—XIV Olympiad, London, England, V Olympic Winter Games, St. Moritz, Switzerland*, edited by Asa S. Bushnell, 45–47, 355–383. New York: USOA, 1949. http://library.la84.org/6oic/USOC_Reports/1948/USOCReport1948Pt4.pdf.

Vennochi, Joan. "An Olympic-Sized Ethical Dilemma." *Boston Globe*, June 8, 1999.

"Vermont Launches Business, Cultural Exchanges with Geneva, Switzerland." *Bennington Banner*, July 27, 1977, 3. https://www.newspapers.com/newspage/63952688.

"Votes for Sale—The Olympic Meddlers." *The Australian*, December 19, 1998.

Wade, Stephen. "Takeda Corruption Probe Sullies 2020 Olympics and IOC." *Washington Times*, January 14, 2019. https://www.washingtontimes.com/news/2019/jan/14/japan-olympic-official-takeda-denies-corruption-al/.

Walden, Laura. "Christophe De Kepper Named to Succeed Lacotte as the IOC's Director-General." *Sports Features.com*, April 5, 2011. Originally available at http://www.sportsfeatures.com/olympicsnews/story/48410/christophe-de-kepper-named-to-succeed-lacotte-as-the-iocs-director-general. See archived page at https://web.archive.org/web/20180425031821/http://www.sportsfeatures.com/olympicsnews/story/48410/christophe-de-kepper-named-to-succeed-lacotte-as-the-iocs-director-general.

Watson, Robert P. Updated by Larry Maloney. "Appendix B: The U.S. Olympic Committee." In *Encyclopedia of the Olympic Movement*, edited by John E. Findling and Kimberly D. Pelle, 499–508. Westport, Conn.: Greenwood, 2004.

Wenn, Stephen R. "Growing Pains: The Olympic Movement and Television, 1966–1972." *Olympika: The International Journal of Olympic Studies* 4 (1995): 1–22.

———. "A History of the International Olympic Committee and Television, 1936–1980." PhD diss., Pennsylvania State University, 1993.

———. "IOC/USOC Relations and the 2009 IOC Session in Copenhagen." In *Rethinking Matters Olympic: Investigations into the Socio-Cultural Study of the Modern Olympic Movement; Proceedings of the 10th International Symposium for Olympic Research*, edited by Robert K. Barney, Janice Forsyth, and Michael Heine, 60–75. London, Ontario: International Centre for Olympic Studies, 2010.

———. "Lights! Camera! Little Action: Television, Avery Brundage and the 1956 Melbourne Olympics." *Sporting Traditions: Journal of the Australian Society for Sports History* 10, no. 1 (1993): 38–53.

———. "A Long and Winding Road: IOC/USOC Relations and the Amateur Sports Act." *Olympika: The International Journal of Olympic Studies* 24 (2015): 1–46.

———. "An Olympian Squabble: The Distribution of Olympic Television Revenue, 1960–1966." *Olympika: The International Journal of Olympic Studies* 3 (1994): 27–47.

——. "Peter Ueberroth's Legacy: How the 1984 Los Angeles Olympics Changed the Trajectory of the Olympic Movement." *International Journal of the History of Sport* 32 (January 2015): 157–71.

——. "Richard Pound's Dilemma: Sub-Saharan Africa Television Rights and the 1992 Barcelona Olympics." *Olympika: The International Journal of Olympic Studies* 6 (1997): 25–50.

——. "Riding into the Sunset: Richard Pound, Dick Ebersol, and Long-Term Olympic Television Contracts." In *Bridging Three Centuries: Intellectual Crossroads and the Modern Olympic Movement; Fifth International Symposium for Olympic Research*, edited by Kevin B. Wamsley, Scott G. Martyn, Gordon H. MacDonald, and Robert K. Barney, 37–50. London, Ontario: International Centre for Olympic Studies, 2000.

——. "Rivals and Revolutionaries: Avery Brundage, the Marquess of Exeter and Olympic Television Revenue." *Sport in History* 32 (June 2012): 257–78.

——. "Television Rights and the 1976 Montreal Olympics." *Sport History Review* 27 (November 1996): 111–38.

——. "A Turning Point for IOC Television Policy: U.S. Television Rights Negotiations and the 1980 Lake Placid and Moscow Olympic Festivals." *Journal of Sport History* 25 (Spring 1998): 87–118.

Wenn, Stephen, Robert Barney, and Scott Martyn. *Tarnished Rings: The International Olympic Committee and the Salt Lake City Bid Scandal*. Syracuse, N.Y.: Syracuse University Press, 2011.

Wenn, Stephen R., and Scott G. Martyn. "Storm Watch: Richard Pound, TOP Sponsors, and the Salt Lake City Bid Scandal." *Journal of Sport History* 32 (Summer 2005): 167–97.

——. "Tough Love: Richard Pound, David D'Alessandro, and the Salt Lake City Olympics Bid Scandal." *Sport in History* 26 (April 2006): 64–90.

Werdigier, Julia. "Leo Kirch, German Media Giant, Dies at 84." *New York Times*, July 14, 2011. http://www.nytimes.com/2011/07/15/business/media/leo-kirch-is-dead-at-84-headed-media-empire-that-went-bankrupt.html.

Westcott, Tim. "Discovery to Take Majority Control of Eurosport." *IHS Markit*, January 22, 2014. https://technology.ihs.com/484424/discovery-to-take-majority-control-of-eurosport.

Wharton, David. "Olympics Forge Big Sponsorship Deal with Toyota." *Los Angeles Times*, March 13, 2015. http://www.latimes.com/sports/sportsnow/la-sp-sn-olympic-officials-sign-big-sponsorship-deal-20150313-story.html.

——. "USOC Names Los Angeles the Official U.S. Bidder for the 2024 Summer Olympics." *Los Angeles Times*, September 1, 2015. http://www.latimes.com/sports/olympics/la-sp-sn-usoc-los-angeles-2024-summer-olympics-20150901-story.html.

White, Jeremy. "'The Los Angeles Way of Doing Things': The Olympic Village and the Practice of Boosterism in 1932." *Olympika: The International Journal of Olympic Studies* 11 (2002): 79–116.

Who Was Who in America 3 (1951–1960). Chicago: Marquis.

Wiellard, Robert J. "EC Says EBU-Eurosport Deal Violates EC Competition Rules." *AP News Archive*, February 20, 1991. http://www.apnewsarchive.com/1991/EC-Says-EBU

-Eurosport-Deal-Violates-EC-Competition-Rules/id-1f68a90519bc8ae1b2b92fae c144c07a.

"Willi Daume (1913–1996), Sportfunktionär." Undated. http://www.rheinischegeschichte .lvr.de/ persoenlichkeiten/D/Seiten/WilliDaume.aspx.

"Willi Daume (1913–1996), Sportfunktionär: Historiker stellt klar: Daume nur ein Mitläufer." December 1, 2010. http://www.nwzonline.de/sport/historiker-stellt-klar -daume-nur-ein-mitlaeufer_a_1,0,3059693542.html.

Wilson, Stephen. "Big Money, Secret Talks Produce Olympic TV Deal." *Business Journal*, May 8, 2014. http://www.thebusinessjournal.com/news/national/ 11900-big-money-secret-talks-produce-olympic-tv-deal.

——. "Corruption Scandal Likely to Force Changes in IOC." *Kitchener-Waterloo Record*, December 17, 1998.

——. "Disputes Emerge on Eve of Drug Summit." *Associated Press Newswires*, February 1, 1999.

——. "IOC Opens Probe into Salt Lake City Payments." *Associated Press Newswires*, December 10, 1998.

——. "IOC-USOC Revenue Deal Done; U.S. Can Bid for Games." *Seattle Times*, May 24, 2012. http://old.seattletimes.com/html/sports/2018277109_apolyiocusoc .html.

——. "NBC Extends Olympic Deal through 2032 for $7.75 Billion." *Denver Post*, May 7, 2014. http://www.denverpost.com/books/ci_25714725/nbc-extends-olympic -deal-through-2032-7-75b.

——. "NBC Gets 2010, 2012 Olympics for $2.2 Billion." *Pittsburgh Past-Gazette*, June 7, 2003. http://old.post-gazette.com/tv/20030607tvrights0607p4.asp.

——. "NBC Sports Chief Rips John Hancock Boss." *Associated Press Newswires*, June 1, 1999.

——. "No Samaranch Successor in Sight." *AP Online*, February 27, 1999.

——. "Richard Carrión Declares IOC Presidential Bid." *Seattle Times*, May 22, 2013. http://old.seattletimes.com/html/sports/2021032785_apolyiocCarrión candidacy .html.

——. "Rival Cities Want $22m." *Sun-Herald*, December 20, 1998.

——. "Samaranch Prepares IOC Members for 'Painful' Decisions." *Associated Press Newswires*, March 11, 1999.

——. "Toyota Drives onto Olympic Stage in Record Sponsorship Deal." *MailOnline*, March 13, 2015. http://www.dailymail.co.uk/wires/ap/article-2993050/Toyota-signs-global -Olympic-sponsor-long-term-deal.html.

——. "USOC Leaders Appointed to 2 Key IOC Commissions." *San Diego Union-Tribune*, March 11, 2011. http://www.sandiegouniontribune.com/sdut-usoc-leaders -appointed-to-2-key-ioc-commissions-2011mar11-story.html.

Wilson, Wayne. "Los Angeles 1984." In *Encyclopedia of the Modern Olympic Movement*, edited by John E. Findling and Kimberly D. Pelle, 207–15. Westport, Conn.: Greenwood, 2004.

——. "Sports Infrastructure, Legacy and the Paradox of the 1984 Olympic Games." *International Journal of the History of Sport* 32 (January 2015): 144–56.

Winston, Brian. *Media Technology and Society—A History: From the Telegraph to the Internet.* London: Routledge, 1998.

"With Severe Warnings to Two Top Members, IOC Inquiry Closes." *SlamSports*, March 12, 1999. http://www.canoe.ca/SlamOlympicScandalArchive/mar12_wit.html.

"With Vote Approaching, Samaranch Worries about Palace Revolt." *Associated Press Newswires*, March 16, 1999.

Zak, Anatoly. "The Rest of the Rocket Scientists." *Air and Space*, September 2003. http://www.airspacemag.com/space/the-rest-of-the-rocket-scientists-4376617/?no-ist=&page=2.

Zeigler, Mark. "Brazil's Passion Beats Chicago's Sponsorships." *San Diego Union-Tribune*, October 3, 2009. http://www.sandiegouniontribune.com/sdut-brazils-passion-beats-chicagos-sponsorships-2009oct03-htmlstory.html.

———. "Why Can't the U.S. Get an Olympics." *San Diego Union-Tribune*, December 29, 2012. http://www.sandiegouniontribune.com/sdut-why-cant-the-united-states-get-an-olympics-2012dec29-story.html.

Ziegler, Martyn. "IAAF 'Could Not Have Been Unaware of the Extent of Doping in Athletics,' Claims Second Part of Wada Report." *The Independent*, January 14, 2016. http://www.independent.co.uk/sport/general/athletics/ iaaf-could-not-have-been-unaware-of-the-extent-of-doping-in-athletics-claims-second-part-of-wada-a6812261.html.

Zimbalist, Andrew. *Circus Maximus: The Economic Gamble behind Hosting the Olympics and the World Cup.* Washington, D.C.: Brookings Institution Press, 2015.

Index

STEPHEN R. WENN is a professor in the Department of Kinesiology and Physical Education at Wilfrid Laurier University. ROBERT K. BARNEY is professor emeritus and founding director emeritus of the International Center for Olympic Studies at the School of Kinesiology at Western University. They are the authors (with Scott Martyn) of *Tarnished Rings: The International Olympic Committee and the Salt Lake City Bid Scandal*.

SPORT AND SOCIETY

A Sporting Time: New York City and the Rise of Modern Athletics,
     1820–70   *Melvin L. Adelman*
Sandlot Seasons: Sport in Black Pittsburgh   *Rob Ruck*
West Ham United: The Making of a Football Club   *Charles Korr*
Beyond the Ring: The Role of Boxing in American Society   *Jeffrey T. Sammons*
John L. Sullivan and His America   *Michael T. Isenberg*
Television and National Sport: The United States and Britain   *Joan M. Chandler*
The Creation of American Team Sports: Baseball and Cricket, 1838–72   *George B. Kirsch*
City Games: The Evolution of American Urban Society
     and the Rise of Sports   *Steven A. Riess*
The Brawn Drain: Foreign Student-Athletes in American Universities   *John Bale*
The Business of Professional Sports   *Edited by Paul D. Staudohar and James A. Mangan*
Fritz Pollard: Pioneer in Racial Advancement   *John M. Carroll*
A View from the Bench: The Story of an Ordinary Player on a Big-Time Football Team
     (*formerly* Go Big Red! The Story of a Nebraska Football Player)   *George Mills*
Sport and Exercise Science: Essays in the History of Sports Medicine
     Edited by Jack W. Berryman and Roberta J. Park
Minor League Baseball and Local Economic Development   *Arthur T. Johnson*
Harry Hooper: An American Baseball Life   *Paul J. Zingg*
Cowgirls of the Rodeo: Pioneer Professional Athletes   *Mary Lou LeCompte*
Sandow the Magnificent: Eugen Sandow and the Beginnings
     of Bodybuilding   *David Chapman*
Big-Time Football at Harvard, 1905: The Diary of Coach Bill Reid   *Edited by Ronald A. Smith*
Leftist Theories of Sport: A Critique and Reconstruction   *William J. Morgan*
Babe: The Life and Legend of Babe Didrikson Zaharias   *Susan E. Cayleff*
Stagg's University: The Rise, Decline, and Fall of Big-Time Football
     at Chicago   *Robin Lester*
Muhammad Ali, the People's Champ   *Edited by Elliott J. Gorn*
People of Prowess: Sport, Leisure, and Labor in Early Anglo-America   *Nancy L. Struna*
The New American Sport History: Recent Approaches
     and Perspectives   *Edited by S. W. Pope*
Making the Team: The Cultural Work of Baseball Fiction   *Timothy Morris*
Making the American Team: Sport, Culture, and the Olympic Experience   *Mark Dyreson*
Viva Baseball! Latin Major Leaguers and Their Special Hunger   *Samuel O. Regalado*
Touching Base: Professional Baseball and American Culture
     in the Progressive Era (rev. ed.)   *Steven A. Riess*
Red Grange and the Rise of Modern Football   *John M. Carroll*
Golf and the American Country Club   *Richard J. Moss*
Extra Innings: Writing on Baseball   *Richard Peterson*
Global Games   *Maarten Van Bottenburg*
The Sporting World of the Modern South   *Edited by Patrick B. Miller*
Female Gladiators: Gender, Law, and Contact Sport in America   *Sarah K. Fields*
The End of Baseball As We Knew It: The Players Union, 1960–81   *Charles P. Korr*
Rocky Marciano: The Rock of His Times   *Russell Sullivan*
Saying It's So: A Cultural History of the Black Sox Scandal   *Daniel A. Nathan*

The University of Illinois Press
is a founding member of the
Association of University Presses.

———————————————————————

Composed in 10.25/13 Marat Pro
with Trade Gothic LT Std display
by Kirsten Dennison
at the University of Illinois Press
Manufactured by Sheridan Books, Inc.

University of Illinois Press
1325 South Oak Street
Champaign, IL 61820-6903
www.press.uillinois.edu